D1522717

Feminism and Migration

Series Editors:

Peter Li and Baha Abu-Laban

The series publishes original scholarly books that advance our understanding of international migration and immigrant integration. Written by academic experts and policy specialists, each volume addresses a clearly defined research question or theme, employs critical analysis and develops evidence-based scholarship. The series includes single or multi-authored monographs, volumes and edited collections.

The scope of the series is international migration and integration research. Topics include but are not limited to thematic and current issues and debates; comparative research of a regional, national or international nature; the changing character of urban areas in which migrants or refugees settle; the reciprocal influence of migrants/ refugees and host communities; issues of integration and social inequality as well as policy analysis in migration research.

For further volumes:
http://www.springer.com/series/8811

Glenda Tibe Bonifacio
Editor

Feminism and Migration

Cross-Cultural Engagements

 Springer

Editor
Glenda Tibe Bonifacio
Department of Women and Gender Studies
University of Lethbridge
University Drive 4401
Lethbridge, AB T1K 3M4
Canada

ISBN 978-94-007-2830-1   e-ISBN 978-94-007-2831-8
DOI 10.1007/978-94-007-2831-8
Springer Dordrecht Heidelberg London New York

Library of Congress Control Number: 2012931444

Printed on acid-free paper

Springer is part of Springer Science+Business Media (www.springer.com)

*This work is dedicated to the women
who ventured beyond their countries of
origin—to see the world and its hope for
enduring humanity; to survive so that others
may live; to embrace the uncertainties
of fate; and to see through the gains of
returning and leaving—all in the hope
of making a difference.*

Glenda Tibe Bonifacio

Acknowledgements

This book collection is a product of a collective effort. It would not have been possible to complete an international project without the support, cooperation, and patience of all contributors. To them, I owe much thanks and appreciation for a fruitful year journey.

A wonderful group of people helped me in many ways to see this project through. Bev Garnett for her superb administrative skills and warm friendship; Leanne Wehlage for easing other tasks in my department; my colleagues in the University of Lethbridge—Joanne Fiske, Carol Williams, Dayna Daniels, Suzanne Lenon, Tiffany Muller Myrdahl, Catherine Kingfisher, Heidi MacDonald, Jan Newberry, Jennifer Mather, Jacqueline Preyde, and Bonnie Lee—for the immeasurable support I received from all of you which makes Lethbridge a special place to be; and Evelien Bakker and Bernadette Deelen-Mans at Springer for their guidance along the way.

With all of life's challenges in time and in different places, I am deeply indebted to my family for always being there for me. To my husband, Ike, for the understanding and great love for over 25 years; my two youngest daughters, Czyna and Charithe, for the support in the domestic front and friendship beyond the biological bonds; my three university students' daughters, Charmaine, Czarina, and Charelle, for picking up some tasks in the heap of paper trails, and for reminding me that you have your own journeys to make.

Above all, to the Supreme Being, who has many names across cultures but One who surely knows what comes next, for giving me the strength to persevere through difficult moments.

To all of you, my loudest Thank you!

Contents

Contributors

MariaCaterina La Barbera is a research fellow at the Centre for Political and Constitutional Studies and an affiliated researcher at the Center for Human and Social Sciences of the National Spanish Research Council, both located in Madrid. She is an attorney at law and obtained her Ph.D. in Human Rights from the University of Palermo, Italy. Her research interests range from gender and women studies, to human rights, international migration, immigration law, and socio-legal anthropology. She has worked as a staff researcher at the Law School at Berkeley, and as postdoctoral researcher at the Department of Anthropology at Berkeley and the Department of Studies in Politics, Law, and Society at Palermo. She has been a Visiting Fellow at the London School of Economics, the Universidad Taronjers of Valencia, the Institute of Language, Literature and Anthropology of CSIC in Madrid, and periodically spends periods of research at the University of California, Berkeley. Her talks and publications are related to women studies, public and private spheres, feminism/s, intersectionality, cultural differences, "female genital mutilation," Islamic headscarf, and Islamic feminism. Her ongoing research aims at combining legal analysis with the ethnographic fieldwork with the purpose of analyzing whether and how law and politics are involved in the formation and transformation of gender identity of foreign women living in Spain.

Glenda Tibe Bonifacio is an associate professor in Women's Studies at the University of Lethbridge, Canada. She is a research affiliate of the Prentice Institute for Global Population and Economy and the Prairie Metropolis Center (PMC), a Centre of Excellence for Research on Immigration, Integration and Diversity. She is the co-editor of Gender, Religion and Migration: Pathways of Integration (Lexington Books 2010) and Immigration and the Small City (forthcoming UBC Press). Her research interests include gender, migration, citizenship, and the youth bulge. Glenda completed her Ph.D. from the School of History and Politics, University of Wollongong, Australia in 2004; M.A. and B.A. from the University of the Philippines.

Cezara Crisan emigrated from Romania to the U.S. in 1999 and earned her B.A. in Sociology from Purdue University Calumet (2005) and an M.A. in Sociology from Loyola University Chicago (LUC) (2007) where she is completing a dissertation on Eastern European migration to the United States. Since 2007 she has taught at Purdue Calumet as a lecturer for introductory sociology, statistics for the behavioral sciences, and gender roles in modern society. At Purdue University Calumet, she held a 1 year (2009–2010) research position as coordinator evaluator for the Indiana Youth Suicide Prevention Program. She was a recipient of the LUC Fourth Year Fellowship Award (2008–2009) and the Department Merit Award Fellowship (2005–2008). Her current area of interest centers on migration, specifically on the comparative study of Eastern European migration to the United States. Related interests include human trafficking for purposes of sexual exploitation.

Annick Durand-Delvigne is a professor of social psychology at the University of Lille 3. She completed a doctorate from the University of Lille 3 in 1979, and a doctorate of State from the University of Paris V in 1992. She is a member of the EA 4072 PSITEC (Psychology Emotions Cognition Interactions Time), and affiliated with the ADRIPS (Association for the Dissemination of International Research in Social Psychology) and AIPTLF (International Association of Psychology of Work and Organisations). Her main research activities include issues of gender relations, quality of life, and struggles against discrimination. She has authored numerous articles, book chapters and edited books on these issues. She coordinates the French part of the research presented in Chapter 11.

Montse Feu is a Ph.D. candidate in U.S. Hispanic Literature at the University of Houston, Texas. Her dissertation is about a Brooklyn-based newspaper, *España Libre*, published by exiles of the Spanish Civil War. She has a language pedagogy certification from Universitat de Barcelona, a Women Studies certification from the University of Houston, and a School of Criticism and Theory certification from Cornell University. She is an adjunct lecturer in Spanish and the Humanities at University of Houston-Downtown. Her research focuses on migration, the working class, and gender.

Maryam Jamarani has a Ph.D. in Sociolinguistics from the University of Queensland, Australia. She has been teaching in the field of intercultural communication for the past 7 years. She is the author of *Identity, Language and Culture in Diaspora*. Her areas of research are intercultural communication, migrant studies, and acculturation, as well as language and culture contacts. She is currently teaching at the University of Queensland, and is a research fellow at Monash University, Australia.

Laura Menin is a Ph.D. candidate in cultural anthropology at the University of Milano-Bicocca Italy. She has carried out ethnographic research related to gender, Islam and migration, and the forms of migrants' associations and their political participation in public spheres. She is a member of L.A.MI.T (Laboratory of Anthropology of Migration and Transnationalism) of the University of Milano-Bicocca since 2007. She has been a visiting student at the University of Sussex

(UK) for a term in 2008, 2010, and 2011. Her research interests focus on love and intimacy, gendered identity crafting, and trajectories of mobility in the rural region of central Morocco.

Gail Mummert is a professor and researcher in the Center for Anthropological Studies at El Colegio de Michoacán in central-western Mexico. Trained as a demographer and a social anthropologist, she has studied novel forms of family life and gender relations in the face of sweeping social and cultural change throughout rural Mexico in the latter half of the twentieth century. She is the author of a book focussing on transformations in an agrarian community when a factory comes to town, and has also edited a volume on migration between Mexico and the United States, *Fronteras fragmentadas*. Her current research deals with transnational families and their encounters with various nation-states, particularly long-distance care giving arrangements for the young and the old in countries such as Mexico, China, Philippines, and Ecuador.

Jun Nagatomo is an assistant professor at the School of International Studies, Kwansei Gakuin University, Japan, where he teaches anthropological courses. He received a Ph.D. from the University of Queensland in 2009, where he has studied contemporary Japanese migration to Australia as a Rotary Foundation Ambassadorial Scholar since 2005. He received a B.A. from Keio University in 2000 and an M.A. from Seinan Gakuin University in 2003. His publications include: *Japan Club of Queensland 20shunen kinenshi: Ijyu no Katari*, an edited book; *Japanese Queenslanders: A history*, co-authored with Dr. Yuriko Nagata; and "Globalization, tourism development, and Japanese lifestyle migration to Australia," a chapter in *Development in Asia: Interdisciplinary, post-neoliberal, and transnational perspectives*, edited by Derrick M. Nault.

Juliana Nazareth is a psychologist who completed a doctorate in psychosociology at the Federal University of Rio de Janeiro (UFRJ) about the migration of women in Brazil. She is an associated researcher in the Laboratory of Images of the EICOS Program (UFRJ), participating in UNESCO researches, especially about the condition of women. She has presented and written numerous papers on women, migration and the family.

Maria Inacia D'Ávila Neto is a titular professor from Federal University of Rio de Janeiro (UFRJ), an acting UNESCO counselor which coordinates a UNESCO Chair on Sustainable Development in the EICOS Program (UFRJ). She is also a guest professor in EHESS, Ecole des Hautes Etudes des Sciences Sociale, Paris, and in University of Lille 3, among others. She concluded a doctorate in social psychology at the University of Paris VII in 1978, and published a number of books and articles about the conditions of women in many languages. She coordinates the Brazilian part of the research presented in Chapter 11.

Nouria Ouali has a Ph.D. in Sociology from the Université Libre de Bruxelles (ULB), Belgium. She has been a senior researcher at the Centre of Sociology of Work, Employment and Training (METICES-ULB) since 1990. She has participated in and led a variety of European and interdisciplinary research mainly dealing with gender, class, racial and ethnic discrimination in education and employment. She founded and coordinates the Interdisciplinary Research Group on Gender and Migration (GEM), and has published her research findings in a number of international scientific journals and edited volumes. She is the co-editor of Migrants, Ethnic Minorities and the Labour Market Integration and Exclusion in Europe (Macmillan Press LTD, London-New York, 1999). Currently, she is a senior lecturer in sociology of work at the Institut d'Etudes du Travail, Université Lumière Lyon 2 in France.

Jackleen M. Salem is a Ph.D. candidate in the global history program in the Department of History at the University of Wisconsin-Milwaukee. Her research focuses on the history, spread, and growth of Muslim communities in the U.S., women in Islam, the Middle East, and immigration history.

Shweta Singh is an associate professor in the School of Social Work at Loyola University Chicago. Her research and teaching is interdisciplinary. She teaches research and policy in Social Work, global feminism in Women and Gender Studies, and about the Indian Subcontinent in Area Studies. Her research incorporates methods from anthropology, communication, feminism, psychology, and social work into the study and measurement of women and girls' identity. Her current research projects focus on issues of migration, work, education, and well-being and application of web-based media projects to women's rights. Shweta completed a master's degree in social work from The Tata Institute of Social Sciences, Mumbai, India, and doctorate in social work from The University of North Carolina at Chapel Hill, USA. Her international work includes assignments with international development organizations on issues of women's health, development, child rights, and social advocacy.

Katharina Stornig holds a Ph.D. from the Department of History and Civilization at the European University Institute. Her dissertation, entitled "*'All for the greater glory of Jesus and the salvation of the immortal souls!'* German missionary nuns in colonial Togo and New Guinea, 1897–1960," focuses on the transnational history of a Catholic women's congregation in colonial contexts. Her research interests include women's history, colonial history, postcolonialism, and the intersections of gender, race and religion.

Luna Vives is a Ph.D. candidate in the Department of Geography at the University of British Columbia (UBC). Her research explores border control practices and the role that transnational social networks play on the migration of women from Senegal to Spain. She is a UBC Vanier Scholar, a fellow of the German ZEIT Foundation, and a researcher in projects financed by the Spanish government studying the transnational practices of migrant families in the country. Besides her academic work, Luna organized "Women through the border," a collaborative project that documented the recent migration of Senegalese women to Spain.

Alexandra Zavos obtained her Ph.D. from Manchester Metropolitan University on "The politics of gender and migration in an anti-racist group in Athens." She has been engaged for many years in feminist anti-racist politics in Athens and

Manchester and helped organize, together with other Greek and migrant women activists, a 'gender and migration' initiative. She is currently based in Athens and is working as a senior researcher for the EC funded projects GEMIC (www.gemic.eu) and MIGNET (www.mignetproject.eu), coordinated by the Gender Studies Center at Panteion University. Some of her research has been published in *Das Argument* (2006), *Annual Review of Critical Psychology* (2008), and *Feminist Review* (2010, with Helen Kambouri), as well as the edited collections *Gender and Migration: Perspectives and Interventions* (2010, London, Zed), and *The Gender of Migration* (2009, Athens, Metaixmio, in Greek).

Chapter 1
Introduction

Glenda Tibe Bonifacio

Feminism and migration are, in fact, two of the most dynamic social movements since the nineteenth century (Ryan 1992; Massey et al. 1998; Walters 2005; Isaacs 2007; Koser 2007). Both have historically altered social relationships, communities, and nation-states. Feminism—circumscribed in the struggle for equal rights, social justice, and full participation of women (including LGBT)[1] in society—continues to make inroads despite ongoing backlash and sustained conservative politics in the twenty-first century (Faludi 2006; Schreiber 2008). In the same manner, migration—in the context of global human flows caused by economic, political, and environmental factors—remains central to issues of national identity, citizenship, welfare, and security among receiving countries, particularly after 9/11 (Freilich and Guerette 2006; Bailey 2008; Bourbeau 2011). For example, immigration is a high political agenda in Australia, Canada, New Zealand, Western Europe, and the United States (Cornelius et al. 2004). As Anthony Gooch (2009, p. 3) notes, "few phenomena have shaped human history as decisively as migration."

But the distinct feature of migration in the twentieth century is the rise in the "feminization of migration" in Africa, Asia, and other parts of the world (Castles and Miller 1998; Oishi 2005; Crush and Dodson 2010). This phenomenon is shown by the "marked increase in the number of women migrants in recent years, and the proportion of women in relation to the total number of migrants" (Passerini et al. 2010, p. 2). For example, the number of Asian female labor migrants working outside their countries of origin reached 1.5 million in the mid-1990s (Castles and Miller 1998). As of 2006, UN-INSTRAW (2006) reported that women migrants comprised 49.6% of the total global flows, although country-by-country variations existed with 70–80% in some areas. In West

---

[1] This refers to lesbians, gay, bisexual and transgendered persons.

G.T. Bonifacio, Ph.D. (✉)
Department of Women and Gender Studies, University of Lethbridge,
Lethbridge, AB, Canada
e-mail: glenda.bonifacio@uleth.ca

G.T. Bonifacio (ed.), *Feminism and Migration: Cross-Cultural Engagements*,
International Perspectives on Migration 1, DOI 10.1007/978-94-007-2831-8_1,
© Springer Science+Business Media B.V. 2012

Africa, women comprised about 50% of the migrant population in 2010 (Idoko 2010). Records indicate that for over 40 years, women migrants represent about half of the world's migrant population (Zlotnik 2003), and it is only quite recently that scholarly interest on feminized migration reached mainstream discourses (Reysoo 2008).

Feminized flows of human migration also point to the trajectories of work and favored places of destination. Women's work has become a commodity for exchange in the international economy, where carework and the domestic service industry predominate (Parreñas 2001; Lutz 2008; Widding Isaksen 2010). Demand for domestic workers, nannies, caregivers, and nurses in developed countries have resulted in the massive entry of foreign migrant labor, usually sourced out from developing states, under conditions of vulnerability and exploitation (Anderson 2000; Hoy 2003; Lindio-McGovern and Walliman 2009). Wide-ranging manufacturing industries target female workers for their dexterity and cheap labor (Afsar 2003; Budde 2005; Rudnick 2009). Other forms of feminized labor with global dimensions include the trafficking of women for sex purposes and the organized marriage-for-migration schemes (Beeks and Amir 2006; Yang and Lu 2010). Women as "birds of passage" (Morokvašic 1984) traverse rural-urban and transnational migration for hopes of better employment opportunities, safety, and well-being for themselves and their families. Some do follow their husbands or other male members of the family, but many tend to tread on their own.

While feminization of migration is fairly recognized in contemporary migration scholarship, the relationship between feminism and migration is not. This means that while women's migration is well-documented from various disciplinary perspectives, feminism as a form of practice in their lives is not quite established. From July 3–7, 2011, I attended the 11th Women's World Congress in Ottawa, Canada and queried about the relationship between feminism and migration in various sessions. During my session on July 5, the discussion centred on the contested meaning of feminism and the daily challenges of immigrant women who may not have the opportunity to establish solidarity with other women in the initial stages of settlement. Still, in two other sessions in the international women's congress, feminism incites different interpretations and, thus, differing ideas in the context of (im)migrant lives. Some points to the public expression of feminism arising from one's own consciousness of oppression based on, for example, gender, race, and class. That is, feminism requires not only a personal understanding of such oppression but action with other women to foster change. While others reject the word "feminist" in favour of the more neutral term "humanist." I left the huge gathering of feminists, scholars, activists, students, and practitioners with no definite answer on the relationship between feminism and migration. But one thing is sure, feminism is still a powerful concept.

1.1 Feminism and Migration: An Overview

What are the emerging trends leading towards the lines of feminism and migration? A cursory overview of the literature in English sets the trends in "feminist interventions" (Palmary et al. 2010) in migration studies and claim for other interest in its gaps.

Feminism and migration may appear divergent in its path in popular discourse but a closer examination of recent scholarship reveals burgeoning thresholds of inquiry between the two.

Migration is defined as "a permanent or semi-permanent change of residence of an individual or a group of people" (Oderth 2002, p. 2). There are different types of migration flows to include "international, frontierwise, rural-urban, urban-urban, intra-urban, and circulation" (Johnston et al. 2000, p. 504). In outlining the scholarly links between feminism and migration, I limit the confines of migration to international mobility as it clearly demonstrates shift in socio-cultural contexts from which dramatic change in traditional gender roles and aspirations is possible. But this choice does not, however, delimit the potentials of change in internal migrations.

Feminism, Chris Beasley (1999, p. ix) states, "is a troublesome term." Defining *feminism* is complex and "controversial" (Offen 1992, p. 64) as there are divergent approaches and perspectives to base it with. *Feminisms* (Kemp and Squires 1998) is a more appropriate word to encompass these divergences: for example, liberal feminism, socialist feminism, radical feminism, psychoanalytic feminism, postmodern feminism (Beasley 2006, p. 51). Judith Lorber (1998) grouped feminism into three major areas: gender-reform, gender resistance, and gender rebellion. Following these areas of feminist thought and action, Michelle Paludi (2010) elaborates their particular dimensions:

> Gender reform feminism emphasizes similarities between women and men rather than focusing on differences between them. Gender-resistance feminism holds that formal legal rights alone will not end gender inequality; male dominance is too ingrained into social relations. Gender-resistance feminism focuses on how men and women are different—cognitively, emotionally, and socially—and urges women to form women-centred organizations and communities. Gender rebellion feminism looks at the interrelationships among inequalities of sex, race, ethnicity, social class and sexual orientation. (Paludi 2010, p. xv)

Addressing gender inequalities in society seems to be the core value of feminism and the main task of feminists. How does this perspective impact migration?

Perhaps the introduction of gender as an analytical frame has defined the impact of feminist scholarship in migration discourse. Gender is a social construct of roles, behaviours, and values assigned to women and men (Lorber and Farrell 1991). Gender does not exist in isolation but intersects with other identities like race or class, as well as embedded in practices and representations which, basically, refers to the organizing system of power relations in society (Cook 2007; Andersen 2010). Today, gender and migration is not anymore a "neglected area of research" (Halfacree and Boyle 1999, p. 1). The use of various feminist theories in migration research has been sustained since the 1990s, particularly among feminist geographers in understanding, for instance, the politics of scale, mobility, sense of place, and identities (McDowell 1993; Altamirano 1997; Willis and Yeoh 2000; Silvey 2004, 2006).

However, migration is a topic of central interest across disciplines—ranging from economics, political science, cultural studies, anthropology to sociology—that many studies inflecting on gender enhance the theoretical and empirical fields (Brettell and Hollifield 2000; Boyd and Grieco 2003). Anthropology is by far the leading discipline in theorizing the significance of gender in migration, particularly the changing roles of women in migration (Brettell 2000). In historical studies of migration, there is a "flowering of interests" using gender in various scales of analyses—"regional, global, and transnational levels" since the 1990s (Sinke 2006, p. 87). According to Sarah Mahler (2006, p. 27), "ethnographers bring gender from the periphery toward the core of migration studies" although there is much to be done to make it as a "constitutive element of migration." But a gendered view on the political aspects of migration is still "a small body of work" (Piper 2006, p. 133). Nonetheless, gender conceptually becomes the focal point of entry of feminist scholars in migration studies. In this way, feminism seemingly comes about as a theoretical frame of examining the dynamics of migration.

Migration is the epitome of globalization. Esther Ngan-ling Chow (2003) claims that "gender matters" in the study of globalization in the twenty-first century. Its multiple dimensions connect global-local exchanges that recognize gender and other social variables in its modalities and practices. Eleonore Kofman (2004, p. 644) outlines the "gendered global migrations" involving both sides of the migration spectrum—the sending and receiving countries—and the "greater diversity of forms" of female migrations which intersects with the demand for labour, family, and immigration controls. Migrants, Nicola Piper (2008, p. 1) argues, "*leave* and *enter* gendered stratified societies" in various contexts of regulation and entitlements. Collectively, the examination of gender and migration stretches to many aspects such as settlement, integration, citizenship and belonging (Tastsoglou and Dobrowolsky 2006), family and household dynamics (Lawson 1998; Zontini 2010), changing identities (Herzig 2006), health and well-being (Bhugra and Gupta 2011), and economics and development (Gonzalez et al. 2004; Arya and Roy 2006). After the first decade of the twenty-first century, gender in migration studies still continues to fill "a glass half-full" (Donato et al. 2006, p. 3) coming from new insights of human mobility. For Rhacel Salazar Parreñas (2009, p. 10), however, "[t]he mere recognition of gender is not necessarily a feminist practice."

Despite the healthy state of gender in migration studies, Pierrette Hondagneu-Sotelo (2000, p. 112) claims, "immigration and feminism are rarely, if ever, coupled in popular discussion, social movements, or academic research." The rights discourse affecting migrant women, particularly workers, have not been fully recognized by mainstream women's organizations in host societies. According to Hondagneu-Sotelo (2000, p. 112), the "rights of immigrant women have not been embraced as a priority of feminist organizations." Like in the various conceptualizations of feminism, the pathways of resolving the gamut of issues affecting women in society create diversity of actions. Concerns of (im)migrant women tend to be sidelined or ignored. In more ways, the plight of female migrant domestic workers, for example, tend to ran counter with the interests of female employers. Activism of live-in caregivers in Canada, mostly comprised of Filipino women, to ensure their welfare and protection are not supported by mainstream women's organizations in their communities (Kelly 2007; Polanco and Nicholson 2010). Parreñas (2009, p. 1) raises the question, "What do we make of the challenge to feminist alliances posed by the increasing dependence of professional women in richer countries on the labor of domestic workers from poorer countries?" The answer remains to be seen. But it is through the organizing activities and public protests of migrant domestic workers where a new feminist-inspired scholarship begins (Swider 2006; Lyons 2010).

Under a regime of national security and the fear of terrorism in Western societies, immigrant women of certain ethnic background become targets of intense public attacks and media scrutiny (Zayzafoon 2005; Ata 2009) even from women's groups themselves. For example, Muslim immigrant women and their identifiable marker, the *hijab*, are discriminated in Western countries (Haddad and Smith 2002; Karim 2009) and a source of political contentions of belonging (Read 2007; Winter 2008; Fernando 2009). The veil and the right of women to express autonomy is perhaps the most publicly engaged issue fending Muslim immigrant women and other women's groups, including feminists (Fekete 2006; Williams and Vashi 2007; Rottman and Ferree 2008). Because the veiled Muslim woman symbolizes patriarchal oppression and female subordination (Akbarzadeh 2010; Edwards 2010), she embodies the so-called anti-thesis of feminist struggles. Unveiling Muslim women seems to be a desirable campaign as opposed to working toward equality in expressing their identity like those of other women wearing a hat or a bonnet. However, an increasing number of women, feminists' scholars and activists have recently rallied behind the cause of Muslim immigrant women to wear the *hijab* in public spaces and other challenges (Ezekiel 2006; Zine 2006; Macklin 2009; Mookherjee 2009).

Another area of focus traversing the nexus of immigration and feminism is human trafficking for sex purposes. Sex trafficking relates with prostitution; albeit the two differs in modes of operation, Siddharth Ashok Kara (2009, p. 100) notes, "it is undeniable that wherever prostitution is found, there are trafficked slaves forced to provide sex services." Feminists have long been divided about the issue of prostitution as "the profound symbol for the degradation and domination of women" (Shrage 1994, p. 82). Some scholars have positioned trafficking in the "international political economy of sex" (Pettman 1996, p. 185) that caters to the sex tourism industry and hospitality services, including prostitution and mail-order brides (Penttinen 2008). Perhaps sex trafficking has galvanized different women's groups into action and international coalitions (e.g., Coalition against Trafficking in Women, CATW) more than any other issue affecting migrant women (Dewey 2008; Cullen-DuPont 2009; Territo and Kirkham 2010). Many contemporary feminists adhere to abolitionist principles of eradicating prostitution as an instrument of male violence against women and children (Ditmore 2006, p. 6). But a "competing feminist approach" (Lobasz 2010, p. 224) argues that human trafficking is just a part of a huge problem of exploitation of human labor that "it is essential to protect the rights of all trafficked persons, whether victims of forced sex or non-sex labor." Heightened engagements of women's groups across different levels of governance have led to the adoption of policies against human trafficking (Morehouse 2009) and the basis for providing care for victims. By and large, trafficking and migration cross a thin line and discerning which group of women fall into traps of promises for a better future in destination countries remains problematic.

In many receiving countries, migration and feminism are both contending spaces of exclusion and inclusion for particular groups of (im)migrant women with numerous "issues, challenges and paradoxes" (Mathi 2008). The contexts of support and solidarity seem flexible and changing among and between diverse groups of women: some groups join together for a particular cause, while others work on their own. The small but rich scholarly pursuits on feminism as a practice in migration discourse (e.g., Hondagneu-Sotelo 2000; Pratt 2004; Fekete 2006; Merrill 2006; Pojmann 2006; Parreñas 2009) demonstrate the profound potential of this area of study, and the inspiration of this collection.

1.2 Feminist Inspirations

Paraphrasing a popular adage, "one is not born a feminist, but made."[2] A feminist is a person who embraces the principles of gender equality, empowerment, change for social justice, and the recognition that each human being has the ability to positively contribute to society. These aspirations become cogent in structures and practices defined by systems of privilege and oppression in society (e.g., racism, sexism, and classism). Becoming a feminist is a product of where one is located in particular social structures—be it in the family, part of a group or a community in a society—based on panoply of intersecting variables such as gender, race, ethnicity, sexuality, ability, and religion. According to Judith Glazer-Raymo (1999, p. 1), in her opening chapter "becoming a feminist," that "we have to start with women's own experience if we are to understand how profoundly it influences our perspectives, values, attitudes, and role in society."

Migration is personal. Although migration touches families and communities, the experience is deeply personal. One is uprooted from the familiar comfort of "home" to embark on the unknown path in strange lands, often hostile to newcomers. Leaving behind one's cultural locationality of norms and mores to venture into a society embracing a different worldview surely shapes personal beliefs and aspirations. For (im)migrant women, the new cultural modalities in host societies offer many ways to challenge, transform, or negotiate traditional prescriptions of womanhood, women's work, and identities, among others. In doing so, these women, arguably, engage in *feminist practice* and become *feminists* on their own sans the label. By feminist practice, I refer to the "doing" (cf. Heyes 2000, p. 2) in the daily lives of (im)migrant women that questions, alters, compromises, or resists commonly accepted normative practices. Defining acts as feminist practice is, however, complex as it is incumbent upon the material, emotional, and intellectual subjectivities facing the (im)migrant woman. In another work, I call this "lived activism" (Bonifacio 2009, p. 143) in the context of Filipino marriage migrants in Australia: "'Lived activism' emanates from marginality, subordination, and exclusion discovered through a process of daily interactions […] with a dominant culture […]."

---

[2] This is an application of Simone de Beauvoir's famous statement that "one is not born but is made a woman" (Evans 1998, p. 77).

Feminism occurs in multiple spaces of engagement—for example, personal or collective, academic or institutional, national or transnational. Feminism as a practice does not exclude anyone who desires change from existing conditions—be it addressed to oneself or to others. If we follow the logic of the discursive agenda of feminism, personal liberation or empowerment is a precondition for any sustained action for change. One must believe and embrace the cause of any struggle; the individual then becomes the unit of an aggregate body now working for social change. To limit the strand of feminist practice to changing society per se, and not the individual, is to deny the core from which such activism takes place.

Because the word "feminist" or "feminism" is subject to constant backlash in popular media, politics, and the everyday world, its usage lead others to caution. Not to be an instrument of more divisions in society, other well-meaning women tend to use more neutral terms (e.g., humanist and womanist) instead of the "F" word (Rowe-Finkbeiner 2004). I do recognize their purposes for inclusivity and cooperation to embrace a generic cause without the potential of divisive politics. However, following feminist standpoint epistemology (Hartsock 1998; Harding 2004), feminist practice begins with the *"concrete experiences"* of *"what women do"* as "the starting point from which to build knowledge" (Brooks 2007, p. 56). In a world of unequal relations, I urge scholars examining the intersections of feminism and migration to open the possibilities from which feminism takes place in the lives of (im)migrant women. That to ascribe feminism is not only to those who publicly embrace it as an identity for advocacy but also as a practice among different women across cultures. That feminism is a flexible practice not always confined to western constructs (i.e., socialist feminism, radical feminism, etc.) but could be something else in a world of diversity. At best, it describes *"multiple feminisms"* and recognize that "western feminists learn to listen to other women rather than speak for them" (Pojmann 2006, p. 160). As well, an urgent call mandates us that there are other aspects to learn from their lives than their supposed view as victims. Through this perspective, a new feminist paradigm that approaches the lives and conditions of (im)migrant women as active agents of change on their own, within their own communities, and outside cultural and national borders could be recognized.

It is from this vantage that this collection of well-researched chapters set out to explore the ways in which broad conceptions of feminism and migration across cultures relate to women's experiences in migration. Does migration empower (im) migrant women? To what extent does the feminist experiential paradigm "the personal is political" contributes to the involvement of (im)migrant women in certain modes of feminist actions for change? More importantly, are there cross-cultural collaboration or engagements among immigrant (i.e., with permanent residency status) or migrant (i.e., with temporary residency status) women with other groups of women in host communities? These are some of the questions explored by the following chapters in examining the possible ways in which feminism and migration intersect in the varying experiences of (im)migrant women in host societies in different contexts and roles—as wives, mothers, exiles, nuns, and workers. Cross-cultural engagements underscore the points of convergence, interaction, and even disjunctures between (im)migrant women and non-immigrant women. From these nodes, the chapters tease out the meanings, interpretations, and possibilities of feminist practice.

1.3   Synopses of Chapters

This book is divided into four thematic parts: theorizing feminism in migration, contesting identities and agency, resistance and social justice, and religion for change. Part I, *theorizing feminism in migration*, presents three chapters that explore new perspectives in examining the use of concepts, theories, and research practice of feminism in migration. Chapter 2 introduces the notion of "intersectional gender" and the locationality of women in transit. In this chapter, MariaCaterina La Barbera challenges the West versus Third World binaries between gender equality and cultural difference, and uses "multicentred feminism" to incorporate women migrants at the margins. In Chapter 3, Gail Mummert tracks the intersections of feminist thought and migration studies in Mexico since the 1970s. She also focuses on the synergies between the two and their potential for change in the empowerment of Mexican women in society, particularly at the familial level. Chapter 4 looks at multi-sited research in migration research as a tool to build solidarity among women, including researchers. Luna Vives addresses the challenges of multi-sited ethnography and its solid fit in studying the experiences of racialized migrants from Senegal in Spain.

Part II presents the theme of *contesting identities and agency* showcasing five chapters that investigate the ways in which constructed identities are negotiated by (im)migrant women in Australia, Belgium, Eastern Europe, and the United States. Chapter 5 explores the case of Japanese single mothers who decided to remain in Australia after separation or divorce. Jun Nagatomo uses poststructuralist perspectives on agency of these Japanese immigrant women's negotiation of their stigma as single mothers and their sense of identity and belonging in Australia on their own. Chapter 6 focuses on migrant women in Belgium and how their feminist claims have been reduced to identity claims as Muslims. Nouria Ouali traces the evolution of feminist organizations in Belgium after World War II and the inclusion or exclusion of migrant women. Chapter 7 introduces the notion of "hidden feminism" of an immigrant Muslim woman from India in the United States. Shweta Singh elucidates the development of a post-migration identity and the use of agentic conceptualizations in migration that involves crossing over many boundaries—gender, nation, and religion—of self, relationship with others, and being American and *Desi*. Chapter 8 illustrates how Iranian immigrant women encounter differences in Australia. Maryam Jamarani raises the question, "to what extent do Iranian immigrant women benefit from the social rights and freedom available to women in Australia?" Using narratives, Jamarani emphasizes the differing attitudes and values associated with gender between Iran and the host culture, and the extent to which these women negotiate such differences at home, in their own community, and in the larger Australian society. Chapter 9 highlights the transnational experiences of Eastern European (im)migrant women after the fall of communism in 1989. Cezara Crisan follows through the transnational, circular, and return migration of Eastern European women in the United States, how they mediate their experiences to shape socio-cultural environments, and whether their migration contributes to advance feminist ideas and practices in new developing democracies.

Part III presents the theme on *resistance and social justice* with four chapters that demonstrate the ways in which (im)migrant women forge alliances and build grounds for social recognition. Chapter 10 is a historical case of exile activism of Spanish women in New York. Montse Feu analyses the political activism set out in a newspaper, *España Libre*, and how Spanish immigrant and exiled women are represented, including their contribution as working-class women in the struggle against fascism. Maria Inacia D'Ávila Neto, Annick Durand-Delvigne, and Juliana Nazareth outline the initial findings of their intercultural research on immigrant women in France and domestic regional migrants in Brazil in Chapter 11. They examine the common points of realities affecting these two groups of (im)migrant women across two countries; their attempts for social justice and recognition; how networks are utilized to survive amidst constraining socio-economic structures; and the possibilities of feminism in postcolonial contexts. Chapter 12 illustrates the political relationship between Greek and migrant women workers in the anti-racist movement in Greece. Alexandra Zavos centres on how migrant women challenge their marginality and essentialized identities within hierarchies to establish new political modalities of belonging. Chapter 13 highlights the forms of activism rendered by migrant women in Italy. Laura Menin explores the impact of migration on the feminist agenda, particularly the multicultural dilemmas of migrant women's self-organization in Milan.

Part IV presents the theme of *religion for change* with two illustrative chapters that examine the role of religion in changing women's lives. Chapter 14 is a feminist approach to the archival study of nun migration in historical and contemporary contexts. Katharina Stornig explores the cross-cultural engagements of nuns in missions and their empowerment in Catholic Church hierarchy. Chapter 15 underscores the activism of immigrant Muslim women in Chicago. Jackleen M. Salem utilizes feminist theories and oral history methodology to provide a nuanced evolution of Muslim immigrant women's activism from the early 1900s to the present.

This international collection of case studies and various strands of feminist practices in migration fill the gaps in our present understanding of the complexities of migration in the lives of (im)migrant women. The contributors engage us in a continuing dialogue of the significance of feminism across cultures and the forms it take in private and public spheres from the perspectives of different groups of women. It is earnestly envisioned that such dialogue inspires others to the limitless possibilities of "doing" feminism across cultures—by (im)migrant women and with women in host communities. Their engagements offer new ways of thinking and the realities of our interconnected lives.

References

Afsar, R. (2003). Gender, labour market, and demographic change: A case study of women's entry into the formal manufacturing sector in Bangladesh. In B. Garcia, R. Anker, & A. Pinnelli (Eds.), *Women in the labour market in changing economies* (pp. 59–86). New York: Oxford University Press.

Akbarzadeh, S. (2010). The challenge of being Muslim. In S. Akbarzadeh (Ed.), *Challenging identities: Muslim women in Australia* (pp. 1–8). Victoria: Melbourne University Press.

Altamirano, A. T. (1997). Feminist theories and migration research—Making sense in the data feast? *Refuge, 16*(4), 4–8.

Andersen, M. L. (2010). The nexus of race and gender: Parallels, linkages, and divergences in race and gender studies. In P. H. Collins & J. Solomos (Eds.), *The Sage handbook of race and ethnic studies* (pp. 166–187). London: Sage.

Anderson, B. (2000). *Doing the dirty work? The global politics of domestic labour*. London: Zed Books.

Arya, S., & Roy, A. (Eds.). (2006). *Poverty, gender and migration*. New Delhi: Sage.

Ata, A. W. (2009). *Us and them: Muslim-Christian relations and cultural harmony in Australia*. Bowen Hills: Australia Academic Press.

Bailey, R. (2008). *Global issues: Immigration and migration*. New York: Infobase Publishing.

Beasley, C. (1999). *What is feminism? An introduction to feminist theory*. St. Leonards: Allen & Unwin.

Beasley, C. (2006). Speaking of feminism…What are we arguing about? In L. Burns (Ed.), *Feminist alliances* (pp. 35–58). New York: Editionsrodopi B. V.

Beeks, K., & Amir, D. (Eds.). (2006). *Trafficking and the global sex industry*. Lanham: Lexington Books.

Bhugra, D., & Gupta, S. (Eds.). (2011). *Migration and mental health*. Cambridge: Cambridge University Press.

Bonifacio, G. (2009). Activism from the margins: Filipino marriage migrants in Australia. *Frontiers: A Journal of Women's Studies, 30*(3), 142–168.

Bourbeau, P. (2011). *The securitization of migration: A study of movement and order*. New York: Routledge.

Boyd, M., & Grieco, E. (2003, March 1). Women and migration: Incorporating gender into international migration theory. *Migration Information Source*.http://www.migrationinformation.org/feature/display.cfm?ID=106. Accessed July 9, 2011.

Brettell, C. B. (2000). Theorizing migration in anthropology: The social constructions of networks, identities, communities and globalscapes. In C. Brettell & J. F. Hollifield (Eds.), *Migration theory: Talking across disciplines* (pp. 97–136). New York: Routledge.

Brettell, C., & Hollifield, J. M. (Eds.). (2000). *Migration theory: Talking across disciplines*. London/New York: Routledge.

Brooks, A. (2007). Feminist standpoint epistemology: Building knowledge and empowerment through women's lived experience. In S. N. Hesse-Biber & P. L. Leavy (Eds.), *Feminist research practice: A primer* (pp. 53–82). London: Sage.

Budde, R. (2005). *Mexican and Central American L. A. garment workers: Globalized industries and their economic constraints*. Münster: Lit Verlag Münster.

Castles, S., & Miller, M. (1998). *The age of migration: International population movements in the modern world*. London: Macmillan.

Cook, N. (Ed.). (2007). *Gender relations in global perspective*. Toronto: Canadian Scholar's Press.

Cornelius, W. A., Tsuda, T., Martin, P. L., & Hollifield, J. F. (Eds.). (2004). *Controlling immigration: A global perspective* (2nd ed.). Stanford: Stanford University Press.

Crush, J., & Dodson, B. (2010). *Migration, remittances and 'development' in Lesotho* (Migration policy series, Vol. 52). Cape Town: Idasa and Southern African Research Centre.

Cullen-DuPont, K. (2009). *Global issues: Human trafficking*. New York: Infobase Publishing.

Dewey, S. (2008). *Hollow bodies: Institutional responses to sex trafficking in Armenia, Bosnia and India*. Sterling: Kumarian Press.

Ditmore, M. H. (2006). *Encyclopedia of prostitution and sex work* (Vol. 1). Santa Barbara: ABC-CLIO.

Donato, K. M., Gabaccia, D., Holdaway, J., Manalansan, M. I. V., & Pessar, P. R. (2006). A glass half-full? Gender in migration studies. *International Migration Review, 40*(1), 3–26.

Edwards, S. (2010). Defacing Muslim women: Dialectical meanings of dress in the body politic. In R. Banakar (Ed.), *Rights in context: Law and justice in late modern society* (pp. 127–146). Surrey: Ashgate.

Evans, R. (Ed.). (1998). *Simone de Beauvoir's the second sex: New interdisciplinary essays*. Manchester: Manchester University Press.

Ezekiel, J. (2006). French dressing: Race, gender, and the hijab story. *Feminist Studies, 32*(2), 256–278.

Faludi, S. (2006). *Backlash: The undeclared war against American women*. 15th Anniversary ed. New York: Three Rivers Press.

Fekete, L. (2006). Enlightened fundamentalism? Immigration, feminism and the right. *Race & Class, 48*(2), 1–22.

Fernando, M. (2009). Exceptional citizens: Secular Muslim women and the politics of difference in France. *Social Anthropology, 17*(4), 379–392.

Freilich, J. D., & Guerette, R. T. (Eds.). (2006). *Migration, culture conflict, crime and terrorism*. Hampshire/Burlington: Ashgate.

Glazer-Raymo, J. (1999). *Shattering the myths: Women in academe*. Baltimore: The Johns Hopkins University Press.

Gonzalez, G. G., Fernandez, R. A., Price, V., Smith, D., & V , L. T. (Eds.). (2004). *Labor versus empire: Race, gender, and migration*. New York: Routledge.

Gooch, A. (2009). Foreword. In B. Keeley (Ed.), *International migration* (pp. 3–4). Paris: OECD [Organization for Economic Cooperation and Development].

Haddad, Y. Y., & Smith, J. I. (Eds.). (2002). *Muslim minorities in the West: Visible and invisible*. Lanham: Alta Mira Press.

Halfacree, K., & Boyle, P. (1999). Introduction: Gender and migration in developed countries. In P. Boyle & K. Halfacree (Eds.), *Migration and gender in the developed world* (pp. 1–29). London/New York: Routledge.

Harding, S. (Ed.). (2004). *The feminist standpoint theory reader: Intellectual and political controversies*. New York: Routledge.

Hartsock, N. C. M. (1998). *The feminist standpoint revisited and other essays*. Oxford: Westview Press.

Herzig, P. (2006). *South Asians in Kenya: Gender, generation and changing identities in diaspora*. Münster: LIT Verlag Münster.

Heyes, C. J. (2000). *Line drawings: Defining women through feminist practice*. New York: Cornell University Press.

Hondagneu-Sotelo, P. (2000). Feminism and migration. *The Annals of the American Academy of Political and Social Science, 571*(September), 107–120.

Hoy, C. C. (2003). *Empire of care: Nursing and migration in Filipino American history*. Durham: Duke University Press.

Idoko, U. (2010, September). Feminization of West African migration. *West Africa Insight*. http://www.westafricainsight.org/articles/PDF/55. Accessed July 2, 2011.

Isaacs, A. K. (Ed.). (2007). *Immigration and emigration in historical perspective*. Pisa: Edizioni Plus-Pisa University Press.

Johnston, R. J., Gregory, D., Pratt, G., & Watts, M. (Eds.). (2000). *The dictionary of human geography* (4th ed.). Oxford: Blackwell Publishing.

Kara, S. A. (2009). *Sex trafficking: Inside the business of modern slavery*. New York: Columbia University Press.

Karim, J. A. (2009). *American Muslim women: Negotiating race, class, and gender within the Ummah*. New York/London: New York University Press.

12   G.T. Bonifacio

Kelly, P. F. (2007). Transnationalism and political participation among Filipinos in Canada. In L. Goldring & S. Krishnamurti (Eds.), *Organizing the transnational: Labour, politics, and social change* (pp. 215–231). Vancouver: UBC Press.

Kemp, S., & Squires, J. (1998). *Feminisms*. Oxford: Oxford University Press.

Kofman, E. (2004). Gendered global migrations. *International Feminist Journal of Politics, 6*(4), 643–665.

Koser, K. (2007). *International migration: A very short introduction.* New York: Oxford University Press.

Lawson, V. A. (1998). Hierarchical households and gendered migration in Latin America: Feminist extensions to migration research. *Progress in Human Geography, 22*(1), 39–53.

Lindio-McGovern, L., & Walliman, I. (Eds.). (2009). *Globalization and third world women: Exploitation, coping and resistance.* Surrey/Burlington: Ashgate.

Lobasz, J. K. (2010). Beyond border security: Feminist approaches to human trafficking. In L. Sjoberg (Ed.), *Gender and international security: Feminist perspectives* (pp. 214–234). New York: Routledge.

Lorber, J. (1998). *Gender inequality: Feminist theories and politics.* Los Angeles: Roxbury.

Lorber, J., & Farrell, S. A. (Eds.). (1991). *The social construction of gender.* Newbury Park: Sage.

Lutz, H. (Ed.). (2008). *Migration and domestic work: A European perspective of a global theme.* Hampshire/Burlington: Ashgate.

Lyons, L. (2010). Transnational network and localized campaign: The women's movement in Singapore. In M. Roces & L. Edwards (Eds.), *Women's movements in Asia: Feminism and transnational activism* (pp. 75–89). New York: Routledge.

Macklin, A. (2009). Particularized citizenship: Encultured women and the public sphere. In S. Benhabib & J. Resnik (Eds.), *Migrations and mobilities: Citizenship, borders, and genders* (pp. 276–303). New York/London: New York University Press.

Mahler, S. J. (2006). Gender matters: Ethnographers bring gender from the periphery toward the core of migration studies. *International Migration Review, 40*(1), 27–63.

Massey, D. S., Arango, J., Hugo, G., Kouaouci, A., Pellegrino, A., & Taylor, J. E. (1998). *Worlds in motion: Understanding international migration at the end of the millennium.* New York: Oxford University Press.

Mathi, B. (2008, September 25–26). Session 1.6: Migration & feminism: Issues, challenges and paradoxes "mind the gap." International conference on gender migration and development, Manila. www.icgmd.info/sessions/session_1_6/pps_braema_mathi.pps. Accessed July 10, 2011.

McDowell, L. (1993). Space, place and gender relations. *Progress in Human Geography, 17*(2), 157–179.

Merrill, H. (2006). *An alliance of women: Immigration and the politics of race.* Minneapolis: University of Minnesota Press.

Mookherjee, M. (2009). *Women's rights as multicultural claims: Reconfiguring gender and diversity in political philosophy.* Edinburgh: Edinburgh University Press.

Morehouse, C. (2009). *Combating human trafficking: Policy gaps and hidden political agendas in the USA and Germany.* Wiesbaden: VS Verlag.

Morokvašic, M. (1984). Birds of passage are also women. *International Migration Review, 18*(4), 886–900.

Ngan-ling Chow, E. (2003). Gender matters: Studying globalization and social change in the 21st century. *International Sociology, 18*(3), 443–460.

Oderth, R. (2002). *An introduction to the study of human migration.* Lincoln: Writers Club Press.

Offen, K. (1992). Defining feminism: A comparative historical perspective. In G. Bock & S. James (Eds.), *Beyond equality & difference: Citizenship, feminist politics and female subjectivity* (pp. 62–81). London: Routledge.

Oishi, N. (2005). *Women in motion: Globalization, state policies, and labor migration in Asia.* Stanford: Stanford University Press.

Palmary, I., Burman, E., Chantler, K., & Kiguwa, P. (Eds.). (2010). *Gender and migration: Feminist interventions*. London/New York: Zed Books.

Paludi, M. A. (2010). Introduction. In M. A. Paludi (Ed.), *Feminism and women's rights worldwide: Heritage, roles, and issues* (pp. xiii–xviii). Santa Barbara: ABC-CLIO.

Parreñas, R. S. (2001). *Servants of globalization: Women, migration and domestic work*. Stanford: Stanford University Press.

Parreñas, R. S. (2009, May). Inserting feminism in transnational migration studies. *Migrationonline. cz*. Focus on Central and Eastern Europe. http://aa.ecn.cz/img_upload/6334c0c7298d6b396d2 13ccd19be5999/RParrenas_InsertingFeminisminTransnationalMigrationStudies.pdf.Accessed July 10, 2011.

Passerini, L., Lyon, D., Capussotti, E., & Laliotou, I. (2010). Editor's introduction. In L. Passerini, D. Lyon, E. Capussotti, & I. Laliotou (Eds.), *Women migrants from east to west: Gender, mobility, and belonging in contemporary Europe* (pp. 1–20). New York/Oxford: Berghahn Books.

Penttinen, E. (2008). *Globalization, prostitution and sex trafficking: Corporeal politics*. New York: Routledge.

Pettman, J. J. (1996). *Worlding women: A feminist international politics*. St Leonards: Allen & Unwin.

Piper, N. (2006). Gendering the politics of migration. *International Migration Review, 40*(1), 133–164.

Piper, N. (2008). International migration and gendered axes of stratification: Introduction. In N. Piper (Ed.), *New perspectives on gender and migration: Livelihood, rights and entitlements* (pp. 1–18). New York/London: Routledge.

Pojmann, W. (2006). *Immigrant women and feminism in Italy*. Aldershot: Ashgate.

Polanco, G., & Nicholson, C. (2010). Re-construction' from the viewpoint of precarious labour: The practice of solidarity. In J. Pulkingham (Ed.), *Human welfare, rights, and social activism: Rethinking the legacy of J. S. Woodsworth* (pp. 199–220). Toronto: University of Toronto Press.

Pratt, G. (2004). *Working feminism*. Philadelphia: Temple University Press.

Read, J. G. (2007). Introduction: The politics of veiling in comparative perspective. *Sociology of Religion, 68*(3), 231–236.

Reysoo, F. (2008). Ambivalent developments in female migration: Cases from Senegal and Lebanon. In A. L. Van Naerssen, E. Spaan, & E. B. Zoomers (Eds.), *Global migration and development* (pp. 253–268). New York: Routledge.

Rottman, S. B., & Ferree, M. M. (2008). Citizenship and intersectionality: German feminist debates about headscarf and antidiscrimination laws. *Social Politics, 15*(4), 481–513.

Rowe-Finkbeiner, K. (2004). *The F-word: Women, politics, and the future*. Emeryville: Seal Press.

Rudnick, A. (2009). *Working gendered boundaries: Temporary migration experiences of Bangladeshi women in the Malaysian export industry from a multi-sited perspective*. Amsterdam: Amsterdam University Press.

Ryan, B. (1992). *Feminism and the women's movement: Dynamics of social change in social movement, ideology and activism*. New York/London: Routledge.

Schreiber, R. (2008). *Righting feminism: Conservative women and American politics*. New York: Oxford University Press.

Shrage, L. (1994). *Moral dilemmas of feminism: Prostitution, adultery, and abortion*. New York/London: Routledge.

Silvey, R. (2004). Power, difference and mobility: Feminist advances in migration studies. *Progress in Human Geography, 28*(4), 1–17.

Silvey, R. (2006). Geographies of gender and migration: Spatializing social difference. *International Migration Review, 40*(1), 64–81.

Sinke, S. M. (2006). Gender and migration: Historical perspectives. *International Migration Review, 40*(1), 82–103.

Swider, S. (2006). Working women of the world unite? Labor organizing and transnational gender solidarity among domestic workers in Hong Kong. In M. M. Ferree & A. M. Tripp (Eds.), *Global feminism: Transnational women's activism, organizing, and human rights* (pp. 110–140). New York/London: New York University Press.

Tastsoglou, E., & Dobrowolsky, A. Z. (Eds.). (2006). *Women, migration and citizenship: Making local, national, and transnational connections*. Hampshire: Ashgate.

Territo, L., & Kirkham, G. (2010). *International sex trafficking of women and children: Understanding the global epidemic*. Flushing: Looseleaf Law Publications, Inc.

UN-INSTRAW [United nations International Research and Training Institute for the Advancement of Women]. (2006, November 20–21). *Gender, migration, remittances and development*. Fifth coordination meeting on international migration. Population Division, Department of Economic and Social Affairs, United Nations Secretariat, New York. http://www.un.org/esa/population/meetings/fifthcoord2006/P02_INSTRAW.pdf. Accessed July 2, 2011.

Walters, M. (2005). *Feminism: A very short introduction*. New York: Oxford University Press.

Widding Isaksen, L. (Ed.). (2010). *Global care work: Gender and migration in Nordic societies*. Lund: Nordic Academic Press.

Williams, R. H., & Vashi, G. (2007). Hijab and American Muslim women: Creating the space for autonomous selves. *Sociology of Religion, 68*(3), 269–287.

Willis, K., & Yeoh, B. (Eds.). (2000). *Gender and migration*. Cheltenham: Edward Elgar Publishing.

Winter, B. (2008). *Hijab and the republic: Uncovering the French headscarf debate*. Syracuse: Syracuse University Press.

Yang, W., & Lu, M. C. (Eds.). (2010). *Asian cross-border marriage migration: Demographic patters and social issues*. Amsterdam: Amsterdam University Press.

Zayzafoon, L. B. Y. (2005). *The production of the Muslim woman: Negotiating text, history and ideology*. Lanham: Lexington Books.

Zine, J. (2006). Between orientalism and fundamentalism: Muslim women and feminist engagement. In K. Hunt & K. Rygiel (Eds.), *(En)gendering the war on terror: War stories and camouflaged politics* (pp. 27–50). Hampshire: Ashgate Publishing.

Zlotnik, H. (2003, March). The global dimensions of female migration. *Migration Information Source*.http://www.migrationinformation.org/feature/display.cfm?ID=109. Accessed July 2, 2011.

Zontini, E. (2010). *Transnational families, migration and gender: Moroccan and Filipino women in Bologna and Barcelona*. New York: Berghahn Books.

Part I
Theorizing Feminisms in Migration

Chapter 2
Intersectional-Gender and the Locationality of Women "in Transit"

MariaCaterina La Barbera

2.1 Introduction

Catherine MacKinnon (2000, p. 690) states that "feminism did call for rethinking everything." As a crucial concept within feminist theory, gender is used as a tool to subvert the male-centered epistemology and admit women's perspective in the public discourse. Questioning the established structures of male power, feminism goes back to the family and its structure, rethinking the relations between the so-called public and private spheres (Okin 1989). Feminism reveals that the historically established sexual roles are socially constructed, rather than normative and natural. Over the past decades, feminism adopted gender as a category of analysis (Scott 1986) for interpreting the relationship between knowledge and normativity, and subverting the male-centric perspective in law and politics (MacKinnon 1989). Critically reflecting on sexuality and the societal construction of biological difference, feminism re-explores the meaning of equality and its inextricable links with diversity (Scott 1988; Minow 1990). In so doing, feminism focuses on the political relevance of identity (Young 1990) and challenges the usefulness of the categories of neutrality and impartiality of the state to address the issue of difference (Rawls 1971; Nozick 1974; Walzer 1983). Since thinking about gender implies a re-conceptualization of power and difference, some feminist scholars have recently interrogated the idea of secularism of the State. They raised the issue of how to find reasonable accommodations for the different religions and cultures that cohabit in the global contemporary society (Shachar 2001; Benhabib 2004; Phillips 2007; Scott 2007).

This work has been supported by MICINN grant n. FFI2009-08762 and by Instituto de la Mujer and ESF grant n. 06/10.

M. La Barbera, Ph.D. (✉)
Centre for Political and Constitutional Studies,
Plaza de la Marina Española 9, 28013 Madrid, Spain
e-mail: mc.labarbera@cepc.es

Since the end of the 1970s, many feminist scholars (English 1977; Pateman 1983; Kearns 1983; Olsen 1985; Green 1986; Matsuda 1986; McClain 1992; Okin 1994; Lloyd 1995; Scott 1998) recurred to gender as a conceptual tool to criticize the purported universality and gender blindness of classical political theory, and claim the necessity to adopt theories of justice that incorporate women and their body (Okin 1994). Questioning the assumption that the theories of justice should be populated by un-unbodied individuals (Okin 1979; Bell 1983; Kennedy and Mendus 1987), feminist scholars contested the categories of universality, generality, and abstraction. They move away from the idea of atomistic and auto-sufficient subject, and conceive individuals as formed by a complex of interactions with others and society. Locatedness becomes a crucial concept to criticize the idea of abstract and disembodied subject who "viewing from nowhere" (Nagel 1986) gets objective, neutral and universal concepts. In contrast, purportedly neutral concepts are meant as tools for those in power to shape reality.

This chapter analyzes the privileges and power within feminist scholarship as a crucial issue for gender and migration studies. The starting point is that, when feminism defines itself from the Western perspective, and excludes any other vision of gender equality, other women's perspectives are inevitably silenced and negated. In this respect, it is interesting to recall the words of Catherine MacKinnon describing how male/state control over women works by eliminating the capability of women's self-definition. The state authoritatively creates the social order, and ensures the "male" control over women by qualifying, regulating, or prohibiting female sexuality at every level (Mackinnon 1983, pp. 636–644). In MacKinnon's analysis, "male" means "those in power," that is, those who define the conditions of possibility for the others, establishing their living space, constraining their body, distorting their voices, and speaking out for them. The dominant perspective is by nature exclusive: there is no space for other points of view.

By replacing "male" for "dominant," this analysis perfectly describes also how "Western liberal feminism[1]" silences the voices of "Third-world" feminists. To ignore differences among women permits the relatively more privileged women to claim a special authority to speak for all women (Minow 1988, p. 52). Yet, by reproducing male power, Western feminism has been converted into a caricature of the very establishment it intended to challenge (Lazreg 1988, p. 97). The point is, how can Western feminists pretend to speak for all women while not listening

---

[1] When in 1988 Chandra Talpade Mohanty used the expression "Western feminism" for the first time, she explained that the reference to "Western feminism" does not imply that it is a monolith. The categories Western and Third-world feminist are not meant as embodied or geographically defined categories. Rather, they refer to political and analytic sites and methodologies. From this perspective, a woman coming from the Third-world can be a Western feminist in orientation or a European feminist can use a Third-world feminist analytic perspective (Mohanty 2003, p. 4). Western vs. Third World is thus used to distinguish between powerful and privileged communities, on the one hand, and economically and politically marginalized communities, on the other. Yet, while these terms are meant to distinguish the northern and southern hemispheres, power and marginalization obviously do not line up only with geographical space (ibid.).

to other women's voices? Since the 1980s, this asymmetry of power has created
many divides within feminism and posed West/white women against Third-world/
black women.

This chapter challenges the West vs. Third-world binarism within feminist
theory and the related dichotomy that opposes gender equality to cultural difference. The goal is perplexing the core of feminism itself by posing the question of
whether the only path toward gender equality is the Western one. To this end, feminism is represented as a multicentered and multifaceted thought. "Multicentered
feminism" is described as a theoretical frame that incorporates the perspectives of
women from the "margin" and stresses out the interrelatedness of different social
categories that together create women's subordination. To this end, intersectionality
is embraced to address the complex locationality of women who stake at the crossroad of interconnecting conditions of subordination. The concept of "intersectional-gender" is finally proposed as an analytical category useful to conceptualize
the formation and transformation of gender identities of women "in transit."
Approaching gender as situated and particular, this chapter also aims to approach
gender identity in relation to the factors of social identification and discrimination,
such as race/ethnicity, culture/religion, sexuality/body-ability, and educational/
occupational levels. The goal is to contribute to the examination of the relationship
between feminism and migration.

2.2   Challenging the West vs. "Third-world" Binarism

Within the "West vs. the Rest" divide of which the Western public discourse has been
nurtured in the last decade (Scruton 2002), the so-called "Third-world" is too often
imagined as related to fixity, rituality, and barbarity. In particular, "Third-world people" are imagined as constrained to adapt their preferences to the unjust conditions
of their situation, and motivated by their a-critically accepted and unchanging culture
(Okin 1999, p. 126; *contra* Narayan 2000, p. 88). Along this way Third-world is set
as the traditional and exotic *par exellence*. According to the orientalistic discourse,
"Third-world" is depicted as a place where women are subjugated by the patriarchal
society, their preferences are "adaptive," and their culture a cage. As a consequence,
"Third-world women" are usually imagined as sexually oppressed, poor, illiterate,
religion or tradition bounded, and domesticated; in a word, as backward (Mohanty
1988, p. 65). The very term "Third-world women" turned out to stand for "inability
to assert their own voice" and "necessity to be represented" (Alarcón 1990, p. 356).
Within this frame, many feminist scholars conceive gender equality as opposed to
cultural difference. In the context of international migration, the dichotomy of gender equality versus cultural differences has often set Western feminists in speaking
out for migrant women without listening to their need of maintaining their culture
while, at the same time, catching Western societal opportunities.

Yet, many postcolonial feminist scholars point out that the insistent focus on
"Third-world women" as passive victims of their culture leads to deny their agency

and ignores the social changes that they are promoting in their own ways (Spivak 1988; Mohanty 1988; Narayan 1997). They argue that the improvement of women's status has always been an inherent component of colonial powers, and it is still used to discriminate between "Western civilization" and the rest of "underdeveloped or developing countries" (Mani 1987; Ahmed 1992; Shaheed 1995; Yegenoglu 1998; Grande 2004). The category of "colonization" has been used to describe how the discourse on the so-called "Third-world" exploits their experiences as women. Postcolonial feminists represent women's difficulties in emerging both in national narratives and in minority group rights revindication in the diaspora. At the same time, they reveal how paternalistic Western feminist attitude toward "Third-world women" is. In this respect, postcolonial feminism aims at dismantling the discursive "othering" (Spivak 1988, p. 306) that places women as inert material within immutable social structures, and claims for analyzing how women's gender identity is molded through and within the complexity of social structures in which they live in postcolonial nation as well as in diaspora (Mohanty 1988, p. 80).

After the 9/11 Al-Queda attacks on the USA and the 2005 London bombings, within the "West vs. the Rest" discourse, Islam has been represented as the "Other" by definition (Scruton 2002). Since then, the whole debate about cultural differences in Europe focuses on Muslim minorities and their integration (Abbas 2005; Modood et al. 2006; Joppke 2009). As a part of this larger discourse, many feminist scholars express their concerns for the condition of migrant women in Muslim minorities, which are consistently represented as subjugated and passive victims of their patriarchal religion (Cohen et al. 1999). In particular, women wearing the hijab are at center of the discourse on migration and cultural integration (McGoldrick 2006; Scott 2007; Winter 2008; Joppke 2009). Many Europeans feel disturbed, sometimes even threatened, by the presence of Muslim women in the public sphere when they can be identified by their outfit (Henkel 2009). Although many Muslim women wearing the hijab show how it is possible to actively and strategically reinvent the traditional dress code without abandoning their tradition and religion (Droogsma 2007; Kejanlio lu and Ta 2009; Jouili 2009; Moors and Salih 2009; Sandikci and Ger 2010), the image of veiled Muslim women is mostly linked to gender subordination in the European public discourse. As a reification of Islam itself, the hijab has been turned into evidence of the conflict between cultures, and many liberal feminists strongly oppose to it. Yet, Muslim women very often declare that they do not feel represented by Western liberal feminists, which misunderstand their needs, requests and values, and consider their culture and religion as oppressive and discriminatory (Fernea 1998).

The whole political debate about hijab in Europe is constructed on the assumption that, as a condition to achieve the Western standards of gender equality, migrant women from the "Third-world" would be better off giving up their own culture, religion, and tradition (Okin 1999). This argument ignores that the aspects of identity cannot be analyzed as an isolated phenomena. Individuals can neither set aside their gender nor ignore their race, class, and religion as factors that shape their lives (La Barbera 2007). Indeed, to set gender equality against culture, religion, and tradition means to assume that they are uniform, homogeneous, and fixed. Such an approach ignores that all cultures are multiple and contradictory as well as in constant transformation and reshaping. Rather, cultures are animated by internal dissent, differently negotiating new meanings in relation to gender, age, class, race/ ethnicity, religion, disability status, and sexual orientation (Sunder 2002, p. 498). Hence, without questioning the political uses of culture, and without asking who the beneficiaries of "culture" are, it is difficult to understand the way in which women are exploited at the political, economic, and discursive levels. If we do not place the very notion of culture into context and analyze the strategical use of it, the risk is that the effort of "saving women from their backward cultures" could cause them the same damages we are supposedly preventing (Rao 1995, p. 174).

By assuming that gender is a transcultural category—regardless of ethnicity, religion, race, class, sexuality, and age—"Western liberal feminists" tend to neglect that identity is complex, plural, and situated. *Being gendered* is always particular and contexted. If gender is defined as the basic and cross-sectional difference of humankind, it should also be considered that we became women and men through different processes of socialization involving culture, social structures, and power relationships (Butler 1990). When Western feminists wave the flag of the universality of "women's rights as human rights" (Bunch 1990), they impose their own particular model as the norm. The fact that Western feminism represents itself as a universal model, rather than as a culturally specific one, engenders the risk of falling into the same fallacy reproached to liberal political theory (Schutte 2000, p. 59).

If feminism wants to establish alliances that cross over the boundaries of Western countries without exporting/imposing its own models, it is pivotal to recognize that each community is modeled not only by patriarchal structures, but also by internal forms of resistance and subversion. To say it in Michael Foucault's (1990, p. 95) words, "where there is the power there is resistance." In order to bypass the unfruitful dichotomy, such as West vs. Third-word and gender vs. culture, we should leave aside the oppositional construction of feminism as standing for women's good and culture as standing for women's oppression (Volpp 2001; Song 2007; Freedman 2007), and rather ask: what can feminists around the world offer in terms of concepts and strategies of intervention to make the cohabitation of differences possible?

2.3 Multicentering Feminism and Locationality of Women "in Transit"

Feminism is both a social and theoretical movement. As a social movement, feminism aims towards local and global social transformation of the existing structures of power that shape gender subordination in the different social contexts. As a theoretical movement, its goal is to question the relationships of power that cause women's subordination. In this respect, all feminist theories share a main concern: the analysis of women's subordination in gendered relations and the elaboration of conceptual tools and strategies of subversion. Yet, it is impossible to describe feminism as theoretically unitary. Many different epistemological arguments, theoretical or practical approaches, and ethical or political backgrounds have been adopted, ranging from critical theory, political liberalism, analytic philosophy, hermeneutics, structuralism, existentialism, phenomenology, deconstructivism, genealogy, poststructuralism, postcolonial theory, psychoanalysis, semiotics, cultural studies, language analysis, pragmatism, neo-Marxism, and post-Marxism (Dietz 2003, p. 400).

In spite of the evident theoretical and operational diversity within feminism, the idea that not a single feminism but different feminisms exist, has been received by many scholars as a weakening of the feminist movement (Alcoff 1988; Bordo 1990; Benhabib 1995; Mackinnon 2000). Notwithstanding, Judith Butler asserts that the endless debate among feminists on the meaning of "gender" should be recognized as the very heart of feminism (1994, p. 50). From this perspective, the connections and links between women are not innate but built. It is rather the effort to recognize and examine the differences among women—which founds the constructions of coalitions, networks, and alliances for shared goals—that can join women and reinforce feminism as a global and local movement (Harris 1990, p. 615; Davis and Martínez 1994).

Challenging the assumption that variety and diversity are incompatible with unity (Nicholson 1992; Fraser 1995), and taking into account the different voices of feminism, I question here the idea of feminism as a singular and unified theory. I rather describe it as a movement that is, at the same time, coherent and heterogeneous, and that has as many propulsive centers as women concerned with gender justice around the world. To this end, I offer the idea of "multicentered feminism" as a conceptual frame that offers those analytical tools needed to understand diversities among women and, thus, challenge the dichotomy of gender versus culture. Multicentering feminism is here proposed as a strategy to understand the locationality of women "in transit."

Multicentered feminism is an adaptive set of conceptual tools and strategies of action that creates a framework to understand women's locationality within the multiple interlocking systems of subordination in which they live (Jaggar 1983; Sandoval 2000; Baca Zinn and Thornton Dill 2003). The expression *multicentered*— as it is inclusive of different race, culture, and national belongings— points to the idea of multiplicity without placing one aspect above the others. Multicentered feminism includes the emergent perspectives and experiences of women from different national, cultural, religious, and ethnic groups, whose marginalized locationality provide them with vivid insights on selves and society (Baca Zinn and Thornton Dill 2003).

Multicentered feminism takes into account the risks of essentializing gender that has been warned by Black feminists since the late 1970s (Combahee River Collective 1986). Black feminist scholars claim not only that race, culture, and religion are as many foundational elements of identity as gender, but also that all of these are inseparably interconnected (Lorde 1984; Spelman 1988). They argue that the concept of gender is conceptualized from the privileged position of the white, middle-class, heterosexual, Christian-formed, and able-bodied experience, which is assumed as the norm. Insofar as liberal feminists claim that gender is not a negligible aspect of identity, Black feminists assert that their color, economic level, sexuality, education, and body-ability form many crucial elements of gender identity.

Gender essentialism is meant as a form of reductionism that views in gender the only form of women's subordination, minimizing all the other factors of identification and discrimination. Gender essentialism reduces the multiple kinds of discrimination into a problem of arithmetical sum, as if adding racism to sexism could describe the experience of Black women, or juxtaposing racism to sexism and homophobia could explain the experience of lesbian Black women (Lorde 1982; Spelman 1988). Along this way, the experiences of Black women have been fragmented among those that analyze race and those that analyze gender discrimination in a way that compelled them to isolate one single aspect of their identity and offer it as it was a "meaningful whole" (Lorde 1984, p. 120).

Multicentered feminism adopts a de-essentialized notion of gender. Gender de-essentialization allows representing women as a map of interconnecting similarities and differences, in which the body does not fade away, but rather bears a situated social significance that, nonetheless, varies in the different contexts (Nicholson 1994, p. 102). Through this way, multicentered feminism recognizes the causes of discrimination as linked to an inextricable web made up of race/ethnicity, religion/culture, sexuality/body-ability and economic/educational level. Multicentered feminism embraces the concept of being *within/out* and of *intersectional-gender* as conceptual tools for approaching the locationality of women "in transit."

2.4 Locationality of Women "in Transit" as Being *Within/out*

The "politics of location" is considered one of the most important epistemological foundations of contemporary feminist thought (Braidotti 2003). Introduced by Adrienne Rich in the mid-1980s, the politics of location claims for not transcending the corporality, but reconnecting the abstract thinking with particular living bodies. Since patriarchy does not exist in a "pure state," the politics of location addresses when, where, and under which conditions women struggle against discrimination in the specific and different socio-cultural contexts in which they live (Rich 1986, pp. 213–218). The politics of location aims at using all the different socio-cultural conditions of each specific context as conceptual resources to interpret and represent the mechanisms of social interaction and subordination.

Over the last 20 years, the concept of politics of location has undergone several specifications, reformulations, and modifications, and turned out to be extremely fruitful to address the complex subjectivity of migrant women in Western countries (Brah 1996). Is an upper class, British educated woman residing in a city of India, an insider or outsider to rural poverty that affect women in India? Is a second generation migrant woman living in Europe, interacting only with her own ethnic group, an insider or outsider to her culture of origin (Okin 2000, pp. 40–41)? The either/or approach assumes social groups and identities as if they were rigid and static, and seems inadequate for explaining the subjectivities "in transit" that inhabit the post-colonial and globalized societies. To address the social location of being at the border space between groups, Patricia Hill Collins (1998, p. 8) introduced the concept of "outsider-within location" to describe the marginalized condition of Black women who no longer belong to any group and live at the interweaving of multiple systems of subordination.

Neither "insider" nor "outsider," the new social identities that populate the global society, particularly the psycho-socio-political locations of migrant women, come out from the hybridism, multiple belonging, and "borderline-ness." I adopt the term *within/out* to define the particular locationality of women who move across different nation-states and communities and belong to several groups at the same time. Being *within/out* is the borderline locationality of women "in transit." With this term I address their simultaneous inclusion/exclusion in displaced communities as a new social condition in the diaspora, without defining them just as "outsiders." Their "in transit" subjectivity is understandable through the multiple and interacting socio-psycho-political belongings, and the constant negotiation between their cultural minority group and the society at large (La Barbera 2010, p. 70).

In particular, migrant Black women in the West are part of the visible minorities, which simultaneous processes of racialization, genderization, and social classification locate within complicated matrixes of social relationships (Ang-Lygate 1996, p. 152). Black, Muslim women from Third-world countries living in the West represent the culmination of what is being "in transit," *within/out* the borderline between the displaced communities and the host society. They live at the crossroad of intersecting conditions of subordination and represent the ultimate position of social exclusion for being migrant, black, Muslim, and women. For this reason, migrant women from the "Third-world" represent the maximum fragility of the condition of being "in transit." Women "in transit" have to face multiple forms of social exclusion within their community of origin as well as in the host society. They have to fight against internal and external forms of discrimination. They share the culture of their group while fighting against its forms of gender subordination. Indeed, women "in transit" also represent the maximum potential of subversion. They tune their gender identity in the migratory process while reinterpreting their tradition. They do not abandon their religion and culture when searching for gender equality.

As a migrant feminist scholar, I depict the new subjectivity of women "in transit" as a suffered but fruitful locationality, which openness and constant becoming provide a productive space for developing a new political thought. The "in transit" locationality implies the deprivation of the "home protection"—meant as family, town, social network, or nation-state—and the search for new psychological and concrete spaces to settle down. Through a conceptual and emotional re-elaboration of multiple belongings, the existential, psychic, and social condition of being at the borderline is transformed from a marginalized condition of exclusion into a fruitful epistemological position from which to interrogate and theorize individual and group's mechanisms of social exclusion and identification. Through this way, the fragile position of cultural hybridism produces a ground for a strong impulse towards social change. More than a site of discrimination and exclusion, the marginality of being *within/out* is reinterpreted as a speculative space as well as a site of oppositional agency (hooks 1990; Sandoval 2000; Mohanty 2003, p. 106).

Multicentered feminism embraces the concept of "multiple consciousness," welcoming a conception of identity as a compound, developing, and possibly contradictory individual and social process (Harris 1990, p. 584). Understanding multiple identities as "oppositional" (Sandoval 1991, p. 14), it is possible to transform the initial condition of discrimination into a site of emancipation and self-affirmation. The goal is to include and develop the dislocated and dispersed, albeit cogent, discourse produced from the borderline locationality of women "in transit." Thinking about the distinctive locationality of migrant women leads to elaborate new interrelated concepts of what gender and cultural differences mean in the global society, how do they work together, and how do they may be reconceived.

2.5 *Intersectional-Gender*

Within the frame of multicentered feminism, I propose the concept of *intersectional-gender.* Starting from the idea that gender is a transversal category, although not identical over time and across cultures, I regard it convenient to analyze the very concept of gender through the intersectional approach. The aim is to avoid an ethnocentric essentialization when approaching the mechanism of gender formation and transformation in different contexts in which women live. To this end, the concept of *intersectional-gender* is elaborated as an analytical tool (La Barbera 2009).

In 1989, as a result of the vivid debate on both sides of the Atlantic on the interrelatedness of race, class, and gender in shaping women's subordination (Yuval-Davis 2006), Kimberlee Crenshaw (1989) coined the term "intersectionality." Intersectionality is a useful approach to understand the structural and dynamic effects of the interactions between the different forms of discrimination. It specifically addresses how sexism, racism, and classism, along with other discriminatory systems, contribute all together to create and reinforce women's social inequality. Intersectionality recognizes that race and class are always interconnected with gender in a way that makes not only senseless, but also counterproductive to disconnect the analysis of different forms of discrimination. It reveals how policies that separately address discrimination based on race, gender, and class cause the paradoxical effect of creating ulterior and ultimate dynamics of disempowerment (Crenshaw 1989).

Intersectionality refers to the complex, irreducible, varied, and variable effects produced by the interaction of social, economic, political, cultural, and symbolic factors intersecting in each context (Brah and Phoenix 2004, p. 76). For these reasons, it is a crucial concept in order to examine the different dimensions of social life, which are distorted by the single-axis analysis (Hill Collins 2000; Anthias 2002; Brah and Phoenix 2004; Yuval-Davis 2006). Intersectionality offers to social science research a methodology to deconstruct essentialist notions of identity, de-center dominant discourses, and produce situated and critically reflexive knowledge toward a more integrated approach for policy making (Davis 2008). This methodology is well captured by "asking the other question" approach described by Mary Matsuda (1991). Assuming that no form of discrimination stands alone, Matsuda (1991, p. 1189) argues that "asking the other question" promotes awareness of the intersectional dimension of both the evident and hidden structures of discrimination. When dealing with racism, one should ask: "Where is the patriarchy in this?;" when dealing with sexism, one should ask: "Where is the heterosexism in this?;" and, when dealing with homophobia, one should ask: "Where is the classism in this?"

I deem it fruitful to examine not only how race and class *inter*-act with gender and produce multiple interlocking forms of subordination, but also how all the factors of identification/discrimination *intra*-act shaping gender identity. Moreover, the factors shaping identity are not reducible just to gender, race, and class, since culture, religion, ethnicity, sexual identity, body-ability, and economical or educational levels also matter. Yet, placing gender within an endless list of other social categories involves the risk of neglecting that gender crosses all of them. In this respect, the term *intersectional-gender* recognizes the importance of focusing on gender as a determinant aspect of identity, and stressing out its intersectionality as an inherent and constitutive feature (La Barbera 2009). *Intersectional-gender* is an interdependent category that is originated at the interweaving of gender with other categories of social identification. To conceptualize gender as intersectional by itself means that it is connected, *inter*-acting and *intra*-acting with race/ethnicity, sexuality/body-ability, culture/religion, and economical/educational level. I, thus, address the intersectionality of gender as a constitutive rather than an additive process.

The inherent intersectionality of gender is well described by the renowned image of the birdcage used by Marilyn Frye (1983) to describe the intertwined aspect that set women's subordination. When one looks too closely at just one wire of a birdcage, it is impossible to see it as a whole. One can carefully examine the structure of one wire and, notwithstanding, be unable to see why the bird cannot just fly free. Indeed, Frye alerts that, by methodically but separately inspecting each wire, one will still be unable to understand how the birdcage is structured. Only by stepping back, it is possible to see the whole intersections of wires and understand how the bird is trapped (Frye 1983, p. 4).

Although the notion of interrelatedness of gender has been used for a long time in feminist theory, I claim here the strategic importance to coin a new term for a concept that was already in use. Naming creates realities, conjoins and disjoins things by identifying them as distinct or recognizing them as connected (Dewey and Bentley 1949, p. 133). Assuming that words are the tools to create concepts, and concepts are the tools to understand, analyze, interpret, and shape social reality, I argue that the use of *intersectional-gender* strongly and unequivocally asserts the complexity of gender and sheds light on how it is originated and interconnected along with other conditions of social identification/discrimination. The adjectivation of gender as intersectional is intended as a part of a discursive strategy stressing that gender, as an analytical category, is meaningless if it does not take into account all the *inter*-acting and *intra*-acting factors that differentiate and transform women's identities. *Intersectional-gender* recalls that women are subordinated in global and local systems of patriarchy, but they are also involved in the mechanisms of production and reproduction of those systems (Butler 1990). The active and dynamic role of women in perpetuating their own subordination recognizes them as active agents that both reproduce and subvert their subordination. This perspective leads to the awareness that an integrated approach is required for understanding the intertwined factors of discrimination that—as a web of dis/em-powering conditions strictly interconnected—oppress, discriminate, and silence women "in transit."

2.6   Conclusion

Multicentering feminism and welcoming *intersectional-gender* as a conceptual tool challenge the gender versus culture dichotomy that grounds the Western liberal feminist discourse. Listening to the voices of multicentered feminism redeems feminism as a movement capable of offering useful tools for understanding international migration of women and, above all, the tuning of gender identity of women "in transit." The recognition of the situatedness, multiplicity, and inherent intersectionality of gender allows conceiving the issues involving women from non-Western cultures in a way that avoids the risk of ethnocentrism. Abandoning the white, middle class, and Western perspective as the standard would allow to reach a goal that is crucial for the future of feminism, that is, to articulate, negotiate, and recognize the negated identities of women "in transit." Multicentered feminism stresses the importance of shifting our attention towards the marginalized perspectives within feminism. The strategy of moving towards the peripheries—as emotional, physical, and theoretical loci—recognizes the coexistent and conflicting cores of feminism, and converts it into "the very house of difference" where all diversity among women can find their place (Lorde 1982, p. 226).

References

Abbas, T. (Ed.). (2005). *Muslim Britain: Communities under pressure*. London: Zed Books.
Ahmed, L. (1992). *Women and gender in Islam: Historical roots of a modern debate*. New Haven: Yale University Press.
Alarcón, N. (1990). The theoretical subject(s) of this bridge called my back and Anglo-American feminism. In G. Anzaldúa (Ed.), *Making face, making soul/haciendo caras: Creative and critical perspectives by women of color* (pp. 356–369). San Francisco: Aunt Lute Foundation.
Alcoff, L. (1988). Cultural feminism versus poststructuralism: The identity crisis in feminist theory. *Signs, 13*(3), 417–418.
Ang-Lygate, M. (1996). Women who move: Experiences of diaspora. In M. Maynard & J. Purvis (Eds.), *New frontiers in women's studies: Knowledge, identity, and nationalism* (pp. 151–163). London: Taylor & Francis.
Anthias, F. (2002). Beyond feminism and multiculturalism: Locating difference and the politics of location. *Women's Studies International Forum, 25*(3), 275–286.
Baca Zinn, M., & Thornton Dill, B. (2003). Theorizing difference from multiracial feminism. In C. McCann & K. Seung-Kyung (Eds.), *Feminist theory reader: Local and global perspectives* (pp. 353–363). New York: Routledge.
Bell, L. (1983). *Vision of women*. Clifton: Humana Press.

Benhabib, S. (1995). Feminism and postmodernism: An uneasy alliance. In S. Benhabib, J. Butler, D. Cornell, & N. Fraser (Eds.), *Feminist contentions: A philosophical exchange* (pp. 17–34). New York: Routledge.

Benhabib, S. (2004). *The rights of others: Aliens, residents, and citizens.* Cambridge: Cambridge University Press.

Bordo, S. (1990). Feminism, postmodernism, and gender-skepticism. In L. Nicholson (Ed.), *Feminism/postmodernism* (pp. 133–157). New York: Routledge.

Brah, A. (1996). *Cartographies of diaspora: Contesting identities.* London: Routledge.

Brah, A., & Phoenix, A. (2004). Ain't I a woman? Revisiting intersectionality. *Journal of International Women's Studies, 5*(3), 75–86.

Braidotti, R. (2003). *The return of the masters' narratives.* http://www.e-quality.nl/assets/e-quality/publicaties/2003/e-quality.final.rosi%20braidotti.pdf. Accessed March 19, 2010.

Bunch, C. (1990). Women's rights as human rights: Towards a re-vision of human rights. *Human Rights Quarterly, 12*(4), 486–498.

Butler, J. (1990). *Gender trouble: Feminism and the subversion of identity.* New York: Routledge.

Butler, J. (1994). Contingent foundations: Feminism and the question of "postmodernism.". In S. Benhabib, J. Butler, D. Cornell, & N. Fraser (Eds.), *Feminist contentions: A philosophical exchange* (pp. 35–57). New York: Routledge.

Cohen, J., Nussbaum, M., & Howard, M. (Eds.). (1999). *Is multiculturalism bad for women?* Princeton: Princeton University Press.

Combahee River Collective. (1986). *Combahee river collective statement. Black feminist organizing in the seventies and eighties* (1977). Albany: Women of Color Press

Crenshaw, K. (1989). Demarginalizing the intersection of race and sex: A black feminist critique of antidiscrimination doctrine, feminist theory and antiracist politics. *University of Chicago Legal Forum, 14*, 139–167.

Davis, K. (2008). Intersectionality in transatlantic perspective. In C. Klinger & A. Knapp (Eds.), *ÜberKreuzungen. Fremdheit, ungleichheit, differenz* (pp. 19–35). Münster: Westfälisches Dampfboot.

Davis, A., & Martínez, E. (1994). Coalition building among people of color. *Inscriptions, 7*, 42–53.

Dewey, J., & Bentley, A. (1949). *Knowing and the known.* Boston: The Beacon Press.

Dietz, M. (2003). Current controversies in feminist theory. *Annual Review of Political Science, 6*, 399–431.

Droogsma, R. (2007). Redefining hijab: American Muslim women's standpoints on veiling. *Journal of Applied Communication Research, 35*(3), 294–319.

English, J. (1977). Justice between generations. *Philosophical Studies: An International Journal for Philosophy in the Analytic Tradition, 31*(2), 91–104.

Fernea, E. (1998). *In search of Islamic feminism: One woman's global journey.* New York: Doubleday.

Foucault, M. (1990). *The history of sexuality: An introduction.* Harmondsworth: Penguin.

Fraser, N. (1995). False antithesis. In S. Benhabib, J. Butler, D. Cornell, & N. Fraser (Eds.), *Feminist contentions: A philosophical exchange* (pp. 59–74). New York: Routledge.

Freedman, J. (2007). Women, Islam and rights in Europe: Beyond a universalist/culturalist dichotomy. *Review of International Studies, 33*, 29–44.

Frye, M. (1983). *The politics of reality: Essay in feminist theory.* Berkeley: The Crossing Press.

Grande, E. (2004). Hegemonic human rights and African resistance: Female circumcision in a broader comparative perspective. *Global Jurist Frontiers, 4*(2), 1–21.

Green, K. (1986). Rawls, women and the priority of liberty. *Australasian Journal of Philosophy Supplement, 64*, 26–36.

Harris, A. (1990). Race and essentialism in feminist legal theory. *Stanford Law Review, 42*(3), 581–616.

Henkel, H. (2009). Are Muslim women in Europe threatening the secular public sphere? *Social Anthropology, 17*(4), 471–473.

Hill Collins, P. (1998). *Fighting words: Black women and the search for justice*. Minneapolis: University of Minnesota Press.

Hill Collins, P. (2000). Gender, black feminism, and black political economy. *The Annals of the American Academy of Political and Social Science, 568*, 41–53.

hooks, b. (1990). *Yearning: Race, gender, and cultural politics*. Boston: South End Press.

Jaggar, A. (1983). *Feminist politics and human nature*. Totowa: Rowman & Allanheld.

Joppke, C. (2009). Limits of integration policy: Britain and her Muslim. *Journal of Ethnic and Migration Studies, 35*(3), 453–472.

Jouili, J. (2009). Negotiating secular boundaries: Pious micro-practices of Muslim women in French and German public spheres. *Social Anthropology, 17*(4), 455–470.

Kearns, D. (1983). A theory of justice and love: Rawls on the family. *Australian Journal of Political Science, 8*(1), 36–42.

Kejanlioğlu, B., & Taş, O. (2009). Regimes of un/veiling and body control: Turkish students wearing wigs. *Social Anthropology, 17*(4), 424–438.

Kennedy, E., & Mendus, S. (Eds.). (1987). *Women in western political philosophy: Kant to Nietzsche*. New York: St. Martin's Press.

La Barbera, M. C. (2007). Una reflexión crítica a través del pensamiento de Susan Okin sobre género y justicia. *Cuadernos Electrónicos de Filosofía del Derecho, 16*, 1–15. http://www.uv.es/CEFD/16/Barbera.pdf. Accessed June 1, 2011.

La Barbera, M. C. (2009). Intersectionalgender. Thinking about gender and cultural difference in the global society. *Global Studies Journal, 2*(2), 1–8.

La Barbera, M. C. (2010). Género y diversidad entre mujeres. *Cuadernos Koré. Revista de historia y pensamiento de género, 1*(2), 55–72.http://kusan.uc3m.es/CIAN/index.php/CK/articleviewFile/%201039/480. Accessed June 1, 2011.

Lazreg, M. (1988). Feminism and difference: The perils of writings as a woman on women in Algeria. *Feminist Studies, 14*(1), 81–107.

Lloyd, S. (1995). Situating a feminist criticism of John Rawls's political liberalism. *Loyola L.A. Law Review, 28*(4), 1319–1344.

Lorde, A. (1982). *Zami: A new spelling of my name*. Watertown: Persephone Press.

Lorde, A. (1984). *Sister outsider: Essays and speeches*. Trumansburg: The Crossing Press.

MacKinnon, C. (1983). Feminism, Marxism, method and state: Toward feminist jurisprudence. *Signs, 8*(4), 635–658.

MacKinnon, C. (1989). *Toward a feminist theory of the state*. Cambridge: Harvard University Press.

MacKinnon, C. (2000). Points against postmodernism. *Chicago-Kent Law Review, 75*(3), 687–712.

Mani, L. (1987). Contentious traditions: The debate on sati in colonial India. *Cultural Critique, 7*, 119–156.

Matsuda, M. (1986). Liberal jurisprudence and abstracted visions of human nature: A feminist critique of Rawls' theory of justice. *New Mexico Law Review, 16*, 613–630.

Matsuda, M. (1991). Beside my sister, facing the enemy: Legal theory out of coalition. *Stanford Law Review, 43*(6), 1183–1192.

McClain, L. (1992). Atomistic man revisited: Liberalism, connection and feminist jurisprudence. *Southern California Law Review, 65*(3), 1171–1264.

McGoldrick, D. (2006). *Human rights and religion: The Islamic headscarf debate in Europe*. Oxford: Hart Publishing.

Minow, M. (1988). Feminist reason: Getting it and losing it. *Journal of Legal Education, 38*, 47–60.

Minow, M. (1990). *Making all the differences: Inclusion, exclusion and American law*. Ithaca: Cornell University Press.

Modood, T., Triandafyllidou, A., & Zapata-Barrero, R. (Eds.). (2006). *Multiculturalism, Muslims and citizenship: A European approach*. London: Routledge.

Mohanty, C. (1988). Under western eyes: Feminist scholarship and colonial discourse. *Feminist Review, 30*, 61–88.

Mohanty, C. (2003). *Feminism without borders: Decolonizing theory, practicing solidarity.* Durham: Duke University Press.

Moors, A., & Salih, R. (2009). "Muslim women" in Europe: Secular normativities, bodily performances and multiple publics. *Social Anthropology, 17*(4), 375–378.

Nagel, T. (1986). *The view from nowhere.* Oxford: Oxford University Press.

Narayan, U. (1997). *Dislocating cultures: Identities, traditions, and third-world feminism.* New York: Routledge.

Narayan, U. (2000). Essence of culture and a sense of history: A feminist critique of cultural essentialism. In U. Narayan & S. Harding (Eds.), *Decentering the center: Philosophy for a multicultural, postcolonial, and feminist world* (pp. 80–100). Bloomington: Indiana University Press.

Nicholson, L. (1992). Feminism and the politics of postmodernism. *Boundary, 19*(2), 53–69.

Nicholson, L. (1994). Interpreting gender. *Signs, 20,* 79–105.

Nozick, R. (1974). *Anarchy, state, and utopia.* New York: Basic Book.

Okin, S. (1979). *Women in western political thought.* Princeton: Princeton University Press.

Okin, S. (1989). *Justice, gender, and the family.* New York: Basic Books.

Okin, S. (1994). Political liberalism, justice, and gender. *Ethics, 105*(1), 23–43.

Okin, S. (1999). Is multiculturalism bad for women? In J. Cohen, M. C. Nussbaum, & M. Howard (Eds.), *Is multiculturalism bad for women?* (pp. 7–24). Princeton: Princeton University Press.

Okin, S. (2000). Feminism, women's human rights, and cultural difference. In U. Narayan & S. Harding (Eds.), *Decentering the center: Philosophy for a multicultural, postcolonial and feminist world* (pp. 26–46). Bloomington: Indiana University Press.

Olsen, F. (1985). The myth of state intervention in the family. *University of Michigan Journal of Law Reform, 18*(4), 835–864.

Pateman, C. (1983). Feminist critiques of the public/private dichotomy. In S. Benn & G. Gaus (Eds.), *Public and private in social life* (pp. 281–303). New York: St. Martin's Press.

Phillips, A. (2007). *Multiculturalism without culture.* Princeton: Princeton University Press.

Rao, A. (1995). The politics of gender and culture in international human rights discourse. In J. Peters & A. Wolper (Eds.), *Women's rights, human rights: International feminist perspective* (pp. 167–175). New York: Routledge.

Rawls, J. (1971). *A theory of justice.* Cambridge: Harvard University Press.

Rich, A. (1986). *Of woman born: Motherhood as experience and institution [1976].* London: Virago.

Sandikci, O., & Ger, G. (2010). Veiling in style: How does a stigmatized practice become fashionable? *Journal of Consumer Research, 37*(1), 15–36.

Sandoval, C. (1991). US third world feminism: The theory and method of oppositional consciousness in the postmodern world. *Genders, 10,* 1–24.

Sandoval, C. (2000). *Methodology of the oppressed.* Minneapolis: University of Minnesota Press.

Schutte, O. (2000). Cultural alterity: Cross-cultural communication and feminist theory in North-South contexts. In U. Narayan & S. Harding (Eds.), *Decentering the center: Philosophy for a multicultural, postcolonial and feminist world* (pp. 47–66). Bloomington: Indiana University Press.

Scott, J. W. (1986). Gender: A useful category of historical analysis. *The American Historical Review, 91,* 1053–1075.

Scott, J. W. (1988). Deconstructing equality-versus-difference: Or, the uses of poststructuralist theory for feminism. *Feminist Studies, 14*(1), 32–50.

Scott, J. W. (1998). "La Querelle Des Femmes" in the late twentieth century. *Differences: A Journal of Feminist Cultural Studies, 9,* 70–90.

Scott, J. W. (2007). *The politics of veil.* Princeton: Princeton University Press.

Scruton, R. (2002). *The west and the rest: Globalization and the terrorist threat.* London: Continuum.

Shachar, A. (2001). *Multicultural jurisdictions: Cultural differences and women's rights.* Cambridge: Cambridge University Press.

Shaheed, F. (1995). Networking for change: The role of women's groups in initiating dialogue on women's issues. In M. Afkhami (Ed.), *Faith and freedom: Women's human rights in the Muslim world* (pp. 78–103). Syracuse: Syracuse University Press.

Song, S. (2007). *Justice, gender, and the politics of multiculturalism.* Cambridge: Cambridge University Press.

Spelman, E. (1988). *Inessential woman: Problems of exclusion in feminist thought.* Boston: Beacon.

Spivak, C. (1988). Can the subaltern speak? In C. Nelson & L. Grossberg (Eds.), *Marxism and the interpretation of culture* (pp. 271–313). Chicago: University of Illinois Press.

Sunder, M. (2002). Cultural dissent. *Stanford Law Review, 54,* 495–567.

Volpp, L. (2001). Feminism versus multiculturalism. *Columbia Law Review, 101,* 1181–1218.

Walzer, M. (1983). *Spheres of justice: A defense of pluralism and equality.* New York: Basic Books.

Winter, B. (2008). *The hijab & the republic: Uncovering the French headscarf debate.* New York: Syracuse University Press.

Yegenoglu, M. (1998). *Colonial fantasies: Towards a feminist reading of orientalism.* Cambridge: Cambridge University Press.

Young, I. (1990). *Justice and the politics of difference.* Princeton: Princeton University Press.

Yuval-Davis, N. (2006). Intersectionality and feminist politics. *European Journal of Women's Studies, 13*(3), 193–209.

Chapter 3
Synergies Between Feminist Thought and Migration Studies in Mexico (1975–2010)

Gail Mummert

3.1 Introduction

This chapter addresses various points of intersection between feminist thought and migration studies in Mexico from 1975 to 2010 and argues that synergies occurred at these junctures.[1] Mexican female scholars and activists embracing different brands of feminism led the way in opening new discussions and spearheaded collective action, as was the case in other countries during this period. Feminism and migration burgeoned in Mexico in the final quarter of the twentieth century, largely in response to visible strides made in opportunities and expectations for Mexican women in education and the workforce, on the one hand, and to increasing numbers of women and children migrants in the northward flows into the United States (Woo 2001; Alvarez and Broder 2006; Ariza and Portes 2007, p. 15; Ariza 2007, p. 456) and Canada (Mueller 2005), on the other. To what extent did feminist consciousness raising, discourse and analyses contribute to recast the questions posed in migration studies? How did the several phases of migration studies and the emergence of myriad nongovernmental organizations (NGOs), followed by the creation of government agencies to tend to women's issues and migrants' needs, inform debates about women's responsibilities and rights in Mexican society? My goal is to track the convergent trajectories of feminist thought and migration scholarship, focusing on the potential for change that their synergies unleashed.

By means of a selective review of scholarship and policies concerned with issues of female empowerment and, more specifically, the impact of migration on male

[1] I am grateful to Glenda Tibe Bonifacio for encouraging me to broach specific topics included in this chapter as well as for many useful suggestions. Erika Pérez Domínguez was an efficient aide in conducting the interviews and literature review that inform the points raised here.

G. Mummert (✉)
Centro de Estudios Antropológicos,
El Colegio de Michoacán Zamora, Michoacán, Mexico
e-mail: gmummert@colmich.edu.mx

G.T. Bonifacio (ed.), *Feminism and Migration: Cross-Cultural Engagements*,
International Perspectives on Migration 1, DOI 10.1007/978-94-007-2831-8_3,
© Springer Science+Business Media B.V. 2012

and female roles and identities, gender relations and family dynamics, I will raise questions about the mutual engagements and intersecting agendas between feminist academics, governmental and non-governmental actors and organizations dealing with migration from a gendered perspective. As a feminist anthropologist, I situate my inquiry squarely at the familial level. I therefore rephrase the question anxiously posed by so many analysts and politicians: does migration to "the North" contribute to greater gender equity in Mexican families and society by empowering women, both migrants and non-migrants? Rather, I ask: how have male and female members of Mexican families renegotiated their life projects, their sense of home and their duties and obligations within the domestic unit in the wake of feminist movements and scholarship as well as new trends in migration?

My theoretical point of departure is a social constructivist understanding of human interaction. Consequently, I deal with the lives of both men and women touched by migration processes; that is, family members who migrate but also those who stay behind, as well as the wider circle of kin involved in family dynamics. I do so from the perspective of the anthropology of experience (Turner and Bruner 1986), listening to and interpreting narratives of actual lived situations, past and present, and probing into envisioned futures. In addition, while focusing on adults as the prime movers and decision makers, I emphasize the need to also consider children, youth, and the elderly as part of the family unit that engages in and is affected by migration practices. Feminist scholars such as Marcela Lagarde (1990) have shown the insidious gender and generational inequalities within the Mexican patriarchal family, ironically reproduced by women and men alike. This finding underlined the need to develop new methodological tools to consider the agency of subaltern family members, particularly dyads heretofore neglected in migration literature that is heavily focused on the marital couple: grandparents and grandchildren; siblings and half-siblings; and godparents and godchildren.

Several caveats regarding Mexican feminisms are in order.[2] First, it is important to acknowledge and then identify different currents within the late-twentieth and early twenty-first century feminist ranks. These range from a radical wing espousing pro-choice agendas and openly confronting patriarchal institutions (particularly the Catholic Church and the judicial system) on thorny issues such as legalizing abortion and homosexual marriage to moderates who promote greater gender equity by fighting for women's workplace rights, more females in political office and high government posts, and the acceptance of more pluralistic family models. At another ideological extreme of the gamut of feminist currents, some Roman Catholics (including nuns) have rejected their Church's teaching on birth control and espoused pro-choice positions, forming the female group Catholics for the Right to Decide. As historian Anna Macías (1982) has shown, such internal divisions between right-wing, left-wing and center-of-the-road feminists date back to the nineteenth century.

---

[2] As long-time feminist historian Ana Lau (2002, p. 14) has pointed out, we must distinguish feminist theory from feminism as a social movement. Here I focus on the former; however, given that the movement spawned much feminist thinking and vice versa it is essential to briefly characterize the latter.

Second, in Mexico—similar to other countries—class and ethnic divisions have also tended to divide women's movements, bringing certain issues to the fore and relegating others. Poor indigenous and rural women have mobilized for very different reasons than better-off, more educated *mestizo*[3] females living in urban areas. In addition, regional differences in Mexican feminisms are clear. Although the written history of the movement has been overwhelmingly centered in the Mexico City metropolitan area as the seat of the federal government and home to roughly one-fifth of its population (Bartra et al. 2002, p. 6), feminist groups are salient in regions such as the Central-west, the Southeast and the northern border states, often linked to pre-existing academic institutions in key cities.[4]

Thirdly, Mexican feminisms have developed in a transnational crucible, with clear influences from the United States, the rest of Latin America and Europe (Arizpe 1990). For example, feminist scholar Estela Serret (2000, pp. 45–46) attributes the rise of a Women's Liberation Movement in Mexico in the 1970s to the convergence of two factors at the end of the sixties: the incipient citizen consciousness-raising that grew out of democratization demands unleashed by the 1968 student uprisings in Mexico; and the growing influence of feminism in the United States. Furthermore, studies frequently mention pressures from supranational organizations such as the United Nations (and its 1975 Mexico City and 1995 Beijing conferences in particular) as having contributed to bringing controversial gender issues to public attention and forcing the Mexican government to act sooner rather than later on them (Bartra 1999). In addition, delegates representing Mexico at these international gatherings tended to be academics and professionals who were part of growing numbers of feminists working in government and nongovernmental agencies. The progressive shift in academia from parochial women's studies to more inclusive gender studies from the 1990s onward is another product of transnational networking and the financing of projects by international foundations.

Lastly, although battles over Mexican feminisms have been waged almost exclusively by women and for women, the 1990s especially witnessed an incipient coalescence of women and men around certain issues that require changes and efforts on the part of both sexes—for example, the topic of domestic violence (that I will analyze in section three). Some men even formed associations to combat *machismo*[5] and related male violent behaviors by means of workshops such as those implemented by the Collective of Men for Equal Gender Relations (*Colectivo de Hombres por Relaciones Igualitarias* or CORIAC) that operated from 1993 to 2006. In academic circles as

---

[3] *Mestizo* refers to the mixture of Indian and Spanish blood as a result of the conquest of Mexico in the sixteenth century; today the vast majority of Mexico's population falls within this ethnic/racial category.

[4] For example, Guadalajara, Morelia, Colima, Guanajuato, Mérida, Ciudad Juárez, Monterrey and Tijuana.

[5] According to Matthew Gutmann (1996, pp. 222–223), *machismo* is a cultural category in a state of flux. This stereotypical label is commonly used in Mexico to refer to (and sometimes justify) a range of male behaviors including "beatings, sexual episodes, alcohol consumption, dare-devil antics, and the not-so-simple problem of defining the categories of 'men' and 'women.'"

well, an increasing number of men have joined the ranks of women who are politically committed to the study of gender issues and the promotion of gender equity.[6] As long-time militant Eli Bartra (1999, pp. 215–216) recognizes in her argument concerning feminism's autonomy in the 1970s, initially men were banned from discussions and from the movement: "women claimed their right to be in that miniscule space without men in order to better understand their process of consciousness raising and to develop their own forms of struggle."

Before proceeding with the analysis of the crossroads of feminist thought and migration studies, it is essential to lay out the conceptual and theoretical foundations of the gendered and transnational perspective I adopt. Today, largely as a consequence of feminist scholarship that criticized the neglect and devaluation of women's roles in the private and public spheres, there is a wide and growing consensus among scholars in Mexico, the United States and Canada that migration decision making and processes are deeply gendered (Pedraza 1991; Pessar 1999; Szasz 1999; Kanaiaupuni 2000a; Pessar and Mahler 2003; Hondagneu-Sotelo 2003; Donato et al. 2006; Ariza 2007). In Mexico this recognition began to take hold in the 1980s and continues to gain ground in the twenty-first century. In addition, studies of masculinities have mushroomed since the 1990s, posing the key question of how one becomes a man through the migration process (Rosas 2009). This interest in the social construction of gendered identities has, in turn, spawned groundbreaking analyses of gender relations for men and women on the move and for families separated by borders (Hirsch 2003; Hellman 2008; Dreby 2006, 2010; Marroni 2009; Mummert 2009). The quotidian, relational and situational notion of gender I espouse was laid out convincingly by Candace West and Don Zimmerman (1991) in their seminal article; in other words, rather than being an attribute of individuals, gender is accomplished in our routine, daily social interactions whereby we intentionally situate ourselves as men, women or other sexual categories vis-à-vis our fellow humans and construct feminine, masculine, gay, transvestite or other identities.

The transnational gaze in migration studies has broken with bipolar models of push-pull dynamics and origin-destination dichotomies, offering new prisms for viewing how men and women move across borders and plan their lives around different conceptions of time and space. Transnational households are sites of engagement that are particularly relevant to feminist agendas and scholarship, since their male and female household heads organize myriad productive and reproductive activities across international borders that are simultaneously political and cultural in nature.

This chapter is comprised of three sections. The first sketches a chronology of trends and milestones in feminist thought and migration studies in Mexico over a span of 35 years, from 1975 to 2010 (see Table 3.1). This overview shows that academic, governmental and non-governmental institution building served as important catalysts in the quest to understand this critical nexus. The second section deals

---

[6] For example, the editorial board of the journal *debate feminista*, launched in 1990 with a clear goal of linking feminist theory and political agendas, included nine men and eleven women. Likewise, the first issue of *La ventana*, a feminist journal founded in 1995 by the University of Guadalajara, announced a board composed of five men and nine women.

Table 3.1 Chronology and milestones in migration and feminist studies in Mexico (1975–2010)

Year	Migration studies	Feminist studies	Academic and governmental institution building	NGOs and legislation relating to domestic violence
1975–1979	The female migrant treated as a universal category	1975-International Women's Year; First World Congress on Women held in Mexico City	1976- Launching of Journal *fem.*	1979- Support Center for Raped Women (CAMVAC) established in Mexico City
1980–1989	Feminization of migratory streams and undeniable visibility of women and children migrants in media and in data. Recognition of autonomous movements of females	Women's issues centered on workplace equality, legalizing abortion	1983- Creation of Interdisciplinary Women's Studies Program (PIEM) in Mexico City	1984-Women Support Center (CAM) in Colima; Mexican Association of Violence Against Women (COVAC) founded in Mexico City
1990–1999	Gender accepted as an organizing principle of migration. Acceptance of reciprocal relationship between gender relations and female migration. Transnational frameworks popularized	Domestic violence emerged as topic of study, surveys and public policy debates. Gender inequalities understood in the context of multiple forms of inequality. Mushrooming of female activist networks (dealing especially with reproductive health, political parties, indigenous political and cultural rights)	1990- Launching of Journal *debate feminista*. 1992- Creation of University Program for Gender Studies (PUEG) in Mexico City. 1994- Creation of Center of Gender Studies (CEG) in University of Guadalajara. 1994- Creation of Center for Gender Studies (CUEG) in University of Colima. 1995- Launching of journal *La ventana* in University of Guadalajara	1993-Men's collective for gender equity (CORIAC) conducts workshops with violent males. 1993-UN resolution to eliminate violence against women. 1996- First shelter for victims of domestic violence opens doors in Aguascalientes. 1996- First law for Family Violence Prevention and Assistance passed in Mexico City (Federal District). 1997- Reforms to Mexican penal code increased penalties for sexual offenders

(continued)

Table 3.1 (continued)

Year	Migration studies	Feminist studies	Academic and governmental institution building	NGOs and legislation relating to domestic violence
			Consolidation of field by means of programs, journals, books Emergence of a handful of state-level offices for Migrant Affairs in key states of outmigration	1999- UN resolution marks November 25 as International Day for the Elimination of Violence against Women
2000–2010	Shift toward understanding how social construction of gender impacts migratory processes	Women's and children's rights seen as part of the human rights agenda	2001- Launching of Journal *Migraciones Internacionales* in Tijuana 2001- Creation of National Women's Institute (INMUJERES), followed by opening of state-level institutes 2003- Creation of Institute for Mexicans Abroad (IME) 2000–2009 Creation of state-level Institutes for Migrant Affairs and 1 Ministry for Migrants (Michoacán) 2000- Umbrella organization National Coordinator for Migrant Affairs Offices (CONOFAM) founded with 8 states; grew to encompass 29 of Mexico's 32 states by 2010	2000–2006 Passage of laws against domestic violence in almost all states

Sources: see references

with the central issue behind the convergence hypothesis guiding this essay: the debate over female empowerment linked to migration experiences. Early formulations placed this question in a before/after framework for marital couples; that is, in a necessarily linear progression from subordination to empowerment before and after the woman or her husband migrated. Yet, once the debate was recast to encompass complex, convoluted and non-linear migration processes (not just the flows) and considered women without male partners, it became clear that empowerment could be better grasped in terms of a disputed terrain where a gradual reshaping of gender relations and of the ideologies that sustained them took place. I therefore consider how gender relations are renegotiated by women and men involved in migration processes—first those who actually move, then those who stay behind. In either case, the negotiations are played out on stages where divergent discourses between migrants, their families, nongovernmental and state agencies can be discerned and explored. In the third section, I develop two examples of sites of engagement and emerging gender dynamics in the state-family interface: (1) the case of wives and children abandoned by a migrant husband and the pathways they follow to attempt to obtain child support; and (2) female emigration sparked by domestic violence, sometimes leading to asylum-seeking in the United States or Canada. In the conclusions, I argue that feminist thought and cross-cultural networking have contributed to recognition—in academic, activist and policymaking circles—of the need for gendered frameworks for studying and tending to the needs of the intergenerational family unit involved in migration.

3.2 Historical Overview of Two Converging Trajectories: Feminist Thought and Migration Studies

As numerous feminist historians have shown, there have been several waves of feminist struggles in Mexico, the first dating from the late nineteenth century when women in significant numbers championed the fight against *machismo* and for female suffrage, remaining active into the 1930s and 1940s. Largely squashed by lack of male support and reactionary preaching by the Catholic Church that cast feminists as destroyers of traditional family values, women finally earned the right to vote in 1953 but continued to suffer discrimination and limited opportunities (Macias 1982). A second wave, largely detached from the first, emerged in 1972 (Serret 2000, p. 46); although in fact many organizations were formed, this vast mobilization was widely known as the Women's Liberation Movement (*Movimiento de Liberación de la Mujer* or MLM).[7]

---

[7] Several excellent overviews and evaluations of the many organizations formed and paths followed by Mexican feminists—often penned by protagonists—are available in Spanish (Tuñón 1997; Fernández 1998; Bartra 1999; Serret 2000; Lau 2002). Sonia Frias (2009) offers a useful synthesis in the English language of some of the previous authors. See also Lamas et al. (1995).

My purpose in this section is to weave together those strands of feminist thought from this second wave onward that informed migration studies. I begin this overview in the summer of 1975 when the First World Conference on Women in Mexico City offered Mexico's fledgling feminist movement, led by a compact group of approximately thirty women (Bartra 1999, p. 214), an opportunity to make its voices heard. In the wake of the United Nations' declaration of International Women's Year in 1975 and the gathering of thousands of women from around the world in the Mexican capital to promote the advancement of women, debates over their subordinate status in the host country were revived. Activists and scholars attempted to unravel the ideological underpinnings of male privilege and female subordination as a first step toward viewing women as men's equals and creating new opportunities for them (Serret 2000, p. 46; Lamas 1990).

One of the first institutions identified as a culprit in women's subordination was the patriarchal family so deeply ingrained in Mexican society. As sole economic provider and head of household, the *paterfamilias* protected his wife and offspring. Treated as his property and lumped together as non-adults, these members in turn owed him obedience and deference. The patriarch controlled the purse strings and decision making of the family unit. The Catholic Church, which holds great sway among the Mexican population, portrayed this family structure as the ideal, normative one and demonized all others.

Yet, as more and more women entered the paid labor force in the pivotal decade of the 1970s, the notion of the sole male breadwinner crumbled. Demographic studies such as Brígida García and Orlandina de Oliveira (1994) show that a major shift in family life occurred during these years: married women with young children tended to leave the labor market for short periods for childbearing and raising, then continued to earn a salary as working mothers. This trend brought questions of the domestic division of labor to the fore. For example, daycare options (*guarderías*) for the children of working women enrolled in the Mexican socialized medical system emerged in urban areas in 1974, yet these were not immediately accepted since the idea of entrusting youngsters to alternate caregivers was rejected by the population at large, preferring care by loving, close relatives in the home (preferably grandmothers or aunts). Clearly, working women faced a double shift (*doble jornada*) since they continued to assume major responsibility for child care and housework while engaged in a paid job outside the home.

The convergence of the 1975 reigniting of the feminist movement and soaring numbers of working women sparked the empowerment debate, one that raged during the 1980s and continues in myriad guises today. Did labor force participation empower Mexican women by catapulting them into the public sphere and giving them earning power, as it had elsewhere in the Western world? Or, did it simply double their load, as they juggled workplace responsibilities with those of housewife and mother, with little or no "help"[8] from their spouses? Also, what was the

---

[8] Generally, when Mexican men participate in household and other social reproductive tasks, they and their wives portray this as "helping," since the primary responsibility is deemed a female one. Inversely, some working women use the same term to describe their income-generating activities, given the male provider ideal (Gutmann 1996, p. 157; Rojas 2008).

impact on the well-being of young children when mothers left the home to do salaried work? Not surprisingly, these questions were hotly debated among feminists, academics and policymakers (Stern 1996).[9] Male bastions like the Catholic Church and the dominant Institutional Revolutionary Party (*Partido Revolucionario Institucional* or PRI) tended to send out signals of alarm over crumbling family values and unsupervised women in public spaces. At the other extreme, feminists fought for workplace rights for the downtrodden *maquila*[10] employees and sought to propagate the idea of salaried work outside the home as a necessity that was compatible with being a mother and a wife. Ironically, many women were disturbed by growing numbers of females entering the labor market since it went against the grain of deep-seated gendered ideologies that dictated marriage and motherhood as primary goals for all women. Therefore, working women tended to justify their participation in the labor force as an economic necessity. This was in fact the case as the 1976 devaluation of the Mexican peso and successive waves of economic crises in the 1980s took their toll on the poor, on working families and even on the middle class.

In such a highly politicized scenario, the migration experiences of growing numbers of Mexican families became particularly relevant to the empowerment debate. Movements within Mexico's borders (notably from the countryside to the cities in the 1950s and 1960s), but also northward to the United States (and most recently to Canada) appeared to set the stage for new opportunities for female mobility and empowerment. One of the most common explanations of this shift is the notion of "contamination": in the cities or in the United States women on the move came into contact in the workplace, schools, churches and communities with other women (compatriots and non-Mexicans) more versed in women's rights. From men's perspectives especially, these other women "contaminated" the new arrival with their ideas (González-López 2005, pp. 221–223; Córdova et al. 2008, pp. 196–197).

At the same time, migration unleashed a pressing need for couples to renegotiate the terms of the household division of labor and decision making processes, as men and women carried out unfamiliar and highly gendered tasks in new cultural situations. For example, lone men living in close quarters with other men and without their wives were forced to cook, clean and grocery shop for themselves. On the other hand, women left behind faced unprecedented daily decision making about family affairs during long-term absences of their husbands. Thus, diverse regions of Mexico with high levels of outmigration—from tiny hamlets to large cities—were deemed fertile ground for a reshaping of gender relations and for questioning underlying gender ideologies. Studies of this opportunity-need nexus mushroomed in a

---

[9] These debates were revisited in 1995 when the Mexican delegation to the Fourth World Conference on Women prepared its platform for Beijing, generating evaluations of two decades of progress made in gendered perspectives in the social sciences. For a view of gender in Mexican social demography, cf. García et al. (1999).

[10] *Maquila* refers to the globalized assembly plants concentrated along the United States-Mexico border (and now throughout the country) that tend to hire young, female low-skilled migrants from the provinces.

variety of academic disciplines (Correa 2009).[11] The fields of anthropology, sociology, women's, and gender studies are among the most prolific and therefore constitute the empirical and ethnographic foundation for arguments made in this essay.[12]

Paradoxically, one of the first institutions attuned to tensions derived from dramatically changing gender and intergenerational relations in migrant families was the Catholic Church. As mentioned before, many feminists consider it to be a stronghold of reactionary thought and androcentric preaching, as the Church hierarchy struggles to contend with perceived threats to its ideal Mexican family model. In certain dioceses with high levels of outmigration, priests developed skills and organized workshops to tend to the specific needs of migrant families facing prolonged physical separation and marital woes associated with lack of communication, fears of infidelity, differences of opinion concerning childrearing patterns, and dire economic straits, to name a few.[13]

Scholarship on how gender relations changed with migration focused mainly on the marital couple and examined gender relations before and after migration. The general assumption was of an antagonistic relationship between the sexes whereby whatever ground the wife gained, the husband necessarily lost. Mixed findings were reported (Mummert 1988; Hondagneu-Sotelo 1994; Espinosa 1998; Malkin 1999; Szasz 1999; D'Aubeterre 2000c; Barrera and Oehmichen 2000; Ariza 2007; Córdova et al. 2008; Correa 2009). The majority of studies—not surprisingly conducted primarily by women researchers—proclaimed that migrant women as well as wives and daughters remaining in Mexico did indeed develop new skills (e.g., money management, dealing with a variety of interlocutors, including men) and enjoy new freedom of movement and decision making.[14] At the other extreme, a few analysts argued more pessimistically that migrant women were not empowered; rather they became more isolated from their strong female networks in Mexico and relegated to the domestic sphere (Malkin 1999). In fact, many stay-behind wives did not seem to decide anything of significance since they simply followed the dictates of their husbands thousands of miles away, communicated to them

---

[11] In her study of an indigenous Nahuatl community in rural Puebla, Leticia Rivermar (2008, p. 74) expresses this nexus very clearly: "We have seen that for the people of Xoyatla international migration has challenged all areas of community organization; it has meant the possibility and the necessity to update the group's organization in the absence of many of the town's inhabitants."

[12] Although outside the purview of this chapter, feminist historians have systematically challenged prevailing androcentric accounts of Mexican history and proven that women participated in the building of colonial, revolutionary and modern Mexico. A collective of U.S. and Mexican-based scholars avid for debate formed the Network of Scholars on Women and Gender in Mexican History (REDMUGEN) and has held five international congresses since 2001.

[13] Dealing with the needs of their migrant family parishioners has been called "pastoral care for migrants." Although the World Day for Migrants and Refugees was instituted by Pope Pius X in 1914, it has taken on renewed vigor since Pope John Paul II emphasized tending to marginalized peoples. I hypothesize that its' most recent popularity is also a response to increasing competition with Protestant churches steadily gaining ground in Mexico and particularly among migrants to the North.

[14] Mercedes González de la Rocha (1993, p. 317) dubbed this "the power of absence." In her anthropological case study conducted in a rural area of Jalisco state, she cited examples of complicity between wives and daughters that served to circumvent or openly defy the absent father's denial of permission for the young women to work or study.

by telephone (Vizcarra et al. 2009, p. 213; Pérez 2009, p. 119). A third position found in the literature reviewed was that certain aspects of marital and family dynamics have changed while others remain intact (D'Aubeterre 2000c, p. 66; Mancillas and Rodríguez 2009, p. 58; Mummert 2010c, pp. 293–295). If any consensus may be drawn from these seemingly confusing results, it would be that empowerment is not a guaranteed byproduct of the migration experience; rather it is a result of many factors. In order to unravel these, it is essential to distinguish the negotiations of gender relations by migrant women as opposed to those carried out long-distance by females who stayed in Mexico.

3.3   Reshaping Gender Relations Through Migration

In migration studies women who leave and women who stay have long been considered two distinct categories of analysis. This dichotomy is ubiquitous from Ina Dinerman's seminal study (1982) comparing "migrants and stay-at-homes" to Gail Mummert's (1988) landmark review of research on women migrants and wives of migrants in Michoacán as well as recent ethnographies of transnational migrant circuits such as Pérez (2009). However, from an experiential perspective, the two categories may overlap across time for the same individual: for example, a stay-at-home wife migrates at her husband's beck or autonomously; a wife who migrated northward returns to Mexico. In addition, these overlaps are not necessarily one-time occurrences; they may be repeated over time as families move across borders. Nevertheless, the distinction is analytically useful to unravel the key question of how gender relations are in fact reshaped through processes of migration.

3.3.1   Women Who Leave

Given that early migration studies took women into account only if they themselves were movers, attention turned first to migrant wives who began to join their husbands in the North. In the Mexican case, this trend began in the 1960s but intensified sharply in the 1980s when new immigration legislation was introduced in the United States (notably the Simpson-Rodino Act passed in 1986), facilitating legalization for qualified, longtime migrants and family reunification processes. These wives, although seen as non-autonomous migrants dependent upon male decision making and largely ignored in studies by male researchers, in fact often prodded their husbands to take the necessary steps toward family reunification in the United States. This "discovery" was made possible once more female scholars took an interest in family and migration studies and actually conducted in-depth interviews with women migrants and included them in surveys (González de la Rocha 1993; Goldring 1996; Barrera and Oehmichen 2000; D'Aubeterre 2000a, 2000b; Hirsch 2003; Malkin 2004). Breaking down androcentric assumptions such as this one is a clear example of synergies between feminist scholarship and migration studies.

By the 1980s there was visible evidence that new groups of female migrants (unaccompanied by men) had entered the northbound streams: press reports (Alvarez and Broder 2006), surveys, census figures and United States Border Patrol detainee data all pointed in this direction. Often these women's circumstances and motives for emigrating differed from those of their male counterparts as well as from those of the aforementioned migrant wives: escape from domestic violence (González-López 2005, 57) or the stigma of spinsterhood, single mothers hoping to establish a better life for their offspring and perhaps find a new male partner; young single females who having worked for a salary in Mexico felt ready to try their luck in the North. The passive female migrant model was thus discarded and studies followed specific categories of women along the paths of migration: never married ones as well as those estranged from their partners (including those stigmatized as "abandoned" by the husband), widows or divorcees (Malkin 1999; Fagetti 2000; Hirsch 2003; Córdova et al. 2008; Boehm 2008).

Since the late 1980s, one segment of these new female migrants is comprised of temporary, documented workers recruited by employers in the United States or Canada by means of bilateral governmental agreements. The women chosen for these slots as "guest workers" tend to do seasonal agricultural work or food processing in highly controlled labor settings, in the hope of proving themselves to be dexterous, efficient laborers who will then be individually "invited" to return the following year. Though a clear numerical minority among women migrants, these thousands of women have been extensively studied by researchers from Mexico, the United States and Canada since they constitute an inversion of the traditional male migration pattern (Preibisch 2000; Basok 2002; Barndt 2002; Vidal et al. 2002; Griffith 2002; Smith-Nonini 2002; Preibisch and Hermoso 2006; Becerril 2007; Suárez 2008). In fact, recruiters favor single and married mothers, under the assumption that their family responsibilities will motivate them to work long hours for low pay and assure their return to Mexico once the season is over. Studies of this flexible workforce and their living conditions in the three countries that signed the North American Free Trade Agreement (NAFTA) in 1992 illustrate how feminist activists-scholars have uncovered the vulnerability of workers in global food chains as well as the complicity of the government agencies involved in workforce selection and control (Basok 2002; Barndt 2002; Preibisch and Hermoso 2006; Becerril 2007).

Openly critical of these schemes to "flexibilize" the female work force to meet the ever-changing needs of capital, an increasing number of academics have become engaged in grassroots organizing with labor unions or non-governmental organizations fighting for migrants' rights (Stephen 2007). This is particularly true in the case of trinational (Canada-U.S.-Mexico) teams of analysts who, thanks to tripartite funding sources, have painstakingly pieced together the different parts of the puzzle.[15]

---

[15] For example, the study "Transnational Work, Labour-related Gender Policies and Family Organization: Mexican Women Transmigrants in Canada and United States," funded by the Ford Foundation through the Interinstitutional Program of Studies on the North American Region (*Programa Interinstitucional de Estudios sobre la Región América del Norte* or PIERAN) at El Colegio de México, involves researchers from Mexico (Ofelia Becerril, Elizabeth Juárez), the United States (David Griffith, Ricardo Contreras) and Canada (Kerry Preibisch, Evelyn Encalada).

Similarly, studies of the seafood processing plants along the Atlantic coast of the United States conducted by researchers in contact on both sides of the U.S.-Mexico border have been instrumental in documenting how globalization logics have used agencies at the federal, state and local levels to channel Mexican women migrants into particular labor market niches that do not recognize their skill levels nor their basic human rights as legally contracted workers (Vidal et al. 2002; Smith-Nonini 2002; Suárez 2008; Montoya 2008).

Despite the diversity characterizing the female migrant population, a clear picture of them as catalysts of change in gender relations has emerged, bolstered by support from settlement countries' government agencies and legal systems. "In the North, the woman gives the orders!" is an aphorism Mexican migrant men ruefully repeat (Hirsch 2003, p. 180). They complain that in the United States, their women can count on government aid for their young children as well as police protection in the event of a husband "disciplining" his spouse with the use of force—an act that would be defined as domestic violence by authorities there. Understandably, men long accustomed to gendered privileges and higher social status tended to prefer the status quo in gender relations, dragging their feet on issues such as sharing housework and child care or allowing their wives mobility and equal say in family decision making. In general, Mexican women perceived gains in autonomy and self-image through migration and salaried labor; they feared that, if the family returned to Mexico, they would lose these advantages and fall back into the old pattern of subordination (Hondagneu-Sotelo 1994). Wearing the shawl (*rebozo*), with which women traditionally covered their heads and carried loads (including babies) in rural Mexico, was seen as a powerful symbol of this subordination to men and to the husband's family. Accordingly, migrant women rejected the *rebozo* when they returned, even if only for visits. Men, on the other hand, foresaw increased social prestige and a recuperation of male privilege in the dream of return "home" to Mexico. Thus, many couples were split along gendered lines regarding the return migration project (Espinosa 1998), especially if US-born grandchildren were involved since they tended to be magnets that pulled the grandmothers toward permanent settlement in the United States (Hondagneu-Sotelo 1994).

3.3.2 Women Who Stay

Women who stay behind have received less attention from migration scholars but have benefitted from feminist grassroots organizations interested in promoting female empowerment, for indigenous peoples and for *mestizos* (Suárez and Zapata 2004, 2007; Torres 2008). However, with the diffusion and adoption of transnational frameworks for Mexican migration studies in the 1990s (Mummert 1999), researchers had new ways of understanding how family members who stayed behind also were involved in and affected by processes of migration. Analysts turned their gaze to the stay-behind wives and their children. Given the longtime predominant pattern of male circular migration, these spouses (or future ones in the case of fiancées) far outnumbered the migrant women, yet had been largely overlooked in research. In fact, women and other family members who stayed were now recognized as "anchors" of kin- and community-based networks that enabled the male migrant to go North (Kanaiaupuni 2000b). In other words, they began to be viewed as active agents rather than passive ones (Mummert 2003).

Clearly, the husband's departure paved the way for and necessitated renegotiating the privileges and responsibilities of each partner, thus rethinking marital power relations. In the male's absence, the wife became *de facto* head of household, often raising the children single-handedly, channeling remittances toward household consumption and—if possible, investment in productive ventures—which might raise the family's standard of living (Mummert 1988). If, however, remittances were sporadic, insufficient or not forthcoming, wives and mothers were forced to find a way to generate income to support the family. "It is as if one were a widow!" (Córdova et al. 2008, p. 165) was a common complaint of migrant wives in the rural communities analyzed extensively in burgeoning anthropological case studies (Curiel 2002; Cordero 2007; Correa 2009); these women often felt overwhelmed by the magnitude of their new responsibilities and the loneliness of being without their men. "Now I am the man and the woman" (Fagetti 2000, p. 123) is another poignant refrain reported in the literature (Boehm 2008) which alludes to the transgression of gendered spaces and ideologies that the wife of a migrant was forced to undertake in order to fulfill her principal role as a good mother and wife. Ironically, her comings and goings were scrutinized by in-laws and others to assure that they remained faithful to their absent husbands. This heightened surveillance and constant suspicion of infidelity became unbearable for many, who pointed out how they were called upon to assume additional duties without societal recognition for their efforts (Torres 2008). In some cases, it was a factor in the wife's decision to attempt to accelerate family reunification in the North or at the very least to live independently from her in-laws, as in the real-life testimony offered by Judith Hellman (2008, p. 45) with the title "Marta: The Tyranny of In-Laws." In other instances, it added insult to injury and led to depression and other emotional traumas for the wife of the migrant (López 2008).

Greater mobility in the public sphere and participation in community affairs have been used as measuring sticks of female empowerment. In the case of wives of migrants, this has occurred as part of individual or collective awakenings, sometimes accompanied by intervention by researcher-activists, such as that reported in Centolia Maldonado and Patricia Artía (2004) for the indigenous Mixtec region of southern Mexico; or by church-related groups as was the case in the Purhépecha Indian highlands of Michoacán studied by Ana Lucía Torres (2008). In addition, in indigenous communities where male outmigration is rampant, the grandmothers and mothers who remain are key actors in time-honored rituals and thus are empowered as guardians not only of the social reproduction of the family but of the village's sense of tradition and community ties as well (Curiel 2002).

3.4   Feminist Thought and Action: Cross-Border Collaboration at the Gender-Migration Nexus

In this section, I exemplify how collaboration (increasingly cross-border) between feminists, NGOs, government agencies, and migration experts has opened new avenues for women's empowerment. The examples concern two groups that are particularly vulnerable to suffering in the migration process: (1) wives and children of migrant men who fail to receive remittances and (2) victims of domestic violence who migrate. I have chosen these two issues due to my recent personal involvement with them, while engaged in research to identify and address specific needs of three potentially vulnerable groups in migration settings: women, children and the elderly (Mummert 2010b).[16]

3.4.1   Abandoned Wives and Children in Limbo

Though not an entirely new phenomenon, cases of abandoned spouses and offspring have come to greater public attention since the turn of the twenty-first century. Dependent upon remittances promised by the male migrant in compliance with his responsibility to support them from afar, the number of wives and children not receiving money from the husband-father seem to be on the rise according to press reports and studies conducted in key high-emigration states such as Michoacán, San Luis Potosí, Veracruz, and Zacatecas. Due to the work of feminist scholars and religious organizations that have reported this problem, some Mexican state-level institutes or ministries for migrant affairs have recently included orientation about child support claims in the range of services offered to wives of wayward migrants. In addition, the signing of bilateral agreements at the federal levels has united the U.S. and Mexican judicial systems in the common cause of the children receiving financial support from their fathers.

Ethnographic studies in particular have underlined the social stigma placed on abandoned wives who find themselves in this predicament by no fault of their own (Ramírez 2000; Rivermar 2008; Córdova et al. 2008; Vizcarra et al. 2009). Derogatory labeling of these women is common and includes such terms as: abandoned (abandonada), left behind (dejada), pushed aside (largada), failure (fracasada) (Córdova et al. 2008, p. 193). As shown above, in the patriarchal family model, females lacking male protectors are particularly vulnerable in Mexican society since they bear the brunt of unwanted sexual advances from other men who consider them sexually available as well as malicious gossip by women who deem them potential marriage breakers. Abandoned wives also find themselves at the mercy of surveillant in-laws who tend to be highly critical; tensions with the

---

[16] Since 2008 I have collaborated with lawyers as an expert witness in three Mexican women's asylum cases in the U.S. and authored an expert affidavit on child abuse in Mexico for the Center for Gender and Refugee Studies (Mummert 2010a).

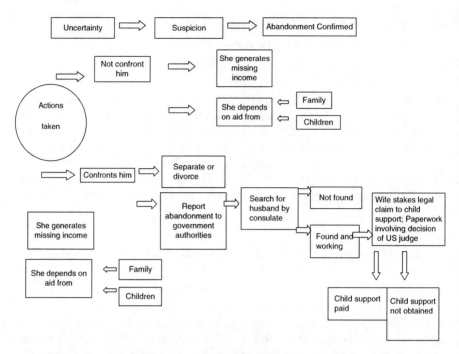

Fig. 3.1 Pathways of the wife abandoned by her husband who migrated to the United States (Source: Interviews with Mexican consulate officials (Philadelphia, 19 October 2009; Chicago, 17 May 2011) and with employees of Michoacan's Ministry for Migrant Affairs (11 January 2010), and State Delegation of the Ministry of Foreign Affairs (6 August 2010))

mother-in-law or spouse's sisters (with whom they live given patrilocal residential customs) may become unbearable and even lead to physical abuse. Leticia Rivermar (2008, pp. 69–76) reports how female in-laws may actually contribute to marital break-up which means that the wife is forced out of the house of her parents-in-law. In her study of a rural community in Michoacán, Tamara Martínez (2008, pp. 180–183) emphasizes how the mother-in-law is one of the foremost guardians of the patriarchal social order, controlling the flow of remittances and information.

When migrant men fail to fulfill their family obligations, what recourse does the wife have to force him to do so? Figure 3.1 maps out the various pathways an abandoned wife with children to feed may follow and some of the roadblocks she faces. Often plagued by lack of communication with her spouse, initially she will go through a series of phases ranging from disbelief to suspicion before reaching final confirmation of the fact that she is on her own. This may be due to job loss, illness or even the death of her husband, but most commonly to a shirking of the parental and marital commitment, often linked to the formation of a new relationship and sometimes even a second family in the North. Once her worst fear has been confirmed, she may opt to confront her spouse or not, either to urge him to formalize the separation in a divorce or silently accept her fate.

If she decides to seek the aid of the Mexican government in locating the wayward husband in the United States, two pathways are available. First, she provides the liaison offices in her state of residence in Mexico with her husband's address or general whereabouts and this information is channeled to the Ministry of Foreign Affairs in Mexico City. Once located by consular personnel, the spouse is formally asked to appear at the nearest consulate and is admonished about his family obligations. This "backing" of the abandoned wife by the Mexican government constitutes a new type of intervention in migrant family affairs, one heretofore associated only with the United States government. As one female employee interviewed in Michoacán explained: "Often the husband sees that the wife is not alone and agrees to pay."

However, if this official reminder does not succeed in prodding the husband to definitely mend his ways (sometimes the payments come for only a few months), the wife may then decide to file a legal claim in Mexican civil courts for child support (a step involving considerable paperwork which is facilitated by the agency in her state of residence). With the 1992 signing of a bilateral reciprocity agreement regarding the Uniform Reciprocal Enforcement of Support Act (URESA) providing the legal framework for cooperation between the Mexican and United States' legal systems, the child support case is channeled through diplomatic networks to the consulate nearest the husband's place of residence. Justified in the best interest of the children involved, a lengthy legal procedure unfolds. In the best case scenario, the claim actually produces the desired results: a United States judge orders that the child support payment be docked from the father's paycheck and this amount is channeled by check to the wife through the same governmental structure. This support is due until the child reaches the legal age of adulthood in Mexico, at eighteen. Of course, an irresponsible husband-father may attempt to avoid detection by United States authorities by moving to another state, thus changing the legal jurisdiction and delaying possible resolution.[17]

Abandoned wives of migrants may despair and lose hope in the legal process or fear retaliation on the part of the husband. Clearly, the obstacles are formidable and the 100–200 new legal claims initiated each year (mostly from Michoacán, Guanajuato, Baja California and Distrito Federal) are relatively few compared to the estimated thousands of abandoned spouses and offspring. Although year-by-year data was not available from the General Office of Protection for Mexicans Abroad of the Ministry of Foreign Affairs, officials interviewed estimated an average 1 year delay for claims to be solved. Employees in Michoacán admitted that to date few cases have been resolved favorably for the wife and offspring.[18] Despite the difficulties in obtaining child support, there has been a steady increase in claims filed since 1998 in states with high levels of outmigration (see Table 3.2). This is initially the result of word-of-mouth and publicity on the part of women's and migrant agencies

---

[17] This information was provided in interviews conducted by the author with staff of the General Division of Protection for Mexicans Abroad of the Mexican Ministry of Foreign Affairs, Mexico City, August 20 and October 20, 2010.

[18] Interviews conducted by Erika Pérez Domínguez in 2010 with state-level officials in Michoacán's Ministry of Migrant Affairs and Ministry of Foreign Affairs, Morelia.

Table 3.2 Mexico: Requests for child support presented by abandoned wives of migrants in selected states of high emigration

Year	Michoacán	Zacatecas	San Luis Potosí[b]
1994	–	–	37
1995	–	–	25
1996	–	–	29
1997	–	–	35
1998	–	–	54
1999	–	–	74
2000	–	–	81
2001	–	–	98
2002	–	–	82
2003	–	–	84
2004	–	–	36
2005	–	11[a]	–
2006	9	9	–
2007	34	6	–
2008	5	27	–
2009	5	14	–
2010[c]	2	–	–

Sources
Michoacán: Records of the Department for Human Rights and Repatriation of the state-level Ministry of Migrant Affairs
Zacatecas: Annual reports of the State Migration Institute (Instituto Estatal de Migración)
San Luis Potosí: Report of the San Luis Potosí Delegation of the Ministry of Foreign Affairs, cited in Alanís (2008, pp. 82–83)
[a]Only one of these cases was reported as resolved and child support granted
[b]These data fall under a category known as "Economic Aid" that encompasses principally child support but also spousal support (if unable to vie for herself) and support for offspring over age 18 who are students
[c]January–July 2010

in these particular states; then in 2010 the federal Ministry began to distribute leaflets specifying the steps to be taken and the documents required. This example proves that battles for female empowerment and social justice are being waged on an individual basis as a result of feminist debates capturing the attention of government agencies in Mexico and the U.S.

3.4.2 Migration, Asylum-Seeking and Domestic Violence

Gender-based violence was an early concern of Mexican feminists in the 1970s, particularly their campaign towards increasing punishment for rapists and legalizing abortion (Serret 2000, p. 100) (see Table 3.1). Violence against women has, of course, been a deep-seated aspect of patriarchal institutions in Mexico; women's rights have been routinely trampled, from the bedroom to the classroom and the shop floor; in the streets, the courts and in the hospital ward. Family violence in all forms continues to be a pervasive phenomenon in Mexico, involving complex gender dynamics within families and in society at large, as well as entrenched ideas about male and female roles in the public and private spheres.

Domestic violence became a less taboo topic in the 1980s; the tendency to brush it away as an unavoidable byproduct of that most Mexican of institutions, *machismo*, was no longer tolerated. International organizations funded the first shelters for battered women and rape victims (Serret 2000, p. 100) and growing numbers of NGOs addressed this problem as well. By the 1990s, in the wake of Mexico's signing of the United Nations Convention on the Rights of the Child (1990) that required nation-states to protect children against abuse, neglect or abandonment, public opinion became galvanized against violence directed disproportionately toward girls and women. Most importantly, strides were made by feminists in building bridges with newly inaugurated government agencies for women's issues and the health bureaucracy, both of which began to fund surveys and issue reports that measured the prevalence of such violence for the first time. Academics were directly involved in the design and analysis of, for example, the National Survey on the Dynamics of Household Relationships (ENDIREH) conducted in 2003 and the 2006 National Report on Violence and Health released by the Ministry of Health. On the legislative front, the congressional Commission for Gender Equity was formed, and the Law on Domestic Violence and the Law for a Life Free of Violence were passed in Mexico City. Despite these undisputed accomplishments, unfortunately much remains to be done. For example, budgets to combat gender-based violence are earmarked for assistance to victims with little or no funds available for prevention.[19] Although large strides have been made by governmental programs and non-governmental organizations to educate the Mexican population about domestic violence and child abuse, these efforts have had little, if any, impact, especially in rural areas where patriarchal family relations remain intact and governmental services (health clinics and campaigns, police, public schools) are deficient.

Against this backdrop of feminist struggles to constitute gender violence in a problem in need of solutions through alliances between government, NGOs, academics and militants, I consider possible linkages between migration and gender violence, a topic yet to be carefully explored. Structural violence is clearly present in migration and has received greater attention: in the poverty that drives many migrants to leave their homes and in the criminalization of undocumented migrants. Based on an ethnographic study in central Mexico, Jorge Arzate and Ivonne Vizcarra (2007) argue that such structural violence spawns specific forms of gender violence that place wives of migrants in a particularly vulnerable position.

Part of the flow of Mexican women and children across the border into the United States is motivated precisely by women's attempts to escape gender-based domestic violence and begin a new life (González-López 2005, p. 57). More and more cases of

---

[19] This was a conclusion of a workshop that explored linkages between domestic violence and migration (*Jornada sobre Violencia Intrafamiliar y Migración*) held in July 2010 in El Colegio de Michoacán. The recommendation of more funding for prevention was made to the state-level agencies in attendance.

sexual, physical and psychological abuse of women by their fathers and/or spouses are coming to light as some of these victims are assisted in seeking asylum in the US or in Canada on these grounds. As Araceli Calderón (2009) shows in a book of testimonies of Mexican migrant women who have been victims of domestic violence, abuse can occur at various junctures: before migrating, during border crossings, and as a continuing feature of the marital relationship or with a new partner in the United States. Here I will explore the particular case of domestic violence as a detonator of female emigration; that is, as a woman's attempt to extricate herself from physical, emotional and/or sexual violence perpetrated by a father, husband, brother or another male.

Feminist anthropologists were pioneers in bringing this family dynamic and alternative female motive to emigrate to public attention by means of long-term ethnographic fieldwork in specific communities (D'Aubeterre 2000a, 2000b, 2007; Mummert 2003; Córdova et al. 2008; Hellman 2008). However, once in the United States or Canada, these female migrants are not automatically safer, since they are often limited in exercising their rights due to their undocumented status. As previously discussed, it is by word of mouth that they learn help seeking, receive assistance from other women and eventually are referred to a psychological counselor, an NGO, or legal assistance office. From such feminist networks they may learn of the possibility of seeking asylum on grounds of domestic violence.

One such organization that guides domestic violence victims is the Center for Gender and Refugee Studies (CGRS) in San Francisco. It was founded in 1999 and is affiliated with the Hastings College of Law of the University of California. CGRS is the United States' primary source of legal resources and research for gender-based asylum and refugee work. Attorneys representing asylee clients pro bono may request aid from CGRS, providing a case description. In turn, they receive technical assistance consisting of documentary support, affidavits and legal research. These are therefore best-case scenario asylum applications—ones in which competent and committed legal representation has been assured. With this caveat, figures culled from the CGRS database[20] corroborate a clear increase in asylum requests by Mexican citizens from 1998 to 2010 (see Table 3.3). They also unveil a disturbing trend: many asylees (mostly girls) were victims of incest as children in Mexico. Furthermore, 75% (315 cases of a total of 421) of asylum requests by Mexican citizens that came to the attention of CGRS from 1998 to 2010 involved domestic violence, much higher than the overall figure regardless of nationality at 47%.

These real-life stories documented by feminist ethnographers and CGRS data provide clear examples of how long-term feminist agendas and consciousness-raising about domestic violence have brought recognition for a particular, yet little-studied type of female migration: "escapes" sparked by abuse in the home. Clearly, cross-border feminist networking has been crucial in channeling victims toward counseling centers serving immigrant communities where they may receive psychosocial support and be referred to legal aid groups. Inversely, word of mouth

---

[20] The author sincerely thanks Kim Thuy Seelinger and Lisa Frydman, CGRS staff members, for providing these data as well as many helpful insights and suggestions on this topic.

Table 3.3 Number of CGRS-assisted applications for asylum in the United State or Canada presented by Mexican citizens on grounds of domestic violence, 1998–2010

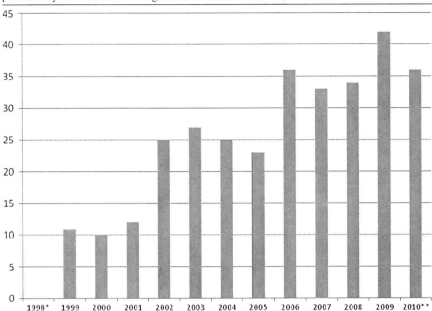

CLARIFICATION: Nine of the 421 cases were presented in Canada. Only 11 of all applicants were males.
* No cases involved domestic violence.
* * January 1 to July 1, 2010

Source: Center for Gender and Refugee Studies database, consulted July 2, 2010

among domestic violence survivors and Mexican women already granted asylum has spread so that sometimes victims go directly to seek out legal representation and may then be referred to counseling groups. Thus, asylum seeking is seen as a chance for women to exit the vicious cycle of abuse and start life anew.

As these two examples of child support and domestic violence issues have proven, women migrants and wives of migrants who find themselves in vulnerable positions have been empowered through experiences of cross-border collaboration involving a wide variety of women (and occasionally men) from very different backgrounds, social classes and political persuasions joining forces in a common cause. This practice of building bridges is stressed by Marta Lamas and colleagues (1995) as one of the most important lessons learned by activists in the various strands of Mexican feminisms, considered by Eli Bartra and Ana Lau (2002, p. 5) to be "the most important social movement of the final decades of the twentieth century."

3.5 Conclusion

This chapter demonstrates that, in Mexico, synergies between migration studies and feminist thought occurred at various junctures and around specific issues. By tracing and assessing the female empowerment through migration debate over several decades, it becomes clear that the twenty-first century researchers who follow Mexican transnational families closely over time as they move back and forth across borders have restated the terms of the controversy. Breaking out of the before/after and win/lose straightjacket and the dichotomy that juxtaposes women who leave/ women who stay, authors such as Robert Smith (2006) and Deborah Boehm (2008) simultaneously explore changing models of masculinity and femininity. Their analyses coin neologisms—"gender moves" (Boehm 2008, p. 16), "gender strategies," "gender bargaining" (Smith 2006, pp. 94, 98)—that attempt to capture the flux involved in daily, tough negotiation as men and women "try on" various models of manhood and womanhood in transnational social fields, thereby actively constructing new forms of transnational life. Boehm (2008, p. 16) aptly states the apparent contradictions inherent in living across borders: "migration results in a complex interplay between males and females- a series of negotiations through which women exercise increased autonomy in some circumstances but also face the reassertion of male dominance and in which males reproduce patriarchal power even as they create new ways to express masculinity."

At the turn of the twenty-first century, this promising line of research embracing transnational frameworks is frontally concerned with the interplay of individual and collective transformations in gender relations, a theoretical issue that heretofore tended to be glossed over in academia. Individualistic frameworks placed exclusive attention on the marital couple, either composed of a migrant husband and stay-at-home wife or both migrants; their offspring were viewed either as those left behind or as the second generation. By means of paradigmatic shifts toward conflict theory, social network analysis, the culturalist turn and gender studies occurring in the 1980s and 1990s (Ariza 2007), today's analysts, activists and even policymakers have been able to view families involved in migrant processes as intergenerational, negotiating units moving within larger household dynamics, affected by and affecting trends in migration flows and policies in the era of globalization.

Bringing potential synergies between migration studies and feminist thought to fruition has required grassroots activism, theoretical discussions and networking among many social actors. Foremost among these have been the feminist researcheractivists (on both individual and collective levels), followed by committed nongovernmental citizen groups, and, finally, employees in government agencies with agenda of promoting gender equity and migrant rights in host societies. More and more of these networks are of a transnational nature and rely upon modern technology to facilitate cross-border contact, thus sharing experiences and expediting results. This trend suggests an emerging question: how have transnational feminist networks and technology use transformed the intersection of Mexican feminist thought and migration studies? How have they recast debates by "shrinking" physical distances and compressing time so that the plight of women and their struggles around the globe become a common agenda, as illustrated, for example, in the global reach of the gender asylum advocacy undertaken by the CGRS, encompassing women and girls not only from Mexico and Central America, but also from Africa and Asia?

Clearly, although the sites of engagement and social actors have multiplied, the feminist struggles for social justice and debates mobilizing Mexican society from the 1970s onwards—notably the women's empowerment through migration debate showcased in this chapter—are ongoing and their nexus with migration studies is only beginning to be explored.

References

Alanís, F. S. (2008). El mapa de la migración potosina a Estados Unidos. Una aproximación al lugar de origen y destino de la emigración del Estado de San Luis Potosí. In F. S. Alanís Enciso (Ed.), *Yo soy de San Luis Potosí!... con un pie en Estados Unidos. Aspectos contemporáneos de la migración potosina a Estados Unidos* (pp. 53–76). Mexico City: El Colegio de San Luis/ Instituto Nacional de Migración de la Secretaría de Gobernación/Consejo Potosino de Ciencia y Tecnología/Miguel Ángel Porrúa.

Álvarez, L., & Broder, J. M. (2006, January 10). More and more, women risk all to enter US. *New York Times*, A1, A23.

Ariza, M. (2007). Itinerario de los estudios de género y migración en México. In M. Ariza & A. Portes (Eds.), *El país transnacional: Migración Mexicana y cambio social a través de la frontera* (pp. 453–511). Mexico City: Instituto de Investigaciones Sociales/UNAM.

Ariza, M., & Portes, A. (Eds.). (2007). *El país transnacional: Migración Mexicana y cambio social a través de la frontera*. Mexico City: Instituto de Investigaciones Sociales/UNAM.

Arizpe, L. (1990). El feminismo y la democratización mundial. *debate feminista, 1*(1), 109–113.

Arzate, S., & Vizcarra, B. (2007). De la migración masculina transnacional: Violencia estructural y género en comunidades campesinas del Estado de México. *Migración y Desarrollo, Segundo semestre, 9*, 95–112.

Barndt, D. (2002). *Tangled routes: Women, work and globalization on the tomato trail*. Lanham: Rowman & Littlefield.

Barrera, D., & Oehmichen, C. (Eds.). (2000). *Migración y relaciones de género en México*. Mexico City: Grupo Interdisciplinario sobre Mujer, Trabajo y Pobreza, A.C./Instituto de Investigaciones Antropológicas/UNAM.

Bartra, E. (1999). El movimiento feminista en México y su vínculo con la academia. *La Ventana, 10*, 214–234.

Bartra, E. et al. (2002). *Feminismo en México, ayer y hoy*. Mexico City: Universidad Autónoma Metropolitana. Colección Molinos de Viento No. 130.

Basok, T. (2002). *Tortillas and tomatoes: Transmigrant Mexican harvesters in Canada*. Montreal: McGill-Queen's University Press.

Becerril, O. (2007). *Lucha cultural por la dignidad y los derechos humanos. Transmigrantes mexicanos en Canadá contendiendo el género, la sexualidad y la identidad*. Ph.D. dissertation, Universidad Autónoma Metropolitana, Unidad Iztapalapa, Mexico City.

Boehm, D. (2008). Ir y venir: Historias transnacionales, trayectorias determinadas por género. In F. S. Alanís Enciso (Ed.), *Yo soy de San Luis Potosí!... con un pie en Estados Unidos. Aspectos contemporáneos de la migración potosina a Estados Unidos* (pp. 93–112). Mexico City: El Colegio de San Luis/Instituto Nacional de Migración de la Secretaría de Gobernación/Consejo Potosino de Ciencia y Tecnología/Miguel Ángel Porrúa.

Calderón, A. (2009). *Rights in a foreign land. Women, domestic violence, and migration. Derechos en tierra ajena. Mujeres, violencia doméstica y migración* (Bilingual edition). Morelia: Secretaría de Cultura del Estado de Michoacán.

Cordero, B. L. (2007). *Ser trabajador transnacional: clase, hegemonía y cultura en un circuito migratorio internacional.* Puebla: Benemérita Universidad Autónoma de Puebla/Consejo Nacional de Ciencia y Tecnología.

Córdova, R., Núñez, C., & Skerritt, D. (2008). *Migración internacional, crisis agrícola y transformaciones culturales en la región central de Veracruz.* Mexico City: Universidad Veracruzana/ CEMCA/Conacyt/Plaza y Valdés.

Correa, J. Y. (2009). *Ahora las mujeres se mandan solas: Migración y relaciones de género en una comunidad transnacional llamada Pie de Gallo.* Mexico City: Plaza y Valdés/Universidad Autónoma de Querétaro.

Curiel, L. C. (2002). *De esas mujeres quiere Dios. Participación femenina en la reproducción comunitaria y la recreación de la costumbre en San Miguel Tlacotepec, Oaxaca.* Master's thesis presented to Centro de Investigación y Estudios Superiores en Antropología Social-Occidente, Guadalajara.

D'Aubeterre, M. E. (2000a). Arbitraje y adjudicación de conflictos conyugales en una comunidad de transmigrantes originarios del estado de Puebla. In L. Binford & M. E. D'Aubeterre (Eds.), *Conflictos migratorios transnacionales y respuestas comunitarias* (pp. 115–145). Puebla: Gobierno del Estado de Puebla/Consejo Estatal de Población/Benemérita Universidad Autónoma de Puebla/H. Ayuntamiento del Municipio de Puebla/Sociedad Cultural Urbavista.

D'Aubeterre, M. E. (2000b). *El pago de la novia.* Zamora: El Colegio de Michoacán/Benemérita Universidad Autónoma de Puebla.

D'Aubeterre, M. E. (2000c). Mujeres y espacio social transnacional: Maniobras para renegociar el vínculo conyugal. In D. Barrera Bassols & C. Oehmichen (Eds.), *Migración y relaciones de género en México* (pp. 63–85). Mexico City: Grupo Interdisciplinario sobre Mujer, Trabajo y Pobreza/Instituto de Investigaciones Antropológicas, UNAM.

D'Aubeterre, M. E. (2007). Aquí respetamos a nuestros esposos: Migración masculina, conyugalidad y trabajo femenino en una comunidad de origen nahua del estado de Puebla. In M. Ariza & A. Portes (Eds.), *El país transnacional: Migración Mexicana y cambio social a través de la frontera* (pp. 513–544). Mexico City: Instituto de Investigaciones Sociales/UNAM.

Dinerman, I. R. (1982). *Migrants and stay-at-homes: A comparative study of rural migration from Michoacán, Mexico* (Monographs Series, 5). La Jolla: Center for U.S.-Mexican Studies, University of California, San Diego.

Donato, K. M., Gabaccia, D., Holdaway, J., Manalansan, M. I. V., & Pessar, P. (2006). A glass half full? Gender in migration studies. *International Migration Review, 40*(153), 3–26.

Dreby, J. (2006). Honor and virtue. Mexican parenting in the transnational context. *Gender and Society, 20*(1), 32–59.

Dreby, J. (2010). *Divided by borders. Mexican migrants and their children.* Berkeley: University of California Press.

Espinosa, V. (1998). *El dilema del retorno. Migración, género y sentido de pertenencia en un contexto transnacional.* Zamora: El Colegio de Michoacán.

Fagetti, A. (2000). Mujeres abandonadas: desafíos y vivencias. In D. Barrera Bassols & C. Oehmichen Bazan (Eds.), *Migración y relaciones de género en México* (pp. 119–134). Mexico City: Grupo Interdisciplinario sobre Mujer, Trabajo y Pobreza/Instituto de Investigaciones Antropológicas, UNAM.

Fernández, A. (1998). Estudios sobre las mujeres, el género y el feminismo. *Nueva Antropología, 16*(54), 79–95.

Frias, S. M. (2009). *Gender, the state and patriarchy. Partner violence in Mexico.* Saarbrücken: VDM Verlag Dr. Müller.

García, B., & De Oliveira, O. (1994). *Trabajo femenino y vida familiar en México.* Mexico City: El Colegio de México.

García, B., Camarena, R. M., & Salas, G. (1999). Mujeres y relaciones de género en los estudios de población. In B. García (Ed.), *Mujer, género y población en México* (pp. 19–60). Mexico City: El Colegio de México.

Goldring, L. (1996). Gendered memory: reconstructions of the village by Mexican transnational migrants. In M. DuPuis & P. Vandergeest (Eds.), *Creating the countryside: The politics of rural and environmental discourse* (pp. 303–329). Philadelphia: Temple University Press.

González-López, G. (2005). *Erotic journeys: Mexican immigrants and their sex lives.* Berkeley: University of California.

González de la Rocha, M. (1993). El poder de la ausencia: Mujeres y migración en una comunidad de los Altos de Jalisco. In J. Tapia Santamaría (Ed.), *Realidades regionales de la crisis nacional* (pp. 317–334). Zamora: El Colegio de Michoacán.

Griffith, D. (2002). El avance de capital y los procesos laborales que no dependen del mercado. *Relaciones, 23*(90), 17–53.

Gutmann, M. C. (1996). *The meanings of macho: Being a man in Mexico City.* Berkeley: University of California Press.

Hellman, J. A. (2008). *The world of Mexican migrants: The rock and the hard place.* New York: The New Press.

Hirsch, J. (2003). *A courtship after marriage: Sexuality and love in Mexican transnational families.* Berkeley: University of California Press.

Hondagneu-Sotelo, P. (1994). *Gendered transitions: Mexican experiences of immigration.* Berkeley: University of California Press.

Hondagneu-Sotelo, P. (2003). Gender and immigration. A retrospective and introduction. In P. Hondagneu-Sotelo (Ed.), *Gender and US immigration: Contemporary trends* (pp. 3–19). Berkeley: University of California Press.

Kanaiaupuni, S. M. (2000a). Reframing the migration question: An analysis of men, women, and gender in Mexico. *Social Forces, 78*(4), 1311–1347.

Kanaiaupuni, S. M. (2000b). *Sustaining families and communities: Non-migrant women and Mexico-US migration processes* (CDE Working Paper: 2000–13). Center for Demography and Ecology: University of Wisconsin-Madison.

Lagarde, M. (1990). *Los cautiverios de las mujeres: Madresposas, monjas, putas, presas y locas.* Mexico City: Dirección General de Estudios de Posgrado, UNAM.

Lamas, M. (1990). Editorial. *debate feminista, 1*(1), 1–5.

Lamas, M., Martínez, A., Tarrés, M. L., & Tuñón, E. (1995). Building bridges: The growth of popular feminism in Mexico. In A. Basu (Ed.), *The challenges of local feminism: Women's movements in global perspective* (pp. 324–347). Boulder: Westview Press.

Lau, A. (2002). "El nuevo movimiento feminista mexicano a fines del milenio." In E. Bartra, A. M. Fernández, & A. Lau (Eds.), *Feminismo en México, ayer y hoy* (pp. 11–41). Mexico City: Universidad Autónoma Metropolitana, Colección Molinos de Viento No. 130.

López, G. (2008, October). *El síndrome de Penélope. Salud emocional, depresión y ansiedad de mujeres de migrantes.* Unpublished paper presented at the Encounter/Workshop Women and migration: the emotional costs (*Encuentro Taller mujer y migración, los costos emocionales.*), Mexico City.

Macías, A. (1982). *Against all odds: The feminist movement in Mexico to 1940.* Westport: Connecticut Greenwood.

Maldonado, C., & Artía, P. (2004). "Now we are awake": Women's political participation in the Oaxacan Indigenous Binational Front. In J. A. Fox & G. Rivera-Salgado (Eds.), *Indigenous Mexican migrants in the United States* (pp. 525–538). San Diego: Center for U.S.-Mexican Studies/Center for Comparative Immigration Studies/University of California.

Malkin, V. (1999). La reproducción de relaciones de género en la comunidad de migrantes mexicanos en New Rochelle, Nueva York. In G. Mummert (Ed.), *Fronteras fragmentadas* (pp. 475–496). Zamora: El Colegio de Michoacán/Centro de Investigación y Desarrollo del Estado de Michoacán.

Malkin, V. (2004). We go to get ahead: Gender and status in two Mexican migrant communities. *Latin American Perspectives, 31*(5), 75–99.

Mancillas, C., & Rodríguez, D. (2009). Muy cerca pero a la distancia: Transiciones familiares en una comunidad poblana de migrantes. *Migraciones Internacionales, 5*(1), 35–64.

Marroni, M. G. (2009). *Frontera perversa, familias fracturadas. Los indocumentados mexicanos y el sueño americano.* Mexico City: BUAP-GIMTRAP.

Martínez, D. T. (2008). *Tan lejos y tan cerca: la dinámica de los grupos familiares de migrantes desde una localidad michoacana en el contexto transnacional.* PhD dissertation, CIESAS, Mexico City.

Montoya, E. (2008). *Remesas, género e inversión productiva. Los negocios remeseros, las mujeres jaiberas en Pamlico, Carolina del Norte y el costo social de la migración en una localidad sinaloense, Gabriel Leyva Solano.* Culiacán: El Colegio de Sinaloa.

Mueller, R. E. (2005). Mexican immigrants and temporary residents in Canada: Current knowledge and future research. *Migraciones Internacionales, 3*(1), 32–56.

Mummert, G. (1988). Mujeres de migrantes y mujeres migrantes de Michoacán: Nuevos papeles para las que se quedan y las que se van. In T. Calvo & G. López (Eds.), *Movimiento de población en el Occidente de México* (pp. 281–295). Mexico City: Centre d'Etudes Mexicaines et Centraméricaines/El Colegio de Michoacán.

Mummert, G. (Ed.). (1999). *Fronteras fragmentadas.* Zamora: El Colegio de Michoacán/Centro de Investigación y Desarrollo del Estado de Michoacán.

Mummert, G. (2003). Dilemas familiares en un Michoacán de migrantes. In G. López Castro & G. Mummert (Eds.), *Diáspora michoacana* (pp. 113–145). Zamora: El Colegio de Michoacán/ Gobierno del Estado de Michoacán.

Mummert, G. (2009). Siblings by telephone. Experiences of Mexican children in long-distance childrearing arrangements. *Journal of the Southwest, 51*(4), 515–538.

Mummert, G. (2010a). *Expert affidavit on child abuse in Mexico.* Submitted to the Center for Gender and Refugee Studies, University of California: Hastings College of the Law.

Mummert, G. (2010b). Growing up and growing old in rural Mexico and China. Caregiving for the young and the elderly at the family-state interface. In N. Long, Y. Jingzhong, & W. Yihuan (Eds.), *Rural transformations and development- China in context. The everyday lives of policies and people* (pp. 215–252). Cheltenham: Edward Elgar.

Mummert, G. (2010c). ¡Quien sabe qué será ese norte! Mujeres ante la migración mexicana hacia Estados Unidos y Canadá. In F. Alba et al. (Eds.), *Migraciones internacionales* (Serie Los grandes problemas de México, Vol. 3, pp. 271–315). Mexico City: El Colegio de México.

Pedraza, S. (1991). Women and migration. *Annual Review of Sociology, 17,* 303–325.

Pérez, M. E. (2009). *Mujeres que se van, mujeres que se quedan. Experiencia migratoria en Tonatico-Waukegan.* Undergraduate thesis, Escuela Nacional de Antropología e Historia, Mexico City.

Pessar, P. R. (1999). Engendering migration studies: The case of new immigrants in the United States. *American Behavioral Scientist, 42*(4), 577–600.

Pessar, P. R., & Mahler, S. J. (2003). Transnational migration: Bringing gender in. *International Migration Review, 37*(3), 812–846.

Preibisch, K. (2000). La tierra de los (no) libres: Migración temporal México-Canadá y dos campos de reestructuración económica neoliberal. In L. Binford & M. E. D'Aubeterre (Eds.), *Conflictos migratorios transnacionales y respuestas comunitarias* (pp. 45–66). México: Gobierno del Estado de Puebla/Instituto de Ciencias Sociales y Humanidades/Benemérita Universidad Autónoma de Puebla.

Preibisch, K., & Hermoso, L. M. (2006). Engendering labour migration: The case of foreign workers in Canadian agriculture. In E. Tastsoglou & A. Dobrowolsky (Eds.), *Women, migration and citizenship: Making local, national and transnational connections* (pp. 107–130). London: Ashgate.

Ramírez, C. (2000). *Buscando la vida: Mujeres indígenas migrantes.* Mexico City: Instituto Nacional Indigenista/Programa de Naciones Unidas para el Desarrollo.

Rivermar, M. L. (2008). *Etnicidad y migración internacional. El caso de una comunidad nahua en el estado de Puebla*. Puebla: Benemérita Universidad Autónoma de Puebla.

Rojas, O. L. (2008). *Paternidad y vida familiar en la Ciudad de México: Un estudio del desempeño masculino en los procesos reproductivos y en la vida doméstica*. Mexico City: Centro de Estudios Demográficos/Urbanos y Ambientales/El Colegio de México.

Rosas, C. (2009). *Varones al son de la migración: Migración internacional y masculinidades de Veracruz a Chicago*. Mexico City: Centro de Estudios Demográficos/Urbanos y Ambientales/ El Colegio de México.

Serret, E. (2000). El feminismo mexicano de cara al Siglo XXI. *El Cotidiano, 16*(100), 42–51.

Smith, R. C. (2006). *Mexican New York: Transnational lives of new immigrants*. Berkeley: University of California Press.

Smith-Nonini, S. (2002). Nadie sabe, nadie supo: El programa federal H2A y la explotación de mano de obra mediada por el Estado. *Relaciones. Estudios de Historia y Sociedad, 23*(90), 55–86.

Stephen, L. (2007). *Transborder lives: Indigenous Oaxacans in Mexico, California, and Oregon*. Durham: Duke University Press.

Stern, C. (Ed.). (1996). *El papel del trabajo materno infantil: Contribuciones al debate desde las ciencias sociales*. Mexico City: El Colegio de México/Population Council.

Suárez, B., & Zapata, E. (Coords.) (2004). *Remesas: Milagros y mucho más realizan las mujeres indígenas y campesinas*, t. 1. Mexico City: Grupo Interdisciplinario sobre Mujeres, Trabajo y Pobreza, A.C. (Serie PEMSA).

Suárez, B., & Zapata, E. (Eds.). (2007). *Ilusiones, sacrificios y resultados. El escenario real de las remesas de emigrantes a Estados Unidos*. Mexico City: Grupo Interdisciplinario sobre Mujeres, Trabajo y Pobreza, A.C.

Suárez, G. (2008). *Entre ires y venires: Reposicionamiento en el grupo familiar de mujeres migrantes despulpadoras de jaiba del municipio de Jalpa de Méndez, Tabasco*, Master's thesis presented to El Colegio de Michoacán, Mexico.

Szasz, I. (1999). La perspectiva de género en el estudio de la migración femenina en México. In B. García (Ed.), *Mujer, género y población en México* (pp. 167–210). Mexico City: El Colegio de México.

Torres, A. L. (2008). *Mujeres esposas de migrantes y su participación en los espacios públicos. El caso de la comunidad indígena purhépecha de Angahuan, Michoacán, México*. Master's thesis presented to Programa Interdisciplinario de Estudios de la Mujer, El Colegio de México, Mexico City.

Tuñón, E. (1997). *Mujeres en escena: De la tramoya al protagonismo (1982–1994)*. México: ECOSUR/UNAM/Porrúa.

Turner, V., & Bruner, E. M. (Eds.). (1986). *The anthropology of experience*. Chicago: University of Illinois Press.

Vidal, L., Tuñón, E., Rojas, M., & Ayús, R. (2002). De Paraíso a Carolina del Norte. Redes de apoyo y percepciones de la migración a Estados Unidos de mujeres tabasqueñas despulpadoras de jaiba. *Migraciones Internacionales, 1*(2), 29–61.

Vizcarra, I., Guadarrama, X., & Lutz, B. (2009). De la migración: Ausencias masculinas y reacciones femeninas mazahuas. *Relaciones, 30*(118), 183–219.

West, C., & Zimmerman, D. (1991). Doing gender. In S. Lorber & S. Farrell (Eds.), *The social construction of gender* (pp. 13–37). Newbury Park: Sage.

Woo, O. (2001). *Las mujeres también nos vamos al Norte*. Guadalajara: Universidad de Guadalajara.

Chapter 4
Fragmented Migrant (Her)Stories: Multi-sited Ethnography and Feminist Migration Research*

Luna Vives

> It took me 4 days—4 days!!—to travel from Spain to Senegal this time. They stopped us at the Spanish border because the driver was wanted by the police and when we arrived at the Mauritanian border we found it closed, so we had to wait until the morning. At least I got to spend *Tabaski*[1] with my people. […] Let me tell you something: it's quite a thing to see you here, in my country, not always Spain, Spain, Spain. Want something to drink? Are you hungry? If you need anything, please let us know. This is Senegal, the country of *Teranga*![2]
>
> (Mame Fatou, 50–60 years old, resident in Spain since 2004)

4.1 Introduction

I was introduced to Mame Fatou in early 2009, when she agreed to participate in a study on Senegalese female migration to Spain. When we first met she was depressed, profoundly homesick, unemployed, and about to lose her status as a legal resident in Spain. As we walked towards the coffee shop where we had our first interview, she recoiled when a teenager yelled at her from across the street: "Hey check it out, it's

*Fieldwork research was funded by a Settling into Motion Scholarship (ZEIT Foundation, Germany), a Vanier Canada Graduate Scholarship (Canada) and a research grant from the Spanish Ministry of Education and Culture. I thank Alex Aylett and Sarah Koopman for their comments and suggestions to earlier versions of this manuscript. Any errors or omissions are entirely my own.

[1] Senegalese term for Eid al-Adha, the Festival of Sacrifice that commemorates Prophet Ibrahim's devotion to God. It is a time to celebrate with family and neighbors.

[2] In Wolof, the language spoken by most people in Senegal, teranga means hospitality. Senegalese often take pride in the country's warm welcoming of strangers.

L. Vives, Ph.D. (✉)
Department of Geography, University of British Columbia (UBC),
Vancouver, BC, Canada
email: lunavives@gmail.com

G.T. Bonifacio (ed.), *Feminism and Migration: Cross-Cultural Engagements*,
International Perspectives on Migration 1, DOI 10.1007/978-94-007-2831-8_4,
© Springer Science+Business Media B.V. 2012

King Kong's wife!"[3] A year later we met again at her home in the outskirts of Dakar. For about 1 hour, one of her grandchildren cried helplessly at the sight of the *Toubab*[4] (myself) that he took for an evil spirit, a *djiné*. At home, Mame Fatou was all laughter and strength, asking about my experiences as a white woman living in and moving around Dakar's impoverished suburbs. She showed me around the house tapping on the solid wood furniture and the three immaculate white leather sofas that have become status symbols in migrants' houses in Senegal. Sipping *ataya* (Senegalese tea) in her living room, surrounded by her family, Mame Fatou chuckled and asked in Spanish: "how do you like *my* country, *Madame Toubab*?"

In this chapter, I draw from this and other encounters to argue that multi-sited research is beneficial for the construction of a "feminist solidarity across borders" (Mohanty 2002)—administrative, racial, cultural, and religious borders—in migration studies. While paying attention to discussions on reflexivity and positionality in feminist scholarship, I aim to go beyond them by proposing that the position of the researcher is a negotiable space. Building more egalitarian relationships in the field does not necessarily require "sameness" (similar identity and/or shared lived experiences between researcher and participant) (Browne 2003; Blake 2007). Instead, empathy, reciprocity, and participation can be built into the research methodology to trigger fairer relations between respondents and researchers. In migration studies, one way to do this is by using multi-sited ethnography, which allows more room for the negotiation of differences, and thus provides a fertile ground for feminist migration research interested in the experience of migrants on the ground. This, in turn, could translate into a more ethical research process consistent with the tenets of feminist scholarship (Bondi 2003; Browne 2003; Domosh 2003; Pratt and Yeoh 2003).

4.2   Within and Beyond Situated Knowledge and Positionality

Academic feminism is committed to producing "scholarship and practices that pay explicit attention to women, gender, and sexuality, and the ways in which other axes of identity are intertwined with these in the relations of power, oppression, and domination that organize and construct the social world" (Brown and Staeheli 2003, pp. 247–248). Knowledge that can be labeled as "feminist" differs from more traditional and mainstream scientific knowledge in at least four ways. First, feminist scholarship rejects the possibility of objective, exhaustive and absolute knowledge (Haraway 1991; Rose 1993; Gilbert 1994). Second, it emphasizes that participation and emotional connection are valid research tools (Bondi 2003; Blake 2007). Third, it aims to deconstruct and eventually debunk the figure of the "master subject" (the judgmental, all-knowing white, bourgeois, and heterosexual male scientist) and

---

[3] Similar racist remarks and behaviors were experienced by all participants.

[4] In Wolof, Toubab means a white person.

to produce knowledge about and from positions of subalter(n)ity (Haraway 1991; Rose 1993; Gilbert 1994; Mohanty 2002). Fourth, the ultimate goal of feminist scholarship is to produce knowledge that leads to action: to make inequalities of power visible in order to contest them (Mohanty 2002). Beyond this rough common ground, feminism is heterogeneous in its purposes and its methods.

One of the main sources of tension in feminist discussions of ethnographic fieldwork is that, while we want to write about and from positions of subalternity, feminist scholars are, overall, a rather privileged bunch (Kobayashi 1994). Given the circumstances, how are we to straddle the many differences that separate participants and researchers, and engage in "read[ing] up the ladder of privilege, [beginning] from the lives and interests of marginalized communities of women" (Mohanty 2002, p. 511) without exploiting them?

Power and difference are central to the feminist project. Feminists do not claim to produce absolute knowledge. Rather, they draw attention to the "situatedness" of their research, and acknowledge their (and all scholars) limited vision of the world and their involvement in complex relations of power (Haraway 1991; Rose 1997). Situated knowledge requires the researcher to address how her complex identity and positionality (her belonging to certain categories of gender, race, socio-economic class, nationality, and so forth) influences each and every stage of the research process. Reflexivity becomes critical to the feminist enterprise. However, if taken too far, the claim for reflexivity (which Gillian Rose (1997) described as "transparent reflexivity") can be criticized on the grounds that it presumes that both self and context can be fully comprehended. Limitations inherent to human knowledge, the dynamism of social relations, and the ever-shifting interaction between the many axes of social differentiation tend to be forgotten when we assume that the understanding of self, other, and context are all fully accessible to us.

Besides the tensions that arise from the unequal relation between researcher and participant on the field, and the limitations of the concepts of reflexivity and positionality, another pitfall of feminist methodological discussions is that participants' agency is rarely problematized, and often not discussed at all (Domosh 2003). Obviously, participants in qualitative research are at least as strategic in their actions as researchers. They do much more than reveal the truth to us: they choose, filter, and shape the information they share, constructing "a productive other" (van Liempt 2007, p. 68) *vis à vis* the researcher. It is thus necessary to move beyond simplistic self-reflexivity to consider how our positionality as researchers combine with participants' identities, positionalities, and interests.

4.3 Rethinking Research Across Difference in Migration Studies

After decades of debate, the question of sameness and difference in fieldwork remains controversial. It has been argued that "auto-ethnography" (research within the researcher's community of reference or research through sameness) results in a more sophisticated understanding of participants' experiences, which are assumed to be similar to those of the researcher. Sameness is also said to allow for more egalitarian relations on the field and facilitate access to hard-to-reach groups (England 1994; Blake 2007). Skeptics of the sameness perspective, on the other hand, point that the "native" may take for granted some of the key elements that shape participants' experiences, because they are an integral part of both participants and researcher's socialisation. Also, were researchers to limit their scientific interest to what they know best through their personal experience, whole sections of the population would be left unrepresented—some of them among the most disempowered groups in society whose circumstances, according to Chandra Talpade Mohanty (2002), are considered fundamental for transnational feminist solidarity. More importantly, sameness is constructed upon an essentialized take on complex identities. Reflecting on this issue, both Melissa Gilbert (1994) and France Winddance Twine (2000) conclude that assuming sameness based on gender or race ignores the relevance of other interlocking axes of social differentiation key to research in the field such as age, socio-economic class, education, citizen/immigrant status, sexuality, religion, and so on.

If complete sameness is impossible and maybe far from ideal, then my argument is that feminist migration studies can (and in fact, should) instrumentalize difference instead of shying away from it. Ideally, research on racialized migrant groups should be conducted by mixed teams to make the best of the insider/outsider positions. To explore the benefits of this approach (proposed, among others, by Twine [2000]), a black Spanish woman of Equatorial Guinean origin named Sesé Sité and I recently carried out ten in-depth interviews with migrant and second generation black women in Madrid. Our objective was to understand their experiences of discrimination in the city (or lack thereof). We found that participants interviewed by Sesé were inclined to present black women as a more or less homogeneous group (a "community"), and articulated their narratives of discrimination around issues of political engagement, beauty standards, and interracial relations. When I (a white Spaniard) interviewed them, however, participants emphasized the heterogeneity of the black population in Spain; existing internal hierarchies along the lines of gender, religion, and legal status in the country (undocumented migrant, legal resident, or citizen); and the challenges of a complex identity, in particular for the second generation. Taken on their own, participants in each set of responses clearly took into account (deliberately or instinctively) the types of discourses we were already familiar with, the type of information that would be relevant to us, and reflected the participants perceptions of who we (the researchers) were. Taken together, both discourses allowed for a much more sophisticated understanding of the issues that we were interested in (Vives and Sité 2010). What emerges is a picture of black women who position themselves strategically within their group of reference (the black community in Spain) and in relationship to the majority of the local population (white), which in this case I represented. Our experience supports the claim that both research through sameness and difference are useful, and at times complementary, approaches to research on race and migration.

4.4   Multi-sited Ethnography

Ethnography is a popular methodological approach in contemporary migration research, and one particularly employed by feminists (Gilbert 1994). Reflecting on the study of world systems, anthropologist George Marcus (1986, 1995) has proposed that contemporary ethnographic work tends to be either intensive and single-sited ("classic") or multi-sited. He labeled the latter "mobile ethnography," arguing that it is a quintessential postmodern methodology arising "from anthropology's participation in a number of interdisciplinary (in fact, ideologically anti-disciplinary) arenas that have evolved since the 1980s" (Marcus 1995, p. 97). According to Marcus, the multi-sited approach placed particular emphasis on "ethics, commitment and activism" (p. 99).

In reality, multi-sited ethnographic work is far from new and it is not necessarily post-modern or politically motivated.[5] However, in the context of a rapidly globalizing world, it becomes increasingly necessary to address the circulation of goods, meanings, and practices from a systemic, transnational, and mobile perspective. This is particularly the case in migration studies. For example: a truly holistic study of Senegalese women's migration to Southern Europe should consider the enormous power differentials between the Global North and the Global South, as well as the key economic and symbolic role that remittances play in source countries (Diop 2008); it should reflect on the tensions that exist between the status of women in communities of origin and destination (Pratt and Yeoh 2003; Dial 2008), and on the role of well-established networks in the migration process (Sinatti 2008; Riccio 2008); finally, this study should relate this phenomenon to the racialization of non-EU (European Union) migrants in Spain (Vives 2008; Vives and Sité 2010) and the increasing securitisation of migration to countries in the Global North (Huysmans 2006; Geddes 2008). Multi-sited ethnography is particularly useful to grasp the interconnectedness of these multiple processes. In fact, it is difficult to imagine a research design able to address these interconnections *without* adopting a multi-sited approach.

The rise of transnationalism as a new "paradigm" in migration studies has triggered greater interest in multi-sited ethnographic work. For example, Margaret Walton-Robert's (2004) fascinating study of marriage and the role of Punjabi transnational networks between India and Canada greatly benefitted from her use of a multi-sited ethnographic methodology). Iria Vázquez Silva (2010) has also used a similar approach to study the transnational domestic duties of Senegalese women reunited with their husbands in Spain. These and other studies using an epistemologically feminist and methodologically multi-sited approach have challenged the implicit masculinization of transnational studies, which remain largely dominated by the study of male migrants (Pratt and Yeoh 2003). And yet, despite the quality of the information gathered, multi-sited ethnography remains a marginal methodological approach.

---

[5] Malinowski's classic 1922 study, "Argonauts of the Western Pacific," provides an early example of a pre-globalization and non-postmodern multi-sited ethnography.

It is true that, like any other research methodology, multi-sited ethnography has important limitations. First, if relying on participants' accounts, this model is only valid for contemporary migration and it requires that participants be alive, able, and willing to talk. Second, the scholar will likely need more time and money (both scarce in academia) to be able to carry out a rigorous study using this methodology, because research sites are more numerous and often far apart. Third, the multiplicity of research spaces may become an obstacle in building relationships of trust with participants, since the researcher is never fully "here" but "There ... and there ... and there!" (Hannerz 2003). Multi-sited research may also require language skills and a certain taste for challenging experiences. Finally, as with traditional single-sited ethnographic work, research carried out in contexts unfamiliar to the researcher bring with them certain risks. And, as other authors have noted, the researcher's (gendered, racialized, exoticized) body may make her a target for sexual harassment, monetary extortion, more or less flattering marriage proposals, or even straightforward racialized discrimination (Warren 2000; Sundberg 2003).

From a theoretical point of view, multi-sited research "tests the limits of ethnography" (Marcus 1995, p. 99), since it does not produce information as steeped into the realities of everyday life as classic single-sited ethnographic work. It does not aim at presenting an all-comprehending explanation of a smaller unit of observation, but a partial explanation of a phenomenon conceived of as part of a much larger system. It could also be assumed that the power of fieldwork is also weakened through its dispersion and that the point of view of the subaltern (the supposedly disempowered migrant) gets lost with so much travelling back and forth (Marcus 1995).

The challenges of multi-sited research are real, but so is its potential. Besides, most of these limitations can be said to affect most other forms of qualitative research methodologies. There has been little reflection, if any, on how to combine feminism and multi-sited ethnography within migration studies. And yet, it is quite possible that multi-sited work is better suited than other qualitative approaches to provide a robust foundation for research on the experience of racialized and gendered international migrants from a feminist perspective.

4.5   Multi-sited Ethnography, Feminist Research and Gendered Migration

This chapter draws extensively from 12 months of ethnographic work conducted in Spain, Senegal, and Morocco between 2009 and 2010. This fieldwork was structured around 15 life histories with Senegalese women living in Spain at the time. I asked these core respondents to put me in touch with members of their social networks that facilitated their migration, both in Spain and in Senegal. Also part of the samples were nongovernment (NGO) workers, government officials and academics who accepted to collaborate in the project as respondents. In total, the sample consisted of 15 life histories, 75 in-depth, semi-structured interviews, and a year of participant observation in core respondents' communities of origin and destination. With this information I was able to trace back participants' journey to their places of origin and reconstruct their travels.

In the following sections, I focus on the impact of using multi-sited ethnography with a feminist twist on three specific aspects of this research: the importance of establishing the broader context of migration (in particular the Spanish migration regime, gender roles, and the media), increased opportunities for reciprocity and participation, and the emergence of strategic agency on the part of migrants.

4.5.1   "Here" and "There" as Interdependent Spaces

Following migrants through different spaces puts the researcher in a good position to understand how identities and positionalities before, during, and after migration shape the opportunities that are open to them—and how these positionalities are tied to processes at a larger scale. If we were to limit our enquiries to the experiences of Senegalese migrant women since their arrival in Spain (a very common approach in migration studies) we would be tempted to cast her in the terms often used in the society of destination: as either victim or criminal (Agustin 2003; Sánchez Leyva et al. 2010). Because of the narrow perspectives used to look into migrants' lives, it is not rare to find studies that portray migrant women primarily as victims of gender violence, domestic abuse or patriarchal family structures (e.g., polygyny); human trafficking; gendered poverty in Africa, and so on. From the perspective of receiving countries, migrant women are also seen as criminals (particularly in the media) insofar as they are often perceived to be in Spanish territory through illegitimate means (as undocumented migrants, illegitimate spouses, fake tourists, or bogus refugees) or to be engaged in some kind of undocumented activity such as underground work in the sex trade (Sánchez Leyva et al. 2010). While none of these assumptions is necessarily false in specific cases, they are by no means an exhaustive description of women's experiences as immigrants. Their limited framing of the issue distorts our understanding of the migratory process. Three examples of how the methodology proposed here may deepen our understanding of migration are briefly discussed below.

4.5.1.1   The Case of the Strawberry Pickers

Multi-sited approach offers insights into how migration is interlocked with other, larger and interconnected processes that impact people's lives in a way extremely hard to grasp through the use of secondary sources. A look at the selection process through which seasonal agricultural workers (in particular, strawberry pickers) were recruited to work in Spain between 2006 and 2008 illustrates how, in order to understand the impact of Spanish legislation on who leaves, who stays, why, and how, we need to reconstruct the migration journey from the point of departure. During that period, government-managed recruitment of Senegalese temporary migrants for agricultural work was largely dominated by women (International Organization for Migration [IOM] 2009). Following previous experiences in Morocco,[6] the Spanish government asked its Senegalese counterpart that healthy women with dependent children and experience working the land be selected and recruited to work in Spain.[7]

Research in Senegal reveals another reality. In practice, corruption during the selection process meant that the characteristics defined by Spanish policymakers had no influence over how women were selected at origin: what counted were their connections to the state bureaucracy in Senegal. Middle-class university students who not even in their wildest dreams saw themselves picking strawberries were recruited, together with pregnant women who arrived in Spain only to give birth days or weeks later.[8] Some women abandoned their group at the airport, before even getting on the buses that took workers to the fields; others ran away before finishing their contracts—in some cases due to sexual abuse on the part of their employers; and roughly 90% never returned to Senegal, according to the experts interviewed for this study. Those who stayed in Spain beyond the extension of their contract automatically became undocumented migrants, and that is all they have become for the Spanish administration and for those scholars who have studied their case. Nothing, however, is being said about how faulty recruitment procedures or a poorly designed legislation have played a role into their becoming "illegal." These aspects only become fully understood when research is done on both ends of migrants' journeys.

4.5.1.2 Family Reunification

About 85% of Senegalese nationals currently living in Spain are young men (Instituto Nacional de Estadística 2010). Because of the gender imbalance, virtually all studies focusing on Senegalese migration to Spain neglect women's experiences and pay no attention to the gender dimension of the phenomenon. But as the group has settled in the country, a growing number of Senegalese women have reunited with their husbands in Spain. The migration of women through family reunification clashes against the differing legal definitions of marriage and family: polygyny is legal (and widely practised) in Senegal, but not in Spain. Since it is up to the migrant already settled to decide who is to join him, competition between spouses back in Senegal can be quite intense. In the impoverished suburbs of Dakar, such as Guédiawaye, up to 90% of the households depend totally or partially on remittances

---

[6] See Juana Moreno Nieto (2009).

[7] Men and single women were thought to be less likely to return after the end of the contract. Based on the interview with an official from the Spanish Bureau of Labour in Senegal, May 2009; interviews with officials from the Ministry of Immigration and Labour in Spain, February 2010.

[8] Interview with representative from the International Organization for Migration in Senegal, May 2009; interview with recruited woman in Senegal, May 2009; interview with representative of the International Labour Organization in Senegal, January 2010.

(Diop 2008). The prosperity implicit in a marriage with a migrant entices families with young daughters, transforming the rules of the marriage market and altering intra-household gender and inter-generational dynamics (Dial 2008; Diop 2008). At the same time, the migration of women married to migrants is strongly discouraged by their families, as it might mean a decrease in the amount and regularity of remittances. This again is a dynamic that cannot be fully understood by researchers based solely in the country of reception.

4.5.1.3 Paulette

The case of Paulette, a Senegalese woman, illuminates the many links that bind origin, transit, and destination in the process of migration. From a poor Muslim family, Paulette was forced into a polygamous marriage with an abusive man she did not love.[9] Since childhood, she had harboured the hope of migrating to that land of milk and honey that she saw on TV: Europe. When, shortly after her marriage, Paulette got pregnant, she said to herself: "either I leave now or I stay here forever." She then negotiated her trip with a local fisherman, who smuggled her through the border in a boat that left the coast of Mbour at 3 am on August 22, 2004. Paulette was one of the pioneers in illegal migration from Senegal to Spain by sea. A year later, black Africans began to arrive by the hundreds to the Canary Islands; others attempted to jump over the razor-wire fences that separate Morocco and the Spanish enclaves of Ceuta and Melilla with more or less luck. The pressure that these migrants put on the border was so intense that it became one of the main factors in the justification of the creation of FRONTEX,[10] the European Union's agency for the coordinated protection of its external borders (Vives 2009). But that night was more important for Paulette than for any of the Euro-bureaucrats that participated in redefining the region's borders. She spent 45 min describing the trip to the Canary Islands in painful detail:

> We were at least eighty people. The boat was very, very large. There were children, women with babies, and men [...]. The first days were ok, but then we run out of water and food. [...] Some people got very badly sunburnt. I don't even want to think about it, because when I do I get a sharp pain here, behind my eyes. The neurologist says that it's the stress that I'm still hung up on what happened in that trip. [...] I don't even remember how long it took us to arrive in Spain. The days were very long [...] [But] the worst were the children: when the mother doesn't eat the milk stops flowing, and children cried all the time.

Two and a half months after our first interview in Spain, I met Paulette's family in Kaolack, a city of 150,000 inhabitants South of Dakar. When her husband told me

---

[9] According to Fatou Binetou Dial (2008), forced marriages are rare in contemporary Senegal, although they still happen. Often marriages are decided by the families and "consented" by the couple, the union between crossed cousins being preferred whenever possible (interview with researcher in Senegal, January 2010).

[10] From the French *Frontières extérieures* or external borders, this is the EU agency responsible for external border security. Its legal name is European Agency for the Management of Operational Cooperation at the External Borders of the Member States of the European Union.

that he had paid over 4,000 euros to buy Paulette a tourist visa and a plane ticket to
Rome, I thought he was saving face. Then her mother and sister[11] insisted that they
had said their farewells to Paulette personally at the airport when she left to join a
cousin in Italy, but shortly after she heard that achieving legal status was easier in
Spain and moved there.

Back in Spain, I asked Paulette why I had been given two different versions of her
trip, and why she had asked her family to tell me the real story. Her answer was: "I
wanted you to understand that I had to look for ways to make my life easier." She said
that upon her arrival in Spain she had spent the last months of her pregnancy at some
friends' home watching TV and trying to learn more about Spanish language and
culture. Only then did she learn about the drama of undocumented migration of black
Africans by sea. She realized that undocumented boat migrants triggered a collective
imaginary of Africa as a place of extreme poverty and desperation and, more importantly, a feeling of Catholic piety towards (in her words) "those poor black people."
At that time, the Spanish government also got involved in a campaign to raise awareness against domestic violence in the country. Paulette then embraced the labels that
she was given as a "black," "poor," "illiterate," "dominated woman," a victim of
domestic abuse and human smuggling who needed to be saved, and made herself
a new persona with them. By all accounts, her appropriation of widely available
gendered, racialized, and postcolonial prejudices served her purposes well.

In summary, the cases of temporary agricultural workers, wives brought to Spain
through family reunification procedures, and Paulette's story point to the potential of
the multi-sited ethnographic approach for the study of gendered experiences of international migration and transnationalism. Without the information collected at the
country of origin and about the migration process itself, our knowledge of the
circumstances under which these women migrated and settled into Spain would have
been incomplete, at best. It is the richness of the discourse that emerges from multi-
sited ethnography that can help us have a more sophisticated understanding of,
among others, the gendered nature of the migration process from beginning to end.

The information gathered using this methodology also provides entry points to
issues of great interest for feminist migration scholarship, such as the precarious
relationship between transnationalism and the advance of gender equity. Geraldine
Pratt and Brenda Yeoh (2003) have argued against the sometimes triumphalist conclusion, on the part of certain feminist scholars, that these two go necessarily together.
Their call for caution certainly applies to this study. Working with Senegalese wives
who have reunited their husbands in Spain, Iria Vázquez Silva (2010) has found that
these migrants' domestic obligations towards their husband's family (particularly
towards their mothers in law) permeate their entire experience of migration. In fact,
it is this obligation which made her participants' lives truly transnational: whenever
their mothers in law needed them, wives would return to Senegal; whenever their

---

[11] In Senegal, people who are emotionally close refer to each other as sister/brother (if they are of
the same age), father/mother (if they are older), or daughter/son (if they are younger) regardless of
the blood relationship. In this case, the woman that Paulette was referring to as her sister was her
best friend and business partner.

husbands requested them in Spain, they would come back to Spain. Gains in gender equity are not to be seen anywhere in this back and forth movement, even though their status in Senegal may have benefited from migration (Vázquez Silva 2010).

4.5.2 Greater Opportunities for Reciprocity and Participation

Reciprocity, a key concept in feminist research (Kobayashi 1994; Mohanty 2002), involves developing a relationship with participants so that the power dynamics between "researcher" and "researched" are problematized. While in many cases the prickly issue of reciprocity may be addressed (if only imperfectly) by offering respondents remuneration for their participation in the study, in feminist research the negotiation is more complex and personal. For example, Kath Browne (2003) described that in her project, respondents (who were also her friends) saw their participation in the study "as 'doing Kath a favour.' Consequently they felt they could ask me for favour in return. These took a number of different forms, from sharing a drink in the pub, to doing numerous odd jobs" (Browne 2003, p. 139). Mona Domosh argues that, more generally, reciprocity implies acknowledging the agency of participants and states that:

> [w]e need to scrutinize the personal knowledges of our subjects just as we do our own: Under what conditions are these truths constructed? For what reasons? Who benefits? [...] By allowing to our interviewees the same subjectivity that we allow ourselves, we create a more fully reciprocal research relationship. (Domosh 2003, p. 110)

Multi-sited ethnography allows ample room for reciprocal relations and, potentially, for participation. While doing my fieldwork, I found participants appreciative of the trouble I was going to in order to understand migrants' lives both in Senegal and in Spain: they saw it as an acknowledgement of their personhood beyond their identity as migrants. This was even more so because participants had the impression that Spaniards were not very interested in Senegal (or in Africa, for that matter) beyond the bad news that appeared in the media. As Sokhna, a Senegalese woman, put it, "Africa remains Africa [in the mind of European journalists]. Africa is not information—it only makes the news if there is hunger or war, otherwise there is no interest whatsoever."

Reciprocity can also take place through the negotiation of formal and informal research spaces (Browne 2003). I was often asked to share information and carry goods across the border and share lunches with families. While for some of these requests extreme caution is advised, acting as a link between migrants and their families can take many shapes, most of which involve little risk. For example, while I was often asked to take unlocked cellphones to Senegal and traditional clothing and letters back to Spain, most commonly I was asked to take pictures of migrant families in Spain to show to their relatives in Senegal, and vice versa (see for example Image 4.1). Basic information on family reunification procedures was also badly sought after.

The reciprocal relations that emerged from these exchanges outside more formal research spaces opened avenues for participation, another tenet of feminist practice,

Image 4.1 One of the many Senegalese families who depend almost entirely on remittances from their relatives in Europe (Photograph by Luna Vives (2009), from the project "Women Through The Border")

which was in this case limited by the temporal constraints of the research project. Participation (and other approaches such as action-research, collaboration or cooperation) results from the acknowledgement that "social research is an explicitly political intervention that not only represents, but constitutes, reality" (Cameron and Gibson 2005, p. 316). This being the case, the researcher may choose to engage in the political struggles of the population she is working with. In my case, soon after the fieldwork began it became obvious that participants deeply resented the negative impact that a biased media representation of Africa and Africans had on migrants' chances as workers and, more generally, as human beings. Because of these representations, interviewees believed neighbours and potential employers saw them as people who "came from the jungle" and had never seen a car or been to school, men and women who must have lived in a sort of timeless and placeless limbo beyond "civilisation" prior to migration. These discourses robbed participants of a very important part of their identity.

Upon some discussion on these issues, a number of the respondents and I got involved in organising "Women Through the Border," a series of activities aimed at educating a Spanish audience on Senegalese history, society and culture; raise awareness about the status of women in Senegal; and provide an accurate account of the migration of women from Senegal to Spain. The activities evolved around a photo exhibit featuring 38 pictures of Senegal (see the promotional poster for the event, Image 4.2). The photographies and captions covered aspects of Senegalese life such as religious and ethnic diversity, polygyny, literacy issues, the pervasiveness of new information technologies, the work of women on the fields as well as

Image 4.2 Promotional flyer for "Women through the Border" in Granada, Spain, November–December, 2009 (Design by Javier Acebal, reproduced with permission from the author)

in office buildings, the roles of men and women in the fishing industry, the different channels used for migration, and migrants' integration into Spanish society. Following the success of "Women Through The Border," participants proposed that we organized a similar project with the goal of shattering the image of Europe as the promise land in Senegal. This second project has yet to materialize.

Reciprocity and political involvement are ideal goals to which we should aspire, but that we may never (or only imperfectly) attain. My own assessment of how much reciprocity and meaningful participation was achieved through this project is uncertain. To begin with, participants could not be integrated into the research design from the beginning, and thus the research questions were defined largely by me (although some of the specific questions addressed by this research were not settled until after I had conducted a number of interviews). It took some time for relations that could be called reciprocal to emerge, and this required complex negotiations of our relationship both in formal and informal settings. Once these were established, however, participation through the project "Women Through the Border" seemed only natural. The project was a success of which participants felt very proud. But, once again, structural constraints reduced the level to which they could claim ownership of the project: some of the most actively involved migrants were (and are, to this day) undocumented, and their names and input in the project remain anonymous upon their request.

4.5.3   The Migrant as a Strategic Agent

As noted before, discussions on reflexivity and positionality have focused on the perspective of the researcher, neglecting participants' own position and engagement with the research process. This is a particular source of concern in the study of South-north migration, because there is already a tendency to write off migrants' desires and aspirations; all that gives migrants accountability for their own actions tends to disappear (Agustín 2003). Responsibility for this can be laid at the feet of media discourses and an excessive attention to the country of destination (Sánchez Leyva et al. 2010). It is also due to the institutional constraints imposed on academic research (Blake 2007). The result is that participants' agency is hidden behind their portrayal as racialized and marginalized migrants.

Generally, researchers in migration studies approach participants as uncritical, almost passive communicators of their migration experience. But just like researchers, migrants are strategic agents who manipulate their identities and narrate their stories with a goal in mind, such as to present themselves in a positive light or to receive some assistance (van Liempt 2007). Neither completely powerless nor in full control of their circumstances, both researcher and participant negotiate a common space that accommodates, on the one hand, the researcher's need to get the story, and, on the other, the participant's resolution to make the most of the situation.

Paulette's story offers a clear example of how migrants make choices when they re-construct their stories. Respondents in this study managed personal information in different ways and towards different means, manipulating it to obtain support, save face, or protect their loved ones. In another example, while doing interviews in Morocco I met Pape, a man in his late forties. He wanted a picture of him in his room to be shown in Spain as part of the "Women Through the Border" exhibit. He did not know anyone living in Spain. But he was clear that the picture should under no circumstances be shown in Senegal: "my family thinks I live like a king here, and I don't want them to know that I live in a house without windows and make my living begging on the street." When he returned to Senegal, he said, it would be in a large car with the most expensive clothing he could afford.[12]

The strategic use of information is not always intended at manipulating other people, as was the case for both Paulette and Pape; most often, it is meant to protect them. Thus Fatou, a middle-aged woman living in Southern Spain, asked me to conceal certain parts of her story from her daughter in Dakar:

---

[12] In the end, Pape's photo was not included as part of "Women Through the Border."

I often think of suicide. I can't sleep at night, and so I lay down, my eyes wide open, asking myself why I must keep on going. Going to the fields every morning, to find, day after day, that my boss doesn't need me, because I'm a woman and men work faster. [...]. So why should I keep on going? Then I *must* remind myself that a good Muslim woman cannot commit suicide, and that I am no one to bend God's will. And I also remember that it's because of the little money that I make that my five children can go to a good school in Dakar, and that they'll succeed where I couldn't. That's why I keep their picture on the wall by the bed, to have their eyes looking at me while I think ... well, of putting and end to so much suffering. [...] You are not to tell this to [my daughter] though, *please* don't tell her.

Despite the hardships they endure, none of these migrants see themselves as victims of a destiny they have not chosen. The label "criminal" also fails to capture their experiences. These migrants have made choices (out of a limited number of options) to shape their lives. To better understand what these options are and how they shape migration, it is necessary to see migrants as what they are: people with experiences prior to and beyond migration, with desires, aspirations, choices, and fears—in short, with agency of their own.

4.6   Conclusion

The feminist perspective continues to be marginal in migration studies. Migration scholarship has become more and more sophisticated through the incorporation of feminists' criticisms, for example by an increased understanding that gender is a constitutive factor of migration (Pratt 2004; Silvey 2004; Walton-Roberts 2004; Mahler and Pessar 2006) or that it is necessary to study the racialisation of migrant populations (Kobayashi 2003; Pratt 2005). Yet feminists are still fighting for mainstream recognition in this body of scholarship.

One of the main obstacles to mainstreaming feminist discourses in migration studies is that the discussion of feminist methodology and epistemology is fraught with anxiety and reflections disconnected from fieldwork practice. Two central concepts of feminist scholarship (positionality and reflexivity) are often approached as theoretical exploits from the comforts of an armchair. Field practice shows that, while these concepts remain theoretically valid and even necessary, they need to be revisited. If, as has been argued here, the reality of ethnographic research is inherently unstable and identities are the result of the dynamic interdependence of many categories of existence, then we should embrace uncertainty and difference and use them to boost the benefits of feminist ethnographic fieldwork for all parties involved. Our positionality as researchers is negotiable; our opportunities to creatively engage with it, virtually endless.

Multi-sited ethnography provides valuable insights into the phenomenon of gendered migration. It is also an important tool for the implementation of feminist principles on the ground and creates ample space for engagement. However, it is an expensive, time and energy consuming methodology that does not work for all projects; it is also a source of anxiety for the feminist researcher who very often must straddle several boundaries—of race, nationality, citizen/immigrant status, religion, and others—which could potentially lead to relations of vulnerability or exploitation. At the same time, multi-sited ethnography facilitates a more holistic understanding of migrants' lives and experiences, aspirations and engagements. More importantly, this methodology opens the door to fully reciprocal relations and participatory research across the spaces that are meaningful for respondents. It is, in other words, an excellent foundation for feminist work in migration studies.

References

Agustin, L. (2003). Forget victimisation: Granting agency to migrants. *Development, 46*(3), 30–35.

Blake, M. K. (2007). Formality and friendship: Research ethics review and participatory research. *ACME, 6*(3), 411–421.

Bondi, L. (2003). Empathy and identification: Conceptual resources for feminist fieldwork. *ACME, 1,* 64–76.

Brown, M., & Staeheli, L. A. (2003). 'Are we there yet?' Feminist political geographies. *Gender, Place & Culture, 10*(3), 247–255.

Browne, K. (2003). Negotiations and fieldworkings: Friendship and feminist research. *ACME, 2*(2), 132–146.

Cameron, J., & Gibson, K. (2005). Participation action research in a poststructuralist vein. *Geoforum, 36,* 315–331.

Dial, F. B. (2008). *Marriage et divorce à Dakar: itinéraires féminins.* Paris/Dakar: Karthala/Crepos.

Diop, M. (2008). Présentation. Mobilités, état et societé. In M. C. Diop (Ed.), *Le Sénégal des migrations: Mobilités, identités et societés* (pp. 13–36). Dakar Étoile/Paris/Nairobi: Crepos/Karthala/ONU-Habitat.

Domosh, M. (2003). Toward a more fully reciprocal feminist enquiry. *ACME, 2*(1), 107–111.

England, K. V. L. (1994). Getting personal: Reflexivity, positionality, and feminist research. *The Professional Geographer, 46*(1), 80.

Geddes, A. (2008). *Immigration and European integration: Beyond fortress Europe?* Vancouver: UBC Press.

Gilbert, M. R. (1994). The politics of location: Doing feminist research at "home.". *The Professional Geographer, 46*(1), 90–96.

Hannerz, U. (2003). Being there ... and there ... and there! Reflections on multi-site ethnography. *Ethnography, 4,* 201–216.

Haraway, D. J. (1991). *Simians, cyborgs and women: The reinvention of nature.* New York: Routledge.

Huysmans, J. (2006). *The politics of insecurity: Fear, migration and asylum in the EU.* New York: Routledge.

Instituto Nacional de Estadística. (2010). *Padrón Municipal 2010.* http://www.ine.es/jaxi/menu.do ?type=pcaxis&path=%2Ft20%2Fe245&file=inebase&L=0. Accessed June 3, 2011.

International Organization for Migration [IOM]. (2009). *Migration au Sénégal: Profil national 2009.* Geneva: Organisation Internationale pour les migrations.

Kobayashi, A. (1994). Coloring the field: Gender, race, and the politics of fieldwork. *The Professional Geographer, 46*(1), 73–80.

Kobayashi, A. (2003). The construction of geographical knowledge—Racialization, spacialization. In K. Anderson, S. Pile, & N. Thrift (Eds.), *Handbook of cultural geography* (pp. 473–484). Thousand Oaks: Sage.

Mahler, S. J., & Pessar, P. R. (2006). Gender matters: Ethnographers bring gender from the periphery toward the core of migration studies. *International Migration Review, 40*(1), 27–63.

Malinowski, B. (1922 [1992]). *Argonauts of the Western Pacific: An account of native enterprise and adventure in the archipelagoes of Melanesian New Guinea.* Taylor & Francis. http://lib. myilibrary.com.ezproxy.library.ubc.ca?ID=9452. Accessed January 4, 2011.

Marcus, G. E. (1986). Contemporary problems of ethnography in the modern world system. In J. Clifford & G. E. Marcus (Eds.), *Writing culture: The poetics and politics of ethnography* (pp. 165–193). Berkeley: University of California Press.

Marcus, G. E. (1995). Ethnography in/of the world system: The emergence of multi-sited ethnography. *Annual Review of Anthropology, 24,* 95–117.

Mohanty, C. T. (2002). "Under western eyes" revisited: Feminist solidarity through anticapitalist struggles. *Signs, 28*(2), 499–535.

Moreno Nieto, J. (2009). Los contratos en origen de temporada: Mujeres marroquíes en la agricultura onubense. *Revista de Estudios Mediterráneos, 7,* 58–78.

Pratt, G. (2004). *Working feminism.* Philadelphia: Temple University Press.

Pratt, G. (2005). Abandoned women and spaces of the exception. *Antipode, 37*(5), 1052–1078.

Pratt, G., & Yeoh, B. (2003). Transnational (counter) topographies. *Gender, Place & Culture, 10*(2), 159.

Riccio, B. (2008). West African transnationalisms compared: Ghanaians and Senegalese in Italy. *Journal of Ethnic and Migration Studies, 34*(2), 217–234.

Rose, G. (1993). *Feminism and geography: The limits of geographical knowledge.* Minneapolis: University of Minnesota Press.

Rose, G. (1997). Situating knowledges: Positionality, reflexivities and other tactics. *Progress in Human Geography, 21*(3), 305–320.

Sánchez Leyva, M. J., Sáiz, V., Fouce, H., & Gómez, P. (2010). Espacio público y estrategias discursivas. La visibilización de las mujeres inmigrantes en el discurso informativo español. In Grupo Interdisciplinario de Investigadoras Migrantes (Ed.), *Familias, niños, niñas y jóvenes migrantes: Rompiendo estereotipos* (pp. 53–65). Madrid: IEPALA.

Silvey, R. (2004). Power, difference and mobility: Feminist advances in migration studies. *Progress in Human Geography, 28*(4), 490–506.

Sinatti, G. (2008). The making of urban translocalities: Senegalese migrants in Dakar and Zingonia. In M. P. Smith & J. Eade (Eds.), *Transnational ties: Cities, identities, and migrations* (pp. 61–76). New Brunswick/London: Transaction Publishers.

Sundberg, J. (2003). Masculinist epistemologies and the politics of fieldwork in Latin Americanist geography. *The Professional Geographer, 55*(2), 180–190.

Twine, F. W. (2000). Racial ideologies and racial methodologies. In F. W. Twine & J. W. Warren (Eds.), *Racing research, researching race* (pp. 1–34). New York/London: New York University Press.

van Liempt, I. (2007). *Navigating borders: Inside perspectives on the process of human smuggling into the Netherlands.* Amsterdam: Amsterdam University Press.

Vázquez Silva, I. (2010). El impacto de la migración en las tareas de cuidado dentro de las familias senegalesas: La emegencia de las 'nueras transnacionales'? *INGURUAK: VII Congreso Vasco de Sociología y Ciencia Política,* 127–142.

Vives, L. (2008, April). *White Europe: A racial reading of the Spanish-European border.* Unpublished manuscript, presented at the Annual Meeting of the Association of American Geographers. Boston.

Vives, L. (2009). Over the fence: The militarization of the Senegalese-Spanish sea border. *African Geographical Review, 28,* 5–9.

Vives, L., & Sité, S. (2010). Negra española, negra extranjera: Dos historias de una misma discriminación. *Revista Estudios De Juventud, 89,* 163–186.

Walton-Roberts, M. (2004). Transnational migration theory in population geography: Gendered practices in networks linking Canada and India. *Population, Space and Place, 10*(5), 361–373.

Warren, J. W. (2000). Masters in the field: White talk, white privilege, white biases. In F. W. Twine & J. W. Warren (Eds.), *Racing research, researching race: Methodological dilemmas in critical race studies* (pp. 135–164). New York/London: New York University Press.

Part II
Contesting Identities and Agency

Chapter 5
Japanese Single Mothers in Australia: Negotiation with Patriarchal Ideology and Stigma in the Homeland

Jun Nagatomo

5.1 Introduction

Australia experienced a dramatic social transformation in the form of a rapid increase in Asian migration in the 1980s and 1990s. In 1991, about 51% of the settler intake was from Asian countries other than the Middle East, compared to 40% in 1984 and 10% in 1972 (Jupp 2002, p. 33). Moreover, Asia—Hong Kong, Vietnam, Philippines and India—dominated four of the six top birthplaces of settlers during the period from 1991 to 1995 (Australian Bureau of Statistics [ABS] 1997). Although relatively fewer compared to other Asian ethnic groups, a significant number of Japanese also immigrated to Australia at around the same time. There were about 5,000 Japanese residents (composed of permanent settlers and long-term residents)[1] in 1980 (Ministry of Foreign Affairs, Japan [MOFA] 1981), which increased to approximately 15,200 in 1990 (MOFA 1991). In 2001, this number increased to 38,400 (MOFA 2001), and by 2005, reached 53,000, or about 25,300 permanent residents and 27,700 long-term residents (MOFA 2005). In 2010, there were 71,000 Japanese residents in Australia, including 37,000 permanent residents and 34,000 long-term (MOFA 2010).

Japanese migration to Australia is characterized by the migrants' motivations. Existing research has revealed that the majority can be regarded as "lifestyle migration." Tetsuo Mizukami (2006) points out in his study on perceptions of Australia

---

[1] A long-term resident, according to the Ministry of Foreign Affairs, refers to any Japanese (other than permanent residents) staying more than 3 months. For instance, it includes Japanese workers in overseas (Australian) offices of Japanese companies, and those in Australia as overseas students, researchers, teachers, and on working holidays.

J. Nagatomo, Ph.D. (✉)
School of International Studies, Kwansei Gakuin University,
Nishinomiya, Japan
e-mail: nagatomo@kwansei.ac.jp

G.T. Bonifacio (ed.), *Feminism and Migration: Cross-Cultural Engagements*,
International Perspectives on Migration 1, DOI 10.1007/978-94-007-2831-8_5,
© Springer Science+Business Media B.V. 2012

among Japanese residents that lifestyle factors such as the attractiveness of a mild climate figure highly in the process of selecting a country of destination. Machiko Sato (2001), in her ethnographic study of Japanese lifestyle migrants to Australia, describes their daily life after immigration. Ryo Tsukui's (2007) research on the leisure practices of middle-aged Japanese migrants in Australia, describes the gap between expectation and reality in having a leisurely life after migration. In his qualitative research of migration and settlement processes of Japanese lifestyle migrants, Jun Nagatomo (2009) emphasizes their relationship with social transformation and the changes of lifestyle values in Japanese society since the 1990s. Nagatomo (2009) also illustrates the interrelationship between tourism experience before migration and the decision to migrate afterwards among Japanese lifestyle migrants to Australia. Although these studies differ in terms of their focus and object of research, there is a consensus that lifestyle is a key factor in contemporary Japanese migration to Australia.

In looking at the demographic profile of the Japanese population in Australia, imbalances in gender and age structure are prominent. Currently, females account for 64.0% of permanent residents and 64.3% of long-term residents (MOFA 2010); the resultant gender imbalance is largely due to the recent migration of Japanese women who have married Australian men (Coughlan and McNamara 1997; Nagata and Nagatomo 2007, p. 29). As the number of Japanese female residents increased, those with failed marriages became noticeable within the Japanese community. There is no demographic data on this point; however, my fieldwork and 5 years of living in Australia suggests that the rate of Australian-Japanese couples whose marriages have broken down is around the same rate, 30%, or slightly lower compared to that of the general Australian population (ABS 2008). Moreover, it is common for most single Japanese women with children to remain in Australia after separation. This phenomenon raises the following questions: Why do they remain in Australia? How do they negotiate their sense of belonging towards Japan as their homeland with that of Australia as their current home? And, how do cross-cultural differences and feminist gains shape their identity as women?

This chapter focuses on Japanese women residing in southeast Queensland, the most common destination of Japanese migrants and tourists in Australia. It illustrates how they negotiate with the stigma of being a single mother in their patriarchal homeland, and their decision to remain in Australia after separation. In exploring the case of Japanese single mothers, this chapter is divided into three sections: theories and methods, including the profile of participants; reasons for remaining in Australia; and sense of belonging and identity.

5.2 Theories and Methods

The notion of agency in feminist discourse aptly relates to the situation of migrant single mothers who remain in the host society after separation. Agency refers to the subjectivity of actions and decision-making by individuals, particularly their reactions toward the constraints of their surroundings. Or, Judith Butler, in *Gender Trouble*, refers to agency as follows:

> The question of locating "agency" is usually associated with the viability of the "subject", where the "subject" is understood to have some stable existence prior to the cultural field that it negotiates. Or, if the subject is culturally constructed, it is nevertheless vested with an agency, usually figured as the capacity for reflective mediation, that remains intact regardless of its cultural embeddedness. (Butler 1990, p. 195)

Using post-structuralist perspectives such as those by Claude Levi-Strauss (1966), Jacques Derrida (1976), and Michel Foucault (1977), Judith Butler (1990, 1997) presents agency and performativity in the social construction of gender. For Butler (1990, 1997), gender can be perceived as performance in a way that gender is socially constructed by the accumulation of discourse on gender ethic as well as repeated acts that are performed "naturally" under the hegemonic practices and norms of heterosexuality. Therefore, Butler (1990, p. 191) criticizes a view on gender as a stable identity, rather, she perceives gender as "an identity tenuously constituted in time, instituted in an exterior space through a *stylized repetition of acts*." Such feminist perspectives on gender and agency have, to a certain degree, impacted on interpretations of migration since the 1980s (Willis and Yeoh 2000).

In studies that expanded the focus of research from the macro level (e.g., push and pull theory, socio-economic study) to the micro level (e.g., gender study of migrants, the role of family in the migration process), the concept of agency provides a theoretical tool to explain individuals' actions and networks at local, national, or global levels. For example, Pierrette Hondagneu-Sotelo (1994) explores gender relations among recently arrived Mexican workers in the United States, arguing that the negotiation within household and social networks after migration could change gender relations as well as power relations. Hondagneu-Sotelo's perspectives on the reconstruction of gender relations in destination countries incorporates the concept of agency as she shows how power relations in family could be changed, and how women could develop autonomy and sense of independence. Sarah Mahler (2011), in studying Salvadoran migrants in Long Island, a New York City suburb, argues that multiple agents and agencies at local and transnational levels are influencing gender relations among them. Geraldine Pratt (2004) interlinks feminist theory to the empirical research on Filipino domestic workers in Canadian society, incorporating agency into the analysis of their practices.

Similarly, migration studies on grassroots network, or "globalization from below," can be seen as both typical and influential in the use of agency. In discussing the possible consequences of globalization, Arjun Appadurai (2001, pp. 16–17) offers a radical view that grassroots globalization, such as that by nongovernment organizations (NGOs) and transmigrants, could weaken the power of nation-states. Ludger Pries (2001) also asserts that grassroots international migrants could develop transnational social spaces. These perspectives recognize the impact of agency in migration, as well as agency in transnational space. Nina Glick Schiller and Georges Fouron (1998, p. 131) propose the emergence of a transnational nation-state based on a perspective that nation-states historically developed trans-border relations emerging from individual agency. Martin Manalansan (2003), in his study of the gay Filipino immigrants in New York, reflects on their own appropriation of effeminacy as agency, while keeping a distance from the styles and practices of the American gay community.

While there are a number of studies in migration that incorporate the notion of agency, the case study of migrant single mothers has been relatively under-examined from this aspect. Most existing research on single mothers, particularly migrant single mothers, perceived them as a vulnerable social group. Common topics about them include single mothers' difficulty in living on a limited income, and their problems in accessing social welfare services. For instance, Valerie Polakow (1993) notes the poverty and lack of social support among single mothers (black and non-black) in the United States. From a similar perspective, Ken Suzuki (2009) describes the relationship between children and their parents in his study of Filipino single mothers in Japan. Susan Holloway and colleagues (1997) examine the cultural factors related to the poverty of low income working mothers in Boston.

The scarce scholarly resources on migrant single mothers also include the following related aspects: the relationship with the homeland after marital breakdown; emotions toward the home society and decision-making process concerning a place to live; and the negotiation with the stigma of being a single mother. By using agency, this chapter shows the unique, subjective and strategic decision-making process of Japanese single mothers who remained in Australia. Their strategic choice shows a form of subjective and flexible action in which prevailing views and power relations between dominant and subordinate social groups are sometimes contested and subverted, thus, allowing a feminist reading of their experiences.

Because there is little research on the factors that entice Japanese single mothers to remain in Australia, a qualitative approach is arguably the most appropriate method to fill this gap. According to Jennifer Mason (1996, p. 4), a qualitative research is, "grounded in an 'interpretivist' position that is concerned with how the social world is interpreted, understood, experienced or produced," and "based on methods of data generation which are flexible and sensitive to the social context in which data are produced." Qualitative methodologies in the social sciences allow highly contextualized research outcomes (Silverman 1993; Payne and Williams 2005). Using this approach enabled me to obtain contextual and experiential data on the factors that explain why Japanese single mothers remain in Australia.

Eleven in-depth interviews were conducted in southeast Queensland, Australia, among Japanese single mothers who were formerly married to Australian nationals. The semi-structured interview questions included their migration experiences, impressions of Australian and Japanese societies and respective lifestyles, and processes through which they chose to remain in Australia after separation. The respondents hold permanent visa status who had been in southeast Queensland for more than 3 years. The women were recruited by snowball sampling who decided the venue for the interview to ensure a relaxed and comfortable environment. Amongst the 11 respondents, 1 was in her twenties, 3 were in their thirties, 5 in their forties, and 2 in their fifties. Seven respondents were employed full-time, 3 were in part-time employment, and 1 was unemployed. I conducted the interviews in Japanese, then transcribed and translated their responses into English. The narratives of these women are integrated in the discussion with assigned pseudonyms.

5.3   Reasons for Remaining in Australia

Martial breakdown and separation involve various challenges for single mothers, mainly financial difficulties and emotional strain. Depending on the cultural context, migrant single mothers are confronted with different levels of marginalization. The choice of residence after separation is, therefore, crucial in mitigating perceived difficulties. Migrant single mothers experience various social interactions with their homeland and host society. In this section, the practical and emotional factors which influenced Japanese single mothers to remain in Australia after separation are discussed. It describes their action as a form of agency as they subjectively chose in which country to live in terms of their respective social systems and ideologies.

5.3.1   Practical Concerns in Remaining in Australia

5.3.1.1   Generous Social Welfare and Job Opportunities in Australia

The Australian social welfare system is generous compared to that in Japan. Households receive financial support from the government in accordance with their income and number of children (e.g., Family Tax Benefits, Child Care Benefit, Rent Assistance, Baby Bonus).[2] Under this system in Australia, it is not a difficult choice for mothers to raise their children alone, even those with income only from part-time employment. In 2005, approximately 20% of children under 15 were living with a single-parent in Australia (ABS 2005). In Japan, on the other hand, single mothers receive a dependent children's allowance (*Jido fujo teate*) of about $400 a month; but they often face financial difficulties. This means-tested assistance was only given to about 11% of single mothers in 2000 (Ezawa and Fujiwara 2005, p. 52). In 2003, among divorced single mothers, only 34% were receiving child support payments from their ex-husbands (Ezawa and Fujiwara 2005, p. 43). Despite having an employment rate of about 85%—higher than the average rate of married mothers in Japan (54%), and the highest among OECD[3] countries—the average income of Japanese single mothers is less than 40% of the average Japanese household income (Fujiwara 2008; Japan Institute for Labour Policy and Training [JILPT] 2009). The differences in the financial situation of single mothers and the welfare systems between Japan and Australia is considered one of the most significant factors in deciding to remain in Australia among Japanese single mothers. Referring to

---

[2] Family Tax Benefit is paid for the cost of raising children, Child Care Benefit supports the cost for child care, and Parenting Payment (about A$500 fortnight) is paid for single parent who raise children under 6 years old. Rent Assistance provides support for the rent to landlords. Baby Bonus is paid to families following the birth or adoption of a child in the amount of A$5,294 in 2010.

[3] OECD stands for the Organization for Economic Co-operation and Development. In 2010, the number of OECD member states is 34, and most of them are industrialized countries.

her impression of Australia, Reiko who is in her thirties, works part-time and goes to school, noted:

> Social welfare systems in Australia are just great. If you are a pensioner, not only public transport, but also electricity and other fees are discounted. Also, if you either work or study a certain amount of time, they pay you twice a week. This would be impossible in Japan.

Similarly, Eriko, in her forties and unemployed, remarked:

> If you are single and have three children, then you would not have to work hard to get by. I hear that there are many Australians who pretend to be single to get social security pensions.

These responses reflect the common impression of Australian and Japanese societies by Japanese women. With poor support from the government, single mothers in Japan are institutionally marginalized under a labor market centered on full-time employment. Although the Liberal Democratic Party (LDP), which has dominated Japanese politics for more than 50 years was defeated by the opposition in 2009, it is still uncertain how the situation of single mothers will improve under the leadership of the new Democratic Party (DP).[4] On the other hand, the Australian social welfare system is considered to be generous for single mothers compared to Japan, and that this perceivable difference in welfare benefits could affect their choice of country after marital breakdown.

Japanese single mothers identify job opportunities and work-life balance in Australia as well as its lifestyle—in particular, fewer full-time job opportunities and low wages in Japan versus Australia's flexible labor market and its easy lifestyle—as other favorable factors. Naoko, in her twenties and working at a Japanese-owned company, remarked:

> I think the lifestyle is very easy here (in Australia). Even if you are unemployed, no one would blame you for that. People change jobs quite often and it is very common to go back to graduate school in the future for your career. In Japan, a full-time job is everything. Once you leave it, you won't be hired as a regular employee by any company. [...] In that sense, as a single mother, Australia is a very good country to live in.

In talking about her part-time job, Rie, who is in her thirties and works as a tour guide, said:

> Above all, in Japan, the wages of part-time workers are too low. In Australia, even a high school kid working at MacDonald's gets fifteen dollars per hour. In Japan, it would be around seven hundred yen—less than half. You could never raise children on that. [...] I can understand a lot of single mothers are now working in the sex industry.

---

[4] In the manifesto during the 2009 election, DP promised to re-start *Boshi-kasan* (aid to single parent household), which had been abolished by LDP government in 2009. DP government's agenda on social welfare is characterized by various kinds of safety nets for those in financial difficulties, such as the unemployed, single parents, and households with children. However, so far their agenda draw criticism from the opposition parties because of few financial resources to achieve their planned social welfare programs.

In talking about working conditions in Australia, Naomi, in her forties and working as a nurse, noted:

> It was really hard to get used to the job, but as a nurse I find that working conditions are very good. I think there is an appropriate division of roles and responsibilities between nurses and other staff. […] Having a secure full-time position, I would not think of returning to Japan.

Employed and unemployed Japanese single mothers found Australia easier to reside in. For those who have employment in Australia, remaining in the country is a practical choice due to job security and financial stability. On the other hand, for those unemployed or living on a part-time income, Australia's generous social security and flexibility in the labor market and career choices make them feel secure and happy to stay in Australia. As Patricia Grimshaw and John Murphy (2005) point out, motherhood and paid work have been combined in Australia in the modernization process. The Australian women's advanced participation in the labor market throughout the twentieth century led to various policy shifts such as generous family benefits and improved employment conditions under patriarchy (Grimshaw and Murphy 2005).

The relatively better situation surrounding women and work in Australia influenced Japanese single mothers to remain after separation. This strategic choice of country can be viewed as a form of agency because single parents are apparently "protected" by a generous social welfare system in Australia. The narratives presented above illustrate that Japanese single mothers "appropriate" their institutionalized vulnerability by using these social benefits to their advantage. Such a perspective, that subordinates the conventional understanding on the relationship between the state and vulnerable single mothers, relates to feminist interpretations of state feminism. For instance, Louise Chappell (2002) studies the interaction between gender interest and the state by exploring feminist engagement in Australia and Canada. In criticizing a conventional view on nation-state as patriarchal and oppressive to women, Chappell (2002, p. 3) presents a view that sees the interaction between feminist engagements and the state as rather "dynamic and co-constitutive." In the case of Japanese single mothers, the benefits gained by feminist engagements with the Australian state provide them with the necessary resources to subvert or resist subordination in Japan.

5.3.1.2 Children and Their Fathers

The issues surrounding children after separation are generally considered as one of the most complicated aspects among divorced couples or those who are contemplating separation. Japanese single mothers consider the welfare of their children as their primary reason for remaining in Australia. In particular, securing contact between children and father, as well as the language and identity of children who grew up in Australia, are the two pressing concerns amongst them. Naomi, in talking about her feelings toward Japan, remarked:

> To be honest, I want to return to Japan. But many practical matters, especially issues concerning my child, do not allow me to do that. My daughter has been living in Australia, and

for her, Australia is home. We speak English to each other at home. [...] I don't know whether or not it is a good choice for my daughter to move to Japan now.

Naomi's comments reflect a typical sentiment of Japanese single mothers in Australia. Taking children back to Japan was considered as a dramatic change that could have a negative impact on their children. The possible language barrier of children born in Australia is an important practical consideration to stay in the country after separation.

Japanese divorced mothers in Australia tend to value father-child relationship, although this is not the same in Japanese society in general. In Japanese society, shared custody is not yet common, as the following data shows. According to the Ministry of Health, Labour and Welfare [MHLW] (2010), in 2010, more than 70% of divorced mothers gained child custody while less than 20% of divorced fathers held parental authority. In Australia, Japanese single parents make use of the "Australian" way of shared custody, and value father-child relationship after separation. Eriko noted the typical view among Japanese single mothers:

Many Japanese parents say that the Australian education system is good, but I want to take my daughter to Japan and stay there for several years for the benefit of her education. Of course, I am planning to return to Australia because we have not divorced yet. But he (husband) is in Sydney, and it is difficult to separate my daughter from him by going to Japan. I also think that communication with the father is an important thing for a child's development.

There is a certain consensus that communication with the father is important for the child's mental well-being. In particular, for those who are separated and yet to divorce, the child's relationship with the father was given due consideration. However, in some cases, it ironically led to emotional complications in the child. For Aya, who is in her forties and works at a Japanese-owned company, the separation was supposed to be a relatively easier one because her husband chose to live within the neighborhood area to help her with daily activities and to see his daughter often. According to Aya, at that time he left them, there was also a slight possibility of reconciliation. But the geographical proximity and frequent contact between father and daughter made her daughter feel lonely. In describing the changes after separation, Aya remarked:

One day I found my daughter crying silently in her room. When I asked her why she was crying, then she said, "I've been shedding as many tears as I can. If I run out of my tears, I cannot cry any more. Is that right, mom?" Now I cannot stop crying because I realized just how sad and lonely we had made her feel.

Similarly, Miho, in her forties and working two casual jobs, expressed her complicated feelings regarding divorce and the relationship between her ex-husband and child:

Although my son goes to my ex-husband's house on weekends and holidays, his new partner is there. I understand that it is important for my son to see him but I don't know if it is appropriate to expose those matters to a child. In Australia separation is very common, but I still feel that there is something wrong about the relationship between my ex-husband and child.

For separated couples, generally speaking, it would be safe to say that the ideal situation would be for children to keep in contact with their parents on a regular basis and for them to live in a nearby suburb, except of course, for those who have experienced domestic violence or similar problems. However, the narrative extracts from Aya and Miho show an ironical situation that the decision to separate while maintaining a close relationship between the ex-husband and children could cause emotional strain and psychological stress on the children.

Of the 11 Japanese single mothers, only 1 disclosed that it was pressure from her ex-husband which forced her to remain in Australia after their divorce. For fathers who have "lost" their children, it is a critical issue for them to remain in contact with their children after separation. In particular, Japan is one of the few countries that have yet to ratify the Hague Convention that protects the right of parents in case either of the parents takes their children back to his/her country without the consent of the other parent. State policies on citizenship and civil rights affect migrant women, especially migrant single mothers. For example, Daiva Stasiulis and Abigail Bakan (2003) illustrate the complex interplay of economic, political and social factors affecting the access to citizenship rights in Canada among migrant women from the Philippines and the West Indies. Feminist scholars interpret citizenship and rights of women as negotiated and contested fields with the interaction between individuals and social institutions (e.g., Dale and Foster 1986; Gordon 1990; Lister 1997). The following case of Reiko shows the reality of an ex-wife and ex-husband who struggle with this institutional and emotional issue. Reiko, in talking about the relationship with her ex-husband, said:

> I think that my ex-husband is a good father to my daughter, but he gets really angry every time we discuss any plans to visit Japan. It is hard to take even a two-week holiday in Japan. He never allows us to return to Japan. In a threatening voice, he says that I will get tangled up in legal action. I guess he is afraid of losing contact with my daughter once we return to Japan.

Reiko demonstrates the depth of the problem of child custody involving different countries. Although Japan's new government under the Democratic Party plans to ratify the Hague Convention, it is unclear whether custody issues like Reiko's will be resolved in the near future.

Remaining in Australia is acknowledged as a practical and realistic choice for Japanese single mothers based on access to social welfare, and the language and identity of Australian-born children. Some of them struggle with children's emotional problems caused by their parents' separation, and the legal pressure from their ex-husbands to remain in Australia to ensure his custody rights. Pressure from an ex-husband is reflective of patriarchal ideological control even after marital separation or divorce. Intimidation and threats of legal action are forms of violence inflicted on vulnerable migrant single mothers. Ex-husbands who are Australian nationals exercise power over them through laws ensuring their rights to patrimony. As a consequence, Japanese migrant single mothers tend to quietly submit to their control. Australian scholar Hilary Astor (1995) posits the view that "silence" of women is a key issue of violence. While no longer directly in an abusive relationship

Japanese single mothers continue to experience male domination through their children. However, at the same time, it is important to note that Australian laws ensure the rights and protection of single mothers and their children as well as children's right to keep relationship with both parents under the Family Law.

5.3.2   Remaining in Australia as an Escape? Negotiating Patriarchal Ideology and Stigma

Japanese society is generally considered as patriarchal (Ueno 2004). It lacks gender equality that seemingly exists in other industrialized countries in the West. However, Japanese society has experienced a growth of feminism from the late 1980s that was triggered by Japan's ratification of the Convention on the Elimination of All Forms of Discrimination against Women (CEDAW) in 1985, and further advanced when the government ratified the Revised Equal Employment Act in 1999. Against this background, Japanese companies reformed their employment systems and practices to incorporate gender equality in the mid-1990s. At the informal level, however, power relations in offices and personal social interactions have not changed dramatically since then. This section explores the subjective factors affecting the decisions of Japanese single mothers to remain in Australia after marital breakdown: the role of patriarchal ideology and stigma of single mothers and work in Japan.

All respondents have had employment experiences in Japan, and yet hold negative representations of the Japanese workplace. These include the busy lifestyle, full-time-employment-oriented system, and Japan's patriarchal ideology. While most of the respondents pointed out practical factors in choosing a place to live after separation, in some cases, the negative impressions of the Japanese corporate society indirectly impact on their decision-making process.

Patriarchal power relations are embodied more commonly in informal daily practices than in the formal structure of the employment system. Most Japanese companies were said to incorporate gender equality in their employment systems since the 1990s. But the prevailing "ethos" of a patriarchal society negatively affects female Japanese workers. Miho, recalled her work experience at a typical large Japanese manufacturing company:

> Even though Japanese companies introduced gender-free employment systems institutionally, I think there remain many unwritten rules in the companies. For instance, if you are a clerical female worker and planning to marry someone, you would be expected to quit the company. When I worked at [company's name], a man said, 'You won't work for many years, anyway, will you?' [...] If we worked at a good large company, then we were seen as single women who had wanted to join the company to find a husband.

In her narrative Miho's colleague asked whether or not she plans to work for many years. However, the question implies a discriminatory assumption that Miho would quit her job soon after getting married. This case demonstrates how more informal aspects of gender discrimination and bias can manifest themselves in everyday workplace conversation. Similarly, in talking about her workplace in Japan, Miyuki, who is in her forties, noted:

> It is impossible to work as hard as Japanese men do. They are forced to work long hours and even on weekends. You are expected to work *for* the company, as the term *kigyosenshi* (company soldier) implies. How can we (women with children) do that? If you are working for a school in Japan, you have to work even on summer holidays. I mean, in Japan holidays are not for teachers—only for students. There are so many documents and boring committees that I think could be organized more efficiently. In Japanese workplaces, particularly at schools, there remain many old systems and ethos. As a matter of fact, most important positions are still held by men.

In relation to her work experience at a large company in Japan, Kayo, a social worker in her forties, remarked:

> Many people say that Japanese workplaces are a man's world, but I don't think so. I used to work as an *OL* (lit: office lady)—a female clerical worker—and there were many OLs around me. It was such an uncomfortable woman's world. I remember there was a middle-aged female worker who thought of herself as a big fish in a little pond. Everyone liked gossiping with each other. […] I think that kind of a woman's world exists because there is a man's world on the other hand.

Kayo demonstrates a male dominated ethos of Japanese corporate society which creates a woman's world at the periphery. However, for those who are in this peripheral world like female clerical workers, human relationships are also based on embedded power structures and practices. Fumie, a woman in her fifties who works as a clerk in Australia, said:

> Talking about job advertisement in Japan, don't you think them terrible? Résumés must have photos attached, and you also have to write whether or not you have a duty of support for your family. Those things, I think, reflect that Japanese companies are not gender free in the true sense.

Kayo and Fumie illustrate some typical sentiments of respondents who had worked for a Japanese company—a negative impression in terms of gender equality. The "gender-free" employment system in Japan is, in reality, still full-time male-oriented. This persisting patriarchal atmosphere in Japanese corporate society relates to Kiyoe Sugimoto's (1997, 1999) study on social welfare in Japan, particularly the social conditions of single mothers. Sugimoto (1997, 1999) asserts that the transition in women's employment since the late 1980s is still based on a patriarchal model that is in turn based on the assumption that men work full time and women do either housework or unskilled part-time jobs. Women's liberation seems difficult to achieve from a male workers' logic in Japanese corporate society—those who pursue gender equality at workplace should work hard as men do— without recognizing particular differences among workers. Christine Delphy (1984) suggests that gender is not a dichotomy of male and female but as a practice of differentiation; and for women, being and acting like men does not necessarily mean their liberation.

Work experiences at Japanese companies shape Japanese single mothers' negative impression of corporate culture in terms of equality in women's working and living conditions. Although women in this study have had no direct experience of gender discrimination in a Japanese workplace which affected their decision to stay in Australia, there were many cases that showed its indirect effect. Most of these focused on the difficulty of getting a full-time job after marriage, or keeping a full-time job while raising children. Aya noted:

> After all, (in Japan) typical or ideal models of women's life have not yet changed much. You have to choose between career woman and housewife. I know there are many alternative ways of working that have become popular among the younger generation. However, if you have children, it would be very hard to work full-time. But, in Australia, we can choose. We have variety of choices such as casual jobs and studying at school, and there is no pressure placed on you because you decide one way or the other. I like this free and open-minded way of thinking on life in Australia.

In talking about the advantages of the Australian lifestyle, Miho, said:

> I feel that the life of a Japanese *salary man* (company employee/salaried worker) and his raising of his children are premised on families with housewives. They get home very late, so who then picks up their children at kindergarten? Who takes care of their meals? It would be a wife to do them all. [...] In Australia, there is no such a role model for a wife. Although my ex-husband pushed me to do all the housework, I know there are many Australian couples who share this.

Gender role expectations of husband and wife have significant differences between Japanese and Australian cultures. Aya and Miho presented negative impressions of the male-dominated Japanese society compared with positive impressions of Australian society. The sense of freedom and gender equality are considered positive benefits of living in Australia. However, in looking at their reasons for separation, many of them suffered from their Australian husband's intransigence in terms of housework, and the most typical case was the power struggle between couples—the Japanese wife expects her Australian partner to be an "Australian" husband (i.e., helpful, family-oriented), while the Australian husband expects their Japanese partner to be a "Japanese" wife (i.e., domestically and sexually obedient, a good housewife). Experiences of this cultural mismatch made Japanese women more aware of freedom and gender equality within a marriage in Australia. According to Delphy (1984, p. 18), patriarchy refers to a system of subordination characterized by power and hierarchy between the sexes as well as the basis of the "domestic mode of production." Delphy views domestic labor as "productive" work; however, it is done for free by "housewives." Expectations of domesticity by Australian husbands toward their Japanese wives circumscribe patriarchy. Japanese wives who expect their Australian partners to be an "Australian" husband tend to be disappointed because of their exteriorization of highly ingrained patriarchal values.

Single mothers in Japan face considerable social stigma as those who "failed" their marriages and, consequently, suffer financial and social disadvantages. When Japanese wives became single mothers in Australia, they chose to maintain a distance from Japan's patriarchal culture and the social stigma associated with single mothers, as well as other possible difficulties upon their return. For instance, Naomi, in talking about her divorce and decision to remain in Australia, remarked:

> When we were discussing separation, I was thinking about where to live. I thought in Australia, more so than in Japan, that I could somehow manage to get by. My (Japanese)

friends in my hometown were saying that I should return, but I thought it would definitely be impossible, because I knew almost every single mother in Japan lives in poverty. I also knew that it is very hard to get a full-time job (in Japan) if you are a single mother. A job I could get in Japan would be a part-time manual laborer.

The generous social welfare system directly affected Naomi's choice to remain in Australia after separation. She recognized the dire economic situation of and stigma attached to single mothers in Japan. Naomi made a strategic choice to remain in Australia based on these practical and social concerns of single parenthood. As a vulnerable social group, migrant single mothers appropriate the benefits of the welfare system to their own advantage by not returning to Japan. Many of them face potential economic difficulties, and their decision to remain in Australia could be viewed as a form of resistance against eventual social marginalization. Japanese single mothers seem to subvert the power relationship—whereby "vulnerable" individuals appropriate the social welfare system to "save" themselves and their children. In this case, migrant Japanese single mothers share the achievements of Australian feminism in the postwar period, particularly those dealing with gender equality, equal job opportunity, and other women's rights on maternity leave and childcare (Simms 1994; Curthoys 1994; Murdolo 1996). Results of Australian feminists' engagements with the state have far reaching implications to the lives of migrant women.

Another important subjective consideration for remaining in Australia is freedom from patriarchal constraints. Japanese single mothers perceive Australian society as less rigid in gender role expectations compared to Japan. Rie, in talking about her current life as a part-time tour guide, noted this difference:

In Australia, it would be no problem living on the income from a casual or part-time job. You will not be blamed for your situation and will not have to feel inferior because of it. However, in Japan, no one thinks you are an *ichininmae* (independent person) if you aren't living off a full-time income or living as a housewife. I feel everyone is strapped into rigid life course models. [...] These days, many housewives go to English language schools or go abroad for *oyako-ryugaku* (accompanying their children while they attend overseas education while their husband remains in Japan). To me, it looks like such a futile effort to escape from their everyday life in Japan. [...] In Australia, I feel it's very easy living here because there is no pressure to follow any particular rigid way of life.

Similarly, Kayo noted:

In Japan, managerial level jobs are dominated by male full-time workers who have been working for the same company for years. Therefore, it is impossible for women who quit their job at a company in order to raise children to work at such levels. Eventually, a woman's life is swayed by life events such as marriage, giving birth to and raising children, and divorce. At the same time, it is also a woman's advantage to be able to have the flexibility to accept such changes and think about new ways of life. I am now living in Australia, something that could be a result of such flexibility. I mean, on the one hand I had to stay here, while on the other hand I wanted to stay here.

Yumiko, who is in her fifties and teaches Japanese, in speaking about her current life, said:

Now I feel so free. When I was with my ex-husband, we moved around so often. I decided for the sake of my children's education, I didn't want to do that anymore. We are separated now, but I enjoy my job here and don't want to leave Australia. I just can't imagine going back to Japan and being the pitiful wife of a *salary man*—writing hundreds of New Year cards to my husband's colleagues and fulfilling so many other such obligations in everyday life.

Rie, Kayo and Yumiko demonstrate that remaining in Australia enabled Japanese single mothers to feel a sense of freedom—from the pressure of following an expected life course as a wife in Japan, as well as from its patriarchal ideology as a whole. Their subjective and partly strategic choice can be seen as that of agency. Remaining in Australia is a way to pursue a sense of freedom away from the social constraints of their homeland. Vera Mackie (2003) notes that Japanese society, throughout the modern era, relegated women to the private sphere, and that gender equality is still far from ideal. On the other hand, in Australia, the negotiation with state patriarchy and feminism was relatively more active than that of Japan, and it led to women's empowerment in the society. For instance, Ann Curthoys (1994, pp. 16–17) shows that feminist movements in the 1970s actually had an impact on parliamentary politics which resulted in favorable decisions for equal pay, childcare, and health care. While there remains a gendered division of labor (Baxter 1998), the relative difference in dealing with gender issues between Australia and Japan closely affected decisions of Japanese single mothers to remain in Australia after separation.

5.3.2.1   Sense of Belonging and Identity

In contemporary migration studies, the theory of transnationalism relates to individuals' construction and maintenance of network and relationships across borders (Glick Schiller et al. 1992; Kearney 1995; Hannerz 1996). It is widely accepted in conceptualizing migrants' multiple senses of belonging after migration. The same applies to Japanese single mothers in Australia; that is, having a sense of belonging between the two countries. But almost all of them still identify themselves as Japanese despite their negative impressions of their home society. In answering the question, "What is Japan to you?" the most common response was "home." More specifically, most of them referred to Japan as the place where their parents reside and that they can return to their home anytime the necessity arises. However, most respondents had a flexible view on a place to live in the long term, particularly after their parents' death. Reiko remarked:

Japan is home and where I will go should it become necessary. That would be if something in particular happened, such as having to take care of my parents or some other situation that required my help.

Naomi also noted:

Although my mother is in her seventies, she can use Skype. In a sense, living in Australia does not differ to living somewhere else in Japan that is far away from home. [...] I don't stick to a certain plan that I will stay in Australia forever—I just think that at this moment, staying here is a better choice for me when I consider my job, social security and my child's relationship with my ex-husband.

The existence of parents in the homeland makes Japanese single mothers in Australia identify with Japan as their home, and more specifically, a place to return to anytime. Following contemporary trends in migration studies, Japanese single mothers are transmigrants with multiple senses of belonging (e.g., Glick Schiller et al. 1992). However, I argue that they are also active agents who appropriate the benefits of a certain migratory destination. This means that their sense of belonging is determined by subjective, strategic, and flexible choices based on consideration of the advantages and disadvantages of remaining in Australia or returning to Japan. Returning to Japan could force them to face financial difficulty and stigma in Japanese society; therefore, staying in Australia after separation could be a strategic choice whereby they make use of the advantage of practical benefits such as job opportunities and social welfare.

This flexible and strategic sense of belonging is reflected on their views about Australian citizenship and their future. Amongst the 11 respondents, there was not a single woman who holds Australian citizenship. The three common reasons include: little difference between Australian citizenship and permanent residency; retention of Japanese legal rights in the event of returning home; and proof of identity as a Japanese. Their reasons raise substantial concerns on the positioning of women in society. For example, the relationship between citizenship and women's lives has been criticized by feminist scholars. Kathleen Jones (1990) points out that the concept of citizenship alienates women and their work. The "gendered nature of citizenship" is based on an assumption that women's work is generally associated with housework taking place in the private sphere while citizenship is related to paid work in the public sphere (James 1992; Rimmerman 1997; Lister 1997; Baxter 1998; Baker 1999). Kayo, in responding to a question on Australian citizenship, noted:

> I don't have any plans to obtain Australian citizenship because it is not all that different to (current) permanent residency, and I just don't feel the necessity of going for it. If I obtained Australian citizenship, it would be difficult to live in Japan for many reasons. It means that I am not Japanese anymore and I guess that could cause many legal difficulties. And, I am Japanese through and through.

In terms of eligibility for receiving social welfare, there is not much difference between Australian citizenship and permanent residency. Many Japanese single mothers in this study referred to suffrage as the only difference between these two. Glenda Bonifacio (2005), in her study of Filipino women in Australia, avers that obtaining Australian citizenship could lead to empowerment to counter racial harassment in the workplace. However, the case of Japanese single mothers shows a clear contrast to the case of Filipino migrants. Since Japan does not recognize dual citizenship, holding a Japanese citizenship means keeping a backup plan of returning to their homeland while they simultaneously benefit from the Australian social welfare and lifestyle even after separation. This sense of flexibility based on security is clearly seen in Aya's remarks:

> Should my parents pass away and I decide to live in Australia forever, I might go for Australian citizenship. But I don't think so. I don't know what's going to happen in my future, but I don't feel the necessity for citizenship so far.

Aya disclosed the strong parental ties with Japan and its effect on her views on Australian citizenship. Remaining in Australia is a good choice among Japanese single mothers based on practical and emotional matters. At the same time, however, keeping the choice of returning to Japan open is also important to them. While returning to Japan does not work well as a backup plan for single mothers, and in fact, many deliberately run from the idea, they remain indifferent to obtaining Australian citizenship and still identify themselves as Japanese. This ironical relationship between their sense of xenophobic nationality and subjective choice of remaining in Australia can be seen as the reflection of the complexity of living as migrant single mothers. More importantly, from a feminist perspective the case of Japanese single mothers in Australia demonstrate their agency to define a better future for them. Japan's patriarchal culture and practices pose as negative factors for their permanent return to homeland. On the other hand, Australia's relatively gender equal atmosphere and generous social welfare system are positive factors. Between these differences in the two societies, Japanese single mothers are subjectively choosing to remain in Australia after separation, taking advantage of its social benefits, and escaping from Japan's rigid patriarchal values, and stigma attached to single mothers in Japan. This form of agency provides useful insights on the type of migrant women negotiating with social and structural constraints.

5.4   Conclusion

This chapter explored the decision of Japanese single mothers in Australia who remained in Australia after separation. Firstly, Japanese single mothers were influenced mainly by practical and subjective factors. The practical factors include the generous Australian social welfare systems, and a flexible labor market which offer career choices for these migrant single mothers. On the other hand, the subjective factors include the negative impressions of Japanese corporate culture and the lack of gender equality in Japanese society as a whole. In some cases Japanese single mothers escape from Japan's patriarchal control and the social stigma attached to single mothers by remaining in Australia after separation.

Japanese single mothers in Australia express belonging and identity between Australia and Japan. This is, however, a result of their strategic and flexible choice in which country to live with their children. From a feminist perspective Japanese single mothers exercise agency by appropriating the benefits accrued to women in Australia. Appropriation of Australian social welfare to "escape" from Japanese patriarchy and stigma in the homeland can be seen as a new form of resistance where power relations between mainstream Japanese male-dominated society and single mothers, as well as between host and home societies, are negotiated and sometimes subverted. It is through the case of Japanese single mothers in Australia that we find particular contexts of individual agency and shared benefits of the achievements of Australian feminism as a consequence of migration.

References

Appadurai, A. (2001). Grassroots globalization and the research imagination. In A. Appadurai (Ed.), *Globalization* (pp. 1–21). Durham: Duke University Press.

Astor, H. (1995). The weight of silence: Talking about violence in family mediation. In M. Thornton (Ed.), *Public and private* (pp. 176–196). Melbourne: Oxford University Press.

Australian Bureau of Statistics [ABS]. (1997). *Australian social trends, 1997*. Canberra: ABS.

Australian Bureau of Statistics [ABS]. (2005). *Australian social trends*. Canberra: ABS.

Australian Bureau of Statistics [ABS]. (2008). *Divorces, Australia, 2007* (Catalogue Number 3307.0.55.001). www.abs.gov.au/ausstats/abs@.nsf/mf/3307.0.55.001/. Accessed January 4, 2010.

Baker, S. (1999). Risking difference: Reconceptualising the boundaries between the public and private spheres. In S. Baker & S. Van Doorne-Huiskes (Eds.), *Women and public policy* (pp. 3–34). Aldershot: Ashgate.

Baxter, J. (1998). Moving toward equality? Questions of change and equality in household work patterns. In M. Gatens & A. MacKinnon (Eds.), *Gender and institutions: Welfare, work and citizenship* (pp. 19–37). Cambridge: Cambridge University Press.

Bonifacio, G. (2005). Filipino women in Australia: Practising citizenship at work. *Asian and Pacific Migration Journal, 14*(3), 293–326.

Butler, J. (1990). *Gender trouble*. New York: Routledge.

Butler, J. (1997). *Excitable speech*. New York: Routledge.

Chappell, L. (2002). *Gendering government*. Vancouver: University of British Columbia Press.

Coughlan, J. E., & McNamara, D. (Eds.). (1997). *Asians in Australia*. Melbourne: Macmillan Education Australia.

Curthoys, A. (1994). Australian feminism since 1970. In N. Grieve & A. Burns (Eds.), *Australian women: Contemporary feminist thought* (pp. 14–28). Melbourne: Oxford University Press.

Dale, J., & Foster, P. (1986). *Feminist and state welfare*. London: Routledge & Kegan Paul.

Delphy, C. (1984). *Close to home* (D. Leonard, Trans. and Ed.). Amherst: University of Massachusetts Press.

Derrida, J. (1976). *Of grammatology* (G. Spivak, Trans.). Baltimore: Johns Hopkins University Press.

Ezawa, A., & Fujiwara, C. (2005). Lone mothers and welfare-to-work policies in Japan and the United States: Towards and alternative perspective. *Journal of Sociology and Social Welfare, 32*(4), 41–63.

Foucault, M. (1977). *Discipline and punish: The birth of the prison* (A. Sheridan, Trans.). New York: Pantheon.

Fujiwara, C. (2008). Single mothers and welfare restructuring in Japan: Gender and class dimensions of income and employment. *The Asia-Pacific Journal: Japan Focus.* http://www.japanfocus.org/-Fujiwara-Chisa/2623/. Accessed March 1, 2010.

Glick Schiller, N., & Fouron, G. (1998). Transnational lives and national identities: The identity politics of Haitian immigrants. In M. Smith & L. Guarnizo (Eds.), *Transnationalism from below* (pp. 130–164). New Brunswick: Transaction Publishers.

Glick Schiller, N., Basch, L., & Blanc-Szanton, C. (Eds.). (1992). *Towards a transnational perspective on migration*. New York: New York Academy of Sciences.

Gordon, L. (Ed.). (1990). *Women, the state and welfare*. Madison: University of Wisconsin Press.

Grimshaw, P., & Murphy, J. (Eds.). (2005). *Double shift: Working mothers and social change in Australia*. Beaconsfield: Circa.

Hannerz, U. (1996). *Transnational connections: Culture, people, places*. London: Routledge.

Holloway, S., Fuller, B., Rambaud, M., & Eggers-Pierola, C. (1997). *Through my own eyes: Single mothers and the cultures of poverty*. Cambridge: Harvard University Press.

Hondagneu-Sotelo, P. (1994). *Gendered transitions: Mexican experiences of immigration*. Berkeley/Los Angeles: University of California Press.

James, S. (1992). The good-enough citizen: Female citizenship and independence. In G. Bock & S. James (Eds.), *Beyound equality and difference* (pp. 43–60). London: Routledge.

Japan Institute for Labour Policy and Training [JILPT]. (2009). *Study on employment support for single-female parent* (JILPT Research Report No.101). www.jil.go.jp/english/reports/documents/jilpt-research/no.101.pdf/. Accessed November 23, 2009.

Jones, K. (1990). Citizenship in a woman friendly polity. *Signs, 15*(4), 781–812.

Jupp, J. (2002). *From White Australia to Woomera: The story of Australian immigration.* Cambridge: Cambridge University Press.

Kearney, M. (1995). The local and the global: The anthropology of globalization and transnationalism. *Annual Review of Anthropology, 24*, 547–565.

Levi-Strauss, C. (1966). *The savage mind.* Chicago: University of Chicago Press.

Lister, R. (1997). Citizenship: Towards a feminist synthesis. *Feminist Review, 57*, 28–48.

Mackie, V. (2003). *Feminism in modern Japan.* Cambridge: Cambridge University Press.

Mahler, S. (2011). Engendering transnational migration. *American Behavioral Scientist, 42*, 690–719.

Manalansan, M. (2003). *Global divas: Filipino gay men in the diaspora.* Durham: Duke University Press.

Mason, J. (1996). *Qualitative researching.* London/Thousand Oaks: Sage.

Ministry of Foreign Affairs, Japan [MOFA]. (1981). *Annual report of statistics on Japanese nationals overseas.* Tokyo: MOFA.

Ministry of Foreign Affairs, Japan [MOFA]. (1991). *Annual report of statistics on Japanese nationals overseas.* Tokyo: MOFA.

Ministry of Foreign Affairs, Japan [MOFA]. (2001). *Annual report of statistics on Japanese nationals overseas.* Tokyo: MOFA.

Ministry of Foreign Affairs, Japan [MOFA]. (2005). *Annual report of statistics on Japanese nationals overseas.* Tokyo: MOFA.

Ministry of Foreign Affairs, Japan [MOFA]. (2010). *Annual report of statistics on Japanese nationals overseas.* Tokyo: MOFA.

Ministry of Health, Labour and Welfare [MHLW]. (2010). *Shinken wo okonau ko no suubetsu nimita rikon.* http://www1.mhlw.go.jp/toukei/rikon_8/repo5.html/. Accessed 10 January 10, 2011.

Mizukami, T. (2006). Leisurely life in a 'wide brown land': Japanese views upon Australia. *Journal of Applied Sociology, 48*, 19–35.

Murdolo, A. (1996). Warmth and unity with all women? Historicizing racism in the Australian women's movement. *Feminist Review, 52*, 69–71.

Nagata, Y., & Nagatomo, J. (2007). *Japanese Queenslanders: A history.* Brisbane: Bookpal for School of Languages and Comparative Cultural Studies.

Nagatomo, J. (2009). *Migration as transnational leisure: The Japanese in southeast Queensland, Australia.* Doctoral dissertation, The University of Queensland, Brisbane.

Payne, G., & Williams, M. (2005). Generalization in qualitative research. *Sociology, 39*(2), 295–314.

Polakow, V. (1993). *Living on the edge: Single mothers and their children in the other America.* Chicago: University of Chicago Press.

Pratt, G. (2004). *Working feminism.* Edinburgh: Temple University Press.

Pries, L. (2001). The approach of transnational social spaces: Responding to new configurations of the social and spatial. In L. Pries (Ed.), *New transnational social spaces* (pp. 3–22). London: Routledge.

Rimmerman, C. (1997). *The new citizenship: Unconventional politics, activism and service.* Boulder/Oxford: Westview Press.

Sato, M. (2001). *Farewell to Nippon: Lifestyle migrants in Australia.* Melbourne: Trans Pacific Press.

Silverman, D. (1993). *Interpreting qualitative data: Methods for analysing talk, text and interaction.* London: Sage.

Simms, M. (1994). Women and the secret garden of politics: Preselection, political parties and political science. In N. Grieve & A. Burns (Eds.), *Australian women: Contemporary feminist thought* (pp. 236–248). Melbourne: Oxford University Press.

Stasiulis, D., & Bakan, A. (2003). *Negotiating citizenship: Migrant women in Canada and the global system*. London: Palgrave.

Sugimoto, K. (1997). *Joseika suru fukushi shakai*. Tokyo: Keisou Shobo.

Sugimoto, K. (1999). *Gender de yomu fukushi shakai*. Tokyo: Yuhikaku.

Suzuki, K. (2009). Zainichi Phiipin-jin single mother to kodomotachi no danzetsu to tsunagari no tsuranarini yorisou. *Iminseisaku Kenkyu, 1*, 124–139.

Tsukui, R. (2007). *The examination of leisure practices and its meanings among middle-aged Japanese settlers in the Brisbane areas*. MA thesis, Griffith University, Brisbane.

Ueno, C. (2004). *Nationalism and gender* (B. Yamamoto, Trans.). Melbourne: Trans Pacific Press.

Willis, K., & Yeoh, B. (Eds.). (2000). *Gender and migration*. Cheltenham/Northampton: Edward Elgar.

Chapter 6
Migrant Women in Belgium: Identity Versus Feminism

Nouria Ouali

6.1 Introduction

After having been a country of emigration, in particular to France and the United States during the nineteenth century, Belgium became a country of immigration after the First World War. Belgium was the receiving country of numerous refugees fleeing fascism and the communist regimes in Italy, Poland and Hungary. During the 1929 economic crisis many of them were sent back to their countries of origin. In the aftermath of World War II the Belgian government organized a massive recruitment of migrant workers through eight bilateral work agreements. The first one was signed with Italy in 1946 in order to recruit thousands of unskilled male workers for the coalmines in Wallonia. Due to an increase in economic growth, demographic needs and pressure from the Italian government, which placed requirements for the safety of its nationals[1] in the work place, the Belgian government found itself under pressure from employers to conclude other bilateral work agreements with Greece, Spain, Morocco, Turkey, Algeria, Tunisia, and the former Yugoslavia (Martens 1976).

This chapter proposes to identify the feminist stakes of women migrant organizations and how their feminist claims have been ignored and reduced to identity claims. Based on the case of women migrant organizations in Brussels, the chapter shows how women migrants[2] contribute to the fight for equality and how Belgian feminist movement started to include their demands in the fight against inhibiting processes of domination. The first section describes the context of migration to Belgium and how the issue of migrant

---

[1] The most serious mining disaster in Belgium occurred in 1956 and resulted in the deaths of 262 men, of which 36 were Italian nationals (Morelli 2004, p. 211).

[2] In this chapter, women migrants generally refer to women who migrated or descendants of migrants. Both may or may not hold Belgian citizenship.

N. Ouali, Ph.D. (✉)
Université Libre de Bruxelles (ULB), Institut de Sociologie,
Centre METICES-Genre et Migration, Avenue Jeanne 44, 1050 Brussels, Belgium
e-mail: nouali@ulb.ac.be

G.T. Bonifacio (ed.), *Feminism and Migration: Cross-Cultural Engagements,*
International Perspectives on Migration 1, DOI 10.1007/978-94-007-2831-8_6,
© Springer Science+Business Media B.V. 2012

women focused gradually on Muslim women. The second section addresses the evolution of feminist organizations since the aftermath of World War II and examines how the feminist movement has dealt with and integrated migrant women in their structures. The third section moves to the critics that migrant women addressed to the feminist movement and analyzes the reasons that led migrant women to create self-organizations. Finally, the chapter concludes that identity claim is not a threat to feminism and considers conditions to redefine a feminist project with migrant women.

6.2   From Invisible Migrant Women to Dominated Muslim Women

Historically, women migrated to Belgium mainly through the family reunification process, particularly after 1974 when the migrant recruitment programme was abolished. Women and children were authorized to join the head of the family, but denied access to the labor market until the end of the 1960s. Family reunification was encouraged because of the foreseen demographic decline in Wallonia. This future demographic decline would jeopardize the social security system, and the long-term financing of retirement pensions (Panciera and Ducoli 1976, p. 26). In this context, the role of migrant women was to serve the objective of "reconstituting the demographic structures" (Delperée and Nols 1958, p. 132). The brochure "*Vivre et travailler en Belgique*" (Living and Working in Belgium) was published in 1964 by the Ministry of Labor, and stipulated that the family reunification had been granted to offer migrant workers an effective family support structure and to create comfort, in order to ensure the physical and psychological regeneration of the workers, and to pave the way for a future labor force. In so doing, women were only seen as a reproductive force that should guarantee the birth of numerous children[3] and take care of their husbands. In 1947, women comprised 40.6% of the foreign population. This reached 49.1%[4] by 2008 due to family reunification since the mid 1970s.[5]

Women contributed to the economy particularly through domestic work. Statistics in 1956 showed relatively few migrant women (especially Italian or Spanish single women) who obtained work permits as domestic workers for the white European

---

[3] Statistics clearly established the huge impact of Italian, Moroccan and Turkish fertility and birthrates on the increasing – population in Belgium. In the 1980s, while the Belgian population decreased (−4.1%), the migrants stemming from South Europe increased slightly (+0.7%), and Moroccan and Turkish population grew significantly (±30% and +20% respectively). During the same period, the average descendant of Belgian women was 1.4 children per woman, 1.2 for EU women, 4.6 for Moroccans and 3.6 for Turkish women (Eggerick et al. 2002, p. 32).

[4] The women's share vary according to ethnic groups.

[5] On 1 January 2008, foreigners made up 9.11% of the 10,666,866 population. The foreign communities with the biggest presence in Belgium are Italians, French, Dutch, Moroccans, Spaniards, Turks and Germans. The foreigners represented 28.1% of the Brussels' population, 9.3% of the Walloons and 5.8% of the Flemish. Since 1985, more than 600,000 foreigners have been naturalized and around 42.5% of foreign-born citizens were granted Belgian citizenship (SPF ETCS 2008, pp. 11–18).

bourgeois families in urban areas (Martens 1976, p. 162). At the end of the 1960s, the work permits legally authorized migrant women and their children to enter the labor market. They were employed in textile and garment manufacturing industries as well as in electronic and food industries. These were economic sectors that would undergo restructuring, thus causing tremendous unemployment after the economic crisis in the 1970s. However, the labor activity rate of migrant women has increased continuously in gaining access to the more precarious, dirty and underpaid jobs; for example, maintenance work in hotels, restaurants and industrial cleaning (Ouali 2008, p. 103).

Since the 1980s the next generation of females coming from migrant families, despite achieving higher levels of education and the acquisition of Belgian nationality, continue to face high rates of unemployment, deskilling, and multiple forms of discrimination. This is more evident among veiled Muslim women. The 1990s were accompanied by an increase in the ageing population, changes in family structures and ways of life (e.g., women's access to labor market, increased spare time and leisure) (Kofman 1999). These factors prompted Belgium to recruit women workers particularly for the healthcare sector in order to satisfy the increased demand for care services like in many other European and developed countries (Raghuram 2006; Sassen 2003).

In the mid 1980s, politicians and media discourses were focused on the Muslim working class originating from Morocco and Turkey. Because of their religion, these ethnic groups were, and still are, perceived as economically and culturally backward and resistant to the western core values of modernity such as democracy, pluralism, secularism, and equality between men and women. Muslim women are "pathologized" and commonly described as victims of their religion and patriarchal traditions, but also seen as the culture and identity carrier of their groups (Yuval Davis 1997). Following the Islamic headscarf affair in France,[6] the Belgian debate also emerged in public schools in 1989. It was argued that the Islamic headscarf signified and confirmed the alleged "incapability" of Muslims to accept the values of modernity. From this time, the Islamic headscarf debates in France and Belgium ran parallel to one another. They brought about on the one hand, legal procedures, ad hoc school regulations and education decrees (French and Dutch speaking community) aimed at banning the Islamic headscarf. On the other hand, this triggered resistance through petitions and demonstrations by, among others, anti-racist groups and Muslim families in order to protest against pupils' expulsion from public schools and the banning of the Islamic headscarf. The Islamic headscarf issue provoked not only the splitting up of the feminist movement but divided society into two camps: a vast majority in favor of the prohibition of the Islamic headscarf and a minority against it (Degavre and Stoffel 2008, p. 9).

Furthermore, the September 11, 2001 attacks of al-Queda on the U.S. additionally stigmatized Muslims. This group is often accused of being communitarians, and viewed as not able to integrate into western society and disloyal to their host countries. In many

---

[6] In 1989, the first headscarf affair started in France when three pupils were expelled from a secondary school because they wore an Islamic headscarf that was considered as infringing secular and republican principles of the public school system (see Gaspard and Khosrokhavar 1995; Scott 2007). From that time, serveral host countries in Europe face similar controversies about the Muslim headscarf and religious insignia in schools and in other public spaces (Lorcerie 2005).

cases, Muslims have indeed been suspected of terrorism (Bousetta and Ouazraf 2002, p. 17). Muslim women's position in these societies are mainly addressed through a cultural approach closely linked to the Islamic headscarf, forced marriage, family codes drawn from Sharia law, honor crimes, virginity and female genital excision. Moreover, Muslim women are described as submissive and under control of Muslim men. Muslim culture and religion is considered as the single factor of women's oppression, and their identity is seen as an enemy of equality and of women's emancipation (Bouteldja 2007; Guénif-Souilamas and Macé 2004, p. 18). Beyond the naturalization of Muslim culture and its stigmatizing impact, this cultural approach takes the ideological direction that the specific oppression of Muslim women is practiced solely by men. Most women (and men) activists remain silent on inequalities faced by Muslim women at school and in the labor market. This silence prevents the questioning of processes, which generate stratifications, hierarchies, inequalities and oppressions (Delphy 2008).

During the past 20 years, the positions of supporters and opponents of religious identity exhibition in the public sphere became more radical and revealed the difficulty to include the Muslim minority in Belgian society, and to recognize them as fully-fledged citizens despite their presence for more than four decades. As Pierre Tevanian (2005, p. 12) underscores, the Islamic headscarf debates are the unhoped-for outlet for latent racism existing in all social groups and political parties.

6.3 Women's Movement and Migrant Women

The status of NGOs (non-governmental organizations) in Belgium is very complex and dense. Associations are a strong component of the Belgian democratic model that considers the necessary and critical role of NGOs. This role is made possible by individuals, who are active, well informed and trained citizens. Members of these NGOs represent different ideological, philosophical and political sensitivities, and are supposed to challenge the state's authority in order to prevent its tendency towards totalitarianism. "Continuing education" is the principle and policy embraced by most of Belgian NGO's to engage "active and informed" citizens. Consequently, three types of association have emerged: self-organizations, institutionalized, and "continuing education" associations.[7]

---

[7] *Self-organizations* are supposed to be independent of the state. Until the 1980s foreigners did not have the right to create their own organizations. From the 1990s, regional governments (Flemish, Walloon and Brussels) have encouraged the self-organization of migrants and ethnic minorities in granting financial support. Religious communities are included in these kinds of organizations. *Institutionalized associations* are (and were) more linked to the political parties such as "Vie féminine"(Women's Life, VF) and "Femmes Prévoyantes Socialistes" (Provident Socialist Women, FPS), which were respectively close to the Christian and Socialist parties, the workers movement, and the mutual benefit organizations (Christian Mutual Benefit and Socialist Mutual Benefit Society). These organizations benefit from the institutionalization of feminism from the mid 1980s. *"Continuing education"* associations are based on the cultural policy devoted to the working class which aims at promoting cultural and individual development through activities like reading and writing courses, social inclusion for popular, youth, and women's movement.

Based on the image of the Belgian state[8] since its creation in 1830, the Belgian women's movement also has the same complex structure and is influenced by different trends and forces. It is a sort of nebula that refers to multiple associations in age, size, financial means and missions, which all aim at fighting for women's emancipation (Plateau 2009, p. 88). From the beginning it has been plural and, according to the circumstances, created alliances beyond social class, ideological, political and cultural (and linguistic) divisions (e.g., for the women's vote or the decriminalization of abortion). Yet, sometimes their allegiance to political parties and workers' organizations made it very difficult to set up of a common front (Jacques 2009, p. 14). If the fight against women's oppression and the achievement for equality are at the core of the feminist struggle, however, the way to address the issues has led to significant theoretical divergences. Many tendencies emerge within the women's movement in Belgium as elsewhere in Europe—liberal feminism, Marxist, radical, cultural, post-modern, and specific groups of black, lesbians, universalists or differentialists, etc. This diversity shows the difficulty in establishing a general theory of female oppression to unite these groups (Degavre and Stoffel 2008, p. 8).

6.3.1   Landscape of the Women's Movement

In the aftermath of World War II, the Belgian government set up a public welfare system, and the means for a social dialogue between employers and trade unions was granted to the workers' movement. At that time Belgian women could not vote yet (conceded in 1948) and still remained under male authority (equality between spouse was not granted until 1976). Thereafter, the mobilization for civil, political, and economic rights became the priority of women's and feminist organizations (Remy 1990; Jacques 2009).

Upon their arrival in Belgium during the late 1950s, the wives of migrants discovered that the landscape of women's organizations was scattered and sparse. This was due to diverse movements linked to World War II like those opposing the pacifists and the pro-war movement. In addition, women's organizations were divided into two camps. One camp supported traditional family values and another camp that purported to advocate for women's independence and emancipation (Jacques 2009). The number of women's associations, however, increased[9] and those in existence were restructured as a result of the new balance of power in the organizations, between the mass association of women and the independent ones. The mass associations of women linked to the Socialist and Christian parties were

---

[8] The Belgian society is mainly divided into four structures: philosophical (religions and laymen), linguistic and cultural (Flemish, French and German communities), ideological (Christian, Liberal, Socialist parties) and social class (peasantry, middle class, working class) (Mabille 1986).
[9] There were 11 women's associations before the 1940s and 5 were founded after 1945 (Jacques 2009, p. 43).

strengthened, and particularly two major rival organizations are still active.[10] The *Ligues Ouvrières Féminines Chrétiennes* (Christian Women Workers' League) which became *Vie Feminine* (Women's Life, VF) at the end of the 1960s, and the *Femmes Prévoyantes Socialistes* (Provident Socialist's Women, FPS) founded in 1922 from the Socialist Mutual Benefit Society (Jacques 2009, pp. 25–26).

The women's movement was very dynamic during the 1950s and succeeded in the elimination of some civil, economic and political forms of discrimination affecting women.[11] In the course of the 1960s the organizations became less reactionary and rested on recently granted rights. The women's mass movement (i.e., VF and FPS) strengthened its bonds with the political parties and working class organizations. That period corresponded to a vigorous social movement due to the restructuring of economic sectors and heavy loss of employment, but a time when more women started entering the labor market.

During the anti-colonial struggle in the 1950s, pacifist and internationalist feminists claimed civic and politic rights for African women, but there was no mention of racial/ethnic dimension within the women's movement. In that period, the Union of the Colonial Women (*Union des Femmes Coloniales*), which was created in 1924, defended the rights of European women and claimed that the rights of the Congolese women should also be respected. It served, nevertheless, the interests of the Belgian colonial project and was a vector of propaganda in favor of the presence of European women in Congo. In regard to the situation of Congolese women, education and morality were the main priorities. According to Catherine Jacques and Valérie Piette (2004, pp. 79–80), "[t]heir objectives are limited to prove that the African woman is an human being deserving interest and consideration and needed to be civilized by the education and moralized."

In 1968, the women's movement commemorated the twentieth anniversary of the women's right to vote in Belgium and seized the opportunity to assess their actions. Although formal equality between men and women had been established, male and systemic resistance and multiple discrimination persisted, particularly in the economic sector. One vivid example was the strike waged by migrant and working class women against the national weapons factory, *Fabrique Nationale*. Due to the gender-based disparity in wages, they successfully launched a debilitating strike under the slogan "Equal work for equal wage." The strike had a European as well as an international echo (Vercheval 2008).[12]

---

[10] The organization close to the Liberal Party remained a minority although they had famous activists such as Georgette Ciselet and Jane Brigode.

[11] For example, the right to vote and to enter in all professions and occupations, the end of the legal incompetence of the spouse, or the abolition of regulations related to prostitution.

[12] The strike triggered, on the one hand, the creation of the international Comity "Equal work for equal wage" which organized press releases and conferences to denounce women's discrimination at work. On the other hand, it brought about a special meeting of the European Parliament in order to assess the application of the regulation of the Treaty of Rome related to wage equality between men and women (Coenen 1991).

In the 1970s, the Belgian women's movement took two trends: on the one hand, one that went along the lines of "neo-feminism" incarnated by the "women's liberation movement" and, on the other hand, the feminism supported by the State through the inclusion of women's demands in the political agenda, the creation of legislation and the implementation of political measurements (quotas, positive actions) to ensure equality (Remy 1990, p. 112). As a rule, the "neo-feminists" mistrust the State and its institutions and wanted to break with first wave feminism, which was perceived as reformist (i.e., VF and FPS) and strongly branded by its moralistic views on sexuality. Neofeminist were more radical and independent from the political parties. Neo-feminist militants fought for women's emancipation and focused on self-autonomy of the female body (e.g. reproductive rights, free sexuality) equality in socio-economic sector (professional segregation and wage inequality), the struggle against violence, and the sharing of domestic tasks. In 1972, advocates of neo-feminism created the National Women's Day, which is celebrated annually on the 11th of November, and created women spaces like women's libraries, shelters and coffee-houses (Peemans-Poullet 1991, p. 75). On the common front, the women's movement still joined forces with various women's organizations and took actions to claim individual rights for social security, measures to better reconcile the professional and private spheres. The glass-ceiling phenomenon commonly faced by highly qualified women and the gender disparity in politics were less popular since it concerned mainly upper and middle class women.

With the emergence of third wave feminism during the first decade of the new millennium, new trends started criticizing the principles of "universal feminism." Black feminism/womanism, gay and lesbians, queer, post-colonial, anti-racist and anti-capitalist movements deconstructed the "woman" subject and sexual identities which exercised a strong influence on the current women's movement. Gender studies welcomed Black feminist and post-colonial scholarship with such scholars as bell hooks (1981), Chandra Mohanty (1988) and Kimberlé Crenshaw (2005). Since then feminists seem ready to affirm diversity in the movement:

> To recognize that women's group is distributed along the axes social class or race/ethnicity—among others, that it is thus divided. It is already the first step towards the recognition of the fact that all women are not exposed in the same way to oppression, that they (white women) can themselves belong to the oppressor group, and that they do not have all the same interests. (Degavre and Stoffel 2008, p. 8)

6.3.2   Migrant Women in the Women's Movement

Migrant women became visible in the Belgian public space from the 1970s onward. The first generation migrant women were mainly housewives, and possessed very low levels of education. For example, the vast majority (95%) of Moroccan migrant women were illiterate. A few migrant women started to emerge in the public eye at the end of the 1960s through their activism within the social movement and the organization of strikes in the textile industry, as a result of economic restructuring (Coenen 1993, pp. 44–45).

Colette Braeckman (1973) describes in particular Moroccan migrant women, as being on their own and are confronted with isolation. She points out that female foreigners benefit from spontaneous movements of welcoming, liking and support from their Belgian neighbors and, above all, from the two main working class women's organizations (i.e., VF and FPS). These working class women's organizations often recommend that personal assistance be given to help migrant women cope with everyday life situations (e.g. housing, education of their children, public administrations, etc.). Thereafter, they invited migrant women to take part in the activities of the organization. Yet, the pathway of inclusion is quite different.

Until the twenty-first century migrant women were basically consumers of services offered by the women's mass movement. They consisted as participants in literacy training, "female" activities such as cooking or sewing, or instruction in how to benefit from cultural or administrative services, and legal advice and support. These services played a crucial role in supporting the rights of first generation migrant women and in their knowledge of the Belgian institutions. From the end of the 1980s, women's organizations started to face difficulties in meeting the demands of the daughters of migrant women and were confronted with refusal of the "maternalist" relationship that had been experienced by their mothers (Cherradi 2004, p. 34; Ouali 2007, p. 5).

6.3.2.1 Women's Mass Movement

Femmes Prévoyantes Socialistes (FPS) and *Vie Féminine* (VF) are the major mass women's movement organizations that approached migrant women's issue in a different way. FPS, founded in 1922, stemmed from the Socialist Mutual Benefit Society, and is very attached to secularism and universalism.[13] FPS viewed particular groups, such as migrants as contrary to the general interest of society. According to FPS, religion is a matter of ones' private life and must not interfere with the public sphere. *Vie feminine*, originated from the *Ligues Ouvrières Féminines Chrétiennes* (Christian Women Workers' League) and emerged at the end of the 1960s. It is a member of the Christian movement, which is composed of trade unions, youth organizations, friendly societies, cultural associations, Christian churches, etc. It created specific groups for youth or migrant women. Although religion constitutes a part of the private sphere, it was recognized as a legitimate part of an individual's identity. As we will see further, these organizations adopted distinguishable approaches of migrant women's issues: universalist and specific.

---

[13] Secularism and universalism are the fundamental beliefs of the Belgian (and international) workers socialist movement. Secularism was embraced in opposition to the Christian movement's very strong influence at the end of the nineteenth century.Universalism supposes that there is no difference between workers and that they must be treated as equals. Any differences (for example sex and ethnicity) are considered as factors of fragmentation of the movement (Jefferys and Ouali 2007, p. 408).

Femmes Prévoyantes Socialistes (FPS)

The universalist approach towards migrant women is reflected in the refusal to take into account any specific demands related to the principle of equal treatment, even if concerns were addressed by FPS (for example undocumented women workers, Moroccan repudiation of spouse,[14] forced marriage, etc.) and some activities organized for them (kitchen or embroidery courses). According to the leaders of FPS, the organization's goal is to fight for women's emancipation, equality and solidarity. It also advocates universal sisterhood, which presupposes all women joining forces to fight patriarchy, poverty, violence against women, and sexual and reproductive rights. FPS defends the principle of equality for all human beings in any constitutional state irrespective of age, sex, ethnicity, and philosophical or religious convictions. Ghislaine Julémont (2008, p. 143) consequently argues that, "It is out of question of admitting neither violence and discrimination against women, nor any bondage in referring to the religious, customary or national rights, and those who misuse them could take advantage under pretext that they are usual."

The solidarity among women is shown vis-à-vis Afghani and Algerian women who are confronted with Islamic fundamentalism. In particular, those women who are subject to stoning because of adultery, rape, honor crimes, sexual mutilation, repudiation or other forms of violence against women. Like in other democratic countries where migrant women from the Third World are settled, FPS confronts any concessions made to the country of origin in terms of religious, customary or national rights (Julémont 2008, p. 143), like the case of Moroccan repudiation. For the leaders of FPS, the actions must be carried out at the intersections of secularism, feminism, citizenship, equality and solidarity, which are considered non-negotiable basic values. They acknowledge that feminism and multiculturalism are compatible only if they are based on secularity (Plasman and Pinchart 2008, p. 156).

In regard to the Islamic headscarf, it is treated through the individual woman's right to own and control her body rather than through the rejection of a religious doctrine. FPS considers the Islamic headscarf as part of the emancipation process, and any concessions made by society would become a vicious spiral of more demands by Muslims. On the ground, Muslim women attending FPS activities are permitted to wear the headscarf, but it is clearly banned for social workers and active leaders within the organization (Plasman and Pinchart 2008). FPS struggles with its identity by claims of Belgian Muslims to their religious rights or non- mixed space for Muslim women. Consequently, the leaders of FPS remain ambiguous on values and principles that became rigid and inflexible, which prevent their understanding of the realities of migrant women and the contemporary stakes of fighting for their empowerment.

From the 1990s, migrant women have criticized the universalistic approach of feminist organizations that excluded their identity and specific concerns. Many of

---

[14] A bilateral agreement on family law was signed in 1991 between Belgium and Morocco which recognized divorce by repudiation in the Belgian legal system.

them are frustrated because both their voices are not heard and their needs are not taken into account. In addition, the indisputable rule of displaying and claiming a Muslim identity, and discussing FPS values are unacceptable for many migrant women and their descendants (Cherradi 2004, p. 45). Consequently, FPS gradually lost its support from migrant working class women. In the 1980s, social workers already noticed a low level of participation of migrant women due to family duties, absence of autonomy, and lack of language skills or literacy. In the past migrant women were recruited through infant care services, summer camps, family planning centers, friendly society, trade unions and employment. Since the 1980s, migrants and minorities (Belgian Sub-Saharan, North African and Turkish) have been faced with considerable exclusion in the labor market, and are mainly employed in the menial labor sector and industrial cleaning where the worst paid and dirty jobs are to be found. Their working conditions and time constraints often make it difficult for migrant women to participate in FPS activities. FPS continues to face difficulties in maintaining links with and the interest of younger migrant women. The women from migrant families are often more concerned with caring for their children and motherhood that is not a part of the feminist project envisioned by FPS (Plasman and Pinchart 2008, p. 158).

Due to pressure from social workers, and the need to reposition its principles and values, the FPS began in 2007 to reflect upon its views regarding feminism and multiculturalism. The social workers want to know how addressing women's demands with different cultures and religious backgrounds within a secular organization, particularly the issues of wearing the Islamic headscarf, or the demand for praying time or access to non-mixed (women only) swimming pools are reconciled. The FPS attempts to understand why it is unsuccessful in reaching out to migrant women (e.g., young women of Moroccan origin). What emerged from their reflections merely strengthened their values and secular identity (Plasman and Pinchart 2008, p. 160).

Vie Féminine (VF)

VF, unlike FPS, adopted a mix of universalistic and a specific approach towards migrant women's issues associated with a strong "bottom up" strategy. This is a strategy that focuses on the working class population where migrant women are overrepresented. In 1947, the Christian workers' movement created a specific "migrant" group apart from those of women, youth and older groups. This was done in order to ensure the reception and the "control" of Italians workers and their family. Historically, VF ran its activities around the group "Action immigrée" (immigrant action), a social service devoted to the reception of migrants which provided support, among others, with schooling and housing. At the end of the 1980s, the "migrant groups" which consisted mainly of Italians, Greeks, Turkish, Moroccan and Spanish, were reorganized because the Christian worker's movement gave priority to the integration of ethnic minorities (i.e., Turks and Moroccans), even if migrants remained a target group. In this context, the "Action *immigrée*" groups ended in 2001 and VF began to reflect upon the issue of interculturality.[15]

During the 1980s, VF recruited social workers and activity leaders[16] from working class ethnic minorities (as well as from groups allied with the Christian worker's movement) that better reflected the diversity of the population. This was fundamental to remain connected with the working class and make possible (and visible) the social mobility of descendants of migrants. In June 2006, this opening strategy led the volunteer workers to elect a woman of Moroccan origin to the presidency, Hafida Bachir. Bachir started her career in 1988 as an activity leader and became General Secretary Deputy of VF in 2003. She had an emblematic trajectory of being a feminist activist, who did not choose to create a specific association that would give a platform to the voice of minority women. Instead she preferred to invest in an existing mass women's structure rather than to be considered a militant in the margins of the Belgian feminist movement.

Under Bachir's presidency, VF opened up the debate on interculturality, which led to this concept being mainstreamed in all their activities and at all levels of the organization. Bachir (2007, p. 5) claims that "Interculturality is a feminist project which aims at questioning all cultures, not solely Muslim and Arabic cultures, which are too often stigmatized and seen as backward" (Bachir 2007, p. 5).[17] In 2001, VF tried to clarify the concept of interculturality within the feminist agenda. It first recognized the richness of cultural diversity (as well as its possible conflicts), and saw it as an opportunity to question and to move forward with intercultural practices. Then, it rejected the culturalist approach that tolerated cultural practices, which are harmful, on the one hand, to women's health, for example, high sugar consumption by pregnant and diabetic women, female genital mutilation, and, on the other hand, to fundamental rights. According to Bachir, the role of VF is to help all women to take a distance from and to adopt a critical attitude towards their culture, and to create the conditions that would provide women with the opportunity to do so (*Vie feminine* 2008). Its feminist project included issues specific to women without abandoning the principles of equality. It supported the fight for the regularization of undocumented women based upon gender-specific criteria, women victims of forced marriage, rape, female genital mutilation and the deprivation of fundamental rights (*Vie feminine* 2008). Yet, there were some limits to the discussion within the organization regarding the moral and physical damage done to women. Bachir (2008, p. 149) states, "One cannot say, "that it is their culture." One cannot tolerate genital excision, polygamy, repudiation and, racism. It is a question

---

[15] This concept is more common in Belgium as well as in French-speaking countries than multiculturalism. Following the work of Carmel Camilleri and Margalit Cohen-Emerique (1989), interculturality in Belgium supposes to question identity of all stakeholders of the relationship and not of ethnic minorities only. Furthermore, among scholars, multiculturalism is often linked to the American model of society that is seen as fragmented, where communities coexist rather than mix.

[16] FPS and members of socialist organizations were, in general, from the white majority.

[17] Statement in *En Marche* (2007), the Christian Mutual Benefit Society Journal (Robert 2007).

of rejecting unjust practices endured by women and not rejecting women. The rejection of the "Other" cannot be tolerated from a feminist point of view."

VF took a stand on the wearing of the Islamic headscarf in schools, repudiation and polygamy. VF discussed the headscarf issue during an entire year and included Muslim women in the debate. They considered the ban to be detrimental to women and not to the chauvinists: Muslim school-age girls would be expelled from schools and adult Muslim women rejected by their employers. Bachir (2008, p. 149) thinks about this issue and that political and religious triumph as:

> [a]ttacking veiled women is not sexism nor feminism, but it is a matter of racism. [...] In stigmatizing the sexism in the Banlieue, we trivialize and we hide the sexism of others. There are not solely Blacks and Muslims who are sexist. The problem is that (white) women and some feminists are also a part of this discourse, which is racist and antifeminist.

Vie Féminine adopted a more open-minded attitude and an inclusive strategy towards migrant women than *Femmes Prévoyantes Socialistes*. Although VF placed clear limits as the respect of women's fundamental rights (repudiation or polygamy) and the protection of women's moral and body integrity (racism, genital excision), it nevertheless chose to discuss the identity issue in order to give women the means to criticize practices, which infringe upon women's rights rather than prevent such debates as done by FPS. The election of a descendant of a migrant family at the head of the organization has certainly contributed to this opening of intercultural relations in VF. The bottom up strategy also exercised an important impact on the capacity of VF to remain in touch with migrant women's' realities.

6.3.2.2 The Feminist Movement

As indicated earlier, the women's movement included more radical associations that broke off from first wave feminists, and were independent from political parties and the state. They were also less popular than the mainstream women's mass organizations. Yet, they have been very active during different periods of the feminist struggle and played an important role in the advancement of women's rights (Remy 1990, pp. 46–53).

During the first decade of the twenty-first century, the feminist movement focused its struggle on breaking the glass ceiling and increasing the representation of women in the sciences and politics. The challenge of the women's movement as a whole was not to recognize the discrimination faced by migrant and minority women in education, housing and employment but to consider it as a societal issue and not as a specific problem. With the exception of some organizations (i.e., VF, COLFEN)[18]

---

[18] COLFEN or *Collectif Femmes en noir contre les centres fermés et les expulsions* (Collective Women in Black against centre of retention and deportation) was created in 1998 after the death of Semira Adamu, a victim of police violence. Until June 2009 COLFEN devoted its tasks to the support of asylum seekers and undocumented migrant women seeking regularization of status and, in particular, for the recognition of rights to women victims of persecutions and discrimination based on sex (COLFEN 2006).

most of these organizations remained silent about the plight of refugees, Black and Muslim women and about those who are confronted with incidents of everyday racism and the continuous violation of their fundamental rights. Consequently, blindness and silence in regard to these issues made feminism less attractive for women facing socioeconomic and cultural inequalities.

According to Nadine Plateau, a woman's rights activist of the 1970s, the feminist movement started to engage with migrant women's issues in the 1990s. This deepened after the Belgian Commission on Intercultural Dialogue[19] was established in 2004 which consulted representatives of feminist associations. Until the process of reflection had begun, the topic of multiculturalism was perceived as an issue affecting only migrant women and addressed specific groups within the feminist movement.

In 2008, Nadine Plateau was shocked when she realized that the famous French-speaking feminist journal *Chronique Féministe* (Feminist Chronic) never published any articles on migrant women in Belgium since its establishment in 1982. For her, this form of ignorance regarding migrant women has several reasons. Firstly, the feminist movement had been predominantly run by upper and middle class white women, and was based on their life experiences, needs and claims. They perceived migrant women as a disadvantaged group rather than as a group consisting of diverse ethnic communities. The second reason was strategic. It was precisely because of its diversity that the movement tended to minimize the "antagonism linked to social and ethnic origins" (Plateau 2009, p. 81) and favor commonalities. Thirdly, the ethnocentrism and the conviction shared by many feminists was that the "Western World" is the main frame of reference in theory and practice (Mohanty 1988). The concept of sharing common values such as Christian legacy, secularism, democracy, and human rights should perhaps increase a feeling of homogeneity within the movement (Plateau 2009, p. 81).

In the 1970s, very few migrant women were considered activists within the feminist movement. The account of the first Belgian Algerian woman, Ouardia Derriche, who joined the French-speaking women's movement in Brussels, demonstrated just how difficult it was to be accepted. During the long course beside the leftist women's movement, her attempt to be closer to autochthonous women failed because they did not perceive her as a full-fledged feminist militant activist. Derriche states:

> The claim of equality was immediately unimaginable and unbearable. I have to show my credentials, to make the vain demonstration of my Universalist and feminist engagement. I was used as an instrument and seen as a foil to them, I have the feeling that I am not recognized as a stakeholder of a truly egalitarian movement. (Derriche 2010, p. 43)

---

[19] *Commission du dialogue interculturel* provided recommendations on different aspects of the lives of migrant and ethnic minorities in Belgian society. The Commission suggested, among others, to improve women's access to information about civil rights, particularly the rules concerning mariage, divorce and child custody. The Commission pleaded to consider children and grandchildren as full-fledged citizens (Delruelle and Torfs 2005).

According to Derriche, this exclusion was common in the leftist militant groups that created not only discomfort among its ranks, but, above all, the women who faced discouragement and disillusionment. She considered that, actually,

> The belonging to feminism, just like democracy, seems experienced by some as a sort of degree of noble lineage, a privilege associated with blue blood that could not agree fully with the commoner's stemming from the Third World and the Muslim groups in particular. (Derriche 2010, p. 43)

A young white Flemish activist, Sara S'jegers, confirms the persistent difficulties around inclusion in the feminist movement, particularly for Muslim women. She explains that as a white non-Muslim woman, she is "naturally" part of the women's movement in Flanders, whereas militant Muslim women in organizations must make themselves clear because the Islamic "culture" is always presented as patriarchal and hostile to women. A Belgian Moroccan Muslim woman, Saliha Berhili, an acquaintance of S'jegers had to, first, prove her devotion to the "women's cause," and, secondly, to prove that issues related to the feminist movement are her absolute priority above all other issues to which she would supposedly be attached: "It was as if she has to prove that she condemned and abjured certain elements of 'the other culture' before membership in the white feminist movement was granted" (S'jegers 2008, p. 126).

There exists no consensus among feminist groups prohibiting women from wearing the Islamic headscarf although the majority is in favor of its ban. Yet, in September 2009, a platform of individual secular feminists from different philosophical and political perspectives protested against the Belgian French-speaking government's[20] determination to ban the Islamic headscarf in schools in the name of feminism and secularism (Platform of Secular Feminists against the banning of the Veil, *Le Soir*, 26 September 2009). This group of feminists denounced using the argument of women's emancipation in order to ban the headscarf, persisting gender-based inequalities, merchandizing of the female body, and violence against all women. Their opposition to the ban was based on different reasons. First, they argued that emancipation cannot be imposed upon anyone, and that economic independence would offer or perhaps create a condition where women have the chance to make individual choices. Second, they believed that the ban on Islamic headscarf would confine young Muslim female pupils to the sole spheres of family and community, which could deprive them of making contact with other cultural models and groups within the larger society. Third, this form of societal isolation would make young Muslim women more vulnerable and situate them in an already very disadvantaged position. "Our conception of secularism supposes the separation of the church and the state but not the separation of believers and non-believers" (Platform of Secular Feminists against the banning of the Veil, *Le Soir*, 26 September 2009). They pleaded for the creation of debates and dialogues to deconstruct stereotypes in all groups and for the rights of all women to wear or remove the Islamic headscarf

---

[20] Belgium is a federal state which consists of the federal government and four regional governments (Flemish, French, Brussels and German).

without pressure. They also made demands regarding respect of fundamental rights of ethnic minorities such as access to and the right to receive an education.

6.4 Critique of the Women's Movement

Although some migrant women's associations existed as of 1975 (e.g., Association of the Moroccan Women), their development occurred mainly during the 1990s, and their membership consisted of migrants from non-European countries such as Angola, Rwanda, Congo (DRC), Latin America, Turkey, Arab states (Maghreb, Lebanon, Palestine, Syria), and Muslims (Moroccan, Turkish or Belgian converts). The leaders and members of these organizations were migrant women aspiring to become more autonomous and to actively participate in debates that concerned them, and defend their interests (Ouali 2010, p. 179). The number of women's associations labeled as cultural or Arabic-Muslim increased dramatically due to the support of regional integration policies that targeted ethnic minorities, particularly in Brussels and in Flanders (Coene 2007, p. 82). These integration policies were aimed at the preservation of culture and identity(ies) of migrants, and thus activities were developed to support this purpose. Arabic language courses were offered, which were not directly linked to the mosques; conferences on the Arab and Muslim women's movement in the Arab world; and music and cinema activities. The struggle against racism and discrimination in schools, the labor market, and the recognition of the rights of migrants also form part of the agenda. One example is the "*Collectif de femmes en Europe*" (Collective of Women in Europe) which was created by the Muslim citizens network *Présence Musulmane* (Muslim Presence). This network campaigned to preserve Muslim identity, to defend religious freedom of Muslims in Europe, and to fight legislation that banned the Islamic headscarf or any discriminatory practices against Muslims (Fournier 2008, p. 3). These associations evolved within the margins of the women's movement for different reasons that will be addressed further in this section.

For the first time in Belgium in October 2006, the feminist movement organized a conference on gender and interculturality in Brussels. Through this conference, women's organizations intended to listen to the needs and grievances of migrant women leaders, and to open up a dialogue. As underlined by a long-standing feminist activist, Nadine Plateau, this "memorable day" presented two important concerns for the women's movement. First, it was severely criticized and questioned the way (White Belgian) feminists treated migrant women. Second, migrant women expressed their will not to be apart from, but to cooperate and create new ways of thinking about feminism in Belgium (Plateau 2009, p. 80).

The issues that were addressed during the conference were not very new among them such as discrimination of minority women in schooling, housing, and employment. For nearly 20 years migrant women had spoken about these issues. Basically, migrant women rejected paternalistic and contemptuous relationships and demanded equality and respect. Muslim women in particular also wanted respect for their

husband and sons, who were and are commonly racialized, criminalized, discriminated against and stigmatized as chauvinist and violent against their women (Ouali
2010, p. 181). The first generation of migrant women complained about being
ordered to leave their chauvinist husbands or having to adopt the Western model of
women's liberation, which excluded identity and religious expressions, all in the
name of secularity. In other words, they were under pressure to choose or to renounce
a part of themselves or of their families that would never have been required from
an "indigenous" white feminist (Ouali 2000, p. 191).

From the 1980s, young activist women from migrant families began to criticize
the feminist movement for not having provided support and promoted concrete
activities to emancipate migrant women. In 1987, for example, three highly skilled
young women from Turkish, Moroccan and Italian background created *La Voix des
Femmes* (Women's Voice) because young girls received inadequate responses to
their problems. They expressed their difficulties "of not being taken seriously" after
having left their homes and families, due to threats of forced marriage or attempted
suicides.[21]

In the 2000s, young Muslim women activists rather questioned the universalist
form of feminism and the alleged "homogeneity" of the women's movement as well
as their hegemonic model of liberation. For the feminist movement, the universal is
seen either as a "sacred" core value of feminism that is to be respected whatever the
cost, or as an ethnocentric value to be redefined. Muslim women activists believe that
the Muslim model of emancipation is not less valid than the Western model since it
is based on Islamic universal values (e.g. equality and social justice). They deplored
the fact that migrant women's voices are often not heard within the feminist movement and that universal sisterhood never existed. Sisterhood is achieved based on the
grounds of human rights and politicized action against patriarchy. In addition, they
condemned feminists who betrayed the liberty of conscience and the individual's
right to own and control ones' own body through the Islamic headscarf debate
(Hamidi 2006, p. 21). Indeed, Muslim feminists have been demonized and solely
perceived as submissive or under the control of fundamentalist networks. Islam and
feminism are seen as contradictory and the activities of Muslim women are viewed
as provocative, extreme propaganda or proselytism (Bouteldja 2009, p. 95). Muslim
feminists consider that the non-Muslim feminist relentless fight against the Islamic
headscarf in the name of equality and secularism is a turning point in the feminist
struggle, and considered it as a clear rupture towards liberation.

The negative image of Muslim, Moroccan or Turkish migrant women as being
submissive and backward, and belonging to an "archaic" culture and religion is also
pointed out in the conference. This cultural devaluation of "other" women in actuality masks sexism that still exists in society (Ouali 2000, p. 192). Thus, the comparison between Muslim and non-Muslim women became the relevant frame of
reference of European progress regarding gender equality. Consequently, this
diverted Western women from the fact that they, too, were and are oppressed by men

---

[21] Statement of the President of the association, Hariyé Balci (1988).

within their own cultures (Volpp 2001, pp. 1212–1214). The focus on Muslim women generated stigmatization, prejudice, racism and discrimination.

Some migrant women raised the issue of the "glass ceiling" or their absence in top positions within feminist organizations despite the fact that many of them were employed as activity leaders, secretaries, cooks or cleaners. They criticized the feminist tendency to analyze inequalities and social problems through the lens of cultural differences (Lefrancq 2008, p. 143). For example, Muslims are stigmatized as perpetrators of honor crimes and are taken to court by some feminist organizations, but fail to take legal action to prevent everyday violence against women.

The Belgian feminist movement has been accused by migrant women leaders and members of women's associations as an intellectual corporatist and elitist group. It seems that a large part of this movement has lost interest in the genuine struggle for social justice of all women since its institutionalization (Derriche 2010, p. 42). Consequently, it has cut ties with people of the popular social movement resulting in the feminist movement becoming more and more distant from the realities of migrant women. To illustrate this point, a militant migrant woman noticed that the most famous women's house in Brussels is located in the core of a Turkish and Moroccan neighborhood. Yet, the house remains only accessible to middle and upper class white women who are mostly indifferent to the issues of school segregation, and to the blatant realm of social inequalities faced by migrant and ethnic minority women (Derriche 2010, p. 43). The feminist mission, according to Leti Volpp (2001), is not concerned with "saving" women from exploitation and subordination in society, but from their own patriarchal and chauvinist culture. In addition, the white women majority is not ready to acknowledge its own advantages and privileges in society (Coene 2007, p. 98) that also serve to oppress other groups of women.

6.5 (Re)building a Feminist Project

A very small part of the feminist movement in Belgium is ready to debate and revisit their model and values of dominant Western feminists in order to cooperate with migrant women. At this stage, although individual contacts have been undertaken between these organizations, but nothing has actually been made to pursue a dialogue that began in the Brussels conference in October 2006. This meeting was an opportunity to acknowledge both the existence of power relations among women within the movement, and the necessity to articulate the inclusion of gender, class and race in future feminist political projects. However, the issue at stake in the women's movement is how to achieve in practical terms a project, which is more inclusive and respectful of migrant women, especially Muslim women, while knowing that the majority of white feminist organizations supported the law banning the Islamic headscarf and the burqa (full-body covering) in the public space, except *Vie féminine* and individual members of the Platform of Secular Feminists. Within this context, one might ponder the question; how is it possible to overcome these divisions while building a future feminist project that is inclusive and respectful of the realities in a multicultural society? The challenge is multi-layered and several important conditions should be addressed by those who criticize the women's movement. Among others, these consist in enlarging the Belgian pluralist model to include migrant groups, making concrete the principle of equality towards migrant women and building solidarity; approaching domination as a complex system where sex, race and class oppression intersect; and changing the gaze towards migrant women and considering women migrants' culture and identities as dynamic but not a threat to feminism.

The Belgian state is defined as pluralist and, in the course of its history, has overcome its numerous divisions based on philosophical, social, political and cultural ground. Pluralism "is not a simple coexistence of opinions and various beliefs but the construction of a common space of dialogue and emancipation, where diversity is the subject of collective debates and is translated into specific institutions" (Delruelle and Torfs 2005, p. 27). Pluralism supposes three things: diversity of opinions and beliefs; opposition and conflict between these opinions; and, finally, debate and search for compromises in order to preserve social cohesion (Faux 2008, p. 4). The women's movement reminds us of this approach that consists of the acknowledgement of divisions, conflicts, and compromises and has proven its effectiveness in overtaking tensions inherent in all groups.

The Belgian women's movement needs to recognize that migrant women are equal and, consequently, fully-fledged citizens, and are also potential feminists regardless of their identity(ies) and religion. Although most of them have Belgian nationality through mixed parentage they are still perceived as foreigners and not legitimate citizens. Their concrete equality could be achieved by looking after a better distribution of material resources and symbolic advantages, fighting racism, establishing democratic relations, and building solidarity among women's organizations. The reality of migrant women's lives is interlaced with poverty, racism, and discrimination that lead to their exclusion.[22]

There is a consensus among feminists that racism is built upon the superiority of western values which impede potential dialogues between migrant women's organizations and the re-definition of priorities and strategies within the women's movement. Feminists need to address domination as a matrix system through which sex, race and class oppression intersect (Collins 1999). One condition of this dialogue entails the acknowledgment of white women's dominant position and privilege within the women's movement, which makes possible the imposition of standards, priorities and strategies that excludes religious identity. Thus, these practices impose secularity as a prerequisite for feminism. Migrant women wish to have their voices heard and not have their questions, concerns and fears marginalized.

The white Western women's movement needs to modify its gaze directed towards migrant women and refrain from seeing their culture and identities as static entities, which threaten feminist goals of liberation. Migrant women need not be solely seen

---

[22] In 2001, the poverty threshold of the Belgian population (less then 777 € a month) was between 9.6% and 10.8%, while those of Turkish and Moroccan ethnic minorities were between 51.1% and 66.7% and 47% and 64%, respectively (Van Robaeys and Perrin 2006).

as submissive, but rather also as resisting patriarchal practices through, among others, economic power. Camille Lacoste-Dujardin (2008) discusses this issue in her latest book about Kabyle migrant women in France and Algeria. She asserts that culture helps individuals enhance their development and not solely oppresses them. Volpp suggests moving away from the devaluating dialectic and instead to move towards a constructive dialogue, which consists of examining,

> [t]he particularity of women's relationships to specific patriarchies, as well as to geopolitical and economic relationships. Attempts to make normative judgments and to change behavior must be premised on the understanding that cultures, including our own, are patriarchal—not more or less so, but differently patriarchal. (Volpp 2001, p. 1217)

All these conditions possibly lead to achieving real "sisterhood" and to rebuilding the future modern feminist project inclusive of all women.

As regards the very complex multi-layered identity claims of migrant women, for example, it cannot be foreseen as a threat to feminism. The emergence of Islamic feminism particularly in Europe and in Western countries shows that, if it seems contradictory, religion does not hinder women's will to fight patriarchy and defend their rights. Through their identity, they try to express their right to criticize the Western model of feminism and experiment their own way of liberation.

References

Bachir, H. (2007, March). Statement in the Christian Mutual Benefit Society Journal. *En Marche*.
Bachir, H. (2008, October–November). Vie féminine, le féminisme et l'interculturalité. *Cahiers Marxistes, 238*, 147–153.
Balci, H. (1988, Février Mars) Interview, *L'antiracisme, 32*, 13–19.
Bousetta, H., & Ouazraf, H. (2002). Le silence des intellectuels de l'immigration nord-africaine. In H. Bousetta (Ed.), *Rompre le silence. 11 septembre 2001–11 septembre 2002* (pp. 15–19). Bruxelles: Labor.
Bouteldja, H. (2007, June). De la cérémonie du dévoilement à Alger (1958) à Ni Putes Ni Soumises: L'instrumentalisation coloniale et néo-coloniale de la cause des femmes. In Collectif Les mots sont importants. *Ni putes ni soumises, un appareil idéologique d'Etat*. http://lmsi.net/spip.php?article320. Accessed January 15, 2010.
Bouteldja, N. (2009). France: Voices of the banlieues. *Race and Class, 51*(1), 90–99.
Braeckman, C. (1973). *Les etrangers en Belgique*. Bruxelles: EVO.
Camilleri, C., & Cohen-Emerique, M. (Eds.). (1989). *Chocs des cultures. Concepts et enjeux pratiques de l'interculturel*. Paris: L'Harmattan.
Cherradi, L. (2004). *L'associatif et les femmes immigrées marocaines. Vers un bilan de 40 ans d'actions*. Bruxelles: Communauté française, Rapport final, février.
Coene, G. (2007). Etre féministe, ce n'est pas exclure! Le pragmatisme féministe dans le débat sur le multiculturalisme en Flandre. *Revue Européenne des Migrations Internationales, 23*(2), 79–105.
Coenen, M.-T. (1991). *La grève des femmes de la F.N. en 1966. Une première en Europe*. Bruxelles: POL-HIS.
Coenen, M.-Th. (1993, December). Quel look mon salik!. *Les Cahiers de la Fonderie, 15*, 42–46.
COLFEN. (2006). *Vivre clandestines*. Bruxelles: Agir Féministes.
Collins, P. H. (1999). *Black feminist thought: Knowledge, consciousness and the politics empowerment*. London: Harper Collins.

Crenshaw, K. W. (2005). Cartographies des marges: Intersectionalité, politique de l'identité et violence contre les femmes de couleur. In *Féminisme(s). Penser la pluralité* (pp. 51–82). Cahiers du Genre no 39. Paris: L'Harmattan.

Degavre, F., & Stoffel, S. (2008). La diversité des féminismes, une problématique à part entière. In F. Degavre (Ed.), *Diversité des féminismes* (pp. 7–34). Bruxelles: Université des Femmes.

Delperée, F., & Nols, J. (1958). Croissance démographique et croissance économique: Essai d'application à la région liégeoise. *Revue du Travail, 2,* 127–141.

Delphy, C. (2008). *Classer, dominer, Qui sont les "autres"?* Paris: La Fabrique.

Delruelle, E., & Torfs, R. (2005). *Commission du Dialogue Interculturel.* Bruxelles: INBEL.

Derriche, O. (2010, February). Danser dans le noir [Dancing in the dark]. *Politique, 63,* 41–43.

Eggerick, T., Poulain, M., & Kesteloot, C. (2002). *La population allochtone en Belgique. Recensement général de la population au 1er mars 1991* (Monographie no 3). INS.

Faux, J.-M. (2008, September). *Le "pluralisme confirmé" de la société belge.* Bruxelles: Centre Avec.

Fournier, L. (2008). Le féminisme musulman en Europe de l'Ouest: Le cas du réseau féminin de Présence musulmane. *Revue de Civilisation Contemporaine de l'Université de Bretagne Occidentale*, no spécial "Femmes et militantisme (Europe-Amérique, XIXe siècle à nos jours)." http://www.univ-brest.fr/amnis/documents/Fournier2008.pdf. Accessed January 10, 2010.

Gaspard, F., & Khosrokhavar, F. (1995). *Le foulard et la république.* Paris: La Découverte.

Guénif-Souilamas, N., & Macé, E. (2004). *Les féministes et le garçon arabe.* Paris: Editions de l'Aube.

Hamidi, M. (2006). Le féminisme musulman, un concept revendiqué et controversé. In Paroles de femmes, *Echos Bruxelles Laïque*, 19–21.

hooks, b. (1981). *Ain't I a woman. Black women and feminism.* London: Pluto Press.

Jacques, C. (2009). Le féminisme en Belgique de la fin du 19e aux années 1970. *Courrier hebdomadaire du* CRISP, no 2012–2013, 54p.

Jacques, C., & Piette, V. (2004). Féminisme et société coloniale au Congo belge (1918–1960). In P. Denis & C. Sappia (Eds.), *Femmes d'Afrique dans une société en mutation* (pp. 77–97). Louvain-La-Neuve: Academia Bruylant.

Jefferys, S., & Ouali, N. (2007). Trade unions and racism in London, Brussels and Paris public transport. *Industrial Relations Journal, 38*(5), 406–422.

Julémont, G. (2008). *Femmes Prévoyantes Socialistes. Des combats d'hier aux enjeux de demain.* Bruxelles: Femmes Prévoyantes Socialistes.

Kofman, E. (1999). Female 'birds of passage' a decade later: Gender and immigration in the European Union. *International Migration Review, 33*(2), 269–299.

Lacoste-Dujardin, C. (2008). *La vaillance des femmes. Les relations entre femmes et hommes berbères de Kabylie.* Paris: La Découverte.

Lefrancq, V. (2008, October-November). Diversité et problématiques communes. *Cahiers Marxistes, 238,* 141–145.

Lorcerie, F. (Ed.). (2005). *La politisation du voile en France, en Europe et dans le monde Arabe.* Paris: L'Harmattan.

Mabille, X. (1986). *Histoire politique de la Belgique.* Bruxelles: CRISP.

Martens, A. (1976). *Les immigrés. Flux et reflux d'une main-d'œuvre d'appoint.* Leuven: EVO-PUL.

Mohanty, C. T. (1988). Under western eyes: Feminist scholarship and colonial discourse. *Feminist Review, 30,* 61–88.

Morelli, A. (2004). L'immigration italienne en Belgique aux XIXe et XXe siècles. In A. Morelli (Ed.), *Histoire des étrangers et de l'immigration en Belgique, de la préhistoire à nos jours* (pp. 201–214). Bruxelles: Couleur livres.

Ouali, N. (2000). Affirmation de soi et sécularisation des identités musulmanes. In U. Manço (Ed.), *Voix et voies musulmanes de Belgique* (pp. 189–194). Bruxelles: Facultés universitaires Saint-Louis.

Ouali, N. (2007). *Femmes immigrées en Belgique: Les enjeux pour le mouvement des femmes*. Bruxelles: CEDIL.   http://www.faml.be/dossier-societe/item/49-femmes-immigrées-en-belgique-les-enjeux-pour-le-mouvement-des-femmes. Accessed January 13, 2010.

Ouali, N. (2008). *Migration et accès au marché du travail: les effets émancipateurs sur la "condition" des femmes issues de l'immigration*. Unpublished Ph.D. thesis. Université Libre de Bruxelles, Bruxelles.

Ouali, N. (2010). La lutte contre la domination de sexe, de classe et de race dans les mobilisations des femmes issues de l'immigration. In *Savoirs de Genre: Quel genre de Savoir, état des lieux des études de genre* (pp. 173–188). Bruxelles: Ed. Sophia.

Panciera, S., & Ducoli, B. (1976, January 23). Immigration et marché du travail en Belgique: Fonctions structurelles et fluctuations quantitatives de l'immigration en Belgique – période 1945–1975. *Courrier hebdomadaire du CRISP*, no 709–710.

Peemans-Poullet, H. (1991). *Femmes en Belgique (XIX – XX siècle)*. Bruxelles: Université des Femmes.

Plasman, D., & Pinchart, S. (2008, October-November). Les Femmes Prévoyantes Socialistes: Un projet féministe et laïc. *Cahiers Marxistes, 238*, 155–161.

Plateau, N. (2009). The women's movement and the challenge of interculturality: The case of French-speaking Belgium. In M. Franken, A. Woodward, A. Cabò, & B. Bagilhole (Eds.), *Teaching intersectionality. Putting gender at the centre* (pp. 79–87). Utrecht: ATHENA.

Platform of Secular Feminists. (2009, September 26). Féministes laïques contre l'interdiction du voile. *Le Soir*.

Raghuram, P. (2006). Gendering medical migration: Asian women doctors in the UK. In A. Agrawal (Ed.), *Migrant women and work* (pp. 73–94). New Delhi: Sage Publication.

Remy, M. (1990). *De l'utopie à l'intégration. Histoire du mouvement des femmes*. Paris: L'Harmattan.

Robert, F. (2007, Mars) Nous devons garder notre capacité d'indignation. Rencontre avec Hafida Bachir la nouvelle présidente de Vie féminine. http://www.enmarche.be/Societe/Social/gardons_capacite_indignation.htm.

S'jegers, S. (2008, October–November). Mouvement(s) des femmes en Flandre: Il est temps d'annoncer la couleur. *Cahiers Marxistes, 238*, 119–127.

Sassen, S. (2003). Géo-économie des flux migratoires. *Esprit, 300*, 102–113.

Scott, J. W. (2007). *The politics of the veil*. Princeton/Oxford: Princeton University Press.

SPF Emploi, Travail et Concertation sociale. (2008). *L'immigration en Belgique. Effectifs, mouvements et marché du travail*. Bruxelles: DG Emploi et Marché du Travail.

Tévanian, P. (2005). *Le Voile médiatique. Un faux débat: "L'affaire du foulard islamique"*. Paris: Raisons d'agir.

Van Robaeys, B., & Perrin, N. (2006). *La pauvreté chez les personnes d'origine étrangère en Belgique: un réel problème*. Bruxelles: Fondation Roi Baudouin.

Vercheval, J. (2008). Actions féministes en milieu ouvrier. In F. Degavre (Ed.), *Diversité des feminisms* (pp. 35–44). Bruxelles: Université des Femmes.

Vie Féminine. (2008, February 7). Nos revendications pour que les critères de régularisation tiennent mieux compte de la situation des femmes. *Communiqué de presse*. http://www.ciep.be/documents/Rev.V.F.08. pdf

Volpp, L. (2001). Feminism versus multiculturalism. *Columbia Law Review, 101*(5), 1181–1218.

Yuval Davis, N. (1997). *Gender and nation*. London: Sage Publications.

Chapter 7
Transgression into 'Hidden' Feminism: Immigrant Muslim Woman from India

Shweta Singh

7.1 Introduction

I propose a theoretical argument that transition into *immigranthood* has the potential to be a space for transgression into 'hidden' feminism for women. I argue that *"hidden"* feminism transcends social identity and group associations, that it overcomes the limitations of complex and multiple social group identities and its influence on the formation of women's identity and agency, both within the household as well as outside of it. My argument stems from the analysis of a single immigrant woman's narrative, and application of poststructuralist feminist thought[1] and the "identities of women framework" (Singh 2007a).

I present migration and the development of post- migration identity as a crossing over of multiple boundaries by women, including those of nation, religion, and gender (Noh 2003). The resultant negotiation of changes within these contexts (both the changes resisted and the changes desired by the immigrant woman) establishes a modified position of her as an individual within a group and by default, alters the construction of the group itself by her presence. As a migrant woman encounters the changing roles and expectations in the host society—in intimate relationships, with immediate family members, ethnic group, and with the larger community—the conception of womanhood changes as well; it does not remain static in one's life. Young

---

[1] Poststructuralist thought is an off shoot of the postmodern thinking and its application to textual or content analysis with an intent to highlight the absence of objectivity, critical review of writing itself (deconstruction), and discourse analysis to locate multiple sources of power. In doing so, the binaries and metanarratives are questioned and multiple perspectives are highlighted to question universal truths. Michael Foucault's work on linguistics has been most influential in this field (Gannon and Davies 2006, pp. 71–106).

S. Singh (✉)
Associate Professor, School of Social Work, Loyola University,
Chicago, IL, USA
e-mail: ssingh9@luc.edu

G.T. Bonifacio (ed.), *Feminism and Migration: Cross-Cultural Engagements*,
International Perspectives on Migration 1, DOI 10.1007/978-94-007-2831-8_7,
© Springer Science+Business Media B.V. 2012

first-generation immigrant women who belong to the middle class tend to have more engagement with mainstream culture (i.e., white) through food, clothing, entertainment, and opportunities for education and employment (Dasgupta 1998; Kurien 2005). Despite their social interactions with mainstream society, these young women face conflicting ideas and expectations between the host culture and their own. Such conflict results in personal strain and tensions in relationships, which leads to a process of self-reflection on the intersectionalities of social systems, particularly the status of individuals from marginalized communities. The process culminates in women identifying with new or evolved symbols of womanhood in a conscious effort to break from the old; thus becoming visible in narratives describing women's experiences in the host society, including those with members of the family, partner, ethnic group, and the changing perception of their own ability or agency in facing challenges anew.

I propose an *agentic* conceptualization of immigrant women even when they agree to the decisions made by others. Within the post migration phase, they take on multiple roles, maintaining their own ideas of self and identity while trying to integrate into host cultures (Mahalingam 2005). One of the key aspects of this agency is cultural continuity; the selection of cultural concepts that women execute as a way of grounding themselves and their family after the loss of direct, immediate, and continuous contact with native society. Another dimension of the execution of this agentic role as the primary person responsible for cultural continuity of the family is the divergence in interpreting the above contexts as (a) primary source of support or (b) an obstacle. The rest of the chapter examines these contentions through a single narrative.

This chapter is organized into three main sections. The first section discusses the complex social classification underlying the "immigrant Muslim Indian women" identity in the United States. Next is an examination of various feminist discourses that leads to or overlaps with some of the tenets of hidden feminism. Then the third section presents Nimmi, the woman who is the informant of the study narrative; and the analysis related to her positionality, relationship with her mother, her identity as American, Desi, and Muslim, including her marriage, and trajectories of self-realization. The chapter ends with a conclusion.

7.2   Immigrant Muslim Women from India

The classification of a "Muslim woman from India" contains three complex categorizations: Muslim, woman, and Indian. Grouped together, they imply an identity of marginalization and subjugation in numerous scholarships—a representation of identity subsumes with images of unjust treatment by the household, community, the larger society, as well as the state and associated institutions (Abusharaf 2006; Basu 2008; Yu 2010). This identity emerges from group associations of the individual: belonging to the Eastern-developing world instead of a Northern developed privileged region, being a woman in a patriarchal society, and being a member of the Muslim minority population in the face of a Hindu majority in India (Alam 2007). For Muslim women in India, national independence brought latent social inequality in the following areas: (a) by virtue of being a religious minority in the framework of the larger Hindu society of independent India; and (b) legally sanctioned inequality with men by the codification of Hindu women's rights under the Hindu Marriage Act of 1955, which made Hindu women legally equal to Hindu men, but excluded Muslim women (Subramanian 2010). Muslim women and their lives continued to function under *Shariat* (Sharia) laws—Muslim Personal Law (Shariat) Application Act, 1937 (Lateef 1990; Jones 2010). This illustrates the choices and conflicts between group identities, the choice of Muslim laws like The S*hariat* to maintain and address the perceived threat to Muslim identity, but, at the same time, hinder the formation of women's identity as equal to men within the community (Lateef 1990; Badran 2001; Salime 2008).

These contradictions embodying "Indian Muslim women" affect social movements working against the practice of *purdah* or social seclusion, which have not found universal support amongst Muslim women in India or in the United States (Bauer 2000; Vatuk 2008). It also highlights that Indian national independence created ambivalent realities among Muslim and Hindu women—freedoms ranging from economic to political for the citizens of India's new nation-state might have resulted in negative consequences for a population of Muslim women. Even though Muslim women participated extensively in the Indian women's movements and advocated for gender equality in the Indian Constitution, they have no legal equality, and made more oppressive by the overarching patriarchal character of the Indian society (Jones 2010). Patriarchy in Indian society is visible in practices such as abortion of female fetuses across rural and urban areas, dowry deaths, arranged marriages, falling sex ratio, gender-based wage inequality, female underemployment, rising incidence of sexual violence, dual roles as primary *caregiver* and *breadwinners*, and lower status of Indian women based on the Human Development Index (HDI)[2] (Singh and Jha 1992; Kantikar and Mistry 2000). However, the positioning of women along other social systems within and outside the Indian society mitigates or exacerbates their condition (Singh 2010a).

The consequences of introducing *immigrant* as another category into the identity of a "Muslim Indian woman" in the US adds yet another layer to her perceived lower status, reduced access to resources and relative powerlessness (Brems 1997). However, the complexity of intersectionality and its interpretation in understanding individuals, their choices, and motivations is apparent when we examine the

---

[2] Between 1980 and 2010, India's HDI for the whole population has risen by 1.6% annually from 0.320 to 0.519, which gives the country a rank of 119 out of 169 countries with comparable data. The Gender Inequity Index is a composite index measuring reproductive, labor, and empowerment outcomes for women, and India recorded 0.748 in 2010. This assessment include, maternal mortality rates of 450 per 10,000 women; percentage of population ages 25 or older that has attained secondary or higher education with female/male ratio of −0.528; adolescent fertility rate or birth per 1,000 to women between 15 and 119 years of age was 68.1; share in seats in parliament was .113. (UNDP, http://hdrstats.undp.org/en/countries/profiles/IND.html, accessed March 2011).

position of the individual on the axes of these different contexts and their individual meanings (Harnois 2008).

Women comprise a large part of the increasing Asian immigrant population in America (Reeves and Bennet 2004).[3] Asian women have significant variation in their levels of education, employment, and earnings (Camarota 2005). However, these differences have not been successful in eroding the homogenous conceptualization of Asian women as symbols of their native cultures, within institutional and community settings in the US. Asian women and their culture are considered static and are often cross-referenced for their lower status (Pyke and Johnson 2003). The archetypal Asian woman is perceived through an assortment of generalizations, such as submissive, dependent, and hard working (Kurien 2005). One of the reasons for these enduring prejudices is the fact that within the US, the advocacy of immigrant women's rights is in its natal stage and focuses more on domestic violence and legality of immigration status (Thomas 2000). Compounding the state level lethargy is the limited collective action undertaken by immigrant women groups from the Indian Subcontinent (Baruah 2004). While there are many instances of women's use of collective strategies to counter prejudice in native settings, such as advocacy against religious intolerance of women in leadership roles in Islamic societies (Nagar 2000; Jamal 2005) and movements for financial independence in Bangladesh and Pakistan (Ahmed 2004), there are fewer instances to exercise collective agency by immigrant women within the U.S. Reasons for this could include displacement and re-adjustments, fear of identifying with a *lesser* group, no common concerns among them (Pahl 2005), or simply the quest for a new, non-collectivist identity. These could also be the reasons why the overt declaration of feminist identity or thinking is not common in this group.

7.3   Treading with Postcolonial, Islamic, Cultural, and Global Feminisms: Hidden Feminism

"Hidden feminism" is a new site of individual engagement based on one's own negotiation of social structures and constraints. In exploring this subjective form of empowerment, I use different threads of feminist theoretical discourses that find similar tenets in "hidden feminism" of immigrant women—postcolonial, cultural, Islamic, and global feminisms.

Aafke Komter (1991), in her discussion on gender and power, states that feminism has a problem with poststructuralists as discourse analysis provides the freedom to interpret multiple meanings and multiple pathways to its creation, thus, making it difficult to create a single empowered identity. On the other hand, discourse construction is empowering as it identifies sources of power in the telling of the story as well as the experiencing of the events, thus building an argument for a non-static and non-generic

---

[3] According to the US Census in 2000, there were 20.6 million total numbers of Asian immigrants. In 2008, about 1.6 million immigrants were from India; of this number 45.2% were women (Terrazas and Batog 2010).

subject and subjectivity of woman and womanhood (Chow 2002). For instance, the narrative in my study identifies *family* as a source of powerlessness and *second husband* as the source of her power. However, these sources of her strength and weakness are not readily identifiable using simple frameworks of mainstream feminism or even the intersectionalities of social systems. Discourse deconstruction is likely the only source that allows the space for reconstructing multiple realities in keeping with poststructuralist feminist thought and its method of discourse analysis to draw out the hidden feminist psyche underlying a traditional social identity (Chowdhury 2005).

Christine Saulnier (1996) states that cultural feminism invoked women's traditional imagery as a symbol of power in reaction to comparisons to men in preceding liberal feminist thought with its denial of woman as a different social and biological entity (Brems 1997). Postmodern feminism finds oppression in modern structures; and poststructuralist see oppression in language, creating grounds for subjective constructions of reality and deconstruction of a single, unified objective reality, while, at the same time, identifying power as multifaceted and with multiple origins. Postmodernism and poststructuralism give credence and meaning to *positionality* and deconstruction, thus allowing the reconstruction of the position of weakness and strength for individuals outside or in opposition to the group (Parpart 1993). Therefore, these strands of thought facilitate the identification of hierarchy within smaller groups and provide power to the subject of study to present alternate realities.

Islamic feminism as one of the postmodern expressions of feminism refers to women who cite the teachings in the Quran and Islam as a source of women's rights. In doing so, they refute the modernist ideology that Islam is fundamentalist by nature and allocates women an essentialist subordinate and disempowered identity (Shah 2006). According to Bronwyn Winter (2001, p. 11), the discussion on Islamic identity has been embedded in *orientalist* despise and *multicultural* eulogizing; and the equally problematic *pluralistic* interpretation that draws from a "progressive interpretations of the Quran and the *hadiths*." Miriam Cooke (2000, p. 92) describes Islamic feminism as: "If feminism can be many changing states of consciousness, each reflecting women's understanding of themselves and their situations as related to their social and biological conditions, then it is not bound to one culture." Cooke propounds that feminism is no longer bound to any society and is not exclusive to women and their rights in a Western context; it is a quest and understanding for justice for all women. In keeping with cultural feminism, Islamic and Muslim feminist thought work with religion as a cultural system and create a legitimate space for them within it; this allows them to maintain their religious identity but expands its scope within the social group created by religious affiliations (Hatem 2006).

Global feminism is linked to globalization and problems that have been created from it or exacerbated by it, such as sex trafficking and increasing burden on women in the household (Jamal 2005; Conway 2008). To fight against the powerful structures of a globalizing world, feminists in developing and underdeveloped countries rallied around issues of mutual concern such as violence and health. Applying the premise of "culture and psyche integrating" under "global capitalism and media production" (McHugh 2004, pp. 575–576) feminist theory becomes the rallying point for transnational activism (Noh 2003). The exchange of people and products under the global capitalist economy with migration and transfer of production units has recreated the meaning of colonialism, racism, and neo-imperialism. This has contributed to raising new questions of epistemology and theory that will be meaningful culturally and psychologically to women from similar backgrounds living in diverse contexts; thus, making global feminism emerge as a unifying agenda that has meaning for more than one population and setting (Briggs et al. 2008).

It is difficult to allocate predefined meaning and effect sizes to cultural and material artifacts, global and local ideologies, and the process of social change in reference to women and probably other constituents of society (Hegland 2003; Jackson 2006). For instance, construction of gender does not imply *sameness*, within large groups such as class and religion, nor in smaller ones, like a village. This becomes apparent when the individual narrative and life history is closely examined (Mack-Canty 2004). It is important to respect and provide latitude to the "pre-existing inequities and conditions—cognitive, emotional, and material" (Hughes 2002, p. 594) in developing theoretical propositions that explain phenomena and analytical method that aims to represent realities. This respect and space is difficult in theorizing for large groups, but is easier when dealing with individuals. Hidden feminism, as proposed in this chapter, attempts to depict feminism as lived in practice but remains unarticulated in theory. Small rather than bigger decisions reflect its practice and are visible in family as well as individual outcomes. Bound in individual concerns, practiced only within familiar spaces, such as home or a relationship, with goals only for self, hidden feminism is an individualistic paradigm. Hidden feminism draws from the realm of postcolonial, Islamic, cultural, and global feminisms as it deconstructs modernity and ethics of modern structures; it supports the efforts of maintaining distinct and enabling religious and cultural identity; it accepts that globalization is bringing about changes across the world and influencing gender relations and expectations at micro levels.

In order to ground the ideals into the practical context of social work and intervention, hidden feminism utilizes the identities of women framework and its interdisciplinarity. This means that, "The *identities of women* framework is built around women's construction of self within contexts of individual relevance and does not predetermine the importance or scope of any single context to women's identity and exercise of agency" (Singh 2010a, p. 210). The identities of women framework (Singh 2007a, b, 2010a, b) enables discussion of women's identity formation and agency through the concreteness of the social systems that drive, restrict, and determine the nature of identity and agency manifestation. An immigrant Muslim woman and her complex group associations are an appropriate case study to examine the applicability of the hidden feminism paradigm.

7.4 Nimmi's Narrative

Nimmi Akhtar is a 45-year-old immigrant Muslim woman living with her second husband and five children in the middle-class suburbs of Chicago. She is a first generation immigrant who moved to Chicago with her family, comprised of her parents and younger siblings in 1970. Her parents were of lower middle class who moved from a traditional city of Hyderabad in India to Chicago. She was first married at the age of 16 and has 2 children from her first marriage. She was divorced from her first husband after 12 years, citing a history of differences. She was married to her second husband a couple of years later; he was an office colleague, and she eventually fell in love with him. He was not from her religion; a Hindu man from India who now lived as an immigrant in the US. I met Nimmi at a few social gatherings prior to our interview in August of 2009. My impressions of Nimmi prior to the interview were formed in very limited spaces and interactions. I perceived her as an extrovert and someone who exudes "high energy." Nimmi's narrative is ideal in exploring hidden feminism because she is a first generation immigrant who came into the US along with her family; and is living the dual exposure of her own culture and the host culture while faced with multiple and overlapping systems—i.e., school, family, community, marriage—each carrying tensions that simultaneously become a part of her life.

Nimmi's narrative was part of a small narrative study with six participants that used snowball and purposive sampling method focused on immigrant women from India between the ages of 30 and 45, who could read and write comfortably in the English language. The interview with Nimmi was recorded and later transcribed. The data was collected using a semi-structured interview guide, which provided a uniform structure to individual narratives. Narratives are used to recapture and represent events in the distant or immediate past and link the narrators' reflections of events within a timeframe (Cortazzi 1993). Personal narratives are useful in bringing out the differences in experiences and expression between women living in the same social contexts because each narrative revolves around different set of factors that women consider salient to their identities.

Nimmi had the open-ended interview guide with her for about 2 weeks. She mentioned that she had been thinking about the questions and was "wondering if she would be able to answer some of them," but when we were talking she realized that "she had all these thoughts in her … just waiting to be asked." In keeping with her starting comments, the narrative and the process of participating in the interview, Nimmi appeared to be creating a space; to understand her self through the process.

This section presents the key themes from the narrative using a holistic qualitative data analysis approach (Lieblich et al. 1998). This entailed examining the key phenomenon in the narrative and the concepts of identity and agency transformation through them as perceived by the narrator. The analysis is used to generate relational links and examine the "how" and its relevance to the current contexts (Moen 2006). Nimmi's story has been organized according to the key contexts as interpreted through the narrative analysis (Cortazzi 1993; Lieblich et al. 1998). It starts with the "positioning of self" by Nimmi as a connector through her other contexts. This is followed by a discussion of her relationship with her mother, "being Desi vs. being an American," and "being a Muslim" as contexts for framing her self and her agency. As the final context, Nimmi shares the meaning of "redefining marriage."

7.4.1 Positioning of Self

Nimmi describes herself as "an energetic, vibrant, social, exciting, full-of-life person." The primary contexts of identity that emerged from her narrative were that of an American and her role relationships—a daughter, a wife, a mother, and a Muslim. Nimmi identifies herself as American, her parents as Indian, and her first husband as Pakistani. "My country, I consider America, my parents' country was India, and then there is a third country now involved, which is Pakistan, which has a totally different culture, different etiquettes than India itself. So, it was quite interesting." According to Nimmi, her family was "the first generation immigrants, I would say early '70s is when we arrived here and I was like, maybe, three years old when we started our life here." In Nimmi's narrative, the self is centered in the context of parents and the larger family.

> So, my family included my mom, my dad, my grandmother who is the dictator at that time with the old ways, and then my mom's side, which is her sister, and her brother-in-law and then their daughters. So, that was our entire family. Believe me, that was enough. That was like fifty people right there. You really didn't need to socialize anymore! You have someone over, you have like fifty over. Those were the parties that we used to have, just with families.

She frequently mentions her mother and father as alternate contexts for positioning her self, but her siblings are mentioned only twice, once in reference to her mother having more children: "My mom was managing me and then she ended up having a couple of kids afterwards." Subsequently she mentions her siblings in reference to her own schooling experience.

> It was very difficult when I repeated my kindergarten, my brother joined me, cause we all are one year apart, except for my youngest one. It was a huge gap; I don't know what happened with my parents at that time. What possessed to have one more child after three in a row?

Nimmi focuses on both her achievements and her appearance in cognizance of self. The social recognition of self as a physically attractive and, logically, a desirable woman is very important to her. Her own attention to body image seems similar to other women. Studies refute the claim that White women are more likely to be concerned with negative body image as compared to Asian women (Grabe 2006). The mixed findings might be due to the underexplored dimensions of individual contexts for beauty and body among women from Asia and India.

> Like I said, who would wanna befriend a girl who has oil in her hair with two braids with big bows? I looked like a cartoon! So, I really didn't have any friends growing up through fourth grade. . . I always thought that I looked good. I always thought I looked clean, though I had oil in my hair, I showered everyday, I wore clean clothes everyday. These people just look nasty! So, I would never associate with any Indian people because I always had that image that they were and I knew the Patel brothers.

Nimmi's focus on the physical appearance could also be an attempt at trying to create a visible difference between herself and the other "nasty" looking Indians. The imagery of Indians as nasty looking might be a reflection of Nimmi being a discernible minority and her community of reference being non-Indians in her neighborhood and school. The perception of ethnic groups, especially women including South Asian women, in the mainstream popular media and institutions in the 1980s might have been narrower and even more "*othering*" experience than the NBC sitcom *Outsourced*.[4] In other words, the western depiction of beauty and looks has been critiqued in feminist literature as being "white and blond" and "thin and seductive," while South Asians are *Mehndi, nose ring bearing*, sexual objects of fetish (Durham 2001). These representations have been analyzed as influential in creating body imaging in American Diaspora (Sengupta 2006; Dunkel et al. 2010). There is another aspect of this disassociation that is related to the construal of self as different across cultures: the Asian collective emphasizes interdependence and interconnectedness while the Western leans towards establishing the uniqueness and difference of self from the group (Markus and Kitayama 1991). Nimmi might be in this way embracing both the difference from her own community and the similarity with the visible "white" culture.

The identified contexts for Nimmi's positioning of self highlight her choices and ability of making these choices that are most relevant to self even if these are sites of struggle intertwined with the larger socio-political context. The awareness of self as an agentic form is the roots of hidden feminism—that remains purposeful even though it is not confrontational to work towards framing self within what the individual perceives as the most enabling context. In doing so, she links the postcolonial realization of Western bias and identifies cultural sources that facilitate the mechanisms for negotiating one's self with the larger collective.

7.4.2 Relationship with Mother

Nimmi's narrative identifies her mother as a context from who she wants to separate herself and her identity. In her entire narrative, Nimmi wants to acknowledge her mother only in contrast to her self-image and identity. For instance, she constructs herself as a learner and wants to belong in the host culture, compared to her mother whom she portrays as "staying- in-the- house," meeting only her relatives, and not even able to drive. She does not allocate much agency or elements of *doing* to her mother; even in describing the birth of more children. She describes her mother as having "ended up with two more kids"; and "managed me" to refer to her mother's role as the primary caregiver in Hyderabad while her father was in the United States. Nimmi's narrative disassociates her mother from being an active decision maker in both conditions, i.e. childbirth and caregiver.

---

[4] *Outsourced* was a TV sitcom from September 23, 2010 to May 12, 2011. It was a work place comedy revolving around a call center of a customer services operation of a US entertainment company in India managed by a 'White' American Todd. The show poked fun at the typecast 'ugly Americanism' that was culturally insensitive and obviously racist even as it presented the contrived realities of Indian workers framed in an ambiguous social commentary on the phenomenon of outsourcing of work from the US to India (Walker 2010).

Nimmi does not seem to understand her mother's orientation and personality, but makes notes of different aspects of her mother's limitations that made her life difficult in the United States. She said, "my mom didn't know any English at all." Her inabilities are linked to the challenges that Nimmi feels she had to face in her life.

> [...] My mom couldn't drive . . . She couldn't speak English. It was very tough for me to even stay on after a Math club, only if I had my transportation, the bus ride home, was I allowed to do that.
> Oh, the microwave, my mom, growing up, my mom was one of those people that she had to keep up with the [trends]. She had to have the number one thing at the number one time, immediately. When the first show comes out in the movie, she would be the first person there 'cause it's the first show first day and the first person to see it. That's how she was in the appliances and everything that came out like a microwave.

Nimmi articulates her resentment of a number of these limitations and her mother's decision not to learn English, not to drive, or buying a microwave without reading about how to use it. Nimmi allocates the same kind of agency to her mother as she does herself. Her interpretation of her mother's actions is not cognizant or forgiving of the adjustment process to a new country, with limited schooling, and conflicting social and cultural values that contributed to her limited choices. In studies of intergenerational continuity to maintain ethnic identity, women are responsible for maintaining the home country's culture (Dasgupta 1998). From one generation to the next, there is considerably more biculturalism and more resistance to maintaining rigid ethnic identities and maternal control, which often leads to mental health issues like depression in second-generation women (Verghese and Jenkins 2009). In Nimmi's expression, the differences in the level of integration and assimilation between her mother and herself appear to be their choices as an outcome of changing gender roles, economic status, and age at migration. Interestingly, this represents Nimmi's biases toward her mother. Because her mother is the authority figure in the household, Nimmi finds it difficult to identify the structural issues behind her choices.

> At the age of five, we didn't know the language; we didn't know the dressing code. So, my mom would send me in my native attire. Yes, the salwar kurtas (native dress) and the two [braids] with the tail and everything; with the whole nine yards. So, that's how I went to school.

Nimmi highlights the paradox about her mother who is trendy in buying material things, but was unwilling to let go of cultural artifacts like oiled braids as a hairstyle.

> So, growing up, I didn't really see anybody else growing through the same thing I did, probably because my mom wasn't very social. She only hung around the family that she had. Now, she realizes that she should have branched out to other Indian families and what not, because they were much more embracing, I think, of the American culture than my family was.

Nimmi seems socially confined, largely due to her mother limiting her social network to her ethnic community, particularly her extended family. She contends that her mother's lack of exposure to mainstream society was the primary reason that led to her early marriage.

[…] because of the fact that she [mother] didn't have the exposure, that fear (Americanism) kept on growing and growing. So, at the age of ten, is when she started looking for someone for me to marry.

Her mother's approach to parenting was very different from Nimmi. For her mother, daughters were a source of worry and her primary concern was to get them married.

My mom had two girls, and for her, it was like oh my God! Since I was a girl, they just kept on saying "How we gonna get her married? When should we start looking?"

Nimmi implies that her mother expressed dissatisfaction with their preferred men (Muslim and Indian or Pakistani) not selecting her, and expresses frustration that her mother did not understand that they rejected her because she was a child.

For the love of God, I'm like 10–11 years old, and these people were like 27! Naturally, they would say no like normal human beings. What they gonna do? Tied me like a rattle around the legs or what? The ankle? Just a little toy? So, naturally, they were saying no because I was very young. My mom didn't get it still.

Finally, when her father asked her to marry a doctor from Pakistan who was studying medicine in America, she said yes even though her mother tried to prevent it as he was likely to be rigid and a poor fit with Nimmi's temperament. However, Nimmi was frustrated with her mother and preferred her father's choice.

So, they somehow got the picture and my mom ended up showing me the picture and she's like this is the guy! Do you really want to do this? He had a beard like down to here. This is a Muslim guy from Pakistan . . . When a Muslim guy has a dark spot over here . . . indicates . . . they pray five times a day . . . are very, very strict. So, my mom showed me the picture, she goes, do you really want to marry this guy? He won't let you wear makeup. He won't let you do this. He won't let you do that. I said, "But dad is saying this is what's best for me." "Oh, your dad doesn't know anything. Why don't we get someone a little bit more high-flying, a little bit more fashionable, because that's what you are" I looked at her and I said, "You know what, mom . . . " I didn't really trust my mom's judgment at the point; because she had prodded me and paraded me around so much that I was just like enough with her. This is the first time my dad approached me on something. So, I looked at my dad and I looked at my mom, to dad, I said, "I trust your judgment. Do what you need to do."

In reference to her parenting, Nimmi uses her mother as an example of what she is today and what parenting should be. Nimmi's embracing of her domestic role appears in contrast to her mother and not the typical stepping away from a "doing" gender perspective, in a radical feminist interpretation of housework (Fox and Murray 2000). The meaning of home, household and housekeeping have been examined to support the feminist interpretation of the hours and type of women's labor at home. The positioning of identity in reference to home has been mostly considered a symbol of patriarchal social system (Lau 2006). Inequities in division of labor in the household have been highlighted in gender studies and feminist scholarship. For example, Scott Coltrane (2010, p. 791) revisits some of her earlier arguments to discuss both paid and unpaid labor within and outside the household in the same space, and to examine household labor in the context of social structure of the household, family relationships, and the market. The explanations for her mother's limited association with household work might be explained in part by the joint family structure; Nimmi's grandmother lived in the household and their extended family lived close by. On the other hand, Nimmi's own explanation of her caregiving and housework is embedded in both narrative of love and the market economy, in which she does not hold a paid job. According to Coltrane, the explanations of domestic labor continuing to be a woman's burden need theoretically complex and methodologically integrated research where the meso and macro environmental and individual factors need to be identified, conceptualized, and measured to understand this phenomenon. Greer Litton Fox and Velma McBride Murry (2000), in their critique of family studies, identify the need to incorporate more socio- political context in situating families within their broader social environment, and the role of covert and overt power in the division of household labor and caregiving work. Nimmi's description of her household position should be seen in reference to her second marriage and lack of paid employment. The meaning of home and housework seems more complicated as a site for unpaid labor, which is similar to migrant woman being depicted as a site for cheap labor in highly regulated economic systems that monitors wage and work structure (Shi 2009).

> It's not in my cousins or my aunts like my mom used to be when we used to come home, nobody was home. Food was always made. Fresh food was always made. My grandma used to be home, but my mom was never home. She's always across the street with my cousins. Me, I'm home. I realize that's my job. I'm a stay-at-home mom, what do I do? I'm here to see them. I'm here to warm up food for them, talk to them, tell them hey, how was your day? What did you do? What happened?

The insistence on differences between her mother and Nimmi consistently highlights the important role played by her mother in the formation of her identity: a contrast and oppositional. The patriarchal normative does not rise above her preference towards her father and his opinion. The post-structuralist realm of non-normative ideology that stakes its "commitments to continual contestation, disruption" appear visible in Nimmi's narrative (Nash 2002, p. 416) and add credence to hidden sources of power and the ability of discourse analysis to unearth them.

7.4.3 Being American vs. Being Desi

A *Desi* means someone from the same country and is loosely used to describe people from India, Pakistan, and Bangladesh living in the US Being *Desi* is mixed-up in Nimmi's cognition of identity. Family, Indian, community, and *Desi* are interchangeable terms in Nimmi's association with her Indian origins. In addition, unlike her negative references of her mother, these references of her Indian identity are diverse and appear more confusing to negotiate.

> [...] The difficulties I think my parents had while growing up is how much do you let your child assimilating to the environment without losing your religious and your cultural beliefs. What I have found based on that fear; they went on the extreme of being very strict. So, the way I had it, nice childhood, I was surrounded by lots of cousins and family, while I really didn't have a lot of interactions with the *goras*, *goras* meaning the American people.

Though I was practically short of three years, born and raised here, I am an American by all means and standards. However, there's always that distinction the white people and then us. I wasn't assimilated in the US either. If you really look at me, I don't really fit very well into *gora* (white) crowd, the Americans nor do I really fit into the Desi crowd, the one that has just recently started to come influx.

Again, the juxtaposition of being "an American by all means and standards" is followed by "there's always that distinction, the white people and then us." In addition, Nimmi notes that her interaction with the *goras* (Whites) was limited because her cousins and family surrounded her. Nimmi interprets Americanism in a consistently positive light: "[…] [parents] never really went into the details, the processes, the procedures of the *gora* way, the American way. Everything was like fast, fast." The "details and (right) procedures" with being American, while not reading instruction manuals and doing things in a hurry and unplanned was Indian. She talks about her parents not knowing how to use the microwave and taking her for her engagement to a Muslim holy city of Mecca but unaware that menstruating girls are not allowed to the pilgrimage. Nimmi seems very clear in her belief that the norm should be the American way. This is well illustrated in the discussion of dating:

Normal tendency in high school, those are the years parents kinda give you the freedom to kinda test the water and see and explore. Dating is allowed. That's what Americans do. That's the normal thing to do is to allow you to date, to have you develop the skills to see if you like someone. Are they good? Are they a good person or what you like, what you don't like whether be with dating, whether be with clothing, whether be with foods. Social exposure, anything like that. Activities also add to your social skills. I had none of that. Everything that I acquired was on my own by looking and observing.

Early on in the narrative, Nimmi identifies her parents' fear of becoming acculturated to the American way of life. She reemphasizes her parents' behaviors as being motivated by fear of "Americanization" a number of times during the interview. According to Nimmi, the meaning of girl and girlhood in the *Desi* Indian society is a burden.

That's something that is much different in my childhood versus the other children that grew up around me, the people I had in Islamic school. Most of the people that grew up with me from the Islamic school, all have arranged marriages. I would say good 85 percent of them have arranged marriages because that was the good-nice-Indian-girl way to do it, to marry whom your parents look up or find.

She compares her own experience of having a girl child, which exemplifies the difference between her and *Desi*.

I think in the Indian culture . . . a girl born in nuclear family itself is a big thing because it seems to be more of a burden. Now that I've grown up, I realize that that was stupid [whispered]. I've got a girl myself but I'm so happy that I've got a girl. They are just so much more sensitive, so much more cuddly and much more caring in nature. Not that my boys aren't.

It was difficult to assimilate in the mainstream American society as the Indian community was very small and hence conspicuous as *Desi* immigrants in Chicago. Difficulty in accessing ethnic groceries or Hindi movies was a case in point:

At that time, in the early 70s, there were very, very few Indians . . . Patel Brothers opening up . . . was the only Indian store. It was on Devon that we would go and travel to . . . to get our groceries. Now . . . there's any [number of] Desi store, Indian store where you can get groceries and your ingredients and what not. I remember the first VHS cassette of Indian movie. The VHS itself was like $890 or something. It was a big deal because parents talked about it. Each cassette that you rented for an Indian movie was $10. Can you imagine $1 DVD now versus a $10 cassette.

Learning the English language and the culture is a big step in Nimmi's identity formation as a way of being socially recognized by her peers, for example, at school. She ridicules her predicament and that of her siblings due to her parents' insistence that they learn their native language. Now, however, she appreciates her grasp of her native language of Hyderabadi Urdu.

Growing up here [USA] was very different because when we came, my mom didn't know any English at all. My dad did, obviously, because he was educated here as well. They were very bent upon us learning the [native] language so that's all they spoke to us in. So, when we entered into kindergarten, to our dismay, nobody else spoke the language. So, it was just absolutely wonderful that we didn't know the language. So the teachers and us [we] would be talking in signs, I remember that in kindergarten, specifically. That was very difficult. It was so difficult that I never said this to anybody; not anybody knows this . . . The fact is, I had to repeat kindergarten because the first year that we were here, we knew none of the alphabets!

"I was at the top of my class," Nimmi confides. Losing a year in repeating kindergarten was not a big issue. Her pride is apparent in all her academic accomplishments, learning the English language, making "A" grades as an excellent student:

I think in fifth grade, I realized what grades meant. Laurina Cruz, I will never forget her . . . little girl that inspired me in fifth grade to shoot for As. I remember we got our report cards in fourth grade, everybody was like what did you get? . . . Really, I didn't have many friends because like I said . . . I looked like a cartoon! . . . grades, that that's something important. That's something everybody's looking up to. Laurina Cruz always gets the attention. Guess what? She's gonna have some competition next year and sure enough, in sixth grade, I was her toughest competition. Because I was getting the higher grade, I was being noticed. Not for my two braids with oil, but for the fact that I was an honor student now. I was getting all A [grade]s. So, I was known and I was always the one who first raised my hand (before) the rest in studies. So, that's when I made my mark in my early childhood. That's what I remember and that carried on through middle school.

Nimmi's narrative includes meeting her first *gora* friend:

[…] Her name is Kathy . . . and she is just an amazing human being, both husband and wife. My first *gora* friend. Literally, my first *gora* friend and I made that friend after I had two children.

I interpret this section of her narrative as her conscious choice of selecting "being American" as the more enabling context for positioning her self, and as a better fit for the exercise of her agency. It also afforded her some form of social recognition in the American mainstream society that had been her goal. She feels that meeting a "White" friend is a criterion for being considered part of mainstream society, and that she was able to accomplish it only after she had given birth to two children. Thus, she eventually accomplished her goal of being a part of "mainstream America" but it took much longer than it should have.

So, the joke around the entire organization is the "Wrath of Akhtar." If you do not follow the processes and procedures that Nimmi has laid down, you will suffer the wrath of Akhtar. I was a very, very aggressive person and I climbed up the ladder when I was working very, very fast because of my energetic and go-getting personality. That's who I was, but I didn't realize it. Isn't that funny?

While married to her first husband, Nimmi reflects on herself in the context of mainstream society, school, and work, but, interestingly, not her family or first marriage. She finds her *Desi* roots as exemplified in her first marriage: "I was so down deep, bottomless pit of self-esteem, [it] was like so low." Or, the time when her family were finding a groom for her at the age of 10:

When my dad sent down (for) me [and] said, "There's this proposal. What do you think?" Being the goody-two-shoes that I was, the straight A [s]student and listened to everything they (parents) had said, all I had asked them is enough, I don't want to be prodded in front of people, to be dressed and made a big deal out of it, and the rejection. Not having them call back and whatever.

Nimmi identifies the centers of powers in her life: husband, father, and culture. Their control comes from the same sources that inhibited her exercise of agency due to gendered expectations at home and the ethnic community—the patriarchal expectations of femininity and womanhood. Patriarchy is the exercise of power and control of men over women by constructing acceptable gender norms in society; the family is its primary institution for training women to follow the roles of daughter, marriage, and mothering (Bhasin 1993, 2003). The identification of men as sources of power and culture as the measure of conformity adds to the existing substantial body of work that discusses patriarchy in societies like India. Sonalde Desai and Leste Andrist (2010) discuss marriage as a site for gender reproduction given that dowry, age of marriage, and kinship prominence in marriage-related decision making are factors that contribute to continued gendered constructions of marriage. Inherent with this discussion is the feminist take on sexuality and its control as key aspects of patriarchy, including the selection of age of marriage at the onset or before puberty (Abraham 2001).

The extension of patriarchal set up in families post migration to U.S. is also a well-documented fact that is highlighted through the sporadic instances of honor killing and domestic violence in immigrant families (Ahmad et al. 2009; Yu 2010). Farha Ahmad and colleagues (2009), in their study of victims of domestic violence, propose that the increased dependence upon the family and limited access to the community and social support as reasons for continuance of patriarchal practices in South Asian families. The overarching influence of discrimination originating in experiences and identity associated with ethnicity, race, and class make gender itself secondary in populations of migrant women (Smith and Mannon 2010). According to Yu Shi (2009), the construction of patriarchy, tradition, and femininity undergo reconceptualization due to the influence of globalization and the new status as marginalized immigrants who need to fall back on their "culture" as a form of strength and community in host cultures.

In this context, hidden feminism adds to the transnational and postfeminism discourse with reference to this population of *immigrant, Indian, Muslim woman* (Noh 2003). Of necessity, this is a complicated context, given the old and the new norms and institutions and their processes that are modified relative to each of the categories that a woman locates herself in. The neoliberal and consumerist sensibilities that are framed on the continuum of opposition, sympathy, and identification with ethnic groups complicate the process by which choices and subjectivities are formed (Butler and Desai 2008).

7.4.4 Being Muslim

Being Muslim is an important part of Nimmi's identity today. She has developed it in keeping with what she believes is right and states "then I had to do it their way, today, I do it according to what I believe is the right way to do it." She has negotiated with herself the space and relationship as a Muslim (Chakraborty 2009). At the onset, it was again her parents' fear of "Americanization" that motivated them to push her into attending an Islamic school, where she made really good friends. Nimmi also discusses her conversation with God when she was at *Kaba*, the holy place for Muslims, to marry the doctor her father had selected for her.

> Anyway, we ended up going there and I had to sit on the side. Here I am, looking at God. I really believe in faith. I have very, very strong faith because we were constantly exposed to Islamic religion stuff, which I still do to this day, but then, I had to do it according to their way; today, I do it according to what I believe is the right way to do it. So, sitting there in the Kaba. I was looking at the Kaba, it was beautiful! It was just the best time in my entire life, so peaceful! It was just beautiful! I'll never forget it and I sat there and I prayed. I said, "I don't know what's going on. You know what's going on. So, please just take care of me. Make sure he doesn't beat me, he's not a drunkard and if he's religious, I don't mind. I don't mind because I love you and I want to embrace You."

But she distinguishes her practice of religion from that of her parents:

> I've never once said to [my children] that if you talk to a girl, it's a sin or if you talk to a boy, it's a sin. I've never actually put religion in them and that's a bad thing too because that's important part of my life. My faith is very important to me, but I didn't want them to be restricted by that . . . So, now I've started at the age of thirteen, I would say, two or three years ago, when I learned that my parenting skills had to go to the other two. That's when I started kinda feeding in the religious part to them slowly, not the way my parents did.

She has a liberal attitude compared to her parents; that is demonstrated in her allowing her Muslim daughter to sleep over in a Hindu house. Religion seems to have more meaning in her life as her present husband is a Hindu. However, religious differences tend to be the primary reason for arguments in her present marriage.

> So, it's very, very different. I think the Hindus and the Muslims always stay away from each other . . . Now, I married into the family, for God's sake. Once was a taboo, here I'm living the life. I'm living the taboo.

Overall, Nimmi views religion in this way:

> [...] Look at what your religion teaches you. Your religion teaches you to live amongst everybody in harmony and what can you take that's good and positive . . . Evil is all around us! God damn it, go back home. Don't live here then. You made conscious decision to be here. I made a conscious decision to live here and be an American. So, therefore, my

children will be American Muslims. It's together. It's not one before the other. I can say Muslim Americans, I can say American Muslims; it doesn't make a difference.

Religion is an important dimension in the lives of many immigrants as a "vehicle in their community formation and identity re-composition" (Mohammad-Arif 2005, p. 67). The increased role of organized religion and religious- based organizations being active in the Indian Subcontinent is another reason why the importance of religion in the lives of South Asian Muslim immigrants has grown. In examining the development of a religious identity, Aminah Mohammad Arif (2005) draws upon her research with three generations of Muslim women; she traces a pathway of conformity and Americanism and rebellion against immigrant parents followed by a quest for self during college and a slow embracing of the religious and multicultural identity. According to Mohammad-Arif (2005), the first generation immigrants become more religious after the birth of children as a way of maintaining their identity. John R. Bowen explicates (2004, p. 879), this is a possibility as the practice and increased identification with Islam among immigrant groups is a continuation of their search for self in *global public space* and is increasingly plural. He adds, "Islam complicates current lines of transnational analysis by emphasizing its own universal norms and its practices of deliberating about religious issues across national boundaries and in need of transnational" (Bowen 2004, p. 880).

7.4.5 Redefining Marriage

Nimmi lived with so many personal and social constraints with her first husband, a Muslim. She finally realized the unbearable living conditions with her Muslim husband and the contradictions within her. She quotes her friend who visited her at home during her first marriage: "Nimmi . . . you were very different. You were waiting for him hand and foot. That's not you!" She believed she was unprepared for this marriage, to someone she found "doesn't even have proper social etiquettes . . . I had to develop those." Then the conflict between three cultures—Pakistani, Indian, and American—was complex. Nimmi states:

> […] because I was immersed in all Pakistani people. There's no Indian people at all. They are all Pakistanis. They are not Indians. So, that in itself was all different and not to mention this person dying inside of me, which was more American than Pakistani, or more Indian than Pakistani, so imagine all that! It was very chaotic. It was very tough, tough time in my life.

Nimmi considered her first marriage as a time for growing up; the second marriage as her space for finally having fun. Nimmi's first marriage was arranged to a man from the same religious background, and from the neighboring country of Pakistan. The first marriage lasted for 7 years. She married her second husband 2 years later. Even though she had survived after her divorce without support from her family, she credits her second husband with helping her find herself. Nimmi gives him credit for showing her a newer life that was more in harmony with what she thought of herself.

> […] It was amazing! For the first time in my life, I thought I didn't even realize how many feelings I have inside in me. All this wonderful stuff that he exposed me to … So, he made me realize as a person, who I am, what I am, the purpose of me and the purpose I have with my children, but I was having so much fun with him.

She expressed her feelings of being a good mother to her two children from her first marriage only after she became an *individual* and created an identity for herself. In her own words, in 1997, when she took the decision to leave her husband, was when she felt better able to understand *parenting* as a concept, too.

> I think it's because of that generation having that belief that you can't assimilated into this environment. Our generation will extinct. My question for them today is why bring us here? Why did you leave your country and bring us here and subject us to all of this. That's my question.

7.5 Trajectories of Self Realization

Nimmi Akhtar's narrative highlights the importance of ascertaining the contexts of the socio-psychological environment and their potential for providing the space for identity realization. It emphasizes the need for developing relevant questions about age and culture. In other words, disaggregating further the binary typologies of young and old, Muslim and Hindu into smaller, intersecting, and overlapping contexts will be able to elicit truer responses and meaningful knowledge to inform important concepts like identity and agency. The thematic organization of Nimmi's narratives present outright rejection of the context provided by her mother; the confusing association of the context of her *Desiness,* her Indian culture; the negotiated, reflective, and controlled context of her marriage and her religion; and the complete acceptance and centering of her identity around the context of being an American.

For Nimmi, the realization of who she is and what she wants appears to have found space very early on in her childhood. Being exposed to alternate forms of selfhood and the experience of being uprooted from her cultural roots through migration, after which she was denied the space which would allow her to explore and be any of the possible selves that she craved generated conflicts—the consequent reflection on her positioning and location within the different social systems of family, school, community, and the larger American society. Her reflections demonstrate the contradictions between her own aspirations and actual experiences. The process of reflection by itself is a tool to create a perception of control over her life, which makes it easier to live with her choices, many, contradicts with what she really want to be or do with her life. For instance, Nimmi continued to prioritize the contexts of family, and being a "good" person as perceived in her cultural contexts of *girlhood, Indianhood,* and *Muslimhood*; but she was able to fulfill her aspirations for social recognition by expressing an American identity through the contexts of school and work.

Embracing a preferred identity that was in opposition to her perception of her mother's identity and the construction of doing and being as *agentic* is how she expresses her hidden feminism. It highlights the role of differences within the same group, and particularly among women living in the same household. In the Indian Subcontinent, the role of older women (i.e. mother-in-laws, mothers, and grand-mothers) in the life of younger women is complex. The underlying tension between them emanates from the power of older women within households and in the community. Traditional female power comes from being feminine in performing tradi-tional roles and responsibilities; a change in the process implies a change in household configurations of power and authority. Older women feel threatened about being usurped in the pathways to empowerment; any change raises questions about the validity of cultural gender role positions. Thus, in the same household, women seek different pathways for empowerment, in reference to their positional-ity and location (Singh 2007a, 2010a). In another work, I raised this comment:

> Kandiyoti (1988) suggests that women in East and South East Asian and African Sub Saharan communities engage in "patriarchal bargaining" to maintain their existing power in the household. Even then, interpretations of power processes drawn from a single social system as represented by a household can be misleading. (Singh 2010a, p. 174)

Nimmi's difficulty in identifying with being an Indian could stem from the fact that her only references for *Desi* seem to be her extended and immediate family; a context that she believes hindered her identity and agency. The absence of immi-grant culture in "mainstream America," described as Christian, White, and to a cer-tain extent, Black America, in the cultural artifacts and social institutions such as media or politics, could have compounded the marginalized status of her *Desi* group identity. In contrast, Nimmi's experience of academic achievement within the schools provided the scope for identity realization and strengthened her affiliation to her American identity (Rodriguez 2007). In this case, stereotyping forces a col-lective identity as Asian, its invisibility in mainstream communities and the conun-drum of choosing an identity between the two primary races of being Black or White in America, as illustrations of discrimination and prejudice against immi-grants (Dhingra 2004). However, women's experiences with discrimination vary based on their position in society along different demographic continuums, such as age group and education level (Marshall et al. 1998). For instance, young women in colleges feel discriminated against by males from their own community if they ven-ture into cross-cultural dating (Saint Louis et al. 2000). In Nimmi's case, the dis-crimination came from within her family and the larger ethnic group, since her goal was to identify more with the American mainstream society. Gender by itself might not be that crucial now in American culture but Nimmi perceives gender as the pri-mary context of discrimination against her within her family.

Nimmi's location along the class continuum raises this question: Does the same process of identity formation happens when one is in the lower class and does not have the privilege of resources like education and employment, and exposure to the mainstream world? The response is not simple; it requires the tracing of the trajec-tory of similarly positioned individuals who can meet the same criteria along the "pre-existing inequities and conditions—cognitive, emotional, and material" (McHugh 2004, p. 594).

Poststructuralist critique of "feminist universalism" and "gendered essentialism" (Hesse-Biber 2007) informs the premise that institutions and their policies and practices are not neutral towards different groups. Institutions and their policies carry within them historical and ideological legacies that affect each member differently (Ray 2003). Media is another example that misrepresents the *other* (Johnson et al. 2004). Radhika Parmesawaran (1996) asserts that in the process of highlighting the discrimination and unequal playing field in native cultures of immigrant women, the media reinforces a subservient and marginalized identity for them, even within the host cultures. Parmesawaran also identifies an additional negative corollary of this kind of media coverage—the hesitation of immigrant women to participate in mainstream culture for fear of backlash from their native culture and community. While the truth of oppressive practices such as dowry cannot be denied (Bhopal 1997), a one-dimensional focus on reality can result in distortion. According to Kamla Viswesaran (2004, p. 485), "women become women in ways as complex and diverse as the world's sexual orientations, class, and religious and cultural formations might suggest." She further asserts that the creation of a victim or an empowered entity for all womanhood is a denial of the structural inequity and individual pathways to addressing them.

For immigrant populations like the Asian-Americans, there is a complex interaction process between family, schools, neighborhood, religion, and other social systems. For instance, there are apparent conflicts between the school and the family around acceptable values, such as encouraging individualism and authoritarian parenting (Atzaba-Poria et al. 2004). Rachel Hall (2002) found in her study of immigration experiences of women with the British version of Immigration and Naturalization Services (INS) that the common perception (misconceptions) of the typical H1B 2 visa (husband's worker visa dependent woman) is a traditional, legitimate, not entirely deserving candidate for immigration, who is able to migrate due to the system of arranged marriages. She further notes that inherent within this "legitimate" identity is distrust by immigration officials of women who do not fit the conventional perception of women as spouses of "professional or qualified or employed" (Hall 2002, p. 55) men. On the other hand, acculturation is propagated as the process of orienting new immigrants to the American way of life through a systemic orientation to the mainstream culture and value systems. However, the individual pathways are studied adequately and therefore, the secondary, peripheral, and *uncontrolled* effects of schooling and interaction of schooling with other systems, such as family, religion, gender, and neighborhood remain under explored in this population.

The context of gender among immigrants from India, Pakistan, and Bangladesh is explored by comparing acculturation success and levels of conflicts between social systems (Dion and Dion 2001, 2004). Conflicting hypotheses and results are found in scholarly research on the desired nature and level of acculturation among immigrant girls with the host culture (Ryder et al. 2000; Salant and Lauderdale 2003; Varghese and Jenkins 2009). The underlying premise is that the freedom of identity expression and agency offered within the modern host society are in contrast with the traditional and constrained expressions of agency and identity within the home and ethnic community. The concepts of gender typicality and gender contentedness (Smith and Leaper 2005) also merit exploration within the process of acculturation in immigrant girls particularly, as the two systems of western and traditional Asian culture are rigidly interpreted. From a rudimentary feminist interpretation, their negotiation is in itself an empowering process that is conscious of the "felt" experiences of intersections of gender and ethnicity.

7.6   Conclusion

Studying hidden feminism is a challenging task, as it is only ever articulated individually within closed circles of women, based on a homogenizing ethnic identity to draw upon. The perspective in this chapter uses poststructuralist feminism to identify the newer contexts, associations, and relevant social systems for immigrant women. It proposes that both positive and negative outcomes are associated with migration, as illustrated by increased freedom and opportunities or increased dependence on husbands. These are considered instrumental in the development of hidden feminism. In Nimmi's life, the exposure to another culture gave her options to choose an alternate self and identity than the one proscribed within the norms of her Muslim family. However, to realize that desired identity she needed to form a constructive interpersonal relationship through her second husband, something that she could negotiate in her culture.

The experiences of women vary depending on their location within the host and home society as well as by women's individual personality and coping strategies. The positioning within native class, culture, politics, and magnitude and nature of exposure to the host cultures are important, instead of presuming a "linear, temporal, and behavioral patterns" (Salant and Lauderdale 2003, p. 76) bases of acculturation. Nimmi postulates her need to explore additional dimensions pertinent to social systems within native and host societies.

This chapter examines the primary group affiliations of nation, family, and religion to understand how an immigrant Indian woman expresses her identity and exercises her agency in the American host society to counter her weaker positions socially, economically, and sometimes legally as a dependent wife. It explores the development of "hidden" agency— i.e., an agency that exists irrespective of contexts and culture. Identity of migrant women traverses the tricky pathway to increased freedom through exposure to more opportunities and under the decreased influence of extended family and community, all of which contribute to but are not easily traceable in motivating one's agency.

Nimmi's narratives lead to identifying the complex pathways to identity change and self-realization that remain largely undocumented, as research on this issue is conducted with small, homogenous samples. Using a poststructuralist feminist perspective allows multiple interpretations of reality and contexts, and identifies a form of feminism that remains hidden from the primary methods of research. By examining Nimmi's identity as an *immigrant, Muslim, Indian, woman,* it explores the pathways of intersecting social contexts and Nimmi's own positioning within them. Finally, through the contexts of her relationship with her mother and position within her second marriage, it shows her transgression into hidden feminism.

References

Abraham, L. (2001). Redrawing the 'Lakshman Rekha': Gender differences and cultural constructions in youth sexuality in urban India. *South Asia-Journal of South Asian Studies, 24,* 133–156.

Abusharaf, A. (2006). Women in Islamic communities: The quest for gender justice research. *Human Rights Quarterly, 28*(3), 714–728.

Ahmad, F., Driver, N., McNally, M. J., & Stewart, D. E. (2009). "Why doesn't she seek help for partner abuse?" An exploratory study with South Asian immigrant women. *Social Science & Medicine, 69*(4), 613–622.

Ahmed, F. E. (2004). The rise of the Bangladesh garment industry: Globalization, women workers, and voice. *National Women's Studies Association Journal, 16*(2), 34–45.

Alam, M. B. (2007). Situating Asian Indian diaspora in the United States: An exploratory study. *Man in India, 87*(1–2), 67–81.

Atzaba-Poria, N., Pike, A., & Barrett, M. (2004). Internalising and externalising problems in middle childhood: A study of Indian (ethnic minority) and English (ethnic majority) children living in Britain. *International Journal of Behavioral Development, 28*(5), 449–460.

Badran, M. (2001). Understanding Islam, Islamism, and Islamic feminism. *Journal of Women's History, 13*(1), 47–52.

Baruah, B. (2004). Earning their keep and keeping what they earn: A critique of organizing strategies for South Asian women in the informal sector. *Gender, Work and Organization, 11*(6), 605–626.

Basu, S. (2008). Separate and unequal Muslim women and un-uniform family law in India. *International Feminist Journal of Politics, 10*(4), 495–517.

Bauer, J. L. (2000). Desiring place: Iranian "refugee" women and the cultural politics of self and community in the diaspora. *Comparative Studies of South Asia, Africa and the Middle East, 20*(1/2), 180–209.

Bhasin, K. (1993). *What is patriarchy?* New Delhi: Kali for Women.

Bhasin, K. (2003). *Understanding gender.* New Delhi: Women Unlimited.

Bhopal, K. (1997). *Gender, 'race', and patriarchy: A study of South Asian women.* Aldershot: Ashgate.

Bowen, J. R. (2004). Beyond migration: Islam as a transnational public space. *Journal of Ethnic and Migration Studies, 30*(5), 879–894.

Brems, E. (1997). Enemies or allies? Feminism and cultural relativism as dissident voices in human rights discourse. *Human Rights Quarterly, 19*(1), 136–164.

Briggs, L., McCormick, G., & Way, J. T. (2008). Transnationalism: A category of analysis. *American Quarterly, 60*(3), 625–648.

Butler, P., & Desai, J. (2008). Manolos, marriage, and mantras: Chick-Lit criticism and transnational feminism. *Meridians: Feminism, Race, Transnationalism, 8*(2), 1–31.

Camarota, S. A. (2005). *Immigrants at mid-decade: A snapshot of America's foreign-born population in 2005.* http://www.cis.org/articles/2005/back1405.html. Accessed March 25, 2010.

Chakraborty, K. (2009). 'The good Muslim girl': Conducting qualitative participatory research to understand the lives of young Muslim women in the bustees of Kolkata. *Children's Geographies, 7*(4), 421–434.

Chow, R. (2002). The interruption of referentiality: Poststructuralism and the conundrum of critical multiculturalism. *The South Atlantic Quarterly, 101*(1), 171–186.

Chowdhury, E. H. (2005). Feminist negotiations: Contesting narratives of the campaign against acid violence in Bangladesh. *Meridians: Feminism, Race, Transnationalism, 6*(1), 163–192.

Coltrane, S. (2010). Gender theory and household labor. *Sex Roles, 63*(11–12), 791–800.

Conway, J. (2008). Geographies of transnational feminisms: The politics of place and scale in the world March of women. *Social Politics, 15*(2), 207–231.

Cooke, M. (2000). Multiple critique: Islamic feminist rhetorical strategies. *Nepantla: Views from South, 1*(1), 91–110.

Cortazzi, M. (1993). *Narrative analysis*. Washington, DC: Falmer.

Dasgupta, S. (1998). Gender roles and cultural continuity in the Asian Indian immigrant community in the US. *Sex Roles, 38*(11–12), 953–974.

Desai, S., & Andrist, L. (2010). Gender scripts and age at marriage in India. *Demography, 47*(3), 667–687.

Dhingra, P. H. (2004). Being American between Black and White: Second-generation Asian American professionals' racial identities. *Journal of Asian American Studies, 6*(2), 117–147.

Dion, K. K., & Dion, K. L. (2001). Gender and cultural adaptation in immigrant families. *Journal of Social Issues, 57*(3), 511–521.

Dion, K. K., & Dion, K. L. (2004). Gender, immigrant generation, and ethnocultural identity. *Sex Roles, 50*(5–6), 347–355.

Dunkel, T. M., Davidson, D., & Qurashi, S. (2010). Body satisfaction and pressure to be thin in younger and older Muslim and non-Muslim women: The role of Western and non-Western dress preferences. *Body Image, 7*(1), 56–65.

Durham, M. G. (2001). Displaced persons: Symbols of South Asian femininity and the returned gaze in US media culture. *Communication Theory, 11*(2), 201–217.

Fox, G. L., & Murry, V. M. (2000). Gender and families: Feminist perspectives and family research. *Journal of Marriage and the Family, 62*(4), 1160–1172.

Gannon, S., & Davies, B. (2006). Postmodern, poststructural and critical perspectives. In H. Nagy Hesse-Biber (Ed.), *Handbook of feminist research: Theory and praxis* (pp. 71–106). Thousand Oaks: Sage.

Grabe, S. S. (2006). Ethnicity and body dissatisfaction among women in the United States: A meta-analysis. *Psychological Bulletin, 132*(4), 622–640.

Hall, R. A. (2002). When is a wife not a wife? Some observations on the immigration experiences of South Asian women in West Yorkshire. *Contemporary Politics, 8*(1), 55–68.

Harnois, C. (2008). Re-presenting feminisms: Past, present, and future. *National Women's Studies Association Journal, 20*(1), 120–145.

Hatem, M. F. (2006). In the eye of the storm: Islamic societies and Muslim women in globalization discourses. *Comparative Studies of South Asia, Africa and the Middle East, 26*(1), 22–35.

Hegland, M. E. (2003). Shi'a women's rituals in Northwest Pakistan: The shortcomings and significance of resistance. *Anthropological Quarterly, 76*(3), 411–442.

Hesse-Biber, S. N. (2007). *Handbook of feminist research: Theory and praxis*. Thousand Oaks: Sage.

Hughes, C. (2002). *Women's contemporary lives: Within and beyond the mirror*. New York: Routledge.

Jackson, P. (2006). Why I'm a Foucauldian. *Journal of Social Issues in Southeast Asia, 21*(1), 113–123.

Jamal, A. (2005). Transnational feminism as critical practice. *Meridians: Feminism, Race, Transnationalism, 5*(2), 57–82.

Johnson, J. L., Bootorff, J. L., Browne, A. J., Grewal, S., Hilton, B. A., & Clarke, H. (2004). Othering and being othered in the context of health care services. *Health Communication, 16*(2), 253–271.

Jones, J. (2010). 'Signs of churning': Muslim personal law and public contestation in twenty-first century India. *Modern Asian Studies, 44*(1), 175–200.

Kandiyoti, D. (1988). Bargaining with patriarchy. *Gender and Society, 2*(3), 274–290.

Kanitkar, T., & Mistry, M. (2000). Status of women in India: An interstate comparison. *The Indian Journal of Social Work, 61*(3), 366–383.

Komter, A. (1991). Gender, power and feminist theory. In K. Davis, M. Leijenaar, & J. Oldersma (Eds.), *The gender of power* (pp. 42–64). London: Sage.

Kurien, P. A. (2005). Being young, brown, and Hindu: The identity struggles of second-generation Indian Americans. *Journal of Contemporary Ethnography, 34*(4), 434–469.

Lateef, S. (1990). *Muslim women in India: Political and private realities, 1890s–1980s.* New Delhi: Kali for Women.

Lau, L. (2006). Emotional and domestic territories: The positionality of women as reflected in the landscape of the home in contemporary South Asian women's writing. *Modern Asian Studies, 40*, 1097–1116.

Lieblich, A., Tuval-Mashiach, R., & Tamr, Z. (1998). *Narrative research: Reading, analysis, and interpretation.* Thousand Oaks: Sage.

Mack-Canty, C. (2004). Third-wave feminism and the need to reweave the nature/culture duality. *National Women's Studies Association Journal, 16*(3), 154–179.

Mahalingam, R. R. (2005). Culture, essentialism, immigration, and representations of gender. *Theory & Psychology, 15*(6), 839–860.

Markus, H. R., & Kitayama, S. (1991). Culture and the self—implications for cognition, emotion, and motivation. *Psychological Review, 98*(2), 224–253.

Marshall, H., Woollett, A., & Dosanjh, N. (1998). Researching marginalized standpoints: Some tensions around plural standpoints and diverse "experiences.". In K. Henwood, C. Griffin, & A. Phoenix (Eds.), *Standpoints and differences: Essays in the practice of feminist psychology* (pp. 115–134). London: Sage.

McHugh, E. (2004). Moral choices and global desires: Feminine identity in a transnational realm. *Ethos, 32*(4), 575–597.

Moen, T. (2006). Reflections on the narrative research approach. *International Journal of Qualitative Methodology, 5*(4), 1–11.

Mohammad-Arif, A. (2005). A masala identity: Young South Asian Muslims in the US. *Comparative Studies of South Asia, Africa and the Middle East, 20*(1), 67–87.

Nagar, R. (2000). I'd rather be rude than ruled: Gender, place and communal politics among South Asian communities in Dar es Salaam. *Women's Studies International Forum, 23*(5), 571–585.

Nash, K. (2002). Human rights for women: An argument for 'deconstructive equality.'. *Economy and Society, 31*(3), 414–433.

Noh, E. (2003). Problematics of transnational feminism for Asian American women. *The New Centennial Review, 3*(3), 131–149.

Pahl, K. (2005). Longitudinal trajectories of ethnic identity among urban low-income ethnic and racial minority adolescents. *Dissertation Abstracts International: Section B: The Sciences and Engineering, 65*(11-B), 6072.

Parameswaran, R. (1996). Coverage of "bride burning" in the Dallas observer: A cultural analysis of the "other". *Frontiers: A Journal of Women Studies, 16*(2/3), 69–101.

Parpart, J. L. (1993). Who is the other?: A postmodern feminist critique of women and development theory and practice? *Development and Change, 243*, 439–464.

Pyke, K. D., & Johnson, D. L. (2003). Asian American women and racialized femininities: "Doing" gender across cultural worlds. *Gender and Society, 17*(1), 33–53.

Ray, K. (2003). Constituting 'Asian women': Political representation, identity politics, and local discourses of participation. *Ethnic and Racial Studies, 26*(5), 854–878.

Reeves T. J., & Bennett, C. E. (2004). We the people: Asians in the United States (Census 2000 Special Reports, CENSR-17). Washington, DC: US Census Bureau.

Rodriguez, A. (2007). Migration and increased participation in public life. *Frontiers, 28*(3), 94–112.

Ryder, A. G., Alden, L. E., & Paulhus, D. L. (2000). Is acculturation unidimensional or bidimensional? A head-to-head comparison in the prediction of personality, self-identity, and adjustment. *Journal of Personality and Social Psychology, 79*(1), 49–65.

Saint Louis, C., Nussbaum, E., Green, J., Jana, R., Mackey, R., Young, A., & Mitchell, C. (2000, July 16). Race: Mixed doubles. *New York Times Magazine.*

Salant, T., & Lauderdale, D. S. (2003). Measuring culture: A critical review of acculturation and health in Asian immigrant populations. *Social Science & Medicine, 57*(1), 71–90.

Salime, Z. (2008). Mobilizing Muslim women: Multiple voices, the Sharia, and the state. *Comparative Studies of South Asia, Africa and the Middle East, 28*(1), 200–211.

Saulnier, C. F. (1996). *Feminist theories and social work: Approaches and applications.* Binghamton: The Haworth Press, Inc.

Sengupta, R. (2006). Reading representations of black, East Asian, and white women in magazines for adolescent girls. *Sex Roles, 54*(11–12), 799–808.

Shah, N. A. (2006). Women's human rights in the Koran: An interpretive approach. *Human Rights Quarterly, 28*(4), 868–903.

Shi, Y. (2009). The formation of a Chinese immigrant working-class patriarchy: Reinventing gendered expectations within the structural confines of US society. *Meridians: Feminism, Race, Transnationalism, 9*(1), 31–60.

Singh, S. (2007a). Deconstructing gender and development paradigm for identities of women. *International Journal of Social Welfare, 16*(2), 100–109.

Singh, S. (2007b). An innovative approach to identity and agency: The case of the Self Employed Women's Association. *Journal of Asian Women's Studies (JAWS), 16*, 51–56.

Singh, S. (2010a). Women's autonomy in rural India: Need for culture and context. *International Social Work, 53*(2), 169–186.

Singh, S. (2010b). Neighborhood—The "outside" space for girls in urban India. *International Journal of Social Welfare, 19*(2), 206–214.

Singh, S. P., & Jha, B. N. (1992). Women's situation in India. In R. B. Mishra & C. P. Singh (Eds.), *Indian women: Challenges and change* (pp. 75–86). Delhi: Commonwealth Publishers.

Smith, R. A., & Mannon, S. E. (2010). 'Nibbling on the margins of patriarchy': Latina immigrants in northern Utah. *Ethnic and Racial Studies, 33*(6), 986–1005.

Smith, T. E., & Leaper, C. (2005). Self-perceived gender typicality and the peer context during adolescence. *Journal of Research on Adolescence, 16*(1), 91–103.

Subramanian, N. (2010). Making family and nation: Hindu marriage law in early postcolonial India. *Journal of Asian Studies, 69*(3), 771–798.

Terrazas A., & Batog, C. (2010, June). Indian immigrants in the United States. *Migration Information Source*. http://www.migrationinformation.org/USfocus/display.cfm?ID=785#10. Accessed March 5, 2010.

Thomas, E. (2000). Domestic violence in the African-American and Asian-American communities: A comparative analysis of two racial/ethnic minority cultures and implications for mental health service provision for women of color. *Psychology: A Journal of Human Behavior, 37*(3–4), 32–43.

UNDP. (2011). International human development indicators—India: Country profile of human development indicators. http://hdrstats.undp.org/en/countries/profiles/IND.html. Accessed March 25, 2011.

Varghese, A., & Jenkins, S. R. (2009). Parental overprotection, cultural value conflict, and psychological adaptation among Asian Indian women in America. *Sex Roles, 61*(3–4), 235–251.

Vatuk, S. (2008). Islamic feminism in India: Indian Muslim women activists and the reform of Muslim Personal Law. *Modern Asian Studies, 42*(2/3), 489–518.

Visweswaran, K. (2004). Gendered states: Rethinking culture as a site of South Asian human rights work. *Human Rights Quarterly, 26*(2), 483–511.

Walker, D. (2010, September 23). Critics weigh in on NBC sitcom 'Outsourced.' *The Times Picayune*. http://www.nola.comtv/index.ssf/2010/09/critics_weigh/_in_on_nbc_sitcom.html. Accessed June 3, 2011.

Winter, B. (2001). Fundamental misunderstandings: Issues in feminist approaches to Islamism. *Journal of Women's History, 13*(1), 9–41.

Yu, Y. (2010). Reframing Asian Muslim women in the name of honor: Neo-orientalism and gender politics in Mukhtar Mai's constructed narratives. *Asian Journal of Women's Studies, 16*(4), 7–29.

Chapter 8
Encountering Differences: Iranian Immigrant Women in Australia

Maryam Jamarani*

8.1 Introduction

Gender as an aspect of identity is a sociocultural construct that is historically, ethnically, situationally and interactionally constituted and negotiated (Eckert 1989; Gal 1994; Ochs 1992; Woolard 1997; Winter and Pauwels 2000). It is defined as the sets of roles, behaviors and expectations that society "associates with being male or female individuals" (Wood 2005, p. 19). Gender relations operates as "one of the major axes of social power" in almost all societies (Bottomley 1992, p. 14). But definitions of masculinity, femininity, and appropriate gender roles and relations are often not shared across cultures. Therefore, gender is one of the areas of identity in which adjustments often occur after migration (Bottomley 1992; Krulfeld 1994). In the case of immigrant women, the challenges to gender roles and relationships within the family depend on the relative status and differential treatment of females between the country of origin and the host society. A more prominent challenge exists when there is a substantial difference in the treatment of women between the two cultures (Jolly and Reeves 2005).

Australia has a long history as an immigrant receiving country. It has been also one of the pioneers in the women's liberation movement (Lake 1999).[1] Australian feminism, however, is largely seen as mainly concerned with issues of the white

*The author wishes to thank Glenda Tibe Bonifacio for her very constructive comments on earlier drafts of this chapter.

[1] Women in South Australia achieved the right to vote and run for office in 1895, and were the first to run for an elected seat in parliament (A Vote of Her Own 2011).

M. Jamarani, Ph.D. (✉)
School of Languages and Comparative Cultural Studies,
University of Queensland, Brisbane, QLD, Australia
e-mail: m.jamarani@uq.edu.au

middle-class women. The problem with this limited interest, according to Sevgi Kilic (1997, p. 33), is that "notions of universal gender experience defined by the terms of experience of a particular group of women (i.e. white middle-class women) effectively obscure other experiences of women from other social groups." The interest in Aboriginal and non-English-speaking background (NESB) women was brought to the fore in 1984, following a conference in Brisbane on "Women in Labour." Even within the macro category of NESB women, the cultural background of each group of women is different and, hence, the practices of gender roles differ from one another.

Migration ushers changes in gender roles, and this appears more significant in the case of married couples. These changes may have critical impact on family dynamics with its negative influence on the traditional power relationship between men and women (Abdulrahim 1993; Benson 1994; Krulfeld and Camino 1994; Darvishpour 1999; Ghorashi 2003). Women from more patriarchal societies like Iran have less social and familial freedom compared to men. Upon entering less patriarchal societies, like Australia, they may gain a greater sense of self, autonomy, independence, self-confidence and start enjoying a better social status. They may question some of the traditional privileges enjoyed by men, and challenge the relations of power between the spouses leading to women's empowerment (Beiser et al. 1988; Carballo 1994; Berry 1997; Graham and Khosravi 1997). However, not all married women moving to more egalitarian societies, tend to aspire more freedom or to make changes in their culturally-prescribed roles. These women may simply follow their husbands without specifically considering possible shifts in gender roles. In this case, migration could even result in enforcing traditional roles between husband and wife.

Iran is a relatively traditional society, governed by Islamic rules and with various ethnic, religious, social, familial, cultural norms and practices imposing limitations on women. Hence, the acculturation process of Iranian women migrating to Australia—a country with relatively more egalitarian laws and rules with respect to gender issues—can influence immigrant women's gender identities and roles, either by entrenching traditional values and roles, or by challenging and changing them.

This chapter deals with the main question: to what extent do Iranian immigrant women benefit from the social rights and freedoms available to women in Australia? These rights pertain to, but are not limited to, employment, social activities, divorce, and child custody. Based on the case of 15 married Iranian immigrant women in Queensland, Australia I will examine the extent to which they have been able or willing to integrate differing sets of values and gender roles between the home and the host culture. The attitudes of these women toward their gender roles and status in the new social context probe the extent to which they engage with the wider Australian society; whether immigrant women from Iran have been able and/or willing to take advantage of the opportunities available to women in Australia.

The 15 Iranian women in this study were between 31 and 55 years of age, and had left Iran within the period of 1984–2004. All had high school diplomas, and 8 had pursued tertiary studies. Eleven were employed, while the remaining 4 were housewives. Except for 1 divorcee, all were married and have children. Their reasons for their migration ranged from marrying their husbands who were already living in Australia, to escaping the social/political insecurity in Iran following the 1979 Islamic Revolution, to their husbands seeking better social and financial opportunities. In all, their husbands made the decision to migrate, and the women simply followed them.

8.2   Theoretical Premises

In the scholarship of migration, immigrant women are subjectively positioned as either "members of families" or as a generalized category of "immigrants." However, a feminist perspective on migration best highlights the situation of this group of immigrants who are mostly ignored in mainstream migration discourse. This study, in general, is informed by postcolonial feminism (Kramarae and Spender 2000; Narayan 2000; McEwan 2001). Unlike feminism in general, postcolonial feminism deals with the gender issue of non-white and non-western women. It gives voice to NESB women, and pays particular attention to ethnic *women* rather than a generalized *woman* issue. The analysis mainly draws on the conceptual framework of "multiracial feminism." This framework is helpful in the analysis of the data in as far as it helps to examine the structures of domination, in particular, through highlighting the social construction of gender in any specific cultural context—and in the case of migrants, with any ethnic background. In using "multiracial feminism" I rely on Bonnie Thornton Dill and Maxine Baca Zinn's (1994, p. 11) definition of the concept whereby it "offers a body of knowledge situating women and men in multiple systems of domination" in which ethnic heritage, racial ancestry and economic status are as important as gender for analyzing the social construction of men and women.

This study is further based on the premise that gender identity involves a dynamic process of becoming through exposure to and interaction with novel social situations, rather than having a static state of being. Haleh Ghorashi (2003, p. 27) argues that the resulting change is "a situated change" in the sense that it occurs through a process of interaction with the current situation, but at the same time involves and is shaped by past experiences. This study of Iranian immigrant women in Australia focuses on "becoming" rather than "being." In other words, the emphasis is on the dynamic process of identity modification as a result of the changes in the social context, rather than a study of identity as a fixed set of attributes. Thus, "constructivism" (Burr 1995) with its emphasis on the process of being constructed provides the theoretical paradigm to emphasize the dynamic relations between identity and culture in migration. Gender as an aspect of identity is socially and ethnically constructed, and, hence, when the social and the cultural context of the individual changes—in the case of migrants—some of the gender attributes are also very likely to be modified. Therefore, a constructivist framework gives us the tools to study the changes that occur in the gender identity of migrants.

The case of Iranian immigrant women in Australia is guided by the notion of *habitus* (Bourdieu 1990; Ghorashi 2003) according to which cultural schemas are formed in the past and consciously or subconsciously control present behaviors. These schemas provide a strong influence in the different aspects of identity formation. And since identity is dynamic, cultural schemas are also likely to change in the process of migration and integration. An important attribute of *habitus* suggests that individuals (immigrants in this case) are not necessarily free to change their identities, even if they are outside of their *former* geographical context. They can, however, modify different aspects of their identities in the process of negotiating with the past and the present. *Habitus,* as a guiding framework among immigrants, comes in the form of their ethnic community in the diaspora, and works as a controlling mechanism when immigrants intend to act according to influences of their present sociocultural context.

8.3 Encountering Differences

Studies on Iranian communities in the United States and Europe (Kamalkhani 1988; Mahdi 2002; Tohidi 2004) report major differences between the roles of women in Iran and women in other European or North American countries. In comparison with women in Iran, women in Australia are better equipped and supported by social and family legislations to enjoy more egalitarian opportunities on familial, social and workplace related levels. Iran is a country with rigid patriarchal sociocultural values and norms, especially with respect to gender roles, and its strong emphasis on the family as the basic social unit. Marriage is encouraged as the first step in the formation of the family, and being a responsible member means carrying out the expected gender roles in order to safeguard the stability of family relations. Article 1105 of the Civil Code of the Islamic Republic of Iran clearly states that "[i]n relations between husband and wife, the position of the head of the family is the exclusive right of the husband." Husbands often have the "undisputed authority [...] [to] supervise the other family members' activities" (Darvishpour 2002, p. 7). Traditionally, the husband is the head of the family and the main economic provider. The perceived sanctity of the family resulted in various sociocultural, familial, and at times legal restrictions that constrain Iranian women from engaging in professional and social activities outside the family. In Article 1108 of the Civil Code, the role of women is defined as "fulfilling the duties of a wife," which translates into bearing children, raising them, and taking care of the family (Darvishpour 2002, p. 281).

A typical traditional woman in Iran performs domestic responsibilities, fulfills the role of mother and wife, and takes care of the family (Toolo and Shakibaee 2000). She would often involve her husband's approval for undertaking activities outside the home. Restrictions imposed on women in Iran suggest that the suitability of their social activities is judged "according to the degree to which they interfere with or draw women away from their family responsibilities" (Higgins and Shoar-Ghaffari 1994, p. 20). In general, women in Iran pursue social activities outside the home in conjunction with their responsibilities as mothers and wives. They would be criticized if these activities come at the cost of not paying due attention to their primary duties at home. Therefore, the social expectations of a woman toward her family make all other individual concerns and interests secondary (Afkhami 1994; Ghaffarian 2001; Kousha 2002). Although there is no direct objection to women working outside the home, a husband can stop his wife from working if he were to claim that, by working, "the woman was not fulfilling" her duties towards her children or her husband (Esfandiari 1994, p. 67). Such a family-oriented attitude makes it difficult for women to improve their social skills outside nonfamilial relations or pursue a career.

When I asked Sara,[2] a resident in Australia for 28 years with two grown up daughters, to rate her individual identity among other aspects of her identity, she was not sure how one could explain individual identity at all. I explained it as: "who I am? And what interests do I have regardless of my responsibilities or what is socially expected from me?" She quickly responded: "so you are talking about selfishness." In answer to the same question, Tara, who had lived in Australia for 4 years and has one teenage daughter, said: "Well, [as an Iranian woman] we do not have individual identity as such. It is rather our family identity which is important." Family identity means one's identity as a mother or as a wife. Tara acknowledged that both men and women are defined through their familial roles, but there is a stark difference between them: men's family identity is only an aspect of their [social] identity, whereas women's identity is almost entirely defined in terms of being a wife and/or a mother. Because women are mainly identified in relation to their family, all that they have achieved, or aspire to achieve as individuals will be assessed against their marital and maternal status. On the other hand, men are not criticized in their pursuit of personal goals as long as they provide financial support for the family.

Sara equated *liking oneself* and *paying attention to one's interest* with *selfishness*. In the cultural schema of Iran, the family and not the individual is regarded as the smallest social unit, close ties with ingroup members is strongly encouraged, and a person is primarily defined as a member of the group rather than as an independent individual. Devotion to the family is regarded as one of the foremost criteria for evaluating a well-behaved, respectable and reliable citizen. Accordingly, Nehzat Toolo and Siavash Shakibaee (2000) note that the individual's interests remain subordinated to the needs of the family.

The women in this study generally disapproved and are critical of the prevalent traditional view in Iran that women are predominantly mothers and wives. Some of them, however, have mixed views about women's status in Iran and their independence in Australia:

---

[2] Iranian women in this study were assigned pseudonyms to protect their identity.

> There is a big difference between the women in Iran and Australia. As a woman, you feel
> that you have more independence and power, here in Australia. (Mahsa, 5 years resident in
> Australia)
>   I believe as a woman you have more financial support from your husband in Iran. In Iran
> it would be OK if you tell your husband that you don't want to work. He just accepts that as
> part of the culture. He has to work even up to twelve hours a day to provide for the family,
> and there is no pressure on women in regard to helping with the financial situation. (Samira,
> 9 years resident in Australia)

By introducing the element of choice ("if you don't want to work") Samira referred to the legal responsibilities of a husband in Iran to provide for his family in Article 1106 of the Civil Code. From a socio-economic perspective, the traditional gendered division of labor results in the significant financial dependence of wives on their husbands. Moreover, the economic dependency of married women on their husbands disempowers them, and reduces "the bargaining position of women in family decision-making" (Moghadam 1994, p. 82).

Australia has relatively lesser discriminatory norms and values toward women compared to Iran, although it can be argued that gender-biases exist (Hinds and Bradshaw 2005; Miliszewska 2006). Migration from Iran to Australia ostensibly provides Iranian women with opportunities to re-evaluate their gender roles and status within the family as well as in the society at large. The Australian context gives them relatively more freedom to engage in social activities that divert their attention from being primarily focused on family responsibilities. Women now have the chance to step out of the social and legal restrictions imposed on them while living in Iran. As a result of migration, Iranian women have the opportunity to change or modify their traditional roles as wives and mothers into more socially active individuals. Tina, 17 years resident in Australia, elaborated on this newfound opportunity in the following way:

> An immigrant is exposed to other values in the new context, and can see beyond their own
> cultural values. As a result, they will no longer believe in the absoluteness of their home
> cultural and social values. Immigrants can go beyond the borders, which were defined by
> their home culture. By becoming aware of different values, an immigrant has the possibility
> of integrating them and coming to a new understanding of themselves and the world, and of
> living accordingly.

The "absoluteness" of the home culture's values is, according to Tina, weakened in Australia, and that immigrants become aware of different values and ways of living. The prospect of moving "beyond" and not restricted by their home culture, which has so far been their controlling system in defining socially acceptable and not acceptable behavior, is a reality. However, Tina introduced the notion of possibility rather than definiteness—an immigrant has the "possibility" of integrating two sets of values and lifestyles. As I will argue in this chapter this possibility does not, on its own, guarantee willingness or an ability to do so. Following Shiva Sadeghi (2006) in her study of Iranian women immigrants in Canada, a change in the social and cultural contexts on their own had not inherently entailed a fundamental transformation in their gender roles and social engagement.

8.4 Social Engagement and Language Proficiency

Language as a tool of communication plays a vital role in preventing or helping people engage in society. But lack of English language did not have a negative impact on the social engagement of Iranian women in this study, as long as they were interacting with other Iranians or working in family-run businesses. The relatively higher potential level of social engagement in Australia, compared to women in Iran, had made them more visible within the Iranian community as well as in the broader Australian community, offering more opportunities to be exposed to life outside the home. This visibility, however, does not necessarily entail understanding or being engaged in the dynamics of the Australian society at large. One of the main reasons for their seeming failure in engaging with and integrating into the mainstream society is their lack of proficiency in the English language. As a result, Iranian women tend to form strong social networks with other Iranian immigrant women rather than with white Anglo women in Australia. Lesser interactions with Australian women reinforce traditional gender roles, cultural norms and values. The ability to speak English is an important factor in facilitating communication with Australians, and integrating into the mainstream labour force or even creating social networks with non-Iranians. Sara, a 21 years resident contrasted the notion of "social presence" or being visible in the community, with "social understanding" in the following way;

> In my opinion, the social presence of Iranian women has definitely improved in Australia. But the social understanding of Iranian women in Australia that I know of, has decreased drastically, because they have been isolated from the wider mainstream society. And that is due to their lack of English language proficiency.

Women in Iran—especially after marriage—are often restricted in their social and professional endeavors. In the Australian context, these external restrictions are to a large extent minimized, and provide women with opportunities to pursue their professional or individual aspirations more freely. Although social mobility and economic independence has made women's role within the family more significant in Australia, the language barrier restricts those with limited English in their capacity to integrate into mainstream society. These women rely largely on their husbands, children or Iranian friends with better English skills. They depend on interpreters even for fulfilling small tasks (e.g., shopping, going to the doctor, paying the bills, banking, and communicating with their children's school), that they would have accomplished on their own in Iran.

Immigrants, as social beings, need to create new social networks and establish new friendship ties in the host society. Proficiency in the host country's language provides them with the means to develop a network with non-Iranians in the new home country, which in turn can result in an enhanced integration. Lack of English language proficiency, however, results in the confinement of NESB women in their socialization to only other people from the same home country/language background in Australia. Sahar, who had very limited English language skills, states "My English is not good enough to have English-speaking friends, and that leaves me with only Iranians." Tina, with a good command of English, described her fellow Iranian women lacking English language proficiency in the following way;

> I know Iranian women who have woven a spider web around themselves and a few other Iranian friends that they have. They are living a life isolated from the broader society [...] because they do not have the English language to communicate with non-Iranian people. They socialize with Iranians, go shopping with Iranians, go to coffee shops with Iranians, and party with Iranians.

Lack of English skills had cause discontent among Iranian women in this study with the quality of their socialization with non-Iranians. As a direct result of being restricted in their choice of friendships, the women with limited English are less confident in their ability to socialize on a level with which they are used to in Iran. Elnaz, a well-known artist back in Iran and taught art at university, described the impact of her basic English language proficiency on her social engagement,

> I don't want to be excluded from the [mainstream] society. I am always making concessions [in the sense of accepting them and not challenging their ideas or arguments] in my encounters with local people, and this is mostly because of my lack of English language . . . I always think I would not have been friends with many of [my Iranian friends here] if we were in Iran. I mean they are not my type, and I would not have chosen them as friends in Iran. As for my Australian friends, I have to make myself accepted by locals. I don't want to be excluded from the [mainstream] society. In my unconscious, I am always making concessions in my encounters with local people [in the sense of accepting them and not challenging their ideas or arguments], and this is mostly because of my lack of English language. I mean when I am with Australians, I change from a challenging person to a concession-making person. I can no longer give what I have knowledge about. Therefore I am put in a position of weakness. Here in Australia I would socialize with whomever I can. I cannot be very selective.

Lack of English language proficiency contributes to lower self-confidence and self-esteem among immigrant Iranian women in Australia. Elnaz expressed different reactions to people or situations she disagreed with or disapproved of, depending on the context. When in the company of Persian speakers, she had the tool of language to express her knowledge and opinion. On the other hand, when in the presence of non-Persian speakers she was deprived of such a tool. As she did not wish to be excluded from the [mainstream] society, she had chosen to make concessions by accepting her English-speaking interlocutors' opinions, rather than forgoing her interactions (however minimal) with her very small circle of three or four non-Iranian friends.

English language proficiency further highlights an important element in hindering or facilitating women's engagement in the wider society. Those with limited English skills, even if they were critical of the restrictions imposed on Iranian women, had been unable to take advantage of their new social setting in Australia and remained isolated. Cheryl Lange (2001, p. 208) notes in her study that language can play the strongest role in the social exclusion of NESB women. Lack of fluency in English marks NESB women as different from the white English-speaking majority, and can cause them not to enjoy "full citizenship" rights for women in Australia. Inability to communicate in English had pushed Iranian women in this study to limit their socialization with other NESB (Iranian in this case) women, and hence behave according to the expected social schema of Iranian culture, according to which the role of women is primarily defined within home and in relation to their husband and children.

8.5   Migration and Women's Independence

The women in this study generally regarded their migration from Iran as an opportunity for moving beyond restrictions imposed by various legal rules, social conventions and norms, limiting their social mobility and freedom. They believed they had more freedom and power as a woman, and they acknowledged the positive role of the general social attitude towards gender in their newly gained status in Australia. Mahsa, a 5 years resident in Australia, saw financial independence as a significant factor in her self-empowerment. Sima, a 17 years resident, further elaborated on the issue of independence in general, in the light of social and legal laws of Australia. Not all the Iranian women in this study, however, approved of, or had been willing to take advantage of, their new socio-cultural setting in regard to their gender roles. Traditional ideas regarding social engagement and family roles, rights and responsibilities of women, as well as the structure of the family, still persisted among some of these Iranian women.

Immigrant Iranian women who hold on to traditional gendered roles, like their counterpart in Iran, saw the negative impact of women's social and professional activities, and their financial independence on the family in Australia. The logic of their argument was that, once women become socially active and independent beyond a certain point, their role as nurturer in the family is likely to take on a secondary importance in relation to their professional lives, and pay less attention to their family (i.e., husband and children). They still follow traditional gender roles, and the primacy of safeguarding the interests of the family over their own individual goals. To them the ultimate benefit of the traditional division of gender roles was the wellbeing of the family and children, best secured by a man "in charge" or as the head of the family. Family, therefore, had remained as a core value even after their migration (Smolicz 1981).

In evaluating the traditional family, Mahtab and Elnaz emphasized their *own* choices in their gender role as opposed to being restricted to it. Mahtab, a 20 years resident in Australia, had the opportunity to work but willingly made the conscious choice to stay at home and take care of her children. She did not aspire a similar professional or social engagement as her husband's. For her, a woman's role is primarily toward her children, which is more important than her professional advancement. To Elnaz, on the other hand, a woman who chooses to stay at home and take care of her children, might be regarded as a "victim" by those women who choose to pursue their social and professional life outside the home. It was significant that she placed emphasis on her choice as a woman in accepting her primary role as a mother. And by accepting, sacrifice her opportunities to develop her individual and social skills. Furthermore, by choosing to do so, she had consciously decided not to own and/or strive to achieve what she refers to as worldly and material commodities. Looking at it from the perspective of multiracial feminism, a change of context from the more traditional Iranian cultural context into a much less traditional context like Australia—did not necessarily cause Elnaz or Mahtab to modify their perspectives on gender roles and responsibilities. They remain steadfast in their traditional and culturally-defined gender role distinction, according to which motherhood (for married women) is more important compared to material and social independence.

8.6 Migration and Divorce

Even if Iranian women in this study lack the necessary English language proficiency to fully integrate into mainstream Australian society, they were able to benefit from the work of generations of "femocrats"[3] and the established "state feminism"[4] to enjoy the freedom and rights similarly available to other women in Australia such as divorce rights, single mother's government payment, and custody rights (Lake 1999). The following discussion centers on the relationship between divorce and migration of Iranian women.

Divorce is a disruption of the family unit where gender roles and gender inequalities are brought to the fore, with respect to rights of each partner and child custody for instance. In the matter of divorce, the situation for Iranian immigrant women in Australia is not the same as the women in Iran. To start with, either party can initiate a divorce in Australia. In contrast, only the husband can divorce his wife whenever he wishes to do so in Iran (Article 1133, Civil Code, Islamic Republic of Iran); a woman does not have the right to divorce without her husband's permission (Darvishpour 2002, p. 6). The exceptional situations where Iranian courts grant the woman the right to initiate the divorce are: if the husband has been absent with unknown whereabouts for 4 years continuously (Article 1029, Civil Code, Islamic Republic of Iran); if the husband is proven to be insane (Article 1121, Civil Code, Islamic Republic of Iran); if the husband is either castrated or is impotent (Article 1122, Civil Code, Islamic Republic of Iran); or, if the husband refuses to pay the cost of maintenance to his wife (Article 1129, Civil Code, Islamic Republic of Iran). Apart from the gender bias in divorce laws, the financial insecurity of women, the stigma attached to divorce, and laws on child custody, all work against women in Iran. As a result of these prescriptions and prohibitions, women in Iran often remain in unhappy marriages. In Australia, however, women who are dissatisfied with their marriage may opt to seek divorce as an alternative, since their situation will be quite different than in Iran. The financial support from the government, and the general social support for divorced women and

---

[3] The term "femocrat" was invented for the distinctly Australian type of feminist bureaucrat and refers to those who entered the federal and state public service in the 1970s as part of the project to translate feminist ideals into government policy (Stetson and Mazur 1995, p. 254).

[4] "State feminism" refers to the "activities of government structures that are formally charged with furthering women's status and rights" (Stetson and Mazur 1995, pp. 1–2).

single mothers in Australia enable Iranian women greater self-confidence and independence. Tara, a recent arrival at the time of the interview was contemplating a divorce, described her marital situation in Iran as a quarrel-dominated relationship where her husband had the power and authority to tell her to leave, while she merely remained a passive recipient of his threats. She was hesitant to initiate a divorce in Iran due to financial considerations and described her situation as:

> Back in Iran, whenever we had a fight my husband used to tell me you can get a divorce and go if you are not happy. But he knew that I would not go for a divorce. If I got divorced, I did not have any money to live on my own.

Based on Tara's account, her husband was convinced that divorce was not an option, and that she would stay with him despite all the difficulties. Tara had a pre-school aged child then and was afraid of losing custody if she pursued divorce. As well, her financial dependence and the discriminatory family laws in Iran worked against making this decision. In Australia, however, she became an active and fearless voice about her marital situation. Tara believed she enjoyed more rights, in particular the financial and legal support from the government with respect to child custody. And this, in turn, empowers her position in the family; "here in Australia I am the one who tells him [my husband], we can get separated if you are not happy."

Financial dependency reduces the bargaining opportunities of women in family disputes. In the absence of any social security provided to divorced women in Iran, financial dependency poses difficulties in the event of a marital break-up. Coming to Australia, however, Tara argued that women become aware of the government financial support for divorced women, and, therefore, find it easier to file for divorce should the situation arise, particularly in cases where women are financially dependent on their husbands.

The stigma of divorce in Iran further deters women from filing for divorce. Tara remarked, "If I got divorced in Iran, I would have been stigmatized as a *motal'aghe* (divorced woman)." The word *motal'aghe* is derived from the word *talaagh* (divorce), but it refers only to a woman who is divorced, and not to a divorced man. In fact, there is no word in the standard Persian vocabulary referring to a divorced man. This indicates that the stigma of divorce—social, family, and individual—affects only women. The extent to which divorce brings shame and stigma to women is expressed in a common Iranian saying:

> /Zan baa lebaaseh sefide aroos mireh khooneh-ye shohar, va ba lebaase sefid (kafan) barmigardeh./
>   A woman goes to her husband's home in white [bridal dress], and comes out in white [burial sheets].

This saying suggests that women should stay in their marriage to the end of their life, in spite of all the difficulties. Although the responsibility to maintain marital ties is placed on both men and women, women are traditionally expected to sacrifice their own personal satisfaction and welfare for the sake of preserving family ties (Toolo and Shakibaee 2000; Kousha 2002; Mahdi 2002).

Since women's roles in Iran are mainly defined within the context of the family, divorced women are often stigmatized on different levels: (a) social (possible loss of social networks and even employment); (b) family (bringing shame to children); and (c) individual (limited opportunities to re-marry and start a new life). At the family level, a divorced mother further compromises the future of her children, especially daughters, through the stigma that her divorce brings to the family. Therefore, parents, and in particular mothers, may stay in unhappy marriages, to protect their children from social isolation.

Marriage in Iran is more than a legal contract and a relationship between two people (Kousha 2002). It is rather a social bond between two families. Divorce is not only seen as the act of disrupting a family unit but also the union between two families, and would negatively affect the extended families on both sides. Couples are often obliged to consider the shame and disruption that this break-up would bring to their families.

Family laws on child custody pose another significant challenge for women seeking divorce in Iran. Tara recognized that the possible loss of custody over her only child was the compelling reason to forego any plans of divorce while she was still in Iran. Child custody legislation in Iran stipulates a division of custody rights into "the [emotional and physical] protection of the child as an individual" (*hizanat*), and "the control and protection of the child's assets" (*wilayat*) (Ebrahimi 2006, p. 463). In the case of divorce, the court initially leaves it to the parents to decide on the *hizanat* of their child. However, if the parents are unable to reach an agreement, the family court intervenes (Ebrahimi 2006). Article 1169 of the Civil Code of the Islamic Republic of Iran states:

> A mother has preference over others for two years from the birth of her child for the [*hizanat*] custody of the child and after the lapse of this period custody will devolve on the father except in the case of a daughter who will remain under the custody of the mother until 7 years.

The mother would, nonetheless, lose her right of *hizanat* if she marries another man or becomes insane (Article 1170, Civil Code, Islamic Republic of Iran). *Wilayat* on the other hand, is the exclusive right of the father, and in his absence this right is given to the *paternal* grandfather. If both the father and paternal grandfather die or are not present, the right then devolves to their (or the court's) appointed executor (*wassi*). The mother has no authority to appoint a *wassi* in this process (Kousha 2002; Ghorashi 2003; Beck and Nashat 2004; Ebrahimi 2006). Consequently, the issue of child custody is a significant factor in dissuading a mother in Iran from pursuing divorce. A mother—like Tara—with less chance of gaining custody of her children after divorce, and unwilling to leave custody to the father, may have no alternative but to stay in an unhappy marriage.

In Australia, on the other hand, mothers have a greater chance of securing custody of their children (currently referred to in Australian family law as *residency*). Within the Australian legal system, when a marriage is dissolved both parents have an equal chance for the custody of their children, provided they are both judged by the family court to be suitable parents in the care of their children. According to the Australian *Family Law Act 1975*, child custody matters are resolved in accordance with the best interests of the child (Council 2000; Carter 2004). Parents are encouraged by the Family Court to come to an agreement about the children's residency order, and the financial maintenance of the child. Although this can prove to be complicated in practice, it is important that the law initially gives an equal chance to parents with respect to custody, unlike in Iran where the father has the sole custody right of children.

Aware of the *residency* law in Australia, Tara states, "Here in Australia, I can be a single mum. I can be financially supported by the government, with, for instance, daycare or school fees as well as a small monthly salary for myself if I do not have a job to raise my child." Although contemplating on divorce during the course of this research Tara had not taken any measures towards filing for divorce.

Overall, the women in this study acknowledged the tremendous difficulties of women pursuing divorce in Iran. For them, it seems easier and less troublesome to think seriously about divorce in Australia. But pursuing a divorce in Australia is not at all easy for these women:

> When I was filing for divorce, my own sister, who has been living here for more than twenty years, was trying hard to dissuade me from divorce, though she knew what a terrible life I was in. She was afraid of the stigma I would bring to myself and to the family. [...] I am aware that the Iranian community talks behind my back about me as a divorced woman. I have even heard that some people say I just got married to my ex-husband, who was a permanent resident in Australia, so that I could come to Australia. But that is not true. I would not jeopardize my emotion just to come to Australia. (Mahsa, 5 years resident in Australia)

Other women like Sahar were also not accepting of divorce as an option:

> There are these types of women who cannot be bothered to work. Then they come here [to Australia] and think, well if I get divorced I can get half of my husband's belongings. And the government also supports me, and pays me. So they would not tolerate the least unhappiness in the marriage and get divorced [...] there are, however, a few cases where women are in real abusive relations and I believe they are doing the right thing to separate [from the husband]. (Sahar, 25 years resident in Australia)

Although social acceptance of divorce and government support for single mothers in Australia makes it easier for Iranian women to consider divorce as an option more readily compared to their counterpart in Iran, the stigma attached to divorce still exists within the Iranian community. Divorced Iranian women in Australia are further criticized as "opportunists": tempted by the financial support from the government; use marriage as a means to immigrate to Australia; or, do not try hard to make the marriage work. On a broader scale, the negative attitude towards divorce still exists among Iranian women in Australia. And many remain inclined in preserving the integrity of the family over a woman's dissatisfaction with marriage.

The centrality of the family has certain repercussions on the practice of divorce. While financial support schemes, as well as a more egalitarian child custody legislation help scaffold women's confidence in contemplating divorce in Australia. The majority of Iranian women in this study maintained a conservative and more traditional view of divorce as a disruption of the family unit. Only one of them, Mahsa, proceeded in filing for divorce and another, Tara, was still considering divorce at the time of interview. Iranian women who applied for divorce were accused of opportunism, of taking advantage of the Australian laws to the detriment of the family.

8.7 Conclusion

The rigid patriarchal family schema practiced in Iran remains dominant in the mindset of Iranian immigrant women even after years of migrating to Australia. Interestingly, however, the women in this study all believe that they have more social freedom and rights compared to women in Iran. In fact, the traditional Iranian family schema, with respect to taking care of the family unit as superior to any other social participation, was still largely favoured by a majority of them. They were skeptical about the impact of women's participation in paid work to the family and welfare of their children in Australia. Attitudes toward gender roles within the family were informed by traditional cultural schema. The interest of the family transcends individual aspirations for professional advancement or wider social engagement with Australian society.

In the case of Iranian immigrant women in this study, the mere availability of certain rights for women (e.g., right for initiating the divorce) in a more egalitarian society like Australia does not make all women pursue this right, especially if traditional cultural schemas are strongly ingrained. In other words, the change of socio-cultural context on its own is not enough to immediately change the gender identity of immigrants toward the family. Immigrant women coming from more patriarchal societies like Iran continue to face difficulties in securing their rights in Australia; individual choice of gaining independence or enjoying more social freedom is often frowned upon by the Iranian migrant community. But Iranian immigrant women value the rights and opportunities accorded to women in Australia and hope that, if the situation arises, they, too, will actually benefit from them.

References

A Vote of Her Own. An exhibition commemorating the centenary of women's suffrage in Western Australia. http://www.ccentre.wa.gov.au/Documents/vote%20of%20her%20own%20-%20primary.pdf. Accessed June 13, 2011.

Abdulrahim, D. (1993). Defining gender in a second exile: Palestinian women in West Berlin. In G. Buijs (Ed.), Migrant women: Crossing boundaries and changing identities (pp. 55–83). Oxford/Providence: Berg Publishers.

Afkhami, M. (1994). Women in post-revolutionary Iran: A feminist perspective. In M. Afkhami & E. Friedl (Eds.), In the eye of the storm: Women in post-revolutionary Iran (pp. 5–18). Syracuse: Syracuse University Press.

Beck, L., & Nashat, G. (2004). Women in Iran from 1800 to the Islamic republic. Urbana: University of Illinois Press.

Beiser, M., Barwick, C., Berry, J. W., da Coasta, G., & Fantio, A. (1988). Mental health issues affecting immigrants and refugees. Ottawa: Health and Welfare Canada.

Benson, J. (1994). Reinterpreting gender: Southeast Asian refugees and American society. In L. A. Camino & R. M. Krulfeld (Eds.), Reconstructing lives, recapturing meaning: Refugee identity, gender, and culture change (pp. 49–75). Basel: Gordon and Breach Publishers.

Berry, J. W. (1997). Immigration, acculturation, and adaptation. Applied Psychology: An International Review, 46(1), 5–34.

Bottomley, G. (1992). *From another place: Migration and the politics of culture.* Cambridge: Cambridge University Press.

Bourdieu, P. (1990). *The logic of practice.* Stanford: Stanford University Press.

Burr, V. (1995). *An introduction to social constructionism.* London/New York: Routledge.

Carballo, M. (1994). *Scientific consultation on the social and health impact of migration: Priorities for research.* Geneva: International Organization for Migration.

Carter, G. B. (2004). *Australian law for the 21st century.* Ashfield: Wensleydale Press.

Civil Code. Islamic Republic of Iran. http://www.alaviandassociates.com/documents/civilcode.pdf. Accessed November 29, 2008.

Council, F. L. (2000). *The best interests of the child? The interaction of public and private law in Australia.* Barton: Family Law Council.

Darvishpour, M. (1999). Intensified gender conflicts within Iranian families in Sweden. *NORA: Nordic Journal of Women's Studies, 7*(1), 20–33.

Darvishpour, M. (2002). Immigrant women challenge the role of men: How the changing power relationship within Iranian families in Sweden intensifies family conflicts after immigration. *Journal of Comparative Family Studies, 32*(2), 271–296.

Dill, B. T., & Baca Zinn, M. (Eds.). (1994). *Women of color in U.S. society.* Philadelphia: Temple University Press.

Ebrahimi, S. N. (2006). Child custody (Hizanat) under Iranian law: An analytical discussion. *Family Law Quarterly, 39*, 459–476.

Eckert, P. (1989). The whole woman: Sex and gender differences in variation. *Language Variation and Change, 1*, 245–268.

Esfandiari, H. (1994). The Majles and women's issues in the Islamic republic of Iran. In M. Afkhaim & E. Friedl (Eds.), *In the eye of the storm: Women in post-revolutionary Iran* (pp. 61–79). Syracuse: Syracuse University Press.

Gal, S. (1994). Between speech and silence: The problematics of research on language and gender. In C. Roman, S. Juhasz, & C. Miller (Eds.), *The women and language debate: A sourcebook* (pp. 407–431). New Brunswick: Rutgers University Press.

Ghaffarian, S. (2001). The acculturation of Iranians in the United States. *Journal of Social Psychology, 126*(6), 565–571.

Ghorashi, H. (2003). *Ways to survive, battles to win: Iranian women exiles in the Netherlands and United States.* New York: Nova Science Publishers, Inc.

Graham, M., & Khosravi, S. (1997). Home is where you make it: Repatriation and diaspora culture among Iranians in Sweden. *Journal of Refugee Studies, 10*(2), 115–133.

Higgins, P. J., & Shoar-Ghaffari, P. (1994). Women's education in the Islamic republic of Iran. In M. Afkhaim & E. Friedl (Eds.), *In the eye of the storm: Women in post-revolutionary Iran* (pp. 19–43). Syracuse: Syracuse University Press.

Hinds, R. W., & Bradshaw, E. R. (2005). Gender bias in lawyers' affidavits to the family court of Australia. *Family Court Review, 43*(3), 445–453.

Jolly, S., & Reeves, H. (2005). *Gender & migration.* Brighton: Bridge.

Kamalkhani, Z. (1988). *Iranian immigrants and refugees in Norway.* Bergen: University of Bergen.

Kilic, S. (1997). Who is an Australian woman? In K. P. Hughes (Ed.), *Contemporary Australian feminism 2* (pp. 30–51). South Melbourne: Longman.

Kousha, M. (2002). *Voices from Iran: The changing lives of Iranian women.* Syracuse: Syracuse University Press.

Kramarae, C., & Spender, D. (Eds.). (2000). *Routledge international encyclopedia of women* (Vol. 3). New York: Routledge.

Krulfeld, R. M. (1994). Changing concepts of gender roles and identities in refugee communities. In L. A. Camino & R. M. Krulfeld (Eds.), *Reconstructing lives, recapturing meaning: Refugee identity, gender, and culture change* (pp. 71–74). Basel: Gordon and Breach Science Publishers.

Krulfeld, R. M., & Camino, L. A. (1994). Introduction. In L. A. Camino & R. M. Krulfeld (Eds.), *Reconstructing lives, recapturing meaning: Refugee identity, gender, and culture change* (pp. ix–xviii). Basel: Gordon and Breach Science Publishers.

Lake, M. (1999). *Getting equal: The history of Australian feminism*. New South Wales: Allen & Unwin.

Lange, C. (2001). Anglo-centrism in multicultural Australia. In P. Crawford & P. Maddern (Eds.), *Women as Australian citizens: Underlying histories* (pp. 178–213). Carlton: Melbourne University Press.

Mahdi, A. A. (2002). Perceptions of gender roles among female Iranian immigrants in the United States. In S. Ansari & V. Martin (Eds.), *Women, religion and culture in Iran* (pp. 189–215). Richmond: Curzon Press.

McEwan, C. (2001). Postcolonialism, feminism and development: Intersections and dilemmas. *Progress in Development Studies, 1*(2), 93–111.

Miliszewska, I. (2006). Gender bias in computer courses in Australia. In E. M. Trauth (Ed.), *Encyclopedia of gender and information technology* (pp. 501–506). USA: Pennsylvania State University.

Moghadam, F. E. (1994). Commoditisation of sexuality and female labor participation in Islam: Implications for Iran, 1960–90. In M. Afkhaim & E. Friedl (Eds.), *In the eye of the storm: Women in post-revolutionary Iran* (pp. 80–97). Syracuse: Syracuse University Press.

Narayan, U. (2000). Essence of culture and a sense of history: A feminist critique of cultural essentialism. In U. Narayan & S. Harding (Eds.), *Decentering the center* (pp. 80–100). Bloomington: Indiana University Press.

Ochs, E. (1992). Indexing gender. In A. Duranti & C. Goodwin (Eds.), *Rethinking context* (pp. 335–358). Cambridge: Cambridge University Press.

Sadeghi, S. (2006). The impact of educational attainment on immigrant Iranian women's perceptions of family gender roles. *Iran Analysis Quarterly, 3*(1), 27–61.

Smolicz, J. (1981). Core values and cultural identity. *Ethnic and Racial Studies, 4*(1), 75–90.

Stetson, D., & Mazur, A. G. (1995). Introduction. In D. Stetson & A. G. Mazur (Eds.), *Comparative state feminism* (pp. 1–21). Thousand Oaks: SAGE Publications.

Tohidi, N. (2004). Iranian women and gender relations among the Iranian immigrants in Los Angeles. In J. Solomon & S. Maasik (Eds.), *California dreams and realities* (pp. 149–159). New York: St Martin's Books.

Toolo, N., & Shakibaee, S. (2000). 'Parted from my origins': Iranian women re-constructing identity. *Studies in Western Australian History, 21*, 101–115.

Winter, J., & Pauwels, A. (2000). Gender and language contact research in the Australian context. *Journal of Multilingual and Multicultural Development, 21*(6), 508–522.

Wood, J. T. (2005). *Gendered lives: Communication, gender and culture*. Belmont: Wadsworth/ Thompson Learning.

Woolard, K. (1997). Between friends: Gender, peer group structure and bilingualism in urban Catalonia. *Language in Society, 26*, 533–560.

Chapter 9
Transnational Experiences of Eastern European Women and Feminist Practices After 1989

Cezara Crisan

9.1 Introduction

In the context of new and developing democracies in Eastern and Central Europe, research accounts on the experience of women in general and (women) migrants from the post-communist states in particular are very scarce. Recent Eastern European scholarship on migration focuses on the dynamics surrounding the ethnicity of migrant populations, rather than gender, race or class, and puts emphasis on the link between internal and external migration. Compared to the extensive research on the earliest waves of Eastern European migrations to the United States (U.S.) and the current focus on recent waves of immigrants from Latin America and Asia, little attention has been given to the Eastern European coming to U.S. after the fall of the Soviet bloc. Furthermore, research on gender and migration has been greatly enriched by the works of scholars from Latin America and Asia but generally overlooks the experience of Eastern European migrant women. From a theoretical standpoint, the experience of immigrants in general and of Eastern European immigrants in particular, has been largely understood at the macro level with the conventional "push and pull" theory and at the micro-level constrained by the assimilationist model. Consequently, the purpose of this chapter is twofold. First it attempts to apply the new transnational model in the interpretation of immigration experience of Eastern European women and their families who migrated to the United States after 1989. Second, it integrates the macro-structural context by presenting the mediating role of women who either returned home or who engaged in circular migration in shaping the socio-cultural environment of their home countries. More specifically, this chapter looks at the effects of immigration on Eastern European migrant women, and the ways in which their immigration experiences advance

C. Crisan, M.A. (✉)
Loyola Univeristy Chicago (LUC) Chicago, IL, USA
e-mail: ccrisa1@luc.edu

G.T. Bonifacio (ed.), *Feminism and Migration: Cross-Cultural Engagements,*
International Perspectives on Migration 1, DOI 10.1007/978-94-007-2831-8_9,
© Springer Science+Business Media B.V. 2012

feminist ideas and practices in their home countries including the form it takes in the context of the new developing democracies in Eastern Europe.

9.2   Methods

Over the course of 2 years, 18 men and women who emigrated from Eastern Europe after 1990 shared their migration stories through in-depth tape recorded interviews. I used the snowball technique to select a non-random sample of respondents in the United States. Participant observation method and data gathered through informal conversations with new immigrants during the past 5 years at various orthodox churches in the areas of Chicago, Northwest Indiana and Michigan allowed me to understand aspects of the dynamic processes related to immigration and settlement of individuals and families coming from Eastern Europe. All except one interview (that had been translated, transcribed and coded in English) occurred in English; however, the informal conversations were conducted in both English and Romanian languages. In the United States, I interviewed 6 Romanian women, 4 Romanian men, 2 women and 2 men from Moldova, 2 Russian women, and 2 Serbian women. Over the phone I interviewed 4 Romanian women engaged in circular migration in Western Europe and 1 returning home from the U.S. after 1 year, and 1 Serbian woman who resided in the U.S. for 9 years and returned home while her husband continues to do temporary work in the U.S.

This chapter is based on an ongoing research where data continue to be collected, and where the findings are limited geographically and by the fact that the sample is not stratified by any other variables than country of origin. Considering these limitations and the narrow literature on recent Eastern European migration, this exploratory study, rather than making generalizations about the overall experience of immigrants from Eastern Europe, aims to point to the issues that transpire from this data collection and to draw trajectories for future research of this immigrant group.

9.3   The Socio-Historical Context of Eastern European[1] Migration

Broadly described, there have been four major historical waves of immigration from Eastern Europe: the first wave from 1880 to 1921, the second wave from 1921 to 1945, the third wave from 1945 to 1989, and the fourth and most recent one, after 1990 (Robila 2010, p. 17). Besides the socio-economic and political contexts that

---

[1]This study mainly focuses on the following countries: the former USSR (including Russia, Moldova, and Ukraine), Romania, Hungary, Bulgaria, and former Yugoslavia.

has shaped these immigrant waves and their settlement patterns abroad, there are a few major variables that have to be taken into account when describing the diversity of these immigrant ethnic groups; a diversity that influences their migration and adaptation patterns.

One major variable is the geographical division of the Eastern European region into five major areas: the Baltic States, Transcaucasia, former Soviet States, Central Eastern Europe, and South Eastern Europe.[2] The second variable presents the cultural elements of language and religion. In terms of geographical location, for example, conditions created in Europe during the First and Second World Wars and then the proximity to the Soviet Union later on, have directly affected the patterns of emigration from different regions of Eastern Europe. But these patterns need to be analyzed in conjunction with the cultural identities of people living in these territories.

The largest ethnic and linguistic group in Eastern Europe is made up of Slavs, but they fall into two main categories in terms of their religion: the Christian Eastern Orthodox (Russians, Ukrainians, Belarusians, Bulgarians, Serbs, and Macedonians) and those associated with the Roman Catholic Church (Czechs, Slovaks, Poles, Slovenes, and Croats). Bosnians, a smaller group, practice Islam (Robila 2010, p. 18). The data collected for this study include respondents migrating to Western Europe and the United States after 1989 from the former Soviet States of Russia, Moldova, and Ukraine as well as from Romania, Hungary, Bulgaria, and former Yugoslavia. While an analysis of their complete patterns of migration is beyond the scope of this study, the socio-historical context of the emigration wave after 1990 will be presented and contrasted with the preceding socialist era, with particular attention to gender roles and relations.

9.4   Gender Roles in Eastern Europe

Women in Eastern Europe entered the job market in great numbers after 1940, and later on during the Communist regimes. They had equal opportunities for employment and encouragement from the Communist Party to pursue professional careers that were not commonly available to women in Western capitalist countries. The communist ideology proclaimed equal rights for men and women, both in education and work without assuming traditional gendered jobs for males and females. Despite this proclaimed ideology, however, the culture of most Eastern European societies assumed very restrictive gender roles, where women were expected to take primary responsibilities within the household including the raising of children, regardless of their employment status.

During the Communist era, the proletarianization of women, like working in factories, was seen as a positive aspect that would allow them independence and

---

[2] Different agencies and organizations developed strategies of theoretically dividing the Eastern European map in order to serve their own research interests.

class-consciousness. But, on the other hand, the male/female dichotomy was very obvious; the "fear" that if women will be raised too independently they might believe that heterosexual marriage and the traditional nuclear family are irrelevant in their lives. Karl Heinz Mehlan (1965) argues in her study of Romanian women at this time that more educated women have less desire to bear children, or about 0.7 per family. This was possibly a result of women's awareness of gender discrimination in Romania.

Many of the countries of the former Soviet bloc had good social policies that were supposed to encourage maternity and the whole social culture of child welfare, but, in practice, discriminated against mothers. The idea of a career was a very difficult endeavor for women in these countries. According to Olga Toth (2004, p. 121), "the idea of a career is alien to the Hungarian women, and that they give priority to the interests of the family over the advancement at work." In Romania, where very strong pronatalist policies had been implemented,[3] many families ended up with more children than they could afford and women's roles and responsibilities became locked to the household. Ironically, these extreme pronatalist policies were generally associated with conservative governments, rather than those claiming to be "Marxists." As a result, thousands of children were born into families that did not have the economic resources to properly care for them, and many were abandoned to state-run orphanages. The unusual tradition of child abandonment and its rationalization as "the government wanted them (the children), so the government should raised them," emerged as a reaction to a depressive and exploitative life endured by the so-called "robot-portrait"— ideal of women in a socialist society.

For the most part, families in Eastern European countries have assumed very traditional gendered roles for men and women. These countries developed family patterns of fertility according to their own situation, but the common trend was that of a man as the head of the household and, overall, the small family of one or two children remained ideal over time. Again, this might seem counter-intuitive because socialist ideology emphasized equality between the sexes and more opportunities for women in some traditionally "male" occupations, such as medicine, factory work, and law enforcement. But in reality, most women still found their position at home which was more alike than different from women in non-socialist societies. Mihaela Robila (2004b, p. 147) shows that "it is expected both formally and informally that women should find their satisfaction primary in family and motherhood. While parenthood is highly desirable for both men and women, household tasks are expected to be performed by women." Recent research on Eastern European families have shown that for countries such as Slovenia, Macedonia, Bulgaria, Moldova,

---

[3]On October 1, 1966, a Romanian government decree severely restricted the right to abortion and left women with no other means for controlling their fertility. All forms of "artificial" birth control were banned, and it was not until the late 1980s that an underground, illegal (black) market for birth control pills and devices began to flourish with such products imported from Hungary and the Yugoslavian Federation countries. However, illegal abortions were commonplace during that whole 23 year period and abandonment of children to state-run institutions was also a way for families to deal with the inability of women to control their fertility.

Ukraine and the rest of the former Soviet countries, the same variation of gender roles are maintained more or less rigidly, with the men assuming the role of breadwinner and head of the family, while women, regardless of their employment outside the house, are responsible for the household tasks as in any patriarchal culture (Filadelfiová 2004; Ule 2004; Robila 2004a, b; Staykova 2004; Bodrug-Lungu 2004; Zhurzhenko 2004). However, the development of a more "westernized" culture with more egalitarian gender roles and social relations emerged after the 1990s.

9.5 Gendered Immigration: Circular and Transnational Migration

The increasingly-used concept of transnationalism has been understood as a new form of migration but is, rather, an old phenomenon (Schiller et al. 1992). Many of the features manifested in both the past and present Eastern European patterns of immigration to America resemble elements of transnationalism. The experience of the recent immigration wave of Eastern Europeans in general and of Eastern European women in particular can be understood within the new analytical framework of *transnationalism* which "[refers] to the civic-political membership, economic involvements, social networks, and cultural identities of (im)migrants and their offspring extending across state-national boundaries and linking people and institutions in two or more locations" (Morawska 2003, p. 611).

Circular migration refers to the ability of migrants to maintain dual-home bases in their country of origin and in the U.S. (Duany 2002). They maintain strong familial, social and political ties with their homeland. While the circulatory type of migration from Eastern Europe is mainly shaped by the labor market forces that regulate the globalized economy, the lack of integration in receiving countries locks them into the margins of society as an emerging servant class, joining the larger and international group of "servants of globalization" (Parreñas 2001a, b) who live outside the "core," even as they are no longer permanently residing outside the "core." Many Eastern European migrants to Western Europe today maintain dual households and lifestyles, but still live in ethnic enclaves outside their country. It seems that they never became fully integrated in the country of destination, and their circular migration (in addition to its immediate economic benefits) tends to be a reaction to ethnocentrism, heightened nationalism in receiving states, discrimination, and alienation.

The experience of circular migration among Eastern Europeans is similar to those of Puerto Ricans' migration to the United States (Perez 2004). Despite their birthright of U.S. citizenship (the fact that they are considered to be U.S. citizens), Puerto Ricans pass ethnic and cultural borders—the geographic, cultural and linguistic contact zones that often differ from formal boundaries of nations, but yet subject to inclusion or exclusion in the imagined American nation (Perez 2004, p. 6). Gina Perez published her ethnographic study on the transnational migration between Chicago, USA and San Sebastian, Puerto Rico in *Near Northwest Side Story* (2004), and finds that Puerto Ricans practice circular migration between the island and the mainland—integrated basically in two economies which has become a successful strategy of survival. This finding challenges the assumption that circular migration is a disruptive strategy and is a major cause of economic marginality. But the case of Puerto Ricans complements the situation of Eastern Europeans in this study that resorted to circular migration as a survival strategy after the fall of the Soviet bloc (Sandu 2005a). As an ancillary point, the elite and the poor are positioned differently in their migration trajectories. In the context of economic globalization, the same practice of a highly mobile lifestyle undertaken to generate income seems acceptable when practiced by the elite, but when practiced by the poor is used to justify their economic marginality.

Puerto Ricans, especially women, tend to resist permanent settlement in the U.S. mainland, and their return migration are driven by more than just economic reasons such as job loss and lack of integration. It is also out of concerns for the safety of their children and the care of older relatives back home, which are traditionally women's responsibilities that sustain their circular migration. Circular migration, as a survival strategy, identifies migration structures not so much in terms of the individual and/or structure as in terms of the community and place. As in this case, it is important to understand the role played by the individual, the community and the regional variables in the selectivity of international circular migration. One variable is social capital, more specifically network capital (i.e., family and community), which provides not only support for travel and accommodation at destination countries (Sandu 2005b) but also the family and community left behind. In most cases the extended relatives and networks of women assume the responsibilities of the migrant woman who is temporarily away from her family.

Using an ethnographic approach, research conducted on immigration of Eastern Europeans suggests that ethnic identities and social networks provide continuity in the structure of emigration before and after 1989. Scholars note a negative association between permanent and temporary migration of Eastern Europeans after 2000: where one type of migration increases, the other type decreases. According to Dumitru Sandu and Oana Ciobanu (2004, p. 6), "the easier the pendular moving abroad (ability to move back and forth), the lower the probability of permanent migration." Dumitru Sandu, Cosmin Radu, Monica Constantinescu, and Oana Ciobanu (2004) also find that social networks facilitate the circular or transnational migration from Romanian villages to Western European countries driven by worsening economic conditions. They identify migration structures not in terms of individuals but of communities and regions. In a further study, Sandu concludes:

> In the case of definitive migration the main unit of reference is the individual, in the case of temporary or circular migration, the role of the local community and the area of origin is much stronger. They operate as a support mechanism for organizing various networks of migration circulation and as the beneficiary or impact are of the emigration. (Sandu 2005b, p. 556)

Ethnic and religious minorities such as Germans, Hungarians and Romas were found to be the most mobile group at the start, and then later, migration became a strategy for survival for the larger population. This observation is relevant but would benefit from further research that takes the interaction of gender, family, and job market into account in analyzing these types of migration. Sandu states:

> […] the secondary and tertiary circular migration from villages aboard was supported by networks created by the first-wave migration and by new transnational network s that develop in connection with various processes such as the definitive migration of Germans, particular forms of globalization such as business, transnational cultural continuities and so on. (Sandu 2005b, p. 569)

Sandu (2005a, b) further notes that there is no hierarchy of importance between human capital and social capital; rather a functional difference between them exists in migration. Human capital refers to the level of education which determine how fast and easy an immigrant will integrate in the work force (Robila 2007, p. 56), language proficiency in the adaptation process (Portes and Rumbaut 2006), and motivation for success that would determine participation in programs for job training to increase the likelihood of landing jobs in the host society (Robila 2010, p. 10). Social capital, more specifically network capital (i.e., family and community), provides support for travel and accommodation at destination countries. However, as migration shifts from temporary to permanent, human capital such as language skills, education and professional knowledge become more essential (Sandu 2005b). Alejandro Portes and Ruben Rumbaut (2006) observe that, unlike in the beginning of the twentieth century, the U.S. is no longer the favored destination country among Eastern Europeans who have less human capital and economic resources. More recent findings of Mihaela Robila (2007) documents that Eastern European immigrants who have more resources (human, social, and economic capital) attempt to migrate to U.S. while those with fewer resources tend to migrate to closer geographical locations such as Western Europe (e.g., agricultural workers leaving for Germany, Italy, and Spain).

Transnational migration shapes places and its characteristics such as ethnic and racial composition, religion, age of migrants, geo-political location, and economic order which regulate specific types of migration. Examples include the following: age (the youngest flow of migrants are oriented toward Italy), religion (a large concentration of Romanian Adventist men work in construction areas near Madrid, Spain) and ethnicity (Romanians of Hungarian ethnicity work in Hungary, while the Roma in Germany and Yugoslavia). Additionally, the geographical location of villages strongly influence migration, where places located near major cities and modern roads are more integrated in transnational spaces (Sandu 2005b). All these factors play a role in determining specific trajectories of migration. Moreover, these factors are tied to economic processes in a dialectical way, where migrants "change" the place to which they migrate, and migration, in turn, changes the characteristics of the place from which they migrated. For example, younger migrants tend to go to Italy because of attractive jobs more suitable to their age, like working in hotels, tourism, and entertainment. The Italian entertainment industry requires a constant change of performers; the "age variable" in this industry becomes a factor in promoting circular migration rather than permanent settlement among young people.

When they return to their own countries, other young people from their villages and towns may seek similar jobs abroad, contributing to the development of a pattern where particular "places of origin" have specific characteristics of work. For example, certain towns might have their young people leaving for Italy, while other towns in another country.

9.6 Gendered Labor: Gendered Migration

In framing these migration patterns in the larger historical context, one major effect of the post communist transition on individuals and families is the steady development of temporary or permanent migration toward Western countries. Previous waves of Eastern European migration (i.e., before the establishment of the Communist regimes) was traditionally led by men. There was uneven migration of men and women during the era of communist regimes, which vary by country of destination. But men still predominates in the process. After the fall of the Communist regimes (i.e., 1989 in Romania), more women began to emigrate as a strategy for survival because of increased unemployment in the new economy (Hughes 2000). Their migration also corresponds to the rise of globalization in general, where the movement of capital and labor has become less restricted over the past 30 years.

Consequently, immigration significantly shifted more from male to female. One major reason for this shift includes the demand for domestic work in advanced capitalist countries. In return, the demand for their labor in other countries helped ameliorate the economic difficulties experienced by their families at home countries where many men were either losing their jobs or taking lower paying jobs. While the push and pull theory can help explain general migration movements, as they did for the past waves of emigration from Europe, the nature of these migration patterns now are different. In the case of transnational migration, the receiving country (mostly to United States) has become a more multicultural society, which allows immigrants to participate in the economy while preserving their ethnic identity unlike those experienced by earlier generations. Hence, they can settle in the U.S. and generally assimilate, while still personally and, through social networks, maintain a major aspect of their ethnicity. However, in the case of circular migration (mostly to Western Europe) the social context is not so permissive for immigrants to assimilate in the host country and, as a result, there are not the kinds of permanent ethnic enclaves of Eastern Europeans in Western Europe. Still, many Eastern European women from rural areas use their social networks for circular migration mostly to Western Europe. Unlike the previous generation of men who migrated to Western Europe, today's migrating women cannot easily find jobs and security that would allow them to sponsor family reunification in the host country. But those coming to the U.S. and Canada are mostly migrating with their families. In both cases, it is less common for women to migrate and then bring their families, in contrast to the patterns of the past, when men could migrate first and then bring their families later. So in both cases, women do not actually exercise full independence within the family, and the empowerment brought by their migration experience is limited not only by the changes in socio-economic and political context but also their gender. Eastern Europeans escaping from the Soviet bloc in the past could request and be granted asylum in a Western country, while now they can freely move and work in these countries. Gender defines their jobs with less economic power and social status.

Feminist literature is rich in examining the experiences of different groups of migrant women around the world, emphasizing the discrimination faced by these workers. Rachel Salazar Parreñas (2001a, b), in *Transgressing the Nation-State: the Partial Citizenship of Migrant Philippine Domestic Workers*, provides more details of how the burden of these migrant workers is doubled by the limitation of their citizenship rights in the receiving country, which constitutes a way of keeping down their already low income and minimizing their possibilities for family reunification. While countries such as Hungary, Slovenia, Romania and Bulgaria are members of the European Union (EU) and, therefore, migrants coming from these countries are EU citizens, their access in the job market remains limited to domestic work and other lower service jobs. Because immigration policies are generally shaped to regulate the labor force (often to fill a labor gap, sometimes to stop an uncontrolled influx), family migration is not always an option among migrant workers. Overall, the *feminization of labor* (using women as a source of cheap labor to maximize profits) is maintained by a gendered labor regime, which in turn supports the global economy. Furthermore, Valentine Moghadam, in *Gender and the Global Economy*, perceives feminization of labor as the main consequence of economic restructuring and explains:

> The world trade in services also favors women's labor migration, in contrast to the demand for men manufacturing workers during the earlier periods of industrialization in Europe and the United States. Mexican, Central American and Caribbean women have migrated to the United States to work as nurses, nannies, and domestics; Filipinas and Sri Lankans have gone to neighboring countries as well as to the Middle East to work as waitresses, nurses, nannies, and domestics; Argentine women have traveled to Italy to work as nurses; and an increasing number of Moroccan, Tunisian, and Algerian women have migrated alone to work in various occupations in France, Italy, and Spain. (Moghadam 2000, p. 137)

Gendered labor is connected to gendered wages, of course, and wage discrimination against women is commonplace all over the world (Moghadam 2000). As the economic well- being for most working class people in the developing world has deteriorated as well as in the "post-Communist" countries of Eastern Europe, this discrimination has intensified. Moghadam, for instance, notes:

> The fact that in Russia and Poland women's unemployment is higher than men's despite women's higher educational attainment and their long work experience is suggestive of the existence of gender bias in labor markets, often influenced by the gender ideology that men are primary breadwinners and more deserving of the better jobs. (Moghadam 2000, p. 133)

A common survival strategy for young, single Eastern European women is to move abroad to Western Europe, Canada, or the United States where there is a demand for domestic work as housekeepers or babysitters (Sandu 2005a, b).

However, many young well-educated girls responding to respectable job advertisements end up working in lesser jobs, sometimes even under conditions of coercion, at the extreme risk of ending up as victims of human trafficking (Feingold 2005, p. 26; Kligman and Limoncelli 2005, p. 118; Raymond et al. 2001).

As industries have privatized in former socialist countries, discriminatory labor markets have pushed women out from the previously inclusive professions (men are now dominating) and occupations, toward lower paying and service sector jobs. For example, gender specifications are a customary feature of job advertising and hiring, as are preference based on marital status in many of these countries. Such gendered practices exclude women from some occupations; concentrate them in other jobs, which contribute to high poverty rates and unemployment for women, and leave them vulnerable to the enticements of traffickers who take advantage of their desire for better working and living conditions abroad (Kligman and Limoncelli 2005, p. 120).

Women migrants from other parts of the globe also face similar challenges; many of them are trafficked across national boundaries. Women migrants who are considered "illegal" are even more vulnerable to quasi-slavery work conditions because they have little, if any, protection from the legal system (Vayrynen 2003). In general, illegal immigration seems increasing due to stricter border controls. It is presumed that the more closed the borders are, the more attractive it is to target these countries; the more human trafficking grows as a share of illegal migration, the greater is the role played by the national and transnational organized crime in this process (Vayrynen 2003). Furthermore, illegal trafficking of people is shaped by the same economic and political forces that facilitate the international labor movement. Host countries benefit from the infusion of hard currency brought by illegal traffickers earning huge profits—all these from the exploitation of migrant people, especially migrant women. The membership in the European Union (which actually created the conditions for the specific case of migration—transnational or circular migration) has become a very complex case in analyzing the relationship between migration and citizenship. But despite the effort on having a coherent intergovernmental immigration policy between the EU members, the circumstances for granting asylum to victims of human trafficking vary.

Other common migration alternative for some Eastern European women seems to be the arranged marriage with a U.S. citizen. Unfortunately, this "alternative" is now a commonly accepted practice in sending countries. Although the practice of "arranged marriage" or "sending the young women away" is not considered a traditional *cultural* practice of these societies, it has become an increasingly accepted *economic* strategy. Traditionally, the common expectation for a young woman is to find a spouse from the same or higher social class, similar age, and with the same ethnic background to whom she would be expected to commit her love, and devote her life as a woman, wife and mother of his future children. The new practice of on-line dating with a foreign citizen (preferably from United States) and the increase in the business of marital matching change the modern values of (marital) love to those of marriage for convenience. The respondents from Russia and Moldova (young women who met their American husbands through on-line dating or through arranged marriage) in this study offer interesting justifications for their decisions to marry:

> *If would have not been for the love I have for my husband, I would have never came to America.* (Natasha G.) [from Russia]

Or,

> *I fell in love with him from the first time we have met.* (Malina R.) [from Russia]

If these behaviors can be rationalized through the discourse of "love," the question remains as to what extent this type of migration is an empowering process for women from this region or not. This could be just one example of the effects of transition from socialism to a new, less stable economic system on existing societal norms.

Eva Kovach and Attila Melegh (2008), in their pioneering work on gender in Eastern Europe, look at the reasons, type and processes of migration and the integration of female migrants. Their study contains important insights, but falls short in fully explaining the ways that globalization and new economic processes impact on gender relations in the lives of migrant women. Broadly discussed, I argue that the term "integration" in European discourse on immigration is analogous to the American concept of "assimilation" since the prejudiced context of ethnic exclusionism accepts the idea of immigrants' general adjustment to the new surroundings but does not envision a complete assimilation of them over time. They remain outside the "core" based on seemingly unchanging constructions of "West" and "East."

There are limited interpretations on how Eastern European women define "freedom" in their experiences of migration. More research deals with the experiences of migrant women from the developing countries and shows the dramatic social consequences of globalization and neoliberal policies affecting especially younger women. According to David Harvey,

> The paths of women's liberation from traditional patriarchal control in developing countries lie either through degrading factory labor or through trading on sexuality which vary from respectable work as hostess and waitress, to the sex trade (one of the most lucrative of all contemporary industries in which a good deal of slavery is involved). (Harvey 2005, p. 159)

In Eastern Europe, there is a need for more research to examine migrant women in the context of new cultural constructions of gender as well as socio-economic conditions that pull Eastern European women out of work in their home countries after 1989. Similar to the "marriage for convenience" type of migration, the same question could be raised as to what extent this type of migration empowers women, especially if looking at the risk and consequences involved in this process.

Many middle-aged Eastern European women, mostly married and mothers, choose to practice circular migration to work in the domestic sector in Western European countries. Their migration is consistent with the current literature on gender and migration in many other parts of the world, increasingly among developing countries. Emigrants, mostly women, are depicted as main actors of migration, with increased attention to the emerging transnational families and the consequences of migration to the children left behind (Parreñas 2001a, b, 2005; Sassen 2002; Spitzer et al. 2003). One common thread in feminist literature focuses on the ways in which the organization of reproductive work (housework, childrearing and elderly care) has been changed in families around the world in the context of the global economy (Ehrenreich and Hochschild 2002) and related issues. Questions include, to what extent have these changes in the global economy created the conditions for the emergence of transnational motherhood? From a utilitarian perspective, who benefits from these changes? What is the likely effect of a generation of children separated for long periods of time from their mothers?

Children left behind by their Eastern European mothers working abroad is a new social reality in many countries. More specifically, the impact of long distance separation inevitably strains family relations and well-being of children. It has created a situation where these children left by their parents in the care of relatives or extended family often tend to develop social and emotional problems, have lower academic performance and engage in delinquency (Shapkina 2010). The ideology of traditional gender norms in Eastern European societies adds more pressure in family relations, where the mother temporary migrates to work abroad, and the father resists assuming women's responsibilities at home. In her absence, another woman in the family (mostly the grandmother) is responsible for doing "women's work" in the household.

Temporary migration is an economic strategy of many Eastern European women working in Western Europe and the U.S. They aim to live relatively modest lives in host societies and send home much of their earnings to their families. Immigration tends to change family dynamics when women emigrate; gender roles seem more egalitarian with women gaining more power in decision-making. However, Eastern European women working in Western European countries who are engaged in circular migration have more opportunity to participate frequently in family decisions because they tend to return home on a regular basis than those working in the U.S. or in Canada. On the other hand, after a period of separation, women working in the U.S. or in Canada might find their children in good care but may have "lost" their husbands to other women and very often are ready to divorce them. Silvia R., from Romania, who had a 1 year visa to the U.S. and worked in jobs well beyond her skills, explains:

> I used to call home very often, we talk over the phone a lot, and he never complained about the fact that I will be working in U.S. for one year, it was a decision we took together. When I returned home, he was ready to divorce me for another woman . . . at least if he would have told me on the phone while I was there. I would have never returned home, I would have done everything to move my daughter to America with me and I would have tried to make a life over there . . . Now I cannot even return back to U.S. . . . If he would have had to raise the child by himself, with no help, this would not have happened . . . But we were helped a lot by grandma.

Not all women who migrated to the U.S. find themselves without a husband or ready to desert them after a period of separation while they work overseas. But Silvia R.'s experience captures the challenges of a woman's position in her family; her better economic position achieved through migration created the conditions for changes in family relations. At the micro–level, this situation usually happens in a cultural context where the women's responsibilities regarding children are customarily taken over by a grandmother or another female member of the family; the husband, in turn, becomes freed from domestic responsibilities other than the authority figure and providing financial support. At the macro-level, the increased divorced rate in Eastern European countries might be also explained in part by the changes at the societal level, as produced by a consumerist culture of the new capitalist system. Women's status has not only become lower now, not only economically and politically, but they have also become increasingly portrayed and perceived as sex objects.[4] For example, even among marriages where women did not migrate, a very common trend after 1990 in Eastern Europe has been the husband divorcing his older wife and leaving his family in order to marry a younger woman. An emerging new culture has evolved that sees women as lesser beings than men, and blames the individual for their failure rather than understanding the broader social disruptions and consequences brought about by migration.

9.7   Gendered Migration's Impact on Gender Relations

Eastern European migrant women tend to adopt a more progressive gender role and attitude while living in Western societies. However, Eastern European men still favor the traditional gender roles for women. Similar to the findings on the Mexican family experience of migration (Hondagneu-Sotelo 1994), major changes in gender relations develop among Eastern European family's permanent migration to the U.S. Eastern European women settle in a more protective, empowering and egalitarian system like the U.S. with less gender discrimination compared to their own countries. A woman from Moldova explains: "*If in America a man beat up women, you call the police; at home we call this tradition.*" While this statement might seem an extreme representation, it does point out that there are socio-cultural practices and legal protections for women in the United States that are not necessarily as common in Eastern Europe. Aside from the cultural, social, and political factors affecting the lives of Eastern European women, the issue of economics is also important. While most of the Eastern European migration to the U.S. after 1990 consists of legal immigrants with the right to gain employment, and often with a high educational background, many Eastern European women tend to work in entry-level positions or low paying jobs well below their skills level and qualifications, although they eventually advance over time (Robila 2008). Personal accounts of respondents in this study confirm that women develop more independence and autonomy after migration, and, thus, result in the exercise of more power in the family.

---

[4]Both in media and in everyday life, women's bodies are constantly scrutinized, and one of the most desirable qualities for women and their first passport for success is a "good looking" body image. Starting with the employment opportunities section of any newspaper that features advertisement such as: "Searching for young, good looking women with good organizational skills." The skills and education required for the position mostly are mentioned secondarily. Media portrayal of women, *even women in politics*, emphasizes very sexualized postures (Tango 2008).

Migration and settlement to the U.S. result in the renegotiation of gender relations in the traditional patriarchal Eastern European family. However, new forms of relations are contingent upon the intersections of social class, age, and educational background of immigrants. For example, husbands in the home country who are better educated tend to adjust to shifting gender relations in the U.S. than those who are less educated. Even as their wives acquired more education and skills in the U.S. with more status or power accrued to them, educated husbands are still more secure in their social class position relative to them. Less educated husbands tend to have diminished power as their wives acquired more education or skills. For example, many immigrants from former Yugoslavia came to the U.S. as refugees from the major wars in the 1990s which included less educated male workers (Robila 2008). Male immigrants from Moldova also tend to have less educational background than those from most of the other Eastern European countries. These men generally find stable blue-collar jobs, while their spouses often acquire more education and skills resulting in higher occupational status. Based on the data collected for this study, migrant families from former Yugoslavia and Moldova tend to report major transformation in family relations and experience most difficulties in maintaining traditional patriarchal practices. It seems that family power tend to become balanced between the husband and wife. Thus, social, economic, and cultural factors contribute to the changing gender relations among Eastern European immigrants.

Changes in gender relations shape the differing opinions between men and women over whether the family should settle permanently in the U.S. One concern is that securing a stable employment is increasingly becoming difficult for men. Also, Eastern European women's independence in the U.S. compared to their traditional gender roles practiced in the home country makes adjustment to American culture challenging. Since the U.S. economic recession in 2008, job market opportunities are unstable and unpredictable. Small businesses provide little opportunities but these do not ensure security as those provided in the immediate post World War II period. Consequently, return migration became a common strategy for many Eastern European families who emigrated to the U.S. after 1989. The mediating roles of women who either returned home or who engaged in circular migration in shaping the socio-cultural environment of their home countries is limited to common cultural practices (i.e., wedding and baby showers) and similar activities that define their position as main agents of transmitting cultural practices from Western/ U.S. to Eastern European culture.

Women's economic and social empowerment through migration and how such experience affects them upon returning home can take different forms. These are contingent upon the migrant women's human and social capital that consequently determine the type of migration (i.e., temporary or permanent) they are engaged in. Professional women and those living in urban areas have more opportunities to engage in international projects in both Western European countries and the United States. Their training experience in the U.S. or Eastern Europe is usually intended to establish similar ventures like operating a business or establishing an organization in the home country. However, many of these projects are related to social work or environmental issues, and although they empower the participants in some ways, their experiences do not fundamentally change the status of women and create a kind of "artificial and limited" political empowerment. Participation in humanitarian activities or engagement in international projects may elevate women's social status, but they remain an isolated group and at the margins of the political arena.

The elderly population of migrant Eastern European women, many of whom are retired with grown up children living in the U.S., undertake a more transitional migration to the U.S. where they can work for a year while living with or near their children. In many former socialist Eastern European countries, people used to retire earlier and were less likely to embrace a new career after that. As a legacy of the old regime, there is a cultural tradition of involvement in raising the grandchildren after retirement. Parents involved in circular migration to Western European countries tend to leave their children in the care of their older parents. However, those who settle in the U.S. are more likely to invite their parents to live with them for up to a year, involving them in the care of their grandchildren. Some of these grandparents gradually change their legal status from visitor to permanent resident and start to balance their own jobs, mostly in their ethnic communities with those of helping their own children. Grandmothers tend to engage the most in transnational migration, because they almost never plan to permanently settle in America. But, on the other hand, they spend very limited time in the home country. Living in ethnic enclaves and attending ethnic churches, they almost never learn English beyond the basic skills they need for traveling and dealing with the American bureaucracy for certain services. Culturally, these elder Eastern European women are major agents in maintaining old traditions, teaching (grand) children the customs of the home countries such as cooking ethnic food and staying strongly connected with events at home through the internet and satellite television. These migrants are also more involved in kin work with relatives back home being in regular contact, sending presents and remittances, and functioning as carriers of American culture.

However, these cultural exchanges are somehow unidirectional, from the home country to the host one, and the opportunity for cross-cultural exchanges that would involve ideas (such as more gender equality) and practices of the host country to home, remain limited to practices such as the wedding showers, baby showers, Valentine's day or other holidays that seem new for the Eastern Europeans. These have become now more popularly adopted and adapted to these societies. For example, the baby showers consist of the gathering of families, including children, women and men, rather than restricted only to women friends. In most of the Eastern European countries, the idea of a feminist is somewhat subversive; the western construction of a feminist as politically engaged or advocate for equality in society remain unpopular.

Another interesting are of interaction occurring in the context of migration is domestic violence. Unlike the latest (feminist) research advanced in Eastern European countries at the intersection of gender and violence during the transition era, the experience of family violence of Eastern European immigrants' remains understudied (Johnson and Robinson 2007). Domestic violence experienced by Eastern European women *after* migration also remains marginal in scholarly discourse. Research on gender politics in post-communist Europe concludes that the values of women's rights lag behind concepts of democracy in civil society. Violence against women in the form of beating, conjugal rape, incest, trafficking sexual harassment and verbal aggression are still widespread (Roman 2001, p. 58). According to Monica Lovinescu (1999), in Romania, feminism for many "true Romanian liberals" is a "hysteria" and "grotesque political correctness coming from American campuses" (cited in Roman 2001, p. 61). Addressing violence against women, like in other countries, remains a feminist challenge.

Studies of immigrant women from Latin and Central America have shown that domestic violence is not higher than the native U.S. population, but exacerbated by the limited language skills, isolation from contact with family and community, uncertain legal status, lack of access to dignified jobs, and experience with authorities in their countries of origin (Menjivar and Salcido 2002). Domestic violence experienced by these groups of immigrant women has also been analyzed in conjunction with women and illegal status, trafficking, fear of deportation and separation from their U.S. born children, which emphasize their oppression at multiple intersecting levels—from the social structural to the institutional, and to the interpersonal (Mendez 2008).

Overall, it is not easy to compare the experiences of Eastern European migrant women to women migrating to the U.S. from Central America for several reasons. First, the migration from Mexico has been a more continuing stream of migration with Latino communities well established in many areas of the U.S. where immigrants are more easily integrated in these communities and in their American life. In contrast, the latest wave of immigration from Eastern Europe, unlike the previous ones, are less connected to the ethnic enclaves and churches established by the older generations. The demographic profile of the newer immigrant waves is also very different from their predecessors. The home societies were largely secularized during the communist regimes in Eastern Europe, and these generations were raised with less contact to religion and to the church institution. With the transition to a new economic and political system, the post-communist, neo-conservative, and ethno-religious nationalist context created a culture where individuals that eventually become immigrants have a very difficult time in "transplanting" their religious experience, and adapting their relationship to a church and the changes in orthodox practices in North America. For example, the "democratic," rather than hierarchical structure, of the church in the host country as well as its lay leadership. The newer wave of immigrants after 1989 are more educated and, in most instances, their educational and professional background allows them to "skip" steps taken by their previous compatriots that used the ethnic enclaves and the church as a buffer in the process of their integration. Also, their white collar professional status, as well as their racial background now resemble more with the white Anglo-Saxon profile, permitting them a higher position in the racialized structure of the American society compared with their older compatriots coming before World War II, mostly peasants coming to America to become blue collar workers, who were often not perceived as "whites" at their time of arrival (Guglielmo 2005).

These characteristics of the newer Eastern European immigrants make them different in many variables from that of immigrants from Mexico and Latin America, and therefore simple comparisons cannot be made. However, the experiences of Eastern Europeans engaged in circular migration to Western Europe, does resemble many of the characteristics of Mexican migration to U.S. In Western Europe, the Eastern European migrant women are largely engaged in domestic work or the entertainment and hotel industry and are more likely to live in the newly founded enclaves. They use the network formed by the previous immigrants from their home communities and are also more likely to encounter xenophobia, and racial or ethnic discrimination.

The general conversation in the sociological field of migration presents the variable of gender in conjunction with the country of origin of women migrants and their marital status. Studies have shown that women's sense of empowerment is facilitated by migration. A common case describes the household division of labor which had not changed significantly after immigrating to U.S., but women gain more confidence as they negotiate their traditional gender roles in the host culture (Zentgraph 2002). It appears that some similarities of experiences could be drawn between Eastern European migrant women and other groups of immigrant women.

9.8   Conclusion

Since the 1990s immigration from Eastern Europe to Western Europe and the U.S. has increased. Unlike the previous wave of emigrants, women from the former socialist countries are more involved in recent waves of migration, brought about by the worsening economic conditions associated with the transition from a socialist economy to a capitalist market economy. The discriminatory labor markets also push women out from well-paid professions toward lower paid, service sector jobs, and the demand for domestic work in advanced capitalist countries. The trajectories of their migration are contingent not only upon their human and social capital but also their age and marital status. Young, single women have more "opportunities" to engage in circular migration to Western Europe where they undertake temporary jobs, or resort to arranged marriages to men in the U.S. or Canada. Many middle-aged, married women leave their children in the care of extended families and find seasonal jobs in Western Europe. Those with more human capital like education and live in urban areas are more likely to migrate with their husband and children to the U.S. Others from rural areas tend to migrate to nearby countries.

Gender relations interact with immigration in multiple ways. This study indicates that the more patriarchal the family is the more dramatic is the change within their families. Because of less discriminatory practices in receiving countries like the U.S., Eastern European women have better opportunities to advance themselves in these countries and become economically independent. The elderly population of Eastern European women is commonly engaged in transnational migration influenced by their migrant children in the U.S. and Canada. They spend from 6 months up to 1 year in the U.S., then return to their homeland for short periods of time and then back to United States. Elderly women invest their resources earned overseas to supplement their pension at home. Besides the ethnic church, the family, especially grandparents, become the main agents of maintaining traditions and culture of their home country.

Framing migration as an empowering process for women still tends to point primarily toward economic empowerment. This applies to Eastern European women engaged in circular migration to Western countries at the expense of separation from their families. In general, immigration and settlement patterns of Eastern European women tend to weaken familial patriarchal structure in terms of exercising decision making power at home. Although many of the culturally-inscribed gendered practices are well preserved, migration and settlement to the U.S. facilitate the renegotiation of traditional gender relations. But new forms of relations are contingent upon the intersections of social class, age, and educational background of immigrants.

Migration of Eastern European women to advanced liberal countries like the U.S. or Canada fosters empowerment, achieved mainly through their economic advancement. While they are still influenced by traditional culture and gender ideology, their migration experiences to Western societies with different cultural, political and social norms about women mark the transition from a life now defined on their own terms, especially concerning the well-being of their children. Having greater economic leverage than their husbands left behind in Eastern Europe, migrant women in circular or permanent migration exercise power in the family. Migration, thus, becomes an avenue to advance gender equality.

References

Bodrug-Lungu, V. (2004). Families in Moldova. In M. Robila (Ed.), *Families in Eastern Europe* (Contemporary perspectives in family research, Vol. 5, pp. 173–186). San Diego: Emerald Group Publishing Limited.

Duany, J. (2002). Mobile livelihoods: The socio-cultural practices of circular migrant between Puerto Rico and the United States. *International Migration Review, 36*(2), 355–388.

Ehrenreich, B., & Hochschild, R. (2002). *A global woman: Nannies, maids and sex workers in the new economy*. New York: Metropolitan Books.

Feingold, A. D. (2005, September/October). Human trafficking. *Foreign Policy, 150*, 26–32.

Filadelfiová, J. (2004). Families in Slovakia. In M. Robila (Ed.), *Families in Eastern Europe* (Contemporary perspectives in family research, Vol. 5, pp. 49–68). San Diego: Emerald Group Publishing Limited.

Guglielmo, T. A. (2005). Review: [Untitled]; Not just black and white: Historical and contemporary perspectives on immigration, race, and ethnicity in the United States. *The Journal of American History, 92*(2), 635–636.

Harvey, D. (2005). *A brief history of neoliberalism*. Oxford: Oxford University Press.

Hondagneu-Sotelo, P. (1994). *Gendered migration: Mexican experience of immigration*. Berkeley: University of California Press.

Hughes, D. (2000). 'The Natasha' trade: The transnational shadow market of trafficking in women. *Journal of International Affairs, 53*(2), 625–626.

Johnson, E. J., & Robinson, C. J. (2007). *Living gender after communism*. Bloomington: Indiana University Press.

Kligman, G., & Limoncelli, S. (2005). Trafficking women after socialism: To, through and from Eastern Europe. *Social Politics: International Studies in Gender, State and Society, 12*, 118–140.

Kovach, E., & Melegh, A. (2008). In a gendered space: Forms and reasons of migration and the integration of female migrants. *Demographia, 5*(50), 26–59.

Lovinescu, M. (1999). Deficitul de democratie. *Romania Literara, 37*. (15/09/1999–21/09/1999).

Mehlan, K. H. (1965). Legal abortions in Romania. *Journal of Sex Research, 1*(1), 31–38.

Mendez, D. S. (2008). Gender on a new frontier: Mexican migration in the new rural mountain west. *Gender and Society, 23*(6), 747–767.

Menjivar, C., & Salcido, O. (2002). Immigrant women and domestic violence: Common experiences in different countries. *Gender and Society, 16*(6), 898–920.

Moghadam, V. M. (2000). Gender and the global economy. In M. M. Ferree, J. Lorber, & B. B. Hess (Eds.), *Revisioning gender* (pp. 128–160). Walnut Creek: Altamira Press.

Morawska, E. (2003). Disciplinary agendas and analytic strategies of research on immigrant transnationalism: Challenges of interdisciplinary knowledge. *International Migration Review, 37*(3), 611–640.

Parreñas, R. S. (2001a). *Servants of globalization: Women, migration, and domestic work*. Stanford: Stanford University Press.

Parreñas, R. S. (2001b). Mothering from a distance: Emotions, gender, and intergenerational relations in Filipino transnational families. *Feminist Studies, 27*(2), 361–390.

Parreñas, R. S. (2005). *Children of global migration*. Stanford: Stanford University Press.

Perez, G. (2004). *The near northwest side story: Migration, displacement & Puerto Rican families*. Berkeley: University of California Press.

Portes, A., & Rumbaut, R. G. (2006). *Immigrant America: A portrait*. Berkeley: University of California Press.

Raymond, G. J., Hughes, D. M., & Gomez, J. C. (2001). *Sex trafficking in the United States: International and domestic trends*. North Amherst: Coalition Against Trafficking in Women.

Robila, M. (2004a). Families in Eastern Europe: Context, trends and variations. In M. Robila (Ed.), *Families in Eastern Europe* (pp. 1–14). Amsterdam: Elsevier.

Robila, M. (2004b). Child development and family functioning within the Romanian context. In M. Robila (Ed.), *Families in Eastern Europe* (Contemporary perspectives in family research, Vol. 5, pp. 141–154). San Diego: Emerald Group Publishing Limited.

Robila, M. (2007). Eastern European immigrants in the United States: A socio-demographic profile. *The Social Science Journal (Fort Collins), 44*(1), 113–125.

Robila, M. (2008). Characteristic of Eastern European immigration in the United States. *Journal of Comparative Family Studies, 39*(4), 545–556.

Robila, M. (2010). *Eastern European immigrant families*. New York: Routledge.

Roman, D. (2001). Gendering Eastern Europe: Pre-feminist, prejudice, an east–west dialogue in post-communist Romania. *Women's Studies International Forum, 24*, 55–66.

Sandu, D. (2005a). Migratia circulatorie ca startegie de viata. *Sociologie Romaneasca, 2*, 5–30.

Sandu, D. (2005b). Emerging transnational migration from Romanian villages. *Current Sociology, 53*(4), 555–582.

Sandu, D., Radu, C., Constantinescu, M., & Ciobanu, O. (2004, November). *A county report on Romanian migration abroad: Stocks and flows after 1989*. Study of Migration. Multicultural Center Prague.

Sassen, S. (2002). Global cities and survival circuits. In B. Ehrenreich & A. R. Hochschild (Eds.), *Global woman: Nannies, maids, and sex workers in the new economy* (pp. 254–272). New York: Henry Holt.

Schiller, N., Basch, L., & Blanc-Szanton, C. (1992). Transnationalism: A new analytic framework for understanding migration. *Annals of the New York Academy of Sciences, 645*, 1–24.

Shapkina, N. (2010). *Gender and social change: Negotiating identities, relations, and movements*. Market Street Room. Formal Paper presented at MSS Chicago.

Spitzer, D., Neufeld, A., Harrison, M., & Hughes, M. (2003). Caregiving in transnational context: "My wings have been cut; where can I fly?". *Gender and Society, 4*(17), 267–286.

Staykova, R. (2004). The Bulgarian family: Specific and development from liking in the village square to love in the "chat". In M. Robila (Ed.), *Families in Eastern Europe* (Contemporary perspectives in family research, Vol. 5, pp. 155–171). San Diego: Emerald Group Publishing Limited.

Tango. (2008). Revista de citit si iubit. *Tango: The magazine to be read and to be loved, 42.* ISSN 1841–7493.

Toth, O. (2004). The Hungarian family. Families in Eastern Europe. *Contemporary Perspectives in Family Research, 5,* 121–139.

Ule, M. (2004). Changes in the family life course in Slovenia. In M. Robila (Ed.), *Families in Eastern Europe* (Contemporary perspectives in family research, Vol. 5, pp. 87–101). San Diego: Emerald Group Publishing Limited.

Vayrynen, R. (2003). *Illegal immigration, human trafficking, and organized crime.* United Nation University; Finland: University of Helsinki; and Indiana: University of Notre Dame.

Zentgraph, K. F. (2002). Immigration and empowerment. *Gender and Society, 16*(5), 625–646.

Zhurzhenko, T. (2004). Families in the Ukraine: Between postponed modernization, neo-familialism and economic survival. In M. Robila (Ed.), *Families in Eastern Europe* (Contemporary perspectives in family research, Vol. 5, pp. 187–209). San Diego: Emerald Group Publishing Limited.

Part III
Resistance and Social Justice

Chapter 10
Transnational Working-Class Women's Activism in New York's Confederated Hispanic Societies (1939–1977)

Montse Feu

10.1 Introduction

Forced to leave Spain because of their support of the Second Spanish Republic, numerous Spanish Civil War exiles joined the Sociedades Hispanas Confederadas (Confederated Hispanic Societies [SHC]) upon their arrival to the United States.[1] In this chapter the confederation's political activism is discussed in a twofold approach. Firstly, I analyze how women were symbolically represented in the confederation's newspaper *España Libre* (Free Spain) through its rhetorical denunciation of fascism and Francoism.[2] Based on the feminist research of Yuval-Davis et al. (1989), Gabriela Baeza Ventura (2006), and Anne McClintock (1993), I highlight the constructed gendered citizenship in *España Libre*: Spanish women's relationship with the exiled nation was defined by their loyalty to men. Secondly, I document how confederate women rallied in New York City's streets denouncing the Spanish military revolt, boycotted consumer goods in order to economically undermine Francisco Franco's dictatorship, and raised funds to aid republican Spain. The second part of my approach shows the diverse strategies working-class women deployed to further the social and political movement of antifascism in exile. Inspired by the feminist studies of Joyce Kaufman and Williams (2007), and Carolina Villarroel (2008), I analyze how women responded within the restrictive patriarchal-exile paradigm and became politically active at the grassroots level, even when they were maintained outside the formal political structure. Women made the most of a paradoxal public

---

[1] Originally known as the *Comité Antifascista Español* (Spanish Antifascist Committee).

[2] *España Libre* understood Francoism as a conservative totalitarian regime in Spain, while interpreted fascism as a movement of social Darwinism and corporatist economy in Europe and Latin America.

M. Feu, Ph.D. (✉)
Hispanic Studies Department, University of Houston,
Houston, TX, USA
e:mail: mmfeulop@mail.uh.edu

G.T. Bonifacio (ed.), *Feminism and Migration: Cross-Cultural Engagements*,
International Perspectives on Migration 1, DOI 10.1007/978-94-007-2831-8_10,
© Springer Science+Business Media B.V. 2012

space reserved for them, and affirmed their position as citizens in their own right, which was decisive support of the confederation's political activism.

This chapter adds to the recuperation of women's collective history, following the work of Mary Nash (1995) and Martha A. Ackelsberg (2005) on women's associations in Spain during and after the Spanish Civil War (1936–1939), and the work of Mercedes Yusta (2009) on women exiles in France. It seeks to address the "collective amnesia" still prevalent regarding women's contribution to Spanish exile politics in the United States.[3]

10.2   Historical Context

In the late 1930s, as Francoist forces encroached on republican territory, republicans began to flee Spain for exile in other lands, including the United States. While exiles are traditionally assumed to be members of social, intellectual, or political elites (Lerner Sigal 2000; Kamen 2007); this was not true for mid-twentieth century Spain. After the war, the Franco regime severely repressed political dissidents. From 1939 to 1950, at least 22,000 Spaniards were executed. Victims ran the gamut from schoolmasters to trade union leaders, and from mayors to republican military commanders (Carr 1992). Half a million republicans of all social classes fled Spain (Kamen 2007). Thus, working-class issues were an integral part of the Spanish-exile culture.

On July 25, 1936, the Spanish exiles organized the Sociedades Hispanas Confederadas (Confederated Hispanic Societies) in Brooklyn, New York. By 1939, the confederation had 135 federated branches throughout the United States and 57,000 members (*Dos buques* 1939).[4] *España Libre* stated that most of the confederates were workers or small business owners who endeavored to aid other Spanish refugees and defended a democratic conception of Spain (*Protegidos* 1940).[5] By 1955, the 60,000 confederates continued to consider themselves members of the working class, as they had done two decades earlier (*Nuestras actividades* 1955).

Spanish exiles found a supportive U.S. civic response to their plight. For the American Popular Front cultural milieu, the Spanish Civil War symbolized the fight for the worker under oppressive political and economic systems (Denning 1998; Ottanelli 2007). When the war started in 1936, the Great Depression of the 1930s had energized American labor movements, which were the ideological force

---

[3]The "collective amnesia" is a phrase used by historian Mary Nash in her seminal work "Two Decades of Women's History in Spain" (1991) to describe the lack of awareness of women's participation in working class politics in the 1930s and 1940s.

[4]According to the U.S. Census Bureau, there were 47,707 Spaniards living in the United States in 1940, and 45,563 in 1950 (Rueda 1993).

[5]Germán Rueda (1993) counts 81% of Spaniards entering the United States from 1873 to 1929 as workers. The Spanish Ministry of Foreign affairs defined the Spanish immigrants established in the United States from 1933 to 1935 as composed of 70% of workers and 15% of merchants (Rueda 1993). According to the Department of Justice, Immigration and Naturalization Service 8,672 Spaniards arrived to the United States from 1936 to 1949; 29.3% declared to be manual workers or merchants, 32.7% declared no occupation, and 38% declared to be professionals (Ordaz Romay 1998).

behind American citizens' contributions to the humanitarian organizations helping republican Spain. Moreover, republican Spain became an icon for the progressives' resistance against the spread of fascism (Ottanelli 2007). In sum, the Spanish republican cause—"the Good Fight"—served as a link for the American Popular Front's consideration of labor unionism and antifascism (Jaffe 2007).

10.3 *España Libre*: The Exiles' Newspaper[6]

As stated in *España Libre*, the confederation's mission was to unite Spanish anarchists, republicans, and socialists in the fight against fascism; to help Spanish refugees and political prisoners; and to work with North Americans and Latin Americans to restore democracy in Spain (*Hay que preparar el regreso* 1939; *Ante el congreso nacional* 1953). The confederation also promoted working-class participation in the struggle, and the general education of this group. International labor movements were also petitioned to work for the republican cause (Rayo 1939). In fact, the confederation obtained the support from several organizations throughout their years of existence.[7]

According to confederates, these goals were best achieved through political literature (*Ante el congreso nacional* 1953). As the confederation's propaganda organ, *España Libre* became an instrument for such political mission, and involved workers in funding the fight against fascism and Francoism. However, to facilitate its role as a forum for the entire progressive community, *España Libre* invited exiles of all social classes to contribute to it. In this manner, the newspaper provided the conditions for a democratic base for exile activism.[8]

España Libre was published weekly from 1939 to 1977. From 1953 until it folded in 1977, the newspaper had irregular publication and circulation.[9] Despite this irregularity, caused by economic difficulties, *España Libre*'s readership spread to all countries where Spaniards took refuge, and clandestinely to Spain.[10] *España*

---

[6]The newspaper has been accessed at the Recovery Project at the University of Houston; at The Library of Congress, Washington, D.C.; and at the Biblioteca del Pavelló de la República, Barcelona.

[7]United Automobile Workers of America (UAW), Spanish Refugee Aid (SRA), Solidaridad Internacional Antifascista (SIA), and Industrial Workers of the World (IWW) were among the organizations that economically and logistically supported Confederated Hispanic Societies' endeavors.

[8]However, confederates were antagonistic towards the Spanish Communist Party because it was considered totalitarian. In fact, in 1939 the newspaper changed its name from *Frente Popular*, under which it had been published since 1936, to *España Libre* to distance itself from the communists. However, *España Libre* continued to individually publish columnists who were "fellow travelers."

[9]*España Libre*'s frequency dropped from weekly to bimonthly in 1962, to monthly in 1963, and finally to one issue every 2 months in 1967. Circulation dropped from 3,000 issues to 1,500 in 1953, and to 2050 in 1965 and 1966. Although modest in circulation, issues were often shared among readers (*A nuestros suscriptores* 1942, p. 5).

[10]The diverse objectives of the confederation were a balancing act: (1) providing information to Republicans, (2) restituting the Republic government, and (3) economically helping refugees and political prisoners. In addition, *España Libre* did not charge some refugees, or economically-challenged exiles, because the newspaper was understood as a service to them. For this reason, an average of the 30% of its circulation was unpaid.

Libre was notable as the only Spanish-language newspaper published in the United States that specifically fought for Spanish democracy throughout the years of the Franco dictatorship.[11] Well-known Spanish, Hispanic, and Anglo intellectuals and politicians, labor leaders, and common people voluntarily contributed to the newspaper.[12] *España Libre* became a combination of political essays, political satires, epic poetry, personal testimonies, and news reports addressed to the exiled community. Finally, when the first post-Franco democratic elections were held in Spain in 1977, *España Libre*'s last issue triumphantly concluded that "the battleground for freedom is now back in Spain" (Granell 1977).

The confederation claimed that it had no political affiliation, and *España Libre*'s editorials often affirmed that the mission of the organization was simply to offer unconditional support to the Spanish Republican Government (*Lo que debe ser* 1939). However, editorials also clearly specified that the confederation supported two Spanish labor associations: CNT (National Confederation of Labor) and UGT (General Union of Workers) (*Lo que debe ser* 1939).

10.4   Gendered Exile Activism

If the shared experience of exile was, on the whole, sufficient to incite different classes to a common denunciation of Franco's dictatorship, and to invite their democratic coexistence, it was not always enough to overcome the leftist patriarchy of the time. Confederate women encountered three particular obstacles to their participation in the formal political structure of exile politics in the United States: their working-class background; the patriarchy ingrained in Spanish culture, even among progressives; and the rhetorical representation of womanhood in *España Libre* that ascribed specific exile roles to them.

España Libre mentioned the working-class condition of confederates and adverted to the difficult financial circumstances of many exiles. While trades were often mentioned when discussing men, there was virtually no information in the newspaper on women's employment. However, it is reasonable to assume that most women, as members of the exiled working-class group, worked in factories as did their husbands, or otherwise performed domestic work. Women workers had fewer opportunities than men to participate in exile activism. They were deprived of the time and knowledge to participate in the formal structure of politics because of the demands of their work and the patriarchal structures and practices that prevailed in exile.

Women exiles were caught in a nation-building project that reproduced the patriarchal structures and practices, and the gendered contradictions of the Spanish Republic. The leftist discourse on women's issues during the Spanish Republic was

---

[11]The Hispanic labor press and many American organizations published newspapers supporting Republican Spain. However, none exclusively focused on it for 38 years. For more on pro-Republic newspapers see Kanellos and Martell, *Hispanic Periodicals in the United States* (2000); and Rey Garcia, *Stars for Spain* (1997).

[12]Hispanic refers here to Latin American and U.S. Hispanic peoples in contrast to Spaniards.

most often based on the traditional Marxist premise that feminism was a bourgeois ideology and that women's liberation was an economic matter, not a gender concern (Magnini 1995). *España Libre* reflected the Spanish left's patriarchal views on feminism. Similarly, the American left in the 1930s and 1940s in the United States were more concerned with empowering the working class and fighting fascism than they were in redressing gender issues (Foley 1993). Such dismissal of women's issues was even more pronounced in the exiled community; it promoted exile only as temporary, and so it was imperative to devote attention to the exile nationalism and antifascist effort. Thus, feminist advocacy that would have helped to alleviate working-class women's gendered responsibilities was put aside.

Nationalism is a form of rhetorical control over women that forces them into patriarchal and traditional roles. Feminist theories of nationalism argue that existing power structures reinforce constructed gender hierarchies, which prevent women from participating in the political process in general (Yuval-Davis et al. 1989; McClintock 1993; Marx 2002). Women are kept from participating in formal politics by the effect of traditional representations of both men and women, which builds "an inherent inequality and relationship of power and dependence which similarly affects women's perceptions of themselves and their roles in the state, especially in times of conflict" (Kaufman and Williams 2007, p. 16).

In exile political activism, women are important symbols used to forward the national project. For example, in Mexican exile literature in the United States, women are subsumed symbolically into the body politic (Baeza Ventura 2006). Mexican women are understood as the carriers and preservers of Mexican cultural practices and values in exile (Baeza Ventura 2006). Specifically, the image of the Mexican woman is manipulated in literature to represent an idealized and gendered exiled nation. In other words, feminist theories of nationalism interpret the socially constructed national identity as gendered (McClintock 1993; Marx 2002), which situates women as "reproducers of the boundaries of ethnic/national groups" or as "signifiers of ethnic/national differences—as a focus and symbol in ideological discourses used in the construction, reproduction and transformation of ethnic/national categories" (Yuval-Davis et al. 1989, p. 7).

In the case of *España Libre*, Spanish national identity was also constructed in gendered terms. During the Second Spanish Republic (1931–1939), the gains of Spanish women signified a loss of men's prerogatives (Caamano Alegre 2004).[13] The conservative sectors of society understood the progressive government of the republican era as a traditional national-identity crisis represented in gendered terms. For example, Francoist propaganda often accused the republicans of "unmanliness." The republicans' sexual identity was questioned because the modern politics of the Republic had opened public spaces for women (Caamano Alegre 2004).

The gender tensions that the Republic's modernity placed on the traditional construction of Spanish masculinity is exemplified in Antonio de la Villa's short story about two republican friends published in April 3, 1941 in *España Libre*. The two

---

[13] Under the 1931 Spanish Constitution, women could vote and stand for parliament. Social reforms, including liberal divorce laws, enhanced their civil rights and employment rights (Graham 1995).

men meet before the Civil War in Spain, and one of them belittles his uncultured and politically disinterested wife: "My blessed wife is a married woman, and this is all she is" (Villa 1942, p. 2).[14] Years later, the two friends meet again, now as exiles in the United States. The husband has remarried, this time to a woman who speaks several languages, knows how to type, and understands Nietzsche's philosophy:

> I am, if in any way possible, even more unfortunate than I was in our Madrid [...][my wife] she thinks herself superior to all, and in the privacy of our home [...] my woman is dry, arid, aggressive; she has no tenderness, no innocence, no feminine candor. (Villa 1942, p. 2)[15]

Like the husband in the story, the short-lived Second Spanish Republic was inspired by modernity, but unable to adapt to it. The Spanish exiled husband mocked the modernity of womanhood in the United States, a similar model for what Spanish republican gender politics was striving for. He sadly invoked a model of femininity defined by submissive domesticity prevalent in nineteenth century Spain.[16]

España Libre's nationalistic discourse employed various rhetorical strategies, among which the representation of women was fundamental. The most significant instance was the reversal of the modern woman prototype, characteristic of the Republic, to the mother of the nation archetype.[17] Anarchist exile Miguel Giménez Igualada wrote a series of articles for *España Libre* addressed to women from 1953 to 1963. These articles promoted their subordinate, traditional roles. Giménez Igualada exhorted women to be guardians of their exiled homes by transforming themselves into "a protected valley, in whose fertile soil your children would blossom in peace and happiness" (1960, p. 3).[18] Women achieved this "fertile home" for the exiled nation through their relationship with men. In Giménez Igualada's narrative, women were "daughters, loyal to their parents; women, loyal to their husbands; mothers, loyal to their children; and finally, friends, loyal to their friends" (1961, p. 3).[19] In other words, by performing roles at home and becoming reliable subjects to men, women were symbolically cultivating the exiled republican culture and nation.

Stereotypes of women as devoted relational caregivers populated the newspaper's news reports. For example, one article claimed that Franco's prisons were full of men "of all walks of life and ages, professors, servants, workers, doctors, lawyers, etc. Women were all wives, mothers or sisters of men who had opposed

---

[14]My translation: *Mi bendita mujer, (...) es una mujer casera de ahí no pasa.*

[15]My translation: *Soy, si cabe, mucho más desgraciado que era en nuestro Madrid [...] se cree superior a todo y en lo íntimo del hogar, [...] La mujer mía de ahora es seca, árida, agresiva, sin ternura, ni inocencia, ni candor femenino.*

[16]The publication of *El ángel del hogar* (The Angel of the Household) by María Pilar de Sinués de Marco in 1859 marked the construction of this archetype.

[17]The archetype of the 'modern woman' developed with *La mujer moderna* (*The Modern Woman*) published by María Lejárraga, under her husband's name, Gregorio Martínez Sierra, in the 1920s in Spain. Carmen de Burgos, Margarita Nelken, and Clara Campoamor are other intellectuals who also demanded improved social conditions for women (Samblancat Miranda 2006).

[18]My translation: *como valle abrigado en cuya fértil tierra de sembradura nazcan y florezcan tus hijos en paz y en alegría.*

[19]My translation: *serás, como hija, leal a tus mayores; como mujer, después, leal a tu marido; como madre, más tarde, leal a tus pichones, y, por fin, como amiga, leal a tus amigos.*

Franco" (*Horrible espectáculo* 1940, p. 2).[20] In fact, the understanding of women as mothers, wives, daughters or sisters was so ingrained in the exile imaginary that columnist Aurelio Pego concluded in 1940 that world peace depended on finding Adolf Hitler a girlfriend. In his satirical style, Pego professed to have found a solution that thwarted Hitler's imperialist threats. Pego assured his readers that Hitler suffered from a peculiar psychosis:

> The common man conquers women; Hitler conquers peoples. A man in love rapes a maiden; Hitler violates nations. The common Don Juan drinks too much good wine, promises everlasting love, and violates virgins. (Pego 1940, p. 8)[21]

In Pego's narrative, nations are blatantly symbolized as women who can be raped, lured, and enslaved. Therefore, the solution to calm Hitler's expansionist passions is to exchange his object of obsession from nations to women. *España Libre* constituted women as exile objects that symbolized not only cultural, but also political boundaries.

In addition to the gendered citizenship displayed in the newspaper, femininity was repeatedly used to belittle Franco, Hitler, Mussolini and Stalin. For instance, cartoons in *España Libre* portrayed Dictator Francisco Franco and his followers with long eyelashes, wearing lipstick and high heels, or holding a rose.

The cartoon shows an effeminate Dictator Francisco Franco characterized by his foreign alliances and football. According to *España Libre*, both violence and football were used by Franco to militarily and culturally dominate Spanish people (*Caricaturizan a Franco en Oslo* 1965, p. 5).

---

[20] My translation: *Los presos [...] eran de todas las condiciones y edades: profesores, sirvientes, obreros, médicos, abogados, etc. Las mujeres eran todas esposas, madres o hermanas de hombre que estaban en la oposición a Franco*

[21] My translation: *El hombre normal conquista mujeres, Hitler conquista pueblos. El enamorado corriente viola doncellas. Hitler viola naciones. El Donjuán ordinario toma unas copas, promete amores eternos y roba virginidades.*

This cartoon illustrates an article on Spanish Falangists in New York in the 1940s. The Falange was a Spanish fascist movement that supported Francisco Franco (*El Spanish House* 1942, p. 9).

The feminine characterization of fascists and Francoists to discredit them evinces the exiles' difficulty in overcoming the gender binaries deeply rooted in the Spanish patriarchal system.

In sum, the representation of arid modern women, self-denying wives, crying mothers, abused girlfriends, or effeminate men, demonstrates that the gender representations in *España Libre* often embraced traditional domesticity and patriarchal values rather than modern and radical progressive ethics. Also, female politicians, authors, and thinkers were seldom mentioned or invited to participate in the newspaper's efforts to overthrow the Franco regime. Thus, the publication also lacked positive female roles for the exiled community.[22]

10.5　Women's Political Activism

Considering the gender representations in *España Libre*, it was notable that women did all sorts of jobs for the republican cause, even performed as amateur artists, stage singers, and dancers.[23] This section shows how the demands of political denunciation allowed women to transform themselves from gendered symbols of the exiled nation to chief agents of grassroots activism in exile. In *España Libre*, women were often revealed not only as makers of history—contradicting their representation in the republican imaginary and consistently negative articles in *España Libre*, as

---

[22]There were some exceptions, such as anarchists Carmen Aldecoa and Federica Montseny, and noted socialist Victoria Kent.

[23]It is important to consider the percentage rate of Spanish immigrant women (18.5%) to Spanish immigrant men (81.5%) who entered the United States from 1899 to 1944 (Rueda 1993).

shown above, but also as having a profound impact on the confederation's successful campaigns. Women's grassroots activism, such as boycotting fascist products and fund-raising, played a crucial role in solidifying transnational solidarity toward democratic Spain, and validating the Spanish working-class identity and culture.

10.5.1 Boycott

Like the American Jewish boycott of German products in the early 1930s, Spanish exiles boycotted Francoist products in the 1940s.[24] In December 1939, 14 women signed an article published in *España Libre* demanding the boycott of fascist and Francoist products sold in the United States (Banyan et al. 1939).[25] Violeta Miqueli González, who also performed as an amateur actress for the confederation,[26] published an article on March 15, 1940, that addressed "Spanish, Czechoslovakian, Polish, and Finnish mothers, all of whom had suffered the horror of seeing their sons cut to shreds by the grapeshot of Hitler, Mussolini, Franco and Stalin" (1940, p. 10).[27] She asked these women not to buy fascist products and to create a female organization that would inform shopkeepers about the need to boycott such products. Also, she proposed that this organization reached as many homes as possible to inform housewives of the boycott. Miqueli González believed this initiative would help fight fascism because "we women can do much good when we forget bourgeois social conventions and, accepting the responsibility of our destiny, we assume a vanguard position" (1940, p. 10).[28] As a result of their advocacy, *España Libre* published advertisements encouraging the boycott of fascist and Francoist products and organized several boycott demonstrations in New York in the 1940s and 1950s.

10.5.2 Women's Participation in Fund-Raising Venues

New York housed many of the organizations which assisted the Spanish Republic (Smith 2007). The International Ladies Garment Workers' Union, American Friends for Spanish Democracy, Medical Bureau and North American Committee to Aid Spanish Democracy, and the Confederated Hispanic Societies led these campaigns (Fernández 2007; Smith 2007). Although confederate associations throughout the United States

---

[24]For more on the Jewish boycott of German products, see Wallace (2007).

[25]The authors were Armiña Banyan, María Bringa, Alba Castilla (daughter of José Castilla Morales), Celeste Cesuraga, Rosa Cesuraga, Josefina Gil, Dolores Llull, Blanca Machado, Amparo Miralles, Peggy Reyes, Emilia Rodríguez, Enriqueta Romeo, Josefina Sánchez, Ana Santana.

[26]*Grandioso será el festival. España Libre* 24 January 1941, 8.

[27]My translation: *Madres españolas, checoslovacas, polacas, finlandesas, madres todas que han sufrido el horror de ver sus hijos despedazados por la metralla de Hitler, Mussolini, Franco y Stalin.*

[28]My translation: *Las mujeres podemos hacer mucho bien cuando olvidamos los convencionalismos de la sociedad burguesa y aceptando la responsabilidad de nuestro destino tomamos una posición de vanguardia.*

were extraordinarily active in their funding efforts to aid republican Spain, fund-raising venues concentrated in New York and New Jersey. *España Libre* enthusiastically covered the confederation's cultural benefit activities, as did other New York City Hispanic newspapers, such as *La Prensa* (The Press) and *Liberación* (The Liberation).

In the decade of the 1940s, the confederation held an average of 39 fund-raising venues per year; at its height, in 1940 and 1941, there were 84 and 82 events respectively.[29] Most of these fund-raising events, which included theater performances, vaudeville shows, dinners, and dances were conducted at the social halls of the constituent organizations. When more space was needed, the Palm Garden Theater or Webster Hall in New York City was rented.[30] These events usually attracted several hundred people and collected, on average, less than $1,000 dollars per event. However, April 14, the anniversary of the Republic, and July 19, the date which commemorated the defense of the Republic from the military revolt by the Spanish people, were solemn dates when the largest theaters and halls were rented, such as Madison Square Garden or Manhattan Hall in New York City. On these occasions, as many as 6,000 people attended, and up to $20,000 were collected.[31] Theatrical shows were accompanied by political and cultural speeches, and other fund-raising activities. Prominent republican politicians and intellectuals were invited to take part in these events and supported them with speeches and performances.[32]

From the 1950s to the 1970s the fund-raising venues progressively diminished in number and in the amount of money collected. On average, the confederation now organized between 10 and 20 events per year, and their meetings were transformed more into social and cultural rather than fund-raising events.[33] Psychological and economic reasons were given in *España Libre* for this growing "apathy" and "pessimism." On one hand, after a decade of almost weekly political speeches and anti-fascist-themed fund-raising events, the exiled community, especially the second generation, had lost interest in political propaganda denouncing Francisco Franco's dictatorship (*Vigorización* 1953). Most importantly, many lost faith in defeating Franco after Spain joined the United Nations in 1955 (*El efecto* 1955). Now that most Spanish refugees felt settled in the United States, the struggle against Franco had begun to fade in importance.[34] Still, numerous exiles sent money to people they knew in Spain, but stopped volunteering in support of the humanitarian and political

---

[29] For the purpose of this study, I have also considered the 21 venues carried out in November and December 1939, after *Frente Popular* transformed into *España Libre*, when the anarchists, socialists and republicans separated from the communists.

[30] In addition, fund-raising picnics and football games were organized in summer.

[31] For example, the rally celebrated in the Manhattan Center on January 8, 1940 (*Camaradas delegados* 1940).

[32] For example, Federico García Lorca's brother Francisco Garcia Lorca and Lorca's niece Laura García Lorca performed in two theatrical events in 1944. The Spanish Republic ambassador to the United States, Fernando de los Ríos, gave 16 speeches for confederate events.

[33] However, 53 fund-raising activities were held in 1958.

[34] The distinction between exile and refugee in *España Libre* is an economic one. A refugee is someone who needs help to get settled outside Spain. Exiles are previous refugees or émigrés who are already settled abroad, and are politically active.

goals of the confederation (*El peligro* 1953). The remaining active and committed members continued the political and humanitarian tasks, such as publishing *España Libre* until democracy was restored in Spain in 1977 (Granell 1977).

Within the constraints of the patriarchal nationalism of exile, women were active in all these fund-raising efforts. Women cooked meals for these venues, sold tickets, prepared decorations, sewed costumes, and helped in the overall organization of the events. Their assiduous work generally remained anonymous. Only a few of their names are revealed in *España Libre*'s obituaries and in a handful of articles. For example, the October 21, 1953 obituary for Dolores Bouveta reads: "Ms. Bouveta dedicated her life until her last moment to the Spanish Republic ... she did not miss any of the events and cooperated daily in all the festivals organized by the affiliated Galicia Committee and by the Confederated Hispanic Societies" (*Dolores Bouveta* 1955, p. 7).[35] An anonymous article of August 28, 1942, praised the "women [who] spend hours cooking ... for free ... having done their duty—their only satisfaction" (*Agrupación Leales Españoles* 1942, p. 5).[36]

Several women became the most popular artists on the confederation's festival stages during the active decades of the 1940s and 1950s. *España Libre* often excused the amateurish performances of the confederates and praised their spirited efforts. As explained in a review published on February 21, 1941, "if there are minor mistakes [in the performance], it is because members have jobs and it is very difficult for them to attend rehearsals" (*Tres representaciones* 1941, p. 5).[37] Maria Cordellat, a Cuban who sympathized with the Spanish Republic, taught piano to confederates on Friday nights and served as the confederation's secretary for several years. She played in 71 different fund-raising venues during the 1940s and the 1950s. A review published in May 24, 1940, claimed that Cordellat and other confederates performing on the stage "act as if they are professionals despite their lack of experience [...] and collaborate selflessly" (*Magnífica* 1940, p. 7).[38] In the same period, Yuyita Concheiro danced Spanish regional dances in a total of 60 fund-raising festivals, as did Carmen López, who also sang. Elena and María Trujillo, both natives from Málaga, Spain (and possibly sisters), danced flamenco and performed as amateur actresses in a total of 34 and 41 artistic festivals, respectively. Fay Torrens danced Spanish regional dances in 34 artistic festivals and performed in several plays. Dorita Montero danced Spanish regional dances in 36 fund-raising festivals, and Leonor Lucas acted in 32 plays.[39] These amateur performers represent only a few of

---

[35] My translation: *La señora Bouveta hasta su último momento dedicó toda su vida en pro del mantenimiento de la República española... no dejó de asistir a todos los actos nuestros y cooperando diariamente y en todas las fiestas organizadas por el Galicia y SHC.*

[36] My translation: *Mujeres que se pasan horas delante de los fogones ...gratuitamente ... sin más recompensa que la satisfacción de haber cumplido con un deber que impone la conciencia.*

[37] My translation: *si hay fallos es porque los componentes tienen que atender a sus labores cotidianas y les es harto difícil atender a los ensayos.*

[38] My translation: *trabajaron como verdaderos artistas, a pesar de ser todos novatos en el arte escénico [...] viene[n] cooperando en nuestras funciones desinteresadamente*

[39] She was Ignacio Zugadi Germendia's romantic partner, a confederate executive member and staff writer of *España Libre*

the many Spanish and Hispanic women who voluntarily danced, sang, and acted in numerous artistic venues to raise funds for the republican cause.

Well-known professional Spanish and Hispanic actors also volunteered by performing *gratis* at these festivals. Benefit venues often had a cast of both amateur and professional artists. Mary Reid, a famous Spanish actress and theater company director, was a staunch supporter of the Spanish Republic (Kanellos 2008). In the 1940s and 1950s, she acted and directed plays for the confederation, and chaired many of the 114 fund-raising events in which she participated. Other famous artists collaborated as well. For example, Spanish singer Consuelo Moreno participated in 66 festivals at the time. Italian soprano Pina Sarro sang in 13 benefit venues. The confederation paid tribute to amateur and professional performers by naming the fund-raising festival celebrated that week after them. Although *España Libre* may not list all the venues in which women participated, it provides some insight into women's importance in raising funds for the confederation's humanitarian and political objectives.

The confederate Agrupación de Mujeres Antifascistas (Antifascist Women's Association) or AMA was founded in October 1939 as a small, non-political organization of Spanish and Hispanic women living in the Bronx (*Agrupación* 1941). The AMA was particularly active from 1939 to 1944.[40] Its first antifascist action was to collect food and toiletries for Spanish refugees held on Ellis Island while in route to Mexico (*Agrupación* 1939).

JUVENTUDES DE A.M.A.

(De izquierda a derecha, de pie:)
Enriqueta Romeo,
Josefina Sánchez,
Peggy Reyes,
Blanca Machado,
Celeste
Gesuraga.
Josefina Gil y
María Bringa.

(Sentadas, de izquierda a derecha:)
Armina Banyan,
Ana Santana,
Evelyn Rodríguez,
Alba Castilla,
Dolores Lull,
Rose Gesuraga y
Amparo Miralles.

The younger members of AMA are pictured here. The upper caption reads left to right the names of the young women standing. The lower caption reads left to right the names of the young women sitting (*Juventudes* 1940).

---

[40] Its president in 1941 was Antonia Pujol, and its representatives at confederate assemblies that year were María Machado and Teresa Castillo. Pujol, a Majorcan woman, was also the cook of the AMA fund-raising dinners.

In the next 5 years, AMA organized 11 fund-raising artistic festivals, 2 theatrical performances, 2 popular dances, and 12 fund-raising dinners. In March 1940, AMA sent 11,500 French francs to republican disabled servicemen exiled in Caussade, France (*Una prueba* 1940). Other women's associations from throughout the United States were also confederated, such as the Spanish American Women's Club of Niagara Falls; the Club Femenino de Marsillon, Ohio; the Damas Auxiliares del Spanish American Citizen's Club, of Bayonne, New Jersey; and the Comité Femenino de Ayuda al Pueblo Español, of East St. Louis, Illinois. They organized an average of three fund-raising artistic festivals per year in the 1940s.

10.6 Community Building

Antifascist associations and venues "played an important and enduring—if often overlooked—role in the evolution of the Spanish-speaking communities in the city" (Fernández 2007, 91), and influenced the creation of a "distinctive New York Latino identity" (Fernández 2007, 91). According to Nicolas Kanellos, the Hispanic press and stage also helped to "fend off the threat of assimilation to Anglo-American culture" (1990, 200) and helped "protecting the home culture and language in exile" (199). Both Politics and language were cohesive factors for the working class Latino identity in New York.

Working-class Spanish exiles found an established working class that (1) was foreign and multiethnic (Freeman 2000; Guglielmo 2010), (2) was living in ethnic neighborhoods (Freeman 2000), (3) did not own real property, a fact that meant that life was "exposed and often communal" (Freeman 2000, 30).[41] The close proximity of the exile community rented living spaces, the confederate organizations' social halls, and the Spanish stores and restaurants in Brooklyn and Lower Manhattan favored the interrelation of the Spanish exiles.

Moreover, working-class women, who performed the arduous work of caregivers in this shared space, were crucial in building community ties.[42] As indicated in *España Libre*, confederate Hispanic and Spanish women closely interacted in the organization of fund-raising venues. According to feminist theories of nationalism, women tend to cross class, race, and religious lines when they involve themselves in political activism (Kaufman and Williams 2007). Thus, confederate women became an extremely important channel in maintaining a collective Hispanic, progressive, working-class identity and in building extensive networks of local solidarity towards republican Spain.

---

[41] New York and Florida were the most common destinations of entry of Spaniards from 1897 to 1944, with 38% and 12%, respectively (Rueda 1993).

[42] See Jennifer Guglielmo (2010) on working-class Italian women's significance in their community in New York in the 1940s.

10.6.1   Working-Class Identity

The confederation staged plays from the Spanish commercial theatrical tradition that had thrived before the Spanish Civil War. Although this tradition catered to working-class and petit-bourgeois audiences, the confederation's stage was most intent on addressing workers' demands. For instance, benefit venues were held on Saturdays and Sundays, but Saturday venues started at 8 p.m. because, as one article published on November 24, 1939 reminded the readers, "most people of the exiled colony work on Saturdays" (*El festival homenaje* 1939, 1). In other words, the venue's space—both accessible and affordable—and the show times took the audience's working-class status into account.

Throughout its 38 years of existence, the confederation succeeded in helping thousands of Spanish refugees. *España Libre's* last issue announced that the SHC had, over the years, collected a total of 2 million dollars to help Spanish refugees (*Cuadro de Honor* 1977). Women's diligent and accessible help in the collection of funds gave the workers a sense of control and success in their fight against fascism and Francoism. Women contributed to the workers' democratic participation in exile activism, which rejected the elite's historically privileged relationship to the state.

10.7   Exiled Women's Political Conscience

Women's activism has been historically linked to peace movements (Kaufman and Williams 2007; Yusta 2009) and has not necessarily been equated with feminist issues. For example, women's activism is often initiated with the traditional imagery of women as mothers and caregivers fighting for peace or humanitarian values, which are not necessarily political (Kaufman and Williams 2007). In the case of the confederate women, maternal values gave them an initial justification for involvement in exile activism.

Before her exile to the United States, Carmen Aldecoa had been the director of the orphanage Iberia in Lyon, France for Spanish refugee children (Aldecoa 1940).[43] In the 1940s, Aldecoa published several articles in *España Libre* to promote funding for child refugees. In the fifth Confederated Hispanic Societies' National Congress, held in New York City in 1941, Aldecoa demanded that funding be spent on humanitarian causes rather than on political propaganda (*El chico de la calle* 1941). As a result, the confederation helped child refugees in France.

---

[43] As a former teacher, Carmen Aldecoa secured herself an adjunct post teaching Spanish in the Romance Languages Department at New York University. She later coordinated the Spanish Teaching Assistants in the 1950s and 1960s (V. Fuentes, Carmen Aldecoa. E-mail message to the author, March 6, 2010). Aldecoa was Jesús González Malo's romantic partner. González Malo, confederated anarcho-syndicalist leader, autodidact, and director of *España Libre* from 1961 to 1965, worked as a welder (Maurín 1966). Aldecoa was described as a professor who "was with the people" (*Grandioso será el festival* 1948).

Although Carmen Aldecoa began her involvement with the confederation reporting about traditional feminine activities, she later developed a more theoretical, political approach within the organization. In 1953 and 1954, Aldecoa gave several political speeches to the exile community, which did not address the support for refugee children, but focused on the cultural and political aspects of exile. She spoke on the role of women in the antifascist effort, remembering women who lost their lives in the fight for democracy in Spain and those who were still incarcerated in Franco's prisons. She implored women in the audience to continue the fight for justice in Spain (*La conmemoración* 1954).

In 1957, Aldecoa published *Del sentir y del pensar* (Of Feeling and Thinking) in Mexico. Her book reviewed the most important figures of Spanish anarchism, and discussed the main Spanish labor newspapers. Her work preserved Spanish labor history that was systematically erased by the Francoist censorship. Aldecoa also noted the didactic function of labor newspapers for workers and advocated a coalition of the working class and the bourgeoisie to effect social change. Aldecoa's exile experience made her reflect on the effects of political propaganda and on the possibility of a democratic state that would involve both the working class and the bourgeoisie as political actors (Aldecoa 1957).

To pursue her political beliefs, Aldecoa traveled several times to Spain as a US exile contact for clandestine syndicalists working with the underground *Alianza Sindical Obrera* (Spanish Labor Alliance [ASO])[44] in the 1960s (González Malo 1962a).[45] In 1961, she chaired the Women's Committee of the confederation. *España Libre* recorded 2 fund-raising festivals organized by the Women's Committee in June 9, 1961 and in February 23, 1962, which collected a total of $1,300 for the Spanish Labor Alliance (*Un éxito completo* 1961; *Gran entusiasmo* 1962).[46] Moreover, Aldecoa was a member of the confederation's International Advisory Committee to help Spanish political prisoners from 1961 to 1964 (Aldecoa 1961; González Malo 1962b).[47] Aldecoa exemplifies how exile, as a political condition, promoted women's activism, and in turn forced them to confront a male-dominated formal political system that had excluded them.

Confederate women like Aldecoa participated in exile activism in ways traditionally not allowed to them. Traditional humanitarian roles gave women legitimacy to actively participate in the confederation. Over the course of their involvement, women became part of the formal political structure of the confederation. For example, female university professors and writers occasionally gave speeches and lectures to confederates on antifascist topics in 1943.[48] In addition, female members

---

[44] As translated in *España Libre*.

[45] United Automobile Workers of America (UAW) supported this alliance with $7,000 (Reuther 1964).

[46] The newspaper did not provide information on the dates the committee was active, nor of its members except its 1962 president: Nieves Vázquez.

[47] The other council members were: Robert Alexander, Ángel del Río, Eugenio Granell, Joaquín Maurín, Francisco Ayala, Víctor Alba (González Malo 1962b).

[48] Amelia del Río gave a lecture on February 12; Violeta Miqueli González, on March 12; and Guillermina Medrano, on August 20.

started to make their voices heard in the confederation assemblies in the 1940s. In an article reviewing the confederation's fifth National Congress, Félix Martí Ibáñez declared that "women representatives and women attending the Congress reminded us with their presence and their words that if men lose heart they only need to look at them to recover their strength of character from the feminine example" (1941, 7).[49] While only Aldecoa and Leonor Lucas were confederate executives in the 1940s, five women had become executive members in 1963 (*Confederated Spanish Societies* 1963).[50] Therefore, women found in exile a public space that promoted their collective political consciousness. Their politicized grassroots context caused women to move from private concerns to state-related issues.

10.8 Feminist Conscience

In *Defying Male Civilization*, Mary Nash (1995) affirms that the Spanish Civil War transformed women's lives as they participated in the public sphere on an unprecedented scale. They undertook new social, economic, and military activities; they organized themselves, and broke with their accustomed isolation from political and public life. Also, women asserted their collective voice in numerous journals and newspapers. Their war efforts not only fought for democracy through an energetic antifascism, but they also "openly question[ned] traditional male monopoly and hegemony in the world of politics" (Nash 1995, 181).

If women have constructed a different identity in the process of becoming politically active (Kaufman and Williams 2007; Villarroel 2008), confederate women's new activist role enhanced their feminist and political conscience, even though they could not always address specific women's issues.[51] Women transformed their identities through their involvement as amateur actors on the confederation's thriving stage or into grassroots undercover leaders. While they inherited a patriarchal relationship with the state, exile activism forced confederate women to reject it or redefine it. The transnational antifascist culture of the 1930s and 1940s in New York facilitated the transformation of women in their relationship to the exiled nation. The result of this transformation was that working women were successful in raising public awareness and contributing funds for Spanish democracy.

In Spain, women organized to provide for the imperatives of war, and had a profound impact on the course of history, despite their subjugated position (Nash 1995; Ackelsberg 2005). In fact, revolutionary periods are crucial for determining the

---

[49] My translation *Muchas mujeres delegadas o asistentes al congreso nos recordaron con su presencia y su palabra que si alguien flaquease en su ánimo entre los hombres, no tendría más que mirarlas a ellas, para recobrar su entereza … del ejemplo femenino.*

[50] The General Secretary was Miguel R. Ortiz, the Assistant Secretary was Jesús González Malo, and the Treasurer was Nieves Vázquez. Georgina Piera, Carmen Conchado, Carmen Kahn, and Magdalena Meijomil were members of confederation's Executive Committee. Carmen Aldecoa was part of confederation's International Advisory Committee.

[51] Some confederate women such as Aldecoa and Miqueli raised gender implications in *España Libre*.

position of women in the nation, as "women who are not empowered to organize during the struggle will not be empowered to organize after the struggle" (McClintock 1993, 77). Similarly, the political needs of exile allowed women to get beyond the private sphere and to occupy grassroots leadership positions, even though they were symbolically portrayed as dependent.

In New York and elsewhere, being in exile advanced the careers of some confederates. While reviews on Consuelo Moreno in the 1930s pinpointed her inexperience on stage (Celonio 1930), she became popular in professional Hispanic theaters in New York after volunteering for the Confederated Hispanic Societies. In 1937 she was contacted by Francoists in New York to work as a spy for them and was offered in reward the protection of her family in Madrid but she refused the offer (González 1937). In the 1940s and 1950s, she became a recognized artist celebrity of the vibrant Hispanic Broadway scene (*Ecos de Broadway* 1954). She even moved to Hollywood for a short time in 1944 (*Consuelo* 1944). In addition, Carmen López opened a dance studio in New York after her amateur involvement in the confederation's artistic festivals (¡*Gloriosa resistencia*! 1959). The public space, therefore, opened to exiled women was extended throughout the duration of their exile and beyond.

10.8.1 Paradoxical Public Space

The exile public space had its own contradictions and paradoxes for women. Though the confederation engaged women politically, it often reinforced traditional patriarchal roles. For example, a beauty contest was one of the exiled community's long-standing annual events, from the 1940s to the 1960s. In addition, staged plays were a mixture of dignified female roles alongside jealous or eccentric, nagging wives that provided comic relief. Women were often equated with the Spanish republican nation; both had to be defended. Although women's representation was manipulated, women also found dignified spaces to participate in social mobilization to help the Republic. On the whole, women increased their profile within the community and made the most of their subordinate position in the patriarchal exiled community to free Spain from the Francoist regime.

10.9 Conclusion

This chapter elucidates the relationship of women with the state, and how exile transforms that relationship.[52] Despite existing patriarchal practices that kept confederate women out of the exiles' formal political structure, women nevertheless transformed themselves into engaged citizens.

---

[52] I would like to thank Dr. Nicolas Kanellos and Dr. Glenda Bonifacio for their helpful suggestions and careful reading. I acknowledge all mistakes are mine.

Initially, the traditional framework of womanhood drew women together to help Civil War refugees. In the course of their involvement, women actively participated in the organization of fund-raising events for the republican cause. They developed their talents as amateur actresses, singers and dancers. In addition to performing and raising funds, as we have seen, their activism often allowed them to participate and lead in the same forums and publications as men; the confederation fostered their citizenship and their own political thought of social change in the framework of antifascism and labor radicalism.

The grassroots politics in which exiled women participated, encouraged transnational solidarity, local community consciousness, and forged a sense of shared culture and identity. Women's participation in the confederation contributed to open a space for an alternative popular culture addressed to exiled workers and focused on antifascist ideology. Thus, women were an extremely important channel for creating a community of support for republican Spain. Their voluntary participation in fund-raising venues was crucial to increase the funding for refugees and political prisoners. Likewise, it was essential in giving the workers a sense of achievement in the difficult conditions of exile.[53]

After the Francoist forces won the Civil War (1939), Spanish women lost their legal and political rights and were brutally persecuted for their participation in leftist movements. In New York, recognition of the women's significant contributions to exile activism was limited by the confederation's patriarchal framework. However, this chapter has shown how exile can provide a new historical experience for women as active political agents. The recovery of their actions and voices in *España Libre* adds to the study of the social history of the Spanish Civil War and women's forms of exile activism. Their public engagement for a cause may appear traditional and within gendered role boundaries, but such took place in exilic migration that no less made their actions significant. Those who seemingly had no power are revealed here as crucial instigators of the exile culture as a whole, modifying the exiled nation as a repository of male exclusiveness.

References

A nuestros suscriptores. (1942, March 20). *España Libre*, p. 5.
Ackelsberg, M. A. (2005). *Free women of Spain: Anarchism and the struggle for the emancipation of women*. Edinburgh: AK Press.

---

[53] As repeatedly mentioned in *España Libre*, Spaniards who escaped from the Franco regime often entered the United States as illegal immigrants. Despite their personal risks if they were ever to return to Spain, Spanish Civil War exiles were not granted the status of refugees by American law. Exile meant for most confederates tragic personal circumstances, such as enduring poverty and the haunting memory of lost relatives and friends in the Civil War, as well as those brutally killed or executed in Franco's prisons. Professor Guillermina Medrano, and exile activist in the United States, declared that exile was especially difficult because she had to endure the fact that her family and friends, who had remained in Spain, were passing away without her being able to go back (Salazar et al. 2006).

Agrupación de mujeres Antifascistas AMA. (1939, October 13). *España Libre*, p. 11.
Agrupación de mujeres Antifascistas AMA. (1941, June 6). *España Libre*, p. 5.
Agrupación Leales Españoles. (1942, August 28). *España Libre*, p. 5.
Aldecoa, C. (1940, May 17). 19 Chemin du Greillon. *España Libre*, p. 12.
Aldecoa, C. (1957). *Del sentir y del pensar*. México: Costa-Amic.
Aldecoa, C. (1961, October 6). En torno a un editorial. *España Libre*, p. 3.
Ante el congreso nacional. (1953, October 23). Editorial. *España Libre*, p. 4.
Baeza Ventura, G. (2006). *La imagen de la mujer en la crónica del "México de afuera"*. Ciudad Juárez: Universidad Autónoma de Ciudad Juárez.
Banyan, A., Bringa, M., Castilla, A., Cesuraga, C., Cesuraga, R., Gil, J., Llull, D., Machado, B., Miralles, A., Reyes, P. Rodríguez, E., Romeo, E., Sánchez, J., & Santana, A. (1939, December 22). Seamos conscientes ¡Boicot a los productos!. *España Libre*, p. 7.
Caamano Alegre, B. (2004). *Mujeres nuevas, viejas ideas: contradicciones y fisuras en la construcción de la feminidad en la II República Española y la dictadura franquista*. Diss, Rutgers University.
Camaradas delegados. (1940, January 12). *España Libre*, p. 6.
Caricaturizan a Franco en Oslo. (1965, September 3). Cartoon. *España Libre*, p. 5.
Carr, R. (1992). *España 1808–1975*. 1969. Barcelona: Ariel.
Celonio, G. (1930, February 22). Revoltillo farandulero. *Gráfico*, p. 5.
Confederated Spanish Societies. (1963, July 5). *España Libre*, p. 7.
Consuelo está por allá. (1944, Mayo 5). *España Libre*, p. 6.
Cuadro de Honor. (1977, May-June). *España Libre*, p. 4.
de la Villa, A. (1942, April 3). El viajero y su sombra. *España Libre*, p. 2.
Denning, M. (1998). *The cultural front: The laboring of American culture in the twentieth century*. London: Verso.
Dolores Bouveta. (1955, October). *España Libre*, p. 7
Dos buques con refugiados españoles para México. (1939, May 12). *La Prensa*, p. 5.
Ecos de Broadway. (1954, July 18). *Ecos de Nueva York*, p. 21.
El chico de la calle. Impresiones del tercer congreso de SHC. (1941, December 5). *España Libre*, pp. 5, 8, 12.
El efecto de nuestra despedida. (1955, November 18). Editorial. *España Libre*, p. 4.
El festival homenaje a Madrid culminó en un éxito sorprendente. (1939, November 24). *España Libre*, p. 1.
El peligro de desaparecer. (1953, August 28). Editorial. *España Libre*, p. 4.
El Spanish House y los pipiolis de la Falange. (1942, September 4). *España Libre*, p. 9.
Fernández, J. (2007). Nueva York: The Spanish-speaking community responds. In P. N. Carroll & J. D. Fernández (Eds.), *Facing fascism: New York and the Spanish Civil War* (pp. 86–91). New York: Museum of the City of New York.
Foley, B. (1993). *Radical representations. Politics and form in U.S. proletarian fiction, 1929–1941*. Durham: Duke University Press.
Freeman, J. B. (2000). *Working-class New York. Life and labor since World War II*. New York: The New Press.
Giménez Igualada, M. (1960, November 4). Tierra de Sembradura. *España Libre*, p. 3.
Giménez Igualada, M. (1961, May 5). Lealtad. *España Libre*, p. 3.
¡Gloriosa resistencia!. (1959, October 16). *España Libre*, p. 6.
González, E. (1937, December 15). Conferenciante en mitin Webster Hall. *Frente Popular*, p. 1.
González Malo, J. (1962a). *Letter to Santamaría. 4 May. Jesús González Malo Papers*. Waltham: Brandeis University Library.
González Malo, J. (1962b). *Letter to Víctor Alba. 5 January. Jesús González Malo Papers*. Waltham: Brandeis University Library.
Graham, H. (1995). Women and social change. In H. Graham & J. Labanyi (Eds.), *Spanish cultural studies. An introduction. The struggle for modernity* (pp. 99–116). Oxford: Oxford University Press.
Gran entusiasmo en nuestro 25 aniversario. (1962, March 2). *España Libre*, pp. 1, 2.

Grandioso será el festival del día de la raza. (1948, October 4). *España Libre*, p. 8.

Granell, E. F. (1977, May-June). El campo de la lucha por la libertad ha vuelto a establecerse en España. *España Libre*, p. 1.

Guglielmo, J. (2010). *Living the revolution. Italian women's resistance and radicalism in New York City, 1880–1945*. Chapel Hill: University of North Carolina Press.

Hay que preparar el regreso a España. (1939, November 10). *España Libre*, p. 5.

Horrible espectáculo ofrece España después de un año de 'victoria. (1940, May 10). *España Libre*, p. 2.

Jaffe, S. (2007). Legacies of the Spanish Civil War in New York. In P. N. Carroll & J. D. Fernández (Eds.), *Facing fascism: New York and the Spanish Civil War* (pp. 172–183). New York: Museum of the City of New York.

Juventudes de AMA. (1940, February 16). *España Libre*, p. 14.

Kamen, H. (2007). *The disinherited. Exile and the making of Spanish culture, 1492–1975*. New York: Harper.

Kanellos, N. (1990). *A history of Hispanic theatre in the united states: Origins to 1940*. Austin: University of Texas.

Kanellos, N. (2008). *The Greenwood encyclopedia of Latino literature*. Westport: Greenwood Press.

Kanellos, N., & Martell, H. (2000). *Hispanic periodicals in the United States. Origins to 1960. A brief history and comprehensive bibliography*. Houston: Arte Público Press.

Kaufman, J. P., & Williams, K. P. (2007). *Women, the state, and war: A comparative perspective on citizenship and nationalism*. Lanham: Lexington Books.

La conmemoración del 14 de abril. (1954, April 23). *España Libre*, p. 8.

Lerner Sigal, V. (2000). *Exilio e historia. Algunas hipótesis generales a partir del caso de los mexicanos exiliados por la revolución mexicana (1906–1920)*. Mexican Studies Program. Center for Latin American Studies. University of Chicago. Working Papers Series 7: 2–21.

Lo que debe ser el órgano de SHC. (1939, November 24). Editorial. *España Libre*, p. 2.

Magnífica representación de La foguera de San Juan. (1940, May 24). *España Libre*, p. 7.

Magnini, S. (1995). *Memories of resistance. Women's voices from the Spanish Civil War*. New Haven: Yale University Press.

Martí Ibáñez, F. (1941, May 12). Después del congreso. *España Libre*, p. 7.

Marx, A. W. (2002). The nation-tate and its exclusions. *Political Science Quarterly, 117*(1), 103–126.

Maurín, J. (1966, January 1). Jesús González Malo. *España Libre*, Suplemento, p. 11.

McClintock, A. (1993). Gender, nationalism and the family. *Feminist Review: Nationalisms and National Identities, 44*(Summer), 61–80.

Miqueli González, V. (1940, March 15). Distintas clases de antifascistas. *España Libre*, p. 10.

Nash, M. (1991). Two decades of women's history in Spain. In K. Offen, R. Roach Pierson, & J. Rendall (Eds.), *Writing women's history. International perspectives* (pp. 381–417). Bloomington: Indiana University Press.

Nash, M. (1995). *Defying male civilization: Women in the Spanish Civil War*. Denver: Arden Press.

Nuestras actividades. (1955, July). *España Libre*, p. 7.

Ordaz Romay, M. A. (1998). *Características del exilio español en Estados Unidos (1936–1975) y Eugenio Fernández Granell como experiencia significativa*. Diss, Universidad Complutense de Madrid

Ottanelli, F. M. (2007). The New York City left and the Spanish Civil War. In P. N. Carroll & J. D. Fernández (Eds.), *Facing fascism: New York and the Spanish Civil War* (pp. 63–69). New York: Museum of the City of New York.

Pego, A. (1940, September 20). Hay que buscarle novia a Hitler. *España Libre*, p. 8.

Protegidos por las notas del Himno de Riego. (1940, February 9). *España Libre*, pp. 1–2.

Rayo, J. (1939, December 8). Sobre el tercer congreso de Sociedades Hispanas Confederadas. *España Libre*, p. 7.

Reuther, V. G. (1964). Letter to González Malo, J. 19 May. Jesús González Malo Papers. Waltham: Brandeis University Library.

Rey García, M. (1997). *Stars for Spain. La guerra civil española en los Estados Unidos*. La Coruña: Edicios Do Castro.

Rueda, G. (1993). *La emigración contemporánea de españoles a Estados Unidos 1820–1950*. Madrid: Mapfre.

Salazar, J., Azkárraga, J. M., Aragó, L. (2006). Guillermina Medrano. *Valencia y la República. Guía urbana 1931–1939*. Resource document. Universitat de Valencia. http://www.uv.es/republica/plano/guiller/entrevista.htm. Accessed July 27, 2010.

Samblancat Miranda, N. M. (2006). Los derechos de la mujer moderna. *Cuadernos Hispanoamericanos, 671*, 7–19.

Sinués de Marco, M. del P. (1859). *El ángel del hogar*. Madrid: Imprenta y estereotipia española de los señores Nieto y compañia.

Smith, E. R. (2007). New York's aid to the Spanish Republic. In P. N. Carroll & J. D. Fernández (Eds.), *Facing fascism: New York and the Spanish Civil War* (pp. 43–51). New York: Museum of the City of New York.

Tres representaciones, tres éxitos. (1941, February 28). *España Libre*, p. 5.

Un éxito completo. (1961, Junio 16). *España Libre*, p. 1.

Una prueba elocuente. (1940, March 1). *España Libre*, p. 6.

¡Vigorización! (1953, April 17). Editorial. *España Libre*, p. 4.

Villarroel, C. (2008). *La mujer Mexicana ante el feminismo: Nación, género, clase y raza en la literatura femenina del destierro (1910–1940)*. Diss. University of Houston.

Wallace, M. (2007). New York and the world: The global context. In P. N. Carroll & J. D. Fernández (Eds.), *Facing fascism: New York and the Spanish Civil War* (pp. 21–29). New York: Museum of the City of New York.

Yusta, M. (2009). *Madres coraje contra Franco. La unión de Mujeres Españolas en Francia, del antifascismo a la Guerra Fría (1941–1950)*. Madrid: Ediciones Cátedra.

Yuval-Davis, N., Anthias, N. F., & Campling, J. (1989). *Woman-nation-state*. New York: St. Martin's Press.

Chapter 11
(Im)migrant Women's Work in France and Brazil: Towards Social Recognition and Social Justice

Maria Inacia D'Ávila Neto, Annick Durand-Delvigne, and Juliana Nazareth

11.1 Introduction

In today's globalized world, women account for a considerable number of immigrants and migrants. This phenomenon is called by scholars as the *feminization of the migratory flows* or of *population dislocations* (Bilac 1995; Boyd 2006; Lisboa 2007) that is emerging as a dominant feature of the twenty-first century (Lutz 2008). The study of migration requires more reflection about women's migration that include, on one hand, the factors of vulnerability and inequality and, on the other, the possibilities of transformations in the social and familiar structures of women's work.

Changes in the international economy since the 1980s together with the labor demands in developed or more progressive communities facilitate particular kinds of women's work. This chapter presents two types of women's work arising from migration: trading of African immigrant women in France and domestic work of Brazilian migrant women in Brazil. It discusses the social inequalities experienced by these groups of women in host societies, including their strategies for survival amidst "othering" practices. The ways in which they negotiate their marginality through cross-cultural interactions are given emphasis.

M.I. D'Ávila Neto (✉)
EICOS Program – Interdisciplinary Studies of Communities and Social
Ecology/Psychology Institute, Federal University of Rio de Janeiro (UFRJ),
Rio de Janeiro, Brazil
e-mail: inadavila@gmail.com

A. Durand-Delvigne
Department of Psychology, University of Lille 3, Lille, France

J. Nazareth
Research Group of Image Laboratory CNPq/EICOS Program, UNESCO
CHAIR on Sustainable development

G.T. Bonifacio (ed.), *Feminism and Migration: Cross-Cultural Engagements*,
International Perspectives on Migration 1, DOI 10.1007/978-94-007-2831-8_11,
© Springer Science+Business Media B.V. 2012

Data is based from the partial results of an intercultural research conducted by the Federal University of Rio de Janeiro (UFRJ), Brazil, and Charles de Gaulle Lille 3 University, France. Although this international research collaboration uses the same theoretical references, each country team pursued an independent collection of data. This initiative aims to promote a deeper understanding about female migration, identify the specificities in each country, and show the similarities and differences between immigrant African women in France and domestic migrant women in Brazil. The theoretical perspectives that permeates the realities of these women rest on the reflections from post-colonial and subaltern studies (Mohanty 1991; Mendoza 2002; Said 2007; Lazarus 2006; Boaventura Santos 2006; Spivak 2008), cultural Studies (Hall 2007), as well as works of social justice theorists like Nancy Fraser (2001) and Axel Honneth (2003). We offer an academic feminist engagement with issues of migration using a collaborative research project as a starting point. That is, as feminist scholars recognizing differences in position and other social categories but united by common interests surrounding (im)migrant women.

We refer to both immigrant women coming from outside the host country, like African immigrants in France, and migrant women coming from within the country, like regional migrants in Brazil—(im)migrants. We point this distinction to clarify that this chapter deals with different groups of women in different countries and with different experiences. However, it is also important to understand their common yet distinct experiences of migration, or what Nazareth (2010) calls as "living in a border": the border of double absence and of double bond. They do not belong to the host society, or even more to the origin society. And, at the same time, they belong to both. They live in a place "between" culture of origin and destination. Thus, the migrant would be, accordingly, always (e)migrant and (im)migrant—someone who comes in, and someone who comes out. There are wide ranging affective experiences and subjective reasons in the process of migration, not only related to their decision to leave. There are also losses and positive gains in their migration, and by speaking to (im)migrant women, we refer to common points in their experiences.

In discussing the initial findings of the intercultural research between France and Brazil, this chapter is divided into six sections: first, the *social justice and women's work in migratory contexts*, which introduces relevant social justice theories and presents some important questions and challenges for feminists about (im)migrant women's work; second, the *intercultural research in local and global contexts*, which outlines the context in which this research was developed; third, the *issues of African immigrants in France*, which shows the realities of Sub-Saharan African immigrant women living in France; fourth, the *regional migrants in Brazil*, which explores the question of internal migration in a country with continental dimensions and the challenges faced by Brazilian migrant women; fifth, the use of *networks as a survival strategy* as well as *comparing networks in France and Brazil* demonstrate the similarities and differences between African immigrant women and Brazilian migrant women; and, finally, *feminism and post-colonial challenge* which provides some conclusions about (im)migration of women from former colonies and the possibilities for feminism.

11.2   Social Justice and Women's Work in Migratory Contexts

The engendering of migration studies enables a nuanced understanding of the factors that create and stimulate migration of men and women. There is now more emphasis in women's motivations beyond the family that includes the search for better living conditions, work, and even their willingness to break with different forms of oppression and exploitation in their countries of origin (Lisboa 2007; Lutz 2008). Migration is a complex decision among women that is not purely explained by economic factors. Besides what could be understood as a quest for social recognition is the desire for new status and dignity; something that at first may seem a bit subjective and particular, but may also be strategic for the transformation of the asymmetrical relations of gender.

According to Axel Honneth (2003), the struggle for recognition is at the base of all social conflicts. He states that "the reproduction of social life is governed by the imperative of mutual recognition" and believes that social recognition is the basic claim and a fundamental concept of social justice (Honneth 2003, 155). Social justice presupposes "intersubjective recognition" (ibid.), a kind of social respect or mutual recognition of differences. In a way social recognition configures itself as a basic premise to overcome any conditions of injustice and, for Honneth (2003), is at the heart of all social conflicts. Nancy Fraser (1997, 2001, 2007) further provides a feminist reading of the question of social justice. Her theory, while not denying the importance of social recognition, goes further by proposing the thesis that social justice also depends on economic disparities, resolved by the process of redistribution (of resources). Thus, Fraser points out that recognition is for cultural injustices as redistribution is to economic inequalities. In practice, these processes intersect and complement each other.

In a more recent work, Fraser (2007) emphasizes the notion of representation as another element of social justice: representation gives political voice to women. It involves the possibility of giving women equal voice in traditional political avenues, and a means for equality of participation in "established political communities" (Fraser 2007, 303). But it also offers the possibility of giving new dimensions for women's claims, even going far from the old boundaries or national frontiers, and extending the claims of economic redistribution and social recognition in a transnational or global perspective. According to Fraser (2007, 304), the new challenge of feminists is to correct the injustice of the meta or the "bad environment" that "arises when the framework of the territorial state is imposed on transnational sources of injustice." She believes that without representation the struggles against other injustices—non-social recognition and poor economic distribution—cannot advance. Thus, gender justice reconfigures itself, in actuality, "as one-dimensional problem, in which redistribution, recognition and representation should be integrated in a balanced way" (Fraser 2007, 305).

This problem of representation, although still contested, fits with the deterritorializing perspective presented by Stuart Hall (2005) as part of the contemporary, global and transnational scenario marked by the weakening of nation-states. This conjuncture shows as a result of "a new type of defensive and racialized national-ism" (Hall 2005, 45). In practice, this is translated as prejudice, discrimination, injustice and violence against the "other"—the culturally different. These exist in addition to the prevailing injustices based on race and gender, "leading to a 'politics of recognition' next to the struggles against racism and social justice" (ibid.). Its relevance is called for in the migration of women from former colonies, and the pervasive disparity between urban centers and poor regions which affect diverse groups of women in the nation-state.

Understanding the status of women in postcolonial states has been central to feminist discourse since the 1980s. Postcolonial feminism or, more appropriately, Third World feminism addresses the totalizing constructions of concepts intended to apply to all women in all cultures. In Breny Mendonza's words:

> They have made possible the analysis of gender, race and sexuality beyond the confinement of national borders and generated the necessary spaces to establish the connections between women of different nations and cultures, but also of different feminisms. (Mendoza 2002, 302)

The experiences of women from postcolonial states compared to women in Western societies are, postcolonial feminists argue, different (see Mohanty 1991; Narayan 1997; Spivak 2008).

An important dimension of postcolonialism is the continued migration of people from the periphery to the center, from the rural to the urban regions. This is the scenario where the increasing rates of female migration takes place and pose par-ticular challenges to feminists in the era of globalization. Stephen Castles and Mark Miller (1993) point out the "feminization of displacement" which configures one of the characteristics of the "age of migration." But this characteristic also indicates an urgency to examine immigration policies and practices in different countries nowa-days because of its undeniable link to the social positioning and vulnerability of (im)migrant women.

Feminization of migration is related to women's work in the global economy. As women in host societies enter the labor force, another group of women take their place in domestic and care work—the *feminized domains* (Parreñas, 2001; D'Ávila Neto and Nazareth 2005; Lisboa 2007; Nazareth 2010)—which configures a global chain of labor (Lisboa 2007; Lutz 2008). Im/migrant women, thus, occupy low skilled occupations and experience more precarious working conditions. The infor-mal service sector provides the main alternative work for poor women, especially (im)migrants. Therefore, there is a link between the majority of female workers and low wages with low status and low occupational mobility. (Im)migrant women usu-ally perform work in the private sphere as domestic workers, and their isolation and economic difficulties pose particular challenges for any collective organization towards empowerment (Lutz 2008). Their situations in unregulated occupations represent a great challenge for feminists working to advance their interests.

If social justice depends on social recognition, as proposed by Axel Honneth (2003), or, if it also depends on redistribution of resources and in political represen-tation as argued by Nancy Fraser (2007), then women's work is an important issue in migration. Immigrant women's precarious work is a key area for social justice;

they compose a group challenged by poor distribution of economic resources among nation-states, and with other women in host societies. These inequalities, however, make it more difficult to promote social justice among diverse groups with competing interests. While the contemporary features of globalization such as "feminization of the workforce," "feminization of poverty" (Lisboa 2007; Nazareth 2003), and "feminization of migration" (Castles and Miller 1993) make a challenging terrain for feminism, these provide the context for the intercultural research of immigrant women in France and migrant women in Brazil.

11.3   Intercultural Research in Local and Global Contexts

Our intercultural research intends to transgress traditional binaries like sameness-otherness, *the first* world- *third world* women, *internal* and *international* migration, *south* or *black* feminism (King et al. 2008). Trying to do a cultural, or a transcultural translation of immigrant women's experiences assumes the impossibility of universalism and recreating frontiers, or unmaking its arbitrariness while also giving voice and visibility to the subalterns. In this sense it is important to focus on the "domination epistemology" (D'Ávila Neto and Cavas 2011) in taking into account the intersections of sex, race and class as proposed by feminists such as Elsa Dorlin (2009) in France or Jurema Werneck (2007) in Brazil. In discussing south feminism or black feminism, Werneck states:

> [...] we should make explicit the practical impossibility of disassociating patriarchy from racism, colonialism, and capitalism—all parts of the same 'package' of western domination over all the other regions in the world. These systems of domination are not structured as chapters or as hierarchies; on the contrary, they operate simultaneously over women, and at times, all too arduously. (Werneck 2007, 100)

The present intercultural research was designed to overcome Eurocentric voices that define some of these binaries. The importance of this kind of initiative resides on the trust and respect among researchers from two different countries, and are considered fundamental in understanding the divisions among migrant women. For example, the separation between internal and international migration is marked by different literatures, concepts, methods and policies. It is imperative to find a balance between general and totalizing theories on "conceptual reductionism and theoretical imperialism" (Pryor 1981 cited in King et al. 2008, 48), noting that,

> Somewhere between these two epistemological extremes—an unattainable theoretical utopia and a myriad of empirical case-studies—some progress needs to be made at the level of what Castles (2007) and Portes (1997) have called middle-range theorization in migration studies. (King et al. 2008, 47)

Separating local and global processes are not anymore realistic in today's world. Internal migration is connected with international movements; one affects the other. However, a number of feminist scholars—including the feminist calls of the South – still refuse to consider global and local concepts simultaneously, presupposing that the transnational could be just a translation from the local, in a kind continuum

(Freeman 2001 cited in Bahri 2006, 328). Considering that "the capital and the industry don't have nationals fronts anymore" (Bahri 2006, 328), it is necessary to understand the importance of local processes and their actors under globalization (Freeman 2001 cited in Bahri 2006, 328; Mendoza 2002). Arjun Appadurai (2005) further indicates that,

> Every deterritorialization is not necessarily covered of a global dimension. In the same way, the imagined lives don't have all as backdrop vast international panoramas. The world in movement also affects minuscule geographical and cultural spaces. (Appadurai 2005, 106)

Using partial results in our intercultural research, the process of globalization leads to issues that affect women in similar ways; those migrating from one continent to another (like the Africans who immigrated to France) and those migrating within the same country (like the Brazilian migrant women). To understand the choices for these different women's groups in both countries, it is necessary to discuss the particularities in a country like Brazil: for example, the continental dimensions, where multiplicity of cultural codes exists besides many different socio-economical realities; and the common reference to many 'Brazils' inside the same country (Minayo 1995). Moreover, in Brazil, as in other parts of the world, there are a growing percentage of women who migrate from poorer regions, like the Northeast, to the more developed regions, like the Southeast, especially to Rio de Janeiro and São Paulo (Nazareth 2009).

Vestiges of the colonization process are still present in Brazil. Its former colonizer, Portugal, managed to build an empire which stood at the periphery of other more hegemonic empires like France and England. Portugal's dubious condition meant being central in relation to the colonies but peripheral to European empires. This semi-peripheral condition brought significant repercussions on the Portuguese identity as well as the Brazilians—the colonized people. Boaventura de Souza Santos (2002) notes that this identity is something between Prospero and Caliban, which in the Shakeasperean allegory describes the psychology of colonization—something between civilized and primitive, colonizer and colonized. Brazilians are supposed to have this double and ambivalent inscription in their identities (Santos 2002). This alludes to some important consequences in the way the richest and central regions of the country view the poorest regions. There are visible traces of dominant and subaltern identities between these regions which appear in different forms of power relationships.[1] For example, the culture of migrant women coming from the Northeast region to the Southeast is frequently seen as imbued with a folklore element or something less developed; they often face "colonial" and dominant treatment when they arrive at the "big cities," the central and more developed parts of the country (Nazareth 2009).

In France, on the other hand, black women participating in this intercultural research are Francophones from Sub-Saharan Africa. They came from former French colonies or countries under former French administration such as Benin, Cameroun, Congo, Togo, Cote d'Ivoire, and Senegal, in which France still maintains a presence expressed by the

---

[1] More developed regions of the country perceive a kind of a "settler" look on the poorest regions in order to see them as backward and less developed. This characterizes an internal repetition of a Eurocentric stance that Brazil has suffered and still suffers (Santos 2002, 2006).

ambiguous phrase "Francafrique" to describe continuity of prototypical French neo-colonialism (Verschave 1998, 2000; Baadikko 2001; Dozon 2003). In the context of current debates on national identity in France, women from Sub-Saharan Africa are less severely stigmatized than women from other Africans regions. They rather represent the "other," quite foreign or exotic but not "dangerous." Their work activity is the production and marketing of handicrafts and Africans products. While this implies a kind of local and official recognition of their culture as they receive sources and subsidies from the French government, it also represents how these women are locked in a polarized and dominated identity (as black women selling Africans stuffs in France).

The two countries, France and Brazil, face internal and international migration movements. Although African and Northeasterner Brazilian women came from relatively similar climatic areas—the semi-arid regions—there are significant differences between them. Aside from gender, those related with race, place of origin, and economic status also carry out important sieves in their lives.

11.3.1 Issues of African Immigrants in France

The countries of sub-Saharan Africa under former French administration, such as Togo, Senegal, Benin, Congo and Cameroun, increased its rate of immigrants to France, from 20,000 in 1962 to 570,000 in 2004, representing 12% of all immigrants in the country (Xavier 2008). It is always difficult to access reliable statistics on the flow of immigrants from Africa and their specificities (ibid), but it is still possible to point to a feminization of immigration from West Africa, Cameroon, Congo, and Senegal, which are among the top ten countries with high female immigration or about 13.6% (compared to 12.3% of men) (Lessault and Beauchemin 2009).

African immigrant women in France raise issues related to their isolation or confinement, and the feeling of being useless. They had always worked in their home country and their present situation depresses most of them. Learning the French language seems not enough for them to integrate in mainstream society. They found a solution based on a kind of solidarity and mutual support through the spontaneous contours of a trade network. Because many of them are married, they face opposition from their husbands: fear that wives will abandon their domestic responsibilities; the impact of their presence in a public space; and the challenge of traditional gender roles, among others. In breaking the cycle of dependency, African women's articulation of their own problems developed into a sort of a voluntary initiative[2] called *Commerce equitable des femmes Africain* (Equitable commerce of African women). This constitutes the creation of kiosks trade fair, with handicraft products produced by most African immigrants, and expanded later with regional products brought directly from Africa.

---

[2] The French team coordinated by Annick Durand-Delvigne started a participatory research with these immigrants from equitable trade within the framework of a project "Développement durable, justice et inégalités sociales: la part des femmes et les enjeux de la reconnaissance sociale" (Sustainaible Development, justice and social inequalities: the women's part in social recognition search) supported by the Maison Européenne des Sciences de l'Homme et de la Société, under an agreement for joint research with researchers from UFRJ.

The African women's initiative highlights a form of equitable commerce; a trading partnership based on dialogue, transparency and respect, where the objective is to achieve gender equity in world trade. It contributes to sustainable development by offering better trading conditions and rights of marginalized producers, especially those found in the South. The African women's venture presents an equitable approach not only to improve wages, but also to give African immigrant women the opportunity to address their isolation, and a chance for others to appreciate their culture and identity through their own crafts. So, it is possible to argue that the explicit aim of this African women's initiative is to gain visibility and recognition for themselves in the host society. These women demonstrated creativity to forge and maintain this initiative although the challenges and difficulties of their precarious economic conditions remain.

The equitable commerce was created by immigrants themselves and, in 2009, got its own space in the city center with support from the municipality of Villeneuve d'Ascq.[3] Previously, they did not have their own space to exhibit their products for some time, and the recognition from the city, earned them an appropriate place to conduct trade. The African women's trade fair is currently made up of a dozen shops at the central space of the city. The kiosks are located on the site of a former shopping center that was renovated in the central district. They sell products manufactured by African immigrant women (jewelry, ornaments, clothing, and food) or purchased in Africa (fabrics, handicrafts, cosmetics, and food).

Somehow the trade fair project mediated problems of social isolation and a strong sense of uselessness among African immigrant women by establishing an informal network and an association. Although still new, their efforts are recognized by local authorities which enable African immigrant women to develop activities linked to trade solidarity; generate income and, thus, facilitate individual empowerment. However, some important concerns related to identity, power and social recognition remain.

While their economic situation is temporarily addressed by their own creativity (but still precarious) and the signs of recognition from their families and host municipality seem in place, their representation in public space is problematic. African women's work in trading is concentrated on this particular site in the city and is solely for African crafts and trades. This presents a real risk of *ghettoization* that encloses a given polarized identity. A division of fair trade that segregates traders and craftsmen exclusively for African migrant representation in society fosters a collective identity dominated by a Eurocentric vision within the aggregate group membership (Durand-Delvigne 1995; Lorenzi-Cioldi 2005). The *ghettoization* of African women's work was apparent in the participatory research conducted with these immigrants by the French team, and seemingly results from their difficulty in integrating to a new culture. What is translated from their social position is a kind of paradox: they want to be recognized for what they do, but, at the same time, the recognition seems to come only if they demonstrate an "African" cast or through the Africanism of the objects and props they produce; and not as a people who are integrated into a new culture, regardless of what is produced as an element of African culture.

[3] This is the city where the Universities of Lille 1, 2 e 3, in the French region of Nord-Pas de Callas are located.

The business opportunity supports those women having difficulty in obtaining a job for the first time, and, in some cases, induces an unexpected gender role reversal: some husbands ultimately resign from their jobs and have become an employee or partner of their wives. The risk is that this gender role reversal is only transient, and that by adapting the traditional gender roles between husband and wife in their original cultures, the man becomes the head of the trading enterprise, while women would then be limited or relegated to a secondary role.

Nevertheless, this collective experience of trading represented an opportunity for these women to gain self-esteem and develop a strong sense of efficacy and accomplishment. The observed changes are also seen as favorable at home, especially having more time to be with their children. Their creativity creates a positive dynamic identity that is forged by a local trading network, and largely translates into a transnational movement: strengthening the links with associations dedicated to women and cooperative structures among African countries. Some of them have also formed associations in their countries of origin, to respond to emergencies and to support women involved in the education of children. Their migration experiences, their individual and collective achievement show concrete impacts on their places of origin. By supporting the community, providing financial aid for families in their village and associations, African women in France contribute to the development of their place of origin, regions and the fight against poverty.

11.3.2   Regional Migrants in Brazil

Figures from the IBGE (Brazilian Institute of Geography and Statistics) (2008) show that the Northeast has the lowest household income in Brazil, about R$680 (in local currency, or about US$340.00) compared to R$1.100 (in local currency, or US$550.00) in the Southeast. The Northeast also presents the highest rate of illiteracy (31.6%), almost double that in the Southeast (15.8%) (IBGE 2008). The number of workers who contributed to social security, indicating the presence of formal jobs and labor guarantees, is also quite disparate, with only 34% in the Northeast compared with 63% in the Southeast (IBGE 2008). These figures help - to portray the idea that there are many 'Brazils' inside the same country (distinct contrasts among the regions in Brazil) and help to explain the regional migration as an alternative for a growing number of northeastern women. Official numbers indicate that of the total of 19.7 million migrants in Brazil in 2007, about 53.5% were from the Northeast or more than 10.5 million; 66.7% of them were in the Southeast (IBGE 2008).

The research in Brazil was based on a group of northeastern women[4] who migrated to the southeast region. Being born in the poorest region of the country and in small

---

[4] Through the support of community associations and from an informal network of about 120 migrant women in Rio de Janeiro, we recruited 19 women to participate in group discussions and individual interviews. Seven women were between 20 and 30 years old and 12 women were over 45 years old. Interviews and meetings were video recorded and were held in local community associations or even in their homes.

cities with no job opportunities, except those few related with public services, it is common among young women in the Northeast regions to think about moving to most developed regions, like the Southeast, especially Rio de Janeiro—a place of their dreams. They increasingly migrate to urban centers in search of better living conditions. Although once in a big town, many of them become vulnerable to low paying jobs, live in poor neighborhoods with little urban infrastructure, and face social exclusion, prejudice and inequalities (Nazareth 2009). This points to the fundamental issue about women's work and the continuities of gender inequalities across spaces—poor women still have little access to education and, consequently, to good job opportunities compared to men (D'Ávila Neto and Nazareth 2005). Access to education is one of the most cited reasons of women's migration in Brazil. But with no appropriate educational qualifications upon migration, they are not able to get a good job, and end up in the service sector usually doing the housework.

Although domestic work is considered precarious among women of the Southeast region, the regional differences that persist through the process of globalization also poses considerable differences between the values assigned in the same housework in different regions of the country. In the Southeast, housework jobs are better paid and most likely to be formalized with certain legal guarantees (Bruschini 2008). The average monthly income of a maid or a nanny in Rio de Janeiro is between R$600 to R$1.200 (in local currency, or about US$300.00 to US$600.00). Even though this rate seems a negligible value, it guarantees those who have signed a formal contract with employers, and represent much more than the average of R$80 (in local currency, or about US$40.00) in the northeast and for those who get only a tip in taking care of the house and children's neighbors without any contract. Many migrant women in our study also disclosed the favorable economic situation of domestic workers in the southeastern regions compared to small Northeastern inner cities like Pirpirituba (PB). There are also more offers of work placement in the southeastern region. In general, housework is perceived as satisfactory by many women in the northeastern inner cities who still dream and plan their own migration to the southeast.

Another related issue of regional migration is what has been called the "cycle of misery and poverty" (Nazareth 2003, 43), involving many young children. With precarious conditions of work and very low wages for women, it is common to see their children leave school prematurely to find work and bring home some money to help their own families. As a result, these children have very low educational levels, and likely face underemployment in the future. It is in the Northeast region where the highest concentration of working children, between 5 and 17 years of age, is found (12.3%), while the Southeast has the lowest (7.9%). Child school leavers are particularly seen among female-headed households who tend to be regional migrants. This is an increasing reality in Brazil.

11.4 Networks as a Survival Strategy

Social networks are of great importance in the study of international migration (Massey et al. 1993). Networks include extended family members, friends, and associates. In the context of regional Brazilian migrants, networks appear as a key strategy in their survival. In addition to practical concerns such as financing of initial migration, marking job interviews, providing accommodation and others, these networks are critical to the psychological adaptation of migrants, who can feel well supported, experience a sense of belonging, and share with other migrants the cultural codes of the Northeast.[5]

Facing significant new challenges in Rio de Janeiro, many migrant women are able to find support and solidarity in informal networks (i.e., in this case, those coming from the same place) which becomes an important mechanism to circumvent the difficulties they usually have to face. These networks not only respond to their more concrete daily adversities, but they also provide support in their more subjective needs, like the longing for family and empathy for being considered the 'other.' Encounter with other migrants, mainly from the same regions or even from the same cities, seems to promote the formation of an intersubjective field, where these women experience belonging, acceptance and identification. To be part of a network is an interesting experience for both, the newcomers and those already better adapted migrants who are able to help others. After all, in a world where migrant women remain in a precarious life, being in these kind of social networks facilitate opportunities to experience social recognition among old and new migrants.

In fact, the migration of these women is itself promoted through a network, which even if informal, is sometimes specialized with basic and specific functions ranging from the financing of the trip to the viability of finding employment and housing. Each new migrant that comes from the same city to Rio de Janeiro brings satisfaction to other migrants, and generates a kind of recognition to those who have contributed in making their migration possible. Who succeeds in helping others migrate demonstrates a differentiated, better established and more prestigious position in the network, configuring a dialectical and reciprocal process. The migrants who set out first in Rio de Janeiro contribute significantly to newcomers in their adaptation and psychological adjustment. On the other hand, the newcomers expand the network of the established migrant in the area, thus increasing the chances of satisfaction and social recognition. For example, the entry in the labor market, although in a precarious way, provides the necessary experience, satisfaction and autonomy which allow migrant women to be part of the consumer market. Being able to afford something is undoubtedly associated with social recognition. But the most important achievement for them is the ability to help their families by sending home regular money and presents.

Although informal, the northeastern migrant's networks exhibit characteristics of cohesion and organization that directly influence the chances of success in migration.

---

[5] In Brazilian society, the cultural codes differ widely in each region. There are typical food, music and rhythms in each region. For example, the Northeastern culture is one of the most vibrant, with a cuisine marked by its own flavors, a unique dance called *forró*, and a specific kind of literature, called *cordel*. Although there are no corresponding English translation of *forró* and *cordel* we can explain that *forró* comes from "for all" but this is still uniquely related to the Northeastern region. *Cariocas* (people born in Rio de Janeiro) are discovering the *forró* and dancing it in parties with a Northeastern rhythm. *Cordel* is something that many *Cariocas* do not know of; its stories are constructed with its own particular cultural references.

As they can facilitate a good adaptation for migrant women, the networks also affect the degree of satisfaction experienced by them. On the other hand, migrant women who have never been part of a network describe the absence of significant links in Rio de Janeiro, and suggest a more negative experience of migration. Brazilian migrant women face similar material and labor conditions, but their support networks made a difference in their lives.

Arguably, social networks could be an important tool to start the social justice process as presented by Fraser (2007), with the three instances of inclusion: redistribution, recognition and representation. If the networks are usually the most efficient way for migrant women to find a job and enter the consumer market, they seem to be important for the beginning of the *redistribution* of resources albeit marginal. *Recognition* in turn can also be enabled among other migrants within the networks, in relation to the family being supported, or be acknowledged by local governments and people in host communities to value a different culture. For instance, a network of Northeasterners in Rio de Janeiro created a few years ago pleaded, in a more structured way, government support for the creation of the Northeastern Traditions Center. Also known as St. Cristovão's Fair, this initiative of migrants ultimately received government support and has become a landmark of the city. This is not only frequented by regional migrants but also by tourists and part of Rio de Janeiro's population that recognizes the uniqueness and importance of Northeastern culture. More importantly, the St. Cristovão's Fair created a situation where migrants are at "home" and *Cariocas* (people who were born in Rio de Janeiro) are the "Others." Furthermore, it is through the networks that migrant women find camaraderie, togetherness, and articulate their needs, configuring a response against the risk of isolation or political weakness (Lutz 2008). This, inevitably, allow for their *representation*. The networks seem to be important tools for collective organization to address daily adversities, enabling many of the necessary conditions to begin the process of migrant women's empowerment in host cultures.

11.4.1 Comparing Networks in France and Brazil

Networks appear as the common factor that crosses the lives of African immigrant women in France and Brazilian regional migrant women. Despite the social, economic and cultural differences between France and Brazil, the mutual support and, more or less, (in)formal articulation of solidarity present an important strategy of survival in the daily lives of immigrant and migrant women. Some significant differences and similarities in these networks, however, are found in the two countries.

The use of networks in both countries varies in degrees of organization and government support. In France, the African women enlisted the support of the municipal government, which gives them the opportunity to develop as a collective trading enterprise. But this successful venture is a consequence of a larger network organization. The networks of African immigrant women in France are more formally organized than the networks of northeastern women in Brazil. Perhaps the Brazilian networks are still more informal, limited to provide the basic needs of regional migrants instead of working towards more strategic needs like collective actions for better wages. It seems that the Northeastern migrant women have not yet realized the power of their networks and the possibilities they may represent. As a result, there is no demand for government intervention in their lives as in the case of African immigrant women in France. Based on our research, the networks of Northeastern migrants in Brazil appear very shy and not very articulate in expressing their demands in public; but they show extreme efficiency in getting around the daily hardships, assist in the migration of others, and increase the satisfaction of migrant women in this process. It is possible, however, to find migrant women from the same region, living in the same neighborhood who had never spoken to each other.

Differences between France and Brazil also point to the motivation for (im)migration. Motivation for regional migration in Brazil include the chance of living better lives in urban centers, search for opportunities to earn higher wages, access to education, and so on. In Africa, on the other hand, scholars of migration (Hass 2007) indicate that motivations for immigration include escape from armed conflict, political contingencies, among others, although there are no precise statistics about these causes leading to migration. Apart from these motivations, it is also important to recognize some assumptions related to the costs involved in international migration and in internal or regional migration (Massey et al. 1993). International migration involves greater distances, more barriers to entry, and possible difficulties to connect with established networks across borders. Maybe the "greater need" involved in international immigrations could explain the better organization of networks among African immigrants in France than those formed by Northeastern migrant women in Brazil. Although there are great distances and difficulties involved in international migrations, it is necessary to confront its corollary—the possible "ease" related to regional migrations. Specifically, in the case of Brazil, even the major and richest region of the country (like the Southeast) cannot guarantee the offer of high quality public systems neither for local people nor for the migrants. Hence, there are also additional difficulties faced by Northeastern migrants made easier by the assistance of their social network.

Nevertheless, it is possible to say that there are many issues that approximate both internal and international migrations (King et al. 2008). In France as in Brazil, the (im) migrants tend to approach other (im)migrants whom they find closer as their equals, or those with whom it is possible to be identified as "others," with diasporic identities. These form part of their network, linking and supporting themselves by creating solidarity joints. Both Africans in France and Northeastern women in Brazil are seen as "others" in their host societies. Both are regarded as subordinated identities with subaltern subjectivities from a Eurocentric standpoint of domination (Santos 2002, 2006). And, in both cases, the traces of their original culture seem to be reinforced and appreciated when they became a (im)migrant in another society. Similarly, Stuart Hall (2003) has described his own experience of just feeling himself as Caribbean once in England.

Another similarity between the two countries and particular groups of (im) migrants under study, is the creation of an economy maintained by networks involved in sending regular remittances to their families and other ventures. Economic activities such as trade fairs help immigrant women to experience satisfaction, recognition, redistribution and empowerment in the host and origin countries. Activities in both countries show the coping process of (im)migrants desiring for recognition of their culture. Their daily "doing and knowing" (Lutz 2008) is an important source of constructing their identity, revealing mechanisms of resistance and creativity. The trade fairs have an important function in developing these identities. However, there is an important difference: while the Africans in France are responsible for the existence and function of the trade fair, which is their main source of income, the Northeastern Brazilians' Fair is associated with leisure times. This Fair was well functioning when they migrated to Rio de Janeiro. Nonetheless, for both groups of women, the trade fairs are the place to meet other (im)migrants, sharing and reinforcing their cultural codes and reinforcing their identities as Africans or Northeasters.

Networks represent social capital (Bourdieu 1980; Portes 2000) directly affecting individual immigrant experiences (Nazareth 2010). It is plausible that, through the international migration of African women to France and the regional migration of women in Brazil, these solidarity networks end up promoting new migrations. Notably, networks also provide psychological support for (im)migrants, especially to women who plan to migrate since those who have migrated serve as an inspiration for them to leave as well. This is a chain process that represents gains for the women involved: mainly, increasing social networks.

11.5 Feminism and Post-colonial Challenge

Feminism successfully ushered thousands of women to join the labor market, created spaces for inclusion of professional activities and their relationship with the public sphere. But Helma Lutz (2008, 6) argues that "a new gender order" as dreamed by the feminist movement is not clearly in sight. The "feminist paradigm" that intends to bring women into the labor market now has to follow the growth of a great paradox: see thousands of poor women, especially migrants, returning to the private sphere, working as maids. At this point, the so-called "post feminist paradigm" that concerns with the challenge of reconciling family and work, seemingly applies to middle-class women who are able to outsource parts of their care work to poor and, mostly, migrant women.

The notion that housework should have been partially offset by men's participation in modern society has, instead, been delegated to other women, setting up a "chain of women's service" (Nazareth 2010, 55). As a consequence, the phenomenon of transnational mothering is reaching staggering numbers nowadays and is creating a kind of outsourcing of affection (Lisboa 2007; Lutz 2008). In Brazil, this takes the *transregional* form, considering the big dimensions of the country and the very significant number of women that migrate each year, from the poorest regions, for example, in northeast to the southeast. This reality fostered by globalization seems to keep afar a feminist collaboration between diverse groups of women (Lutz 2008), although in France and Brazil it seems to reinforce the articulation of "equals" within groups. The feminist postcolonial challenge necessarily involves issues arising from the process of globalization, especially those related to the disadvantaged positioning of (im)migrant women and the possibilities these represent in changing the old patterns of gender relations and practices.

Because migration reveals adverse contingencies and lines of flight or the capacity of (im)migrants to break from oppressive conditions (Mezzadra 2005), it opens prospects for transformation. In this process, there are undoubtedly many losses and obvious vulnerabilities, but this also seems to be a significant symbolic gain for women, pointing to a horizon potentially more egalitarian in host societies. This also shows the agency of female migrants who face difficulties and particular needs, but also has many opportunities or potential to transform themselves. Sandro Mezzadra (2005) note that at the center of theoretical and political discussions about migration, there is a tension between the reality of oppression and the pursuit of freedom, characterizing many of the experiences of (im)migrant women in France and Brazil.

It is important to (re)emphasize the central role of social networks not only in facilitating the stages of the migration process and sustaining its flows, but also the possibilities of transformation they may represent. From the intercultural research in France and Brazil, the networks of (im)migrant women encourage migration, contribute to the strengthening of social relations, help women cope with their daily hardships and difficulties, and foster the shift to more strategic positions and demands in host societies. Networks, therefore, represent a depository of seeds of social change consistent with the ideals feminism—empowerment and social justice (Fraser 2007; Nazareth 2009).

Hence, it is possible that informal networks seek to respond to specific and immediate needs of immigrants and migrants, developing into a more articulated social organization to address more strategic "needs" in host societies. But that is not all. The relevance that networks bring to (im)migrants include the possibility to feel accepted, supported and, at the same time, recognized as "winners"—not just in their migration, but in life, no matter how they define it. It is also possible to argue that through these networks, women see and feel themselves represented in their claims, in their culture away from home.

While constructed in an informal, unconsciously depoliticized way, like the Brazilian migrants, these networks facilitate the negotiation of daily difficulties and prejudices encountered by women, as well as provide psychological and economic support for them. In this manner, social networks enable belonging and social recognition. At this juncture, it is a great opportunity to move feminist goals of meeting postcolonial challenges forward. While social recognition of migrant women is somehow linked with its materiality,[6] it is important to translate their activities in host societies as leading toward empowerment. Honneth (2006, 181) points to the question of "materialization of recognition" which means that social recognition involves presence in human daily lives and the ways it can be materialized in bodies as well as in space. Thus, presenting (im)migrant women with the dialectics of cultural and economic dimensions create representations of a political project with possibilities of transformation within limiting spaces of inclusion.

---

[6] Axel Honneth in his latest works pointed to question of 'materialization of recognition' meaning that social recognition has a presence in human daily lives. Being important to perceive the ways it can be materialized in the bodies and also in the space. To more details see the interview with Axel Honneth in *La societe du mepris* (Honneth 2006).

Consistent with the aims of feminism, (im)migrant women exercise autonomy and agency in their daily lives by utilizing resources such as social networks and economic fairs to ease their settlement and adaptation. The feminization of migration poses continued challenges to feminism, as a movement and a body of thought, and its ensuing examination of the similarities and differences between and among countries. We have particularly shown through our intercultural research that academic engagement links different cultures in transnational and regional perspectives, like France and Brazil, which results in a better understanding of migration in local and global contexts. It is only when these contexts are interconnected could we envision more concrete feminist actions.

References

Appadurai, A. (2005). *Les conséquences culturelles de la globalisation*. Paris: Payot & Rivages.
Baadikko, M. (2001). *Françafrique: l'échec. L'afrique postcoloniale en question*. Paris: L'Harmattan.
Bahri, D. (2006). Le feminisme dans/et le postcolonialisme. In N. Lazarus (Ed.), *Penser Le Postcolonial. Une introduction critique* (pp. 301–330). Paris: Éditions Amsterdam.
Bilac, E. (1995). Gênero, família e migrações internacionais. In M. Patarra (Ed.), *Emigração e Imigração Internacionais no Brasil contemporâneo* (pp. 65–77). São Paulo: FNUAP.
Bourdieu, P. (1980). Le capital social: Notes provisoires. *Acts the la recherché en sciences sociales, 3*, 2–3.
Boyd, M. (2006). Push factors resulting in women decision to migrate. In UNFPA/IOM (Ed.), *Female migrants: Bridging the gaps throughout the life cycle*. New York: UNFPA-IOM.
Bruschini, C. (2008). *Articulação trabalho e família: Famílias urbanas de baixa renda e políticas de apoio às trabalhadoras*. São Paulo: FCC/DPE.
Castles, S. (2007). Twenty-first-century migration as a challenge to sociology. *Journal of Ethnic and Migration Studies, 33*(3), 351–371.
Castles, S., & Miller, M. J. (1993). *The age of migration: International population movements in the modern world*. Basingstoke/London: Macmillan.
D'Ávila Neto, M. I., & Cavas, C. (2011). Diáspora negra: Desigualdades de gênero e raça no Brasil. *Revista Latino-Americana de Geografia e Gênero*. doi:10.5212/Rlagg.v.2.i1.003011.
D'Ávila Neto, M. I., & Nazareth, J. (2005). Globalization and women's employment. *Peace Review: A Journal of Social Justice, 7*(2/3), 215–220.
Dorlin, E. (2009). *Sexe, race, classe—pour une epistemologie de la domination*. Paris: PUF.
Dozon, J. (2003). *Frères et sujet: La France et l'Afrique en perspective*. Paris: Flammarion.
Durand-Delvigne, A. (1995). Gender identity and situations of power. In L. Amancio & C. Nogueira (Eds.), *Gender, management and science* (pp. 43–55). Braga: University of Minho. FAPERJ.
Fraser, N. (1997). *Justice interruptus. Critical reflections on the "postsocialist" conditions*. New York: Routledge.
Fraser, N. (2001). Da redistribuição ao reconhecimento? Dilemas dajustiça na era pós-socialista. In J. Souza (Ed.), *Democracia hoje: Novos desafios para a teoria democrática contemporânea* (pp. 245–282). Brasília: UNB.
Fraser, N. (2007). Mapeando a imaginação feminista: Da redistribuição ao reconhecimento e à representação. *Estudos Feministas. Florianópolis, 15*(2), 240.
Freeman, C. (2001). Is local feminine as global masculine? Rethinking the gender of globalisation. *Journal of Women in Culture and Society, 26*(4), 1007–1037.
Hall, S. (2003). *Da diáspora: Identidades e mediações culturais*. Belo Horizonte: UFMG.
Hall, S. (2005). *Identités et cultures*. Paris: Ed. Amsterdam.

Hall, S. (2007). *Identités et cultures. Politiques des cultural studies.* Paris: Éditions Amsterdam.

Hass, H. (2007). *Le mythe de l'invasion. Migration irrégulière d'Afrique de l'Ouest au Maghreb et en Union européenne.* Travail de recherche de l'IMI. University of Oxford.

Honneth, A. (2003). *Luta por reconhecimento: A gramática moral dos conflitos sociais.* São Paulo: Editora 34.

Honneth, A. (2006). *La societe du mepris. Vers une nouvelle théorie critique.* Paris: La Decouverte.

IBGE (2008). *Fundação Instituto Brasileiro de Geografia e Estatística.* Censo Populacional Ano Base 2007.

King, R., Skeldon, R., & Vullnetari, J. (2008, July 1–3). *Internal and international migration: Bridging the theoretical divide.* Paper prepared for the IMISCOE 'Theories of Migration and Social Change Conference', St. Anne's College, Oxford.

Lazarus, N. (Dir). (2006). *Penser Le Postcolonial. Une introduction critique.* Paris: Éditions Amsterdam.

Lessault, D., & Beauchemin, C. (2009). Les migrations d'Afrique subsaharienne en Europe: Un essor encore limité. *Population & Sociétés, 452.* www.ined.fr. Accessed June, 16 2010.

Lisboa, T. K. (2007, setembro-dezembro). Fluxos migratórios de mulheres para o trabalho reprodutivo: A globalização da assistência. *Revista Estudos Feministas, 15,* 805–821.

Lorenzi-Cioldi, F. (2005). *Les représentations des groupes dominants et dominés. Collections et agrégats.* Grenoble: PUG.

Lutz, H. (2008). Introduction: Migration and domestic work in Europe. In H. Lutz (Ed.), *Migration and domestic work: A European perspective on a global theme* (pp. 1–12). Aldershot: Ashgate.

Massey, D., Arango, J., Graene, H., Kowaouci, D., Pellegrino, A., & Taylor, E. (1993). Theories of international migration: A review and appraisal. *Population and Development Review, 19*(3), 431–466.

Mendoza, B. (2002). Transnational feminisms in question. *Feminist Theory, 3*(3), 295–314.

Mezzadra, S. (2005). *Derecho de fuga. Migraciones, ciudadania y globalizacion.* Madrid: Queimadas Gráficas.

Minayo, M. C. (1995). *Os muitos Brasis: Saúde e população na década de 80.* São Paulo: Hucitec.

Mohanty, C. T. (1991). Under western eyes: Feminist scholarship and colonial discourses. In C. T. Mohanty, A. Russo, & L. Torres (Eds.), *Third world women and the politics of feminism* (pp. 51–80). Indianapolis: Indiana University Press.

Narayan, U. (1997). *Dislocating cultures: Identities, traditions and third-world feminism.* New York: Routledge.

Nazareth, J. (2003). *Na hora que tá em sufoco, um ajuda o outro. Um Estudo sobre Famílias Chefiadas por Mulheres Urbanas de Baixa Renda.* Dissertação de Mestrado, EICOS/UFRJ.

Nazareth, J. (2009). *Trabalho, Família e Redes Sociais: Transformações e Permanências das Relações de Gênero no Contexto da Migração Feminina.* Projeto apresentado no exame de Qualificação como pré-requisito para o cumprimento dos créditos no curso de Doutorado. Programa EICOS/UFRJ.

Nazareth, J. (2010). *Mulheres em movimento: trajetória de jovens nordestinas no Rio de Janeiro.* Tese de Doutorado, Programa EICOS/UFRJ.

Parreñas, R. (2001). *Servants of globalization: Women, migration and domestic work.* Stanford: Stanford University Press.

Portes, A. (1997). Immigration theory for a new century: Some problems and opportunities. *International Migration Review, 31*(4), 799–825.

Portes, A. (2000). Capital social: Origens e aplicações na sociologia contemporânea. *Sociologia, Problemas e Práticas, 33,* 133–158.

Pryor, R. J. (1981). Integrating international and internal migration theories. In M. M. Kritz, C. B. Keely, & S. M. Tomasi (Eds.), *Global trends in migration: Theory and research of international population movement* (pp. 110–129). Staten Island: Center for Migration Studies.

226 M.I. D'Ávila Neto et al.

Said, E. (2007). *Orientalismo: O Oriente como Invenção do Ocidente*. São Paulo: Companhia de Bolso.

Santos, B. (2002). *Between Prospero and Caliban: Colonialism, postcolonialism, and inter-identity*. Luso-Brazilian. Review, XXXIX I1 by the Board of Regents of the University of Wisconsin System.

Santos, B. (2006). *A gramática do tempo para uma nova cultura política*. São Paulo: Cortez.

Spivak, G. (2008). Estudios de la subalternidad. Deconstruyendo la Historiografia. In S. Mezzadra (Ed.), *Estudios postcoloniales. Ensayos funadamentales* (pp. 33–68). Madri: Queimadas Gráficas.

Verschave, F. (1998). *La Françafrique: Le plus long scandale de la République*. Paris: Stock.

Verschave, F. (2000). *Noir silence: Qui arrêtera la Françafrique?* Paris: Les Arènes.

Werneck, J. (2007). Of Ialodês and feminists: Reflections on Black women's political action in Latin America and the Caribbean. *Cultural Dynamics, 19*(1), 99–113.

Xavier, T. (2008). *Les migrations internationales en Europe: Vers l'harmonisation des statistiques. Population & Sociétés, 442*. www.ined.fr. Accessed June 23, 2010.

Chapter 12
Building Alliances: Greek and Migrant Women in the Anti-racist Movement in Athens*

Alexandra Zavos

Because life as a migrant has taught me to believe that to dream you have to wake and not go to sleep.

(Dimitra Malliou, 11th Anti-Racist Festival, Athens)

12.1 Introduction

Anti-racism was introduced in the Greek political context in the 1990s through the efforts of different strands of the Left and bears the marks of leftist discourses and practices. It exhibits an anti-state and worker orientation, aiming its interventions towards the central and public political stage as well as the collectivization of the movement through the organization of large public events (e.g. demonstrations, protest marches, press conferences, and parliamentary debates). With the arrival of significant numbers of migrants from countries of Eastern Europe and Albania, the leftist anti-racist movement developed as a solidarity movement for migrants and refugees and focused its action on fighting for migrants' social and political rights (Glarnetajis 2001; Gropas and Triandafyllidou 2005).

In this chapter, I explore the political relationship between Greek and migrant women activists in the context of an anti-racist group in Athens, which I have anonymized as 'Support Action.' 'Support Action' represents the oldest and most active anti-racist group in Greece. It was founded in 1995 by members of a leftist political group with the purpose of uniting different anti-racist initiatives and individual Greek and migrant activists to campaign for the legalization of migrants in Greece.

*This article is based on research I carried out for my Ph.D. on "The politics of gender and migration in an antiracist group in Athens" at Manchester Metropolitan University, March 2010.

A. Zavos, Ph.D. (✉)
Center for Gender Studies, Department of Social Policy,
Panteion University of Social and Political Sciences, Athens, Greece
e-mail: alexandra.zavos@gmail.com

The group contributed significantly to the politicization of migration and the engagement of public opinion and politicians with adverse conditions that, as a rule, migrants experience in Greece. Nevertheless, this politicization has been established in terms that have excluded migrants themselves, and most notably migrant women, from substantial and equal participation (Zavos 2009).

Importantly, the presence of migrant women in antiracist mobilizations in Athens crosses several boundaries: the gendered boundary of the public domain as a masculinist domain, as well as the gendered boundary of political participation, where, again, mainly men are recognized as political subjects; the gendered boundary of political discourse, where only masculinist, abstract and universalizing narratives are 'properly' political; and, finally, the racialized/nationalized boundary of politics, where—if women do engage in public politics—it is mainly native (Greek) women. Migrant women's public participation in anti-racist mobilizations is circumscribed by Greek leftist political discourses with their limited and discriminating representations of migrants, which the women themselves take up in their move to occupy public space and become more visible. Identifying migrant women's agency in this act of performative appropriation of available discourses is extremely important for recognizing the many ways in which they are actively taking up positions of power.

In my analysis, I focus on representations of women migrants in formal anti-racist discourses that construct essentialized identities and hierarchical subject positions through gendered discourses that invoke stereotypes of the female migrant as victim. On the other hand, drawing on migrant women's political narratives, I demonstrate how migrant women establish visibility and recognition with Greek audiences performatively engendering a new politics of belonging that challenges existing (ethnocentric, racialized, masculinist) hierarchies and entitlements. The data for my analysis are drawn from two sources: the 'Support Action's' official annual anti-racist newsletter, *open borders*, from the date of its fist publication in 1995 to the date of the end of my fieldwork in 2006, which includes in total 17 sixteen-page newsletters; and 8 presentations by Greek and migrant women from a public discussion organized at the 11th Anti-racist Festival in Athens (July 2006). The discussion focused on the topic of "Migrant Women and Domestic Labour." Each of the presentations lasted between 30 and 45 min and was recorded on video, transcribed in Greek and translated into English for analysis.

The critique developed by black and post-colonial feminists since the 1980s (cf. Mohanty 1986; Brah 1996; Mirza 1997) draws attention to the implicit (and explicit) racism, elitism and ethnocentrism of the white, middle-class feminist movement in the West. Normative and normalized ideas about the family, gender roles and gender development, sexuality, labor, class, agency, are denounced as replete with racialized assumptions (Phoenix 1987). While a direct analogy with migrant women's position in the Greek anti-racist movement today cannot be drawn, these debates do, however, offer important insights into the racialized stereotypes and hierarchies that find their way into feminist and anti-racist practices (Lutz 1997; Anthias 2002; Lewis 2006). For example, ideas about the backwardness of migrant women, their fixation in traditional patriarchal family structures, their inability to conceptualize and articulate their problems politically, capture some of the circulating representations of the basic inferiority of (non-western) migrant women. Such notions are constructed out of a number of intersecting dominant discourses regarding, first of all, the 'natural' superiority, progressiveness, emancipation, rationality, liberalism, of the West (as opposed to the obscurantism and authoritarianism of the non-West). Taking this cultural-ideological field into account, the limited and dependent presence of migrant women in anti-racist politics needs to be interrogated in relation to the tacitly accepted gendered, racialized and ethnocentric assumptions structuring established practices of political representation (Lentin 2004).

Against essentializing and homogenizing tendencies inherent in identity discourses, taking an intersectional approach to gender and power relations (Yuval-Davis 2006) allows us to claim the complexity, situatedness, and openness of social positionings. Feminist research on migration looks at the intersections of gender with other social differences in order to understand the positions of (multiple) exclusion and discrimination as well as power and agency that migrant women occupy, not just as gendered but as simultaneously classed and racialized subjects. Intersectionality, then, is claimed both as a multilevel analytical approach and a more sophisticated political orientation (Phoenix and Pattynama 2006, 187).

12.2 Female Migration and Women Migrants in Anti-racist Discourse

In this section, I use written material from pamphlets (*open borders*, *Solidarity to Migrants*) published by 'Support Action' and distributed at the yearly Anti-Racist Festival of Athens as 'Support Action's' official information bulletins, to analyze representations of gender and migration in relation to two modalities of anti-racist discourse: gender as an add-on, and gender as a moral category.

12.2.1 Gender as an Add-on

Rather than addressing gender as a constitutive social relation like class, or 'race,' gender is seen as a (separate) female attribute highlighted against the background of the universal subject of migration, which is genderless, and assumed masculine. Explicit references to gender are organized under the rubric 'female migration' using titles in *open borders* such as: "Women Migrants: Overexploitation, racism and sexism"; "The Migrant Woman Suffers not only from Racism but from Sexism as well"; "The Slave-Trade in Foreign Women Constitutes the Most Beastly Form of Social Barbarism"; "Equal Rights to all Migrant Women." Yet even these references are very short and few. Only 3 out of the 17 pamphlets contain relevant accounts about migrant women, which, in fact, remain unchanged and consistent with the representational motif of victimization, as illustrated by the following excerpts:

> Migrant women constitute the most oppressed category of our society. They are paid less, they are hired with more difficulty and fired more easily, they are dependent not only on their employer, but on their husband or father as well—who usually secure their residence

permit. [...] Foreign women are usually tragically isolated and excluded since they are
subjected not only to the racism and the prejudices of the country they live, but also the
backward (anachronistic) mores and the conservatism of their country of origin... In ethnocentric, classist and patriarchal societies the migrant woman suffers both from racism and
exploitation as well as sexism. (*Solidarity to migrants* n.d. my translation)

The victimization of migrant women is not only linked to racism and exploitation they suffer in receiving countries, but also to patriarchal social relations they
carry with them from their countries of origin.[1] They are represented as more
insecure, exploited, oppressed, vulnerable and victimized than their male counterparts, both by their Greek employers, or pimps, as well as their own (patriarchal
and conservative) men-folk, who keep them in conditions of dependency and control. For example:

Migrant women suffer ... also many prohibitions and discriminations in the family, in the
community, at work etc. from men of the same national origin as them. (*open borders* 1996,
No. 3: 9, my translation)

Moreover, they experience all the sufferings that are procured by the conservative norms of
the societies they come from, as well as the insufferable isolation that being locked inside a
house offers, whether in the from of domestic labour or because of their dependence from
their family (*open borders* 2000, issue 7: 7, English original)

Migrant women as victims can only become visible through their assumed weakness
and are, thus, firmly fixed into positions of fatalistic and inescapable subordination.

12.2.2   Gender as a Moral Category

The fact that gender, where present in anti-racist discourse, is imbued with moral
rather than political meanings is most clearly observed in accounts of trafficking
and sexual exploitation of migrant women. In language that calls up moral outrage,
denunciation and incrimination, trafficking and female migrant prostitution are con-
flated as "slave trade" and represented not only as exploiting, abusive and criminalized work but also as morally blameworthy (Anderson and Andrijasevic 2008).

The slave trade of foreign women constitutes the most brutal form of social barbarism ...
he slave trade of foreign women is certainly directed by 'Greek-spirited' policemen and
foreign or native criminals, but it exists and proliferates because thousands of our fellow
Greek countrymen, under all appearances 'reputable citizens' and 'respectable family men',
demonstrate an excess of brutality and exhibit an equivalent amount of barbarism. (*Solidarity
to migrants* n.d. my translation)

Descriptions of trafficked women as passive victims of male violence to be used,
bought and sold at will, without any resistance or agency on their part, are normative

---

[1] For a critique of the normalized representation of migrant women as victims, and an analysis of
the empowering aspects of migration see Morokvasic (2007).

as far as constructions of gender are concerned. For example, on the issue of trafficking, anti-racist, feminist and mainstream discourses seem to collude in representing migrant women as sex slaves rather than conscious subjects, thereby engendering them politically inoperative (Andrijasevic 2007). Gender signals either a lack (in the case of women) or an excess (in the case of men) of power. Thus, power is located only in the abusive hands of male perpetrators and is represented, not as an aspect of social and political antagonism, therefore also productive and contested, but as a moral quality—the barbaric perversion of 'bad' men. 'Good' men, on the other hand, such as those to be found, we assume, among the rank and file of anti-racist activists, are not implicated in abuses of power. The effect of this denial, in the name of moral outrage, is a political elision. The rendition of migrant women as voiceless victims denies them political subjectivity.

References to trafficking also signal a telling metonymic projection. In the place of the violated female body are positioned not only specific sexually abused women, but the whole countries where they come from.

> The organized slave-trade of women—lucrative as much as the illegal gun trade—flourishes on the ground of sordid poverty, wretchedness, and disintegration of *whole societies*, on the active role of diplomats, policemen and judges and, of course, the 'demand' in behalf of thousands of customers [...] (*open borders* 2005, issue 11: 10, my translation, my emphasis)

As feminist theorists have pointed out (Pettman 1996; Yuval-Davis 1997), gender is implicated in the imaginary construction of the nation-state: if the women of a country are violated, it is assumed that the whole country is violated as well, as if women were the agents of a country's integrity and wholeness. Anti-racist discourse, far from challenging these nationalist assumptions, often reproduces ethnocentric political premises. In the anti-racist discourse of 'Support Action' I have been analyzing, in spite of its empowering intentions, migrant women are infantilized and feminized as 'passive' against the background of an assumed (national, paternalistic, male) 'active' subject.

In the next section, I focus on Greek and migrant women's public performances. In contrast to prevailing representations of victimhood and inferiority, I hope to show the complex and dynamic positioning of migrant women in anti-racist mobilizations and their political agency that points to the potential emergence of new political subjectivities and discourses that resist, subvert and transgress established hierarchies of the leftist anti-racist movement.

12.3 Women's Public Positioning: Performing the Politics of 'Voice'

Domestic work in Greece is a labor sector stratified along class, ethnic and racial divisions, and mainly represented by migrant women. Migrant women are mostly employed either as live-in care workers, or as domestic cleaners (Kambouri 2007).

Because domestic labor, both for migrant and Greek women, is largely informal and unregulated, it is not possible to have a comprehensive, or accurate, view of the situation. Official statistics, which however represent only a small percentage of the actual migrant population and employment in Greece, record 13.2% of the documented migrant population as domestic workers (Organization for Economic Cooperation and Development [OECD] 2007, 73), and 51.8% of the total female migrant population as employed under the category 'services' (Parsanoglou and Tsiamoglou 2008). Regarding national distribution of migrant women domestic workers in the Greek labor market, Dimitris Parsanoglou and Josef Tsiamoglou, elaborating on the 2001 Census, note:

> For Filipino women, employment in the sector of services is an almost exclusive option, since 86.3% of them work in the sector, followed by Ukrainians (66.7%), Poles (64.1%), Moldavians (64.5%), Georgians (59.3%) and Albanians (51.2%). Therefore, even if precise estimations cannot be made about the exact total of migrant women who work in domestic and care services, it would not be inaccurate to assume that this type of employment constitutes a dominant pathway of entrance into the Greek labour market. (Parsanoglou and Tsiamoglou 2008, 94)

Currently, there are no labour or migration policies securing the rights of migrant women domestic workers, and work in this area is carried out under conditions of exploitation and, often, abuse (Theodoridis 2008).

During the 11th Anti-racist Festival in Athens organized by the Joint Committee of Migrants and Anti-racist Organizations in July 2006, a public discussion was presented, with the participation of migrant and Greek women, on the topic of "Migrant Women and Domestic Labour." This discussion represented the culmination of a series of actions on gender and migration that had taken place during the preceding year. It offered an opportunity to present to the Greek public some of the gendered dimensions of migration, and especially to hear the voice of its, up to that point, politically less acknowledged subjects. By taking the stand with migrant women and dedicating a discussion to their particular experiences, this event constituted not only a chance for migrant women to present their problems and claim their rights but also an intervention into the dominant politics of representation practiced by the anti-racist movement.

The panel of the discussion consisted of 3 Greek and 5 migrant women speakers, in various capacities, from different national and socio-economic backgrounds and positions, including Albania, Bulgaria, Philippines, Sierra Leone, and Ukraine. These positions encompassed inequalities of power, status, legitimacy and resources. The moral and political discourses mobilized during this event drew on familiar themes of humanitarianism, victimhood, agency, labor rights, feminism and anti-racism, yet did not fall squarely within traditional (and recognized) leftist anti-racist repertoires. In the case of the 3 Greek women speakers, the performativity of these discourses signaled a liberal subject of rights, speaking out against injustice. In the case of migrant women speakers, the performativity of 'voice' drew on but also challenged the gendered and racialized stereotypes associated with these discourses.

12.3.1 Constructing Authority: 'Experience' vs. 'Institution'

It is indicative that in the narrative frame defined by the public context, two kinds of discursive legitimations prevailed. On the one hand, the authority of political, institutional and academic discourses, which were represented by the Greek women speakers, and, on the other hand, the authority of discourses of 'authentic experience,' was represented by the migrant women speakers. This in itself could be understood as an instance of racialized discrimination. As Rosi Braidotti (2006, 77) points out, marginal others, such as, I would argue, migrant women, are "stuck with the burden of 'authentic experience, empirical 'reality' and real-life socio-economic 'conditions,' thus leaving the task of theorizing to others."

Migrant speakers, on the whole, talked about their own lives, extrapolating their experience to migrants in general or to particular groups of migrants marked by nationality or occupation. All of them, however, grounded, constructed, and validated their claims through the authenticity attached to discourses of 'lived experience.' This rendered them at the same time exposed and vulnerable, but also powerful in being able to claim first hand knowledge of the conditions and relations they were denouncing. Their experience in Greece in general and of working as domestic laborers was negative. They claimed to be—and indeed are—discriminated against, exploited, racialized and stereotyped, excluded or marginalized as migrants, as manual laborers, and as women. While the first and main reason for discrimination against them is understood to be their migrant identity, it is, however, their gendered and classed position that renders them particularly vulnerable to racialized and racist representations (practices and attacks). For example, the figure of a poor working class woman from Albania elicits further identifications—on the part of female Greek employers—of lack of education, refinement, culture, of backwardness, disempowerment and, finally, criminality.

For the Greek women speakers it was always second hand knowledge that was being represented and mobilized, albeit through an intellectual and political discourse that lent authority to their words by virtue of its institutional legitimation. This placed Greek speakers in a paradoxical position of simultaneous power and powerlessness: first of all the 'facts' they were claiming in their arguments were drawn from migrant women's accounts and, therefore, not only lacked the impact of 'authenticity' and emotional identification but also rendered them dependent on migrant women for information. Secondly, they were speaking against other Greek women's practices and politics, and at the same time, were—as Greek women themselves—in a position of accountability vis-à-vis migrant women's accusations. In this sense, Greek speakers were in a quandary to disqualify (other) Greek women as racist (thus setting themselves apart), react against migrant women's accusations (in the sense that not all Greek women are racist exploiting employers etc.), and align themselves with migrant women's struggles (with whom they did not share the same experiences). They faced the impossible task of both standing as/for Greek women and arguing against them.

12.3.2   Political Alliances

The need to meet and collaborate with migrant women from different countries as well as Greek women and Greek women's organizations is identified by Dimitra Malliou, a migrant woman from Albania working in the domestic sector. She invokes the common identity of gender to elicit strategic alliances, since, she argues, all women suffer in different, but parallel positions, from inequality and discrimination. This appeal is tactically sealed by the evocation of the common language of motherhood, which is assumed to unite all women across differences and conflicts.

> I would like a cooperation [collaboration] with the women's groups here, because Greek women know what they want and fight to get it. Eh, we, most [things] we do not know, where to do and what to do. That's why we want a collaboration with all of you. And I close with a question, in every conference and in every assembly meeting when I have in front of me friends, eh Greek women, I say, think that this [woman] too is a mother, when she crosses the limits of tiredness she doesn't have the strength to smile at the child which is waiting for her when she returns home. (Dimitra Malliou, Albania)

Engaging in feminist anti-racist activism from the perspective of developing "feminist transversal politics" (Yuval-Davis 1999), also referred to as "alliance politics" (Haraway 1991; Phoenix 2000), the political objective in the public discussion in Athens in 2006 was to explore and develop a gendered approach that would highlight the richness and multiplicity of different experiences and the potential for action/participation across boundaries and differences. In contrast to the axiomatic political unity based on class or labor identity presupposed by the masculinist anti-racist movement, what was sought was to explore the possibilities for transient and thematic convergences among different political actors engaging in collaborative and circumstantial construction of collective action from 'below.' However, it was not by chance that the issue of commonality (and difference) and the request for political collaboration were raised only by migrant, and not by Greek, women speakers. It indicated a fundamental structural difference of social positioning between the two groups of women speakers, with overlapping and intersecting differences of nationality, culture and class. It was migrant women who 'needed' the support, help, and closeness to Greek women; this was not reciprocated. Greek women, in contrast, were the ones who 'give' support in solidarity. Thus, the two different groups of women were set up not in reciprocal but hierarchical relationships vis-à-vis each other, even in this anti-racist context that assumed a common goal for all.

12.4   Migrant Women's Social Poetics

Migrant women wielded power and gained legibility by drawing on culturally authoritative discursive repertoires, including ideological and gender stereotypes as resources. Their narratives manifested a fundamental ambiguity. They continuously both signaled and blurred the markers of status and difference, thus emerging as inherently ambivalent and non-appropriable (unregulated, unfixable, recalcitrant, non-recuperable) subjects that move in (or produce) the interstices of power, oscillating between victim and agent, supporter and claimant, worker and activist. Strategically, rather than essentially, they articulated subject positions and discourses, used and transformed common victim stereotypes, and, finally, breached the boundaries of cultural intimacy and resignified the national imaginary in inclusive rather than exclusive terms—as workers, mothers, and agents.

12.4.1   Migrant Women as Workers

One of the questions that emerged in the public discussion was to what extent a common identification as exploited workers was possible between migrant and Greek women, or whether, even as this possibility was invoked, it was simultaneously withdrawn through reference to fundamental differences of position and power. Migrant women acknowledged the fact that they shared some of the problems that Greek women face in Greek society, such as gender inequality, and employment precarity in the domestic labor sector, but they stressed that differences between them inhibit any kind of simple gender identification even as they may share the same labor tasks. Indeed, differences among migrant women, based on nationality, class, race, and age, as well as differences among Greek women, made the clear demarcation of these two groups problematic.

> Eh, when we talk about our problems, usually, when we go somewhere to talk about them [she means to some public meeting where they are invited], the retort [disagreement, reaction] is—I'm sorry about the Greek, if I cannot express myself well—that the Greek woman has problems too. And surely she has, and we have to cooperate so they can help us. But when we talk about the facts, on the women's issue Greece is indeed in the last places, in the indices on gender equality, well, consider that the migrant woman's problems escalate very much. And the most important. We talk about labor … Indeed very often the Greek woman too works without insurance, right? But because in Greece the law, sorry, the legal framework, is based on labor [she means proof of labor is the only condition upon which residence and work permits are allowed to migrants], it means, you work, you have stamps [social security signs], you can stay in Greece, you don't have stamps, you will be deported. In other words, there is an essential [or substantial] difference between, this thing, between the two labors, the two categories, how can I say it now, yes. (Dimitra Malliou, Albania)

In fact, positioning against any kind of simple attribution of a collective, homogenized migrant identity, migrant women pointed out that even if dominant significations construct them ubiquitously as "hands" (i.e., servants) there are, nevertheless, significant differences between them such as access to place of origin, that enable or hinder access to different entitlements, resources and relationships.

> It is not possible for this mentality to have passed [taken root], that we only want hands. In other words, the migrant was only the hands. To work in all the conditions you know about [meaning bad], and … at night the Albanian could pop over [she means back home], but the African how can he go to sleep in Africa. This is the issue. (Dimitra Malliou, Albania, domestic worker)

Still, this standpoint (of recognizing differences between women) was not adopted uniformly throughout migrant women's talks because at other moments, it was precisely the common experience of migration constructed as a collective identity that was evoked in order to call for common mobilizations against injustices and discrimination practiced against them.

> Work in the house is hard and heavy. We demand all women you work in the area of domestic labour to have stamps, social security, vacation leave and gift salary. To work eight hours for the jobs for which we have been hired. And to be paid for extra duties. To get unemployment benefits when they fire us, or the employer dies … As our age goes, then we have nothing left. (Lauretta Macauley, Sierra Leone, domestic worker)

12.4.2 Migrant Women as Mothers

For most (but not all) of the migrant women speakers, motherhood was a significant and valued social role, competing to some extent with their worker identity in importance, since it was motherhood that was evoked to justify both their claims for respect and understanding, as well as the decision to migrate and the sufferings endured in the process.

> And in the end, thank you for listening to me … I would like to say … it doesn't matter from the problems … which we found here in Greece. I would like to say that what makes us happy is when we see our children which we once abandoned in Bulgaria … and became both mother and father to them … for them, for their future, and when we see that indeed they finish the Universities, they finish their high-schools, and are well. I want to say, thank you Greece, that you gave us the chance to raise our children (Venelina Marinova, Bulgaria, cleaner)

Becoming both "mothers and fathers" to their children, points to the central—and not secondary or auxiliary—role of migrant women in the family's social and material reproduction, assuming responsibilities traditionally associated with the male role. The success of this undertaking makes Venelina Marinova, a migrant woman from Bulgaria working as a cleaner, proud and strong.

Motherhood was also one of the points where a commonality between migrant and Greek women could be claimed, assuming the overlap of emotional and moral predispositions regarding the centrality of family commitments in one's life (Halkias 2004). Migrant women's affective and strategic appeal becomes a moment of mutual recognition and acknowledgement beyond national differences.

> And I close with a question, in every conference and in every assembly meeting when I have in front of me friends, eh Greek women, I say, think that this (woman) too is a mother, when she crosses the limits of tiredness she doesn't have the strength to smile at the child which is waiting for her when she returns home. (Dimitra Malliou, Albania, domestic worker)

The performance of 'heroic' or 'self-sacrificing' motherhood was meaningful and of tactical importance, not only for alliance building, but also for deflecting criticism (by Greeks or by members of their own communities) of morally reproachable neglect of family duties and children's needs. Many migrant women practice mothering in what, in Greece, would be clearly seen as deviation from the norm. Even though in the dominant discourse of the nation-state the stereotypical mother's role is defined in relation to the nuclear or extended family of kin, in the narrative of another migrant speaker the possibility to take on the role of 'maternal' carer for 'foreign children' in the (material and social) space of the Greek home, marked for her as a site of employment, expands the context of relations within which a woman can approach motherhood.

> I graduate from university at the Philippines, where, after my graduation I had worked in an office for a number of years. Because I wanted to improve my situation I left my country and my family. With great sadness I left my two young children to be taken care of by my parents. Upon my arrival in Greece I worked in the home of a Greek family. And one of my responsibilities was a domestic worker was to take care of their children and all their needs. (Teresita Torevillas, Philippines, live-in domestic worker)

Migrant mothers engender different caretaking practices that mostly involve mothering 'at a distance' and single mothering (Parreñas 2001; Lyberaki 2008). Such practices usually fall under the mark of "normalized absence/pathologized presence" (Phoenix 1987, 51), which based on racialized and classed constructions of gender and motherhood, establishes visibility for different kinds of mothering/parenting only in so far as they are seen to deviate from white middle class norms.

12.4.3   Migrant Women as Agents

To what extent can/do migrant women re-signify, negotiate, or resist prescribed positions? Tracing *how* they made use of the available discourses of victimization and dependence, I highlight how migrant women's narratives strategically challenged stereotypical assumptions about their lack of political agency. For example, Venelina Marinova, working as a cleaner, remarked:

> You yourselves can understand how difficult it is a woman who had another life to change and become the lowest rung [in the ladder] in another country, not knowing either the language, or the life, or nothing, in a strange family, in a strange house. I say this because when she enters, a migrant woman, into a house as domestic help ... first of all she does not know, neither the detergents, nor, it is other in our countries, other here, eee, the chores are other, that is we are all clean but the way of cleaning is different and so on and so on. These details make it hard [for] all of us from the start. (Venelina Marinova, Bulgaria, cleaner)

It appears here that, in relating the challenges and risks migrant women who enter Greek homes as domestic workers face, she is reproducing the common discourses of hardship and alienation. However, her detailed recital of the particulars of this kind of work—which as housework is both familiar to all, and at the same time, for her as a foreigner, strange—introduces a level of intimacy between herself and Greek families/Greek women which her official status as migrant 'other' does not presume. By virtue of her work—a work which is both commonplace and internal to the home/close to the body—she traverses the distance assumed by her different (national) identity and becomes an 'intimate' outsider, in fact one who is entrusted with the task of reproducing that home/body. The intimacy she alludes to is not only gendered, as women's work, but sexualized as well. From this position she can challenge racialized ideas of inferiority and danger attributed to (certain) strangers, such as being unclean or polluted, or even sexually compromising. This allows her to go on to claim that:

> That is, most work in houses, most women work in houses. This risk is not only for the women, it is also for their employers because a man [*anthropos*: human being] comes into the house, strange, it depends, he doesn't know the language first of all, doesn't, know the job well, OK, there is fear from the migrant woman because she doesn't know who she has fallen to in this house, fear there is also from the, and risk, from the employers, the employer. That is, what woman is this, what will she take from us, what can she do to us. (Venelina Marinova, Bulgaria, cleaner)

In a subversive move she reverses the notion of risk from something afflicting mainly migrants to include employers, who are also afraid of having a 'strange person' in their home, their private and guarded personal space. Thus, by utilizing to her advantage the mainstream stereotype of the 'dangerous foreigner,' she brings forward a new aspect of power, the one wielded by migrant women themselves in the space of the employer's home. In moving from her own primary identification as an exploited migrant woman into the opposite position of understanding the employer as well, she gains a sense of her own agency and the other's vulnerability.

Teresita Torevillas specifies her position in the employer's family as that of an object, in an invisible and unrecognized role, who is nevertheless crucial for the reproduction of society.

> [...] domestic work in households is crucial to family life and social support systems, yet is undervalued and invisible. Because of the low status of the work, the range of skills required and the sacrifices it demands of the worker, Greeks are not willing to do domestic work. That's the need to find workers from outside the EU to fill the demand ... Domestic work is special kind of work. Not only because it takes place in the household, but also because of its fundamental importance to the very fabric of society. Without provision or childcare, care for the elderly, cooking and cleaning, how can society function? (Teresita Torevillas, Philippines, live-in domestic worker)

However, by reframing domestic space as a workspace defined by formal relations of employment/exchange, she claims for herself and all "domestic workers" the identity of workers who have rights and not degraded "helpers."

> Domestic helper is not the right word. The word helper must be changed to worker. We are not just helping with the house, we are working. We do full time work as RESPECT[2] says

---

[2] R.E.S.P.E.C.T. (Rights, Equality, Solidarity, Power, Europe, Cooperations Today) is a European network, launched in 2002 by migrant domestic worker's organizations, individuals, and supporters to campaign for the rights of women and men working in private households in EU countries (www.respectnetworkeu.org).

… We migrants from the Philippines and from Asia, Africa and women working as domestic workers must start to bind together to form our own self-organizations. This is the only way that we can demand from employers, from the Greek government, our rights. We demand the respect that we truly deserve. Thank you. (Teresita Torevillas, Philippines, live-in domestic worker)

The issue of the informal relations between migrant women domestic workers and the Greek family, and the blurring of the boundaries between 'relatives' and 'strangers' or 'employees,' is brought up by Lauretta Macauley, another migrant worker/speaker. Such interpellations incorporate women migrants in a relationship of inter-dependence, but at the same time weaken their worker identity.

When there is a special problem they help you, you are family they tell you, and money they give if there is need. They offer it as gift and then they expect that you must not ask for anything. If some woman complains and asks what she is entitled to, leave, gift salary, stamps, they tell you that they helped you when you were in need. You shouldn't talk and demand this, what you are entitled to. It's a trap. When they tell you, you are a member of the family, because this means you don't have other rights. (Lauretta Macauley, Sierra Leone, domestic worker)

As she argues, "being part of the family," a claim often made by Greek women/ employers to refute accusations of exploitation or racism, is a double-edged sword. A migrant woman can find herself in an ambiguous position while working in a Greek family: on the one hand she, informally, receives certain benefits that accrue from her status as purported member of the household, a status nonetheless unilaterally granted by the Greek employers; on the other hand, this precise familiarization cuts her off from her formal labor rights. In other words, the presumably desirable 'insider' status establishes a relationship of incommensurability and not reciprocity, as the interpersonal context would assume. This, migrant women are well aware of. Thus, Lauretta Macauley reproaches the state for not taking care of them, or intervening on their behalf, given that they are, by now, a necessary presence in Greek society.

The Greek state must do something for us women who work in our [she means your] homes, because we are our [again, she means your] strength. (Lauretta Macauley, Sierra Leone, domestic worker)

Here, the performativity of faulty Greek accomplishes a telling semantic shift: the substitution of 'our' with 'your' possessive pronouns in her speech enacts a repossession of dispossessed power and blurs the boundaries of entitlement and belonging: Whose home, whose strength is this? "Ours," that is, migrant women's. By claiming, "we are our [your] strength," she establishes a new position of authority, from which she demands the attention of dominant state power and redefines the interaction between Greek society and migrants in the context of a reciprocal, and not subjugated/subordinated, relationship. The reframing of the relationship between Greeks and migrants in terms of retribution (we take care of your children, you take care of us, or, we need you to help our children study and advance, you need us because we are your strength) and not subjection, determines a new kind of space of coexistence, which entails elements of equality and the demand for mutual recognition.

12.5 Concluding Remarks

Summing up, I argue that the image emerging from the analysis of migrant women's own narratives reverses the dominant stereotype of victimhood and features migrant women as a dynamic part of migration, involving both family and work negotiations. Their agency is not represented in the established and institutionalized leftist anti-racist discourse but is present nevertheless in the ongoing and daily asymmetrical interactions between natives and foreigners which migration catalyses. As Avtar Brah (1996) argues, agency, here, is not understood as an individual voluntaristic act, or even as a conscripted political act, but rather as an aspect of power: "Power is exercised in/ through/by human discursively constituted subjects, and such operations of power are the vary basis of agency. But agency, as we all know, is not voluntaristic but marked by the contradictions of subjectivity" (Brah 1996, 243). In other words, migrant women's agency lies precisely in the continuous negotiation of belonging and 'otherness,' of exploitation and rights, which they exercise as part of the precarity of their existence.

Given the lack of visibility of migrant women domestic workers, both in migration and labor policies, as well as in anti-racist politics in Greece, the opportunity to address some of the most pressing issues of exploitation and rights that these women face, becomes important both for migrant and feminist activists. However, as the tensions between Greek and migrant women speakers highlight, building a feminist politics of alliance within the anti-racist movement comes up against, not only with already established gendered hierarchies and political ideologies, but also differences in status and privilege among Greek and migrant women, which make it difficult to establish a common ground. It is, therefore, only through the acknowledgement of difference that inclusive activism can occur.

Drawing on two kinds of sources of anti-racist discourse on migration—official anti-racist pamphlets by the group 'Support Action' and Greek and migrant women's presentations during a public discussion on migrant women and domestic labor—I have tried to trace the common stereotypes through which migrants in general, and migrant women in particular, are represented in the Greek anti-racist movement, as well as highlight how these discourses are used by migrant women themselves to gain visibility and become legible subjects in public political contexts. Common anti-racist discourses frame migrants unambiguously as victims of neoliberal globalization, employers' exploitation, state and popular racism. Such representations construct migrant women not only as passive objects of state and patriarchal violence, but also place them in the position of backward 'other' to dominant Western conceptions of self-determination and agency. However, as I have argued, migrant women's own appropriation of these discursive interpellations introduces unexpected resignifications of the victim and outsider/'other' stereotypes through which they become recognized as subjects, which blur the boundaries between power and powerlessness, as well as inside and outside, belonging and non-belonging. Such performative reiterations can, therefore, be claimed as acts or practices of citizenship from below (Butler and Spivak 2007; Isin 2008) that challenge established gendered political relations and ethnocentric hierarchies.

References

Anderson, A., & Andrijasevic, R. (2008). Sex-slaves and citizens: The politics of anti-trafficking. *Soundings, 40*(1), 135–145.

Andrijasevic, R. (2007). The spectacle of misery: Gender, migration and representation in anti-trafficking campaigns. *Feminist Review, 86*, 24–44.

Anthias, F. (2002). Beyond feminism and multiculturalism: Locating difference and the politics of location. *Women's Studies International Forum, 25*(3), 275–286.

Brah, A. (1996). *Cartographies of Diaspora. Contesting identities*. Milton Park: Routledge.

Braidotti, R. (2006). *Transpositions: On nomadic ethics*. Cambridge: Polity Press.

Butler, J., & Spivak, G. C. (2007). *Who sings the nation-state? Language, politics, belonging*. London: Seagull Books.

Glarnetajis, N. (2001). Taking a look at the antiracist movement in Greece. In A. Marvakis, D. Parsanoglou, & M. Pavlou (Eds.), *Migrants in Greece* (pp. 391–400). Athens: Ellinika Grammata.

Gropas, R., & Triandafyllidou, A. (2005). *Migration in Greece at a glance*. Athens: ELIAMEP – Hellenic Foundation for European and Foreign Policy. http://www.eliamep.gr/migration/publications-metanasteusi/metanastes-stin-ellada-mia-sinopsi/. Accessed March 29, 2010.

Halkias, A. (2004). *The empty cradle of democracy: Sex, abortion and nationalism in modern Greece*. Durham/London: Duke University Press.

Haraway, D. (1991). *Simians, cyborgs and women: The reinvention of nature*. London: Free Association Books.

Isin, E. (2008). Theorizing acts of citizenship. In E. Isin & G. Nielsen (Eds.), *Acts of citizenship* (pp. 15–43). London/New York: Zed.

Kambouri, E. (2007). *The daily life of female migrants from Albania and Ukraine*. Athens: KEKMOKOP, Gutenberg.

Lentin, A. (2004). *Racism and antiracism in Europe*. London: Pluto Press.

Lewis, G. (2006). Imaginaries of Europe: Technologies of gender, economies of power. *European Journal of Women's Studies, 13*(2), 87–102.

Lutz, H. (1997). The limits of European-ness: Immigrant women in fortress Europe. *Feminist Review, 57*, 93–111.

Lyberaki, A. (2008). *Deae ex Machina: Migrant women, care work and women's employment in Greece* (GreeSE Paper No 20), Hellenic Observatory Papers on Greece and Southeast Europe, LSE.

Mirza, H. S. (Ed.). (1997). *Black British feminism: A reader*. London/New York: Routledge.

Mohanty, C. T. (1986). Under western eyes: Feminist scholarship and colonial discourses. *Boundary 2, 12*(3), 333–358.

Morokvasic, M. (2007). Migration, gender and empowerment. In I. Lenz, C. Ullrich, & B. Fersch (Eds.), *Gender orders unbound: Globalization, restructuring and reciprocity* (pp. 69–98). Opladen/Farmington Hills: Barbara Budrich.

open borders. (1996). No. 3.

open borders. (2000). Issue 7.

open borders. (2005). Issue 11.

Organization for Economic Cooperation and Development [OECD]. (2007). *International migration outlook*. Paris: OECD—SOPEMI.

Parreñas, R. (2001). *Servants of globalization: Women, migration and domestic work*. Stanford: Stanford University Press.

Parsanoglou, D., & Tsiamoglou, J. (2008). National report: The case of Greece. In MIGS, *Integration of female migrant domestic workers: strategies for employment and civic participation*. Nicosia: University of Nicosia Press. http://www.antigone.gr/en/projects/files/INTI%20 Integration%20of%20Female%20Migrant%20Domestic%20Workers.pdf. Accessed July 15, 2010.

Pettman, J. J. (1996). Boundary politics: Women, nationalism and danger. In M. Maynard & J. Purvis (Eds.), *New frontiers in women's studies: Knowledge, identity and nationalism* (pp. 187–202). London: Taylor & Francis.

Phoenix, A. (1987). Theories of gender and black families. In G. Weiner & M. Arnot (Eds.), *Gender under scrutiny: New inquiries in education* (pp. 50–63). London: Hutchinson and The Open University.

Phoenix, A. (2000). Aspiring to a politics of alliance. *Feminist Theory, 1*(2), 230–235.

Phoenix, A., & Pattynama, P. (Eds.). (2006). Editorial: Intersectionality. *European Journal of Women's Studies, 13*(3), 187–192.

RESPECT. www.respectnetworkeu.org. Accessed July 25, 2010.

Solidarity to migrants. n.d.

Theodoridis, A. (2008). Policy recommendations for Greece: Employment rights, civic rights and migration regime. In MIGS, *Integration of female migrant domestic workers: strategies for employment and civic participation.* Nicosia: University of Nicosia Press. http://www. antigone.gr/en/projects/files/INT1%20Integration%20of%20Female%20Migrant%20 Domestic%20Workers.pdf. Accessed July 25, 2010.

Yuval-Davis, N. (1997). *Gender and nation.* London: Sage.

Yuval-Davis, N. (1999). What is transversal politics? *Soundings, 12*, 94–98.

Yuval-Davis, N. (2006). Intersectionality and feminist politics [Special Issue]. *European Journal of Women's Studies, 13*(3), 193–209.

Zavos, A. (2009). Searching for new political subjects: Gender and migration in the anti-racist movement. In D. Vaiou & M. Stratigaki (Eds.), *The gender of migration* (pp. 125–162). Athens: Metaichmio.

Chapter 13
Feminist Desires, Multi-culturalist Dilemmas: Migrant Women's Self-organizing in Milan

Laura Menin

13.1 Introduction

By and large, the experience of migration has been conceived historically as an opportunity for social improvement, emancipation and the upward mobility of people and individuals. Although it may prove to be true in many cases, the ideology implicitly upheld within this representation becomes particularly pervasive when "Third World women" (Mohanty 1984) are subsumed as the subjects of neoliberal discourses on migration. Accordingly, the paths of mobility toward Europe and "the West" writ large represent linear trajectories in the direction of achievement of major freedom and modernity. Such an image, with the assumptions it contains, inhabits the collective imageries and public debates on migration in Italy. Furthermore, it has appeared to be attractive even to some feminist scholars and activists, who have theorized about the increasing participation of women in global mobility in terms of broader possibilities for agency and empowerment. However, the micro-practices by which migrant women endeavor to relocate their lives across manifold symbolic and geographical borders reveal the ambivalent sentiments connected with the lived experiences of migration. Indeed, migrant women's encounter with the Italian nation-state, its material and symbolic borders, sheds light on the multiple forms of exclusion that they experience in their daily lives. Not only are they socially and politically constructed as "migrants" in local discourses on immigration, they are also ethnicized and depicted as "others" within the Italian politics of recognizing cultural diversity which aims to include them (Grillo and Pratt 2002). By highlighting the mechanisms through which the "glocalized" (Robertson 1994) system arranges the forms of organization of women's labor in and out of the household, their lives reveal the entangled hierar-

L. Menin, Ph.D.(✉)
Laboratory of Anthropology of Migration and Transnationalism,
University of Milano-Bicocca, Milan, Italy
e-mail: laura.menin@hotmail.it

G.T. Bonifacio (ed.), *Feminism and Migration: Cross-Cultural Engagements*,
International Perspectives on Migration 1, DOI 10.1007/978-94-007-2831-8_13,
© Springer Science+Business Media B.V. 2012

chies of power that mold the relationships amongst different groups of women, both natives or foreigners.[1] The forms of social and political marginalization that migrant women encounter raise critical questions for Italian feminism. Indeed "labor" and the "household" have historically represented critical concepts within the feminist movement's commitment to the progressive politics of women's liberation and its social critique. Mainly conceptualized as battlegrounds for shifting power relations between the sexes, they turned into spaces of asymmetry *among* women which may compromise the possibilities of paving the way for cross-cultural gendered alliances.

In this chapter, I aim to address a broader reflection on the challenges that the presence of migrant women in Italy and their forms of activism have been posing to neo-feminism[2]—conceived both in terms of analytical and political project—over the last four decades. Firstly, I focus on the impact of migration on feminism in terms of the theoretical tools it developed for broadening the understanding of the experiences of mobility. Secondly, I investigate the political practices that the encounter amongst women with different cultural, national and religious affiliations has generated. Specifically, I reflect on both the possibilities and the cultural dilemmas arising from the intersections of the paths of migrant women's activism and feminist agenda. I discuss these general issues by exploring the ways in which two groups of university-educated women from different countries have attempted to overcome the difficulties they have faced along their paths of integration in the city of Milan, Italy.[3] Notwithstanding the expectations of socio-economic improvement through migration, the encounter of these women with the Italian gendered economy has positioned them within multiple hegemonic discourses and micro-structures of power that have shaped the actual possibility of agency in their daily lives.

---

[1] I consider "native" and "foreigners," as well as "Italian feminists" and "migrant women," as quite general and abstract categories. However, I find it useful to use them in order to shed light on the collective imaginaries and universalist narratives that inhabit debates on migration, women's freedom and empowerment.

[2] In this context, the term "neo-feminism" (or simply "feminism") indicates the second wave women's movement that emerged in Italy during the 1970s. While the late nineteenth century and early twentieth century feminist movement claimed civil and political rights for women, women's liberation movement in 1970s pursued the progressive politics of women's liberation as well, by focusing not only on the notion of equality but also on that of difference. In general, I use the term feminism instead of feminisms to refer to a historical phenomenon that occurred in Italy over the last four decades and conceive it as sets of various theories, standpoints, and projects of political struggle.

[3] The data were based on in-depth interviews with activists and members of associations in Milan and its province as part of a wider research project of the University of Milano-Bicocca and CREAM (Centro di Ricerche Etno-Antropologiche) entitled "Partecipazione Migrante" (Migrants' Participation), coordinated by Prof. Alice Bellagamba and Dr. Mauro Van Aken, and funded by Provincia di Milano. The project, which aimed to explore the multiple forms of institutional participation and migrants' associations in the province of Milan, was carried out between April and June 2007 in several cities and towns. The names of the associations and people I refer to are all pseudonyms. I am deeply grateful to Glenda Bonifacio for commenting on a draft of this chapter in its various stages of development.

Finally, I draw attention to Italian feminist activists' engagement with the notion of "cultural difference" occurring in the search for terrains of encounter among Italian and migrant women. By doing so, I further push towards a rethinking of the tensions between feminism and multiculturalism in terms of recognizing migrant women as "cultural others" that the practices sensitive to cultural difference risk implicitly upholding. While essentialist conceptualizations of a shared experience of being a woman have failed to encompass the interwoven axes of power that differentiate women, the notion of "cultural difference" itself contains some traps as well. Not only do I consider that "*every* feminist struggle has a specific *ethnic* (as well as class) context" (Anthias and Yuval-Davis 1983, 62), but I also argue that the multiculturalist[4] discourses that inform Italian gendered policies seem to prevent further analysis of the ways in which power relations operate within women's daily lives. Thus, I intend to broaden the debates initiated by some liberal feminists (e.g. Okin et al. 1999; Nussbaum 2000) by focusing on the notions of cultural difference and gendered subjectivity. Instead of assuming them as given, I problematize these notions within the field of the everyday social practices and identity politics. I emphasize the manifold, ambivalent and strategic uses of "cultural stuff" (Barth 2000, 12) that different social actors perform, collectively appropriate and mobilize in order to obtain public visibility. In doing so, they negotiate and position themselves in a shared, albeit contingent and asymmetrical, local "political arena" (Fabietti 2004, 300).

13.2   Mobile Subjects: Migrant Women and Feminism in Italy

In recent times, scholars have underscored the increasing feminization of migration flows as a characterizing trait of globalization (Castles and Miller 1993). As Katie Willis and Brenda Yeoh (2000) point out, many studies interpret the experience of migration as a potential for female liberation, since movement is supposed to allow oppressed women to escape from patriarchal and traditional societies. Enthusiastic interpretations of women's mobility in terms of its liberatory potentials are criticized by feminist theorists who emphasize the power relations in which migrant women (and men) are contextually situated within hegemonic discourses on nation, ethnicity and gender (Brah 1996; Pessar and Mahler 2001; Yeoh 2005). Since the 1990s, the theoretical shift from simply "adding women to migration studies" to a sophisticated notion of gender enables scholars to investigate the complex politics that informs everyday life and the subjectivities that are molded in contemporary

---

[4] In the Italian literature on the topic, some scholars stress the difference between the terms "multicultural" and "intercultural" from a theoretical and political perspective. While the former indicates politics and narratives which promote the respect of the cultural, religious and national differences, the latter emphasizes the necessity of an active promotion of dialogue among different cultures.

forms of gendered mobility (e.g., Osella and Osella 2000; Salih 2003). By blurring binary oppositions (i.e. modern *vs.* traditional; liberated *vs.* oppressed), scholars explore the uneasy strategies through which women and men locally renegotiate and accommodate the competing aspirations that shape their encounter with modernity (Mills 1999; Osella and Osella 2006).

These theoretical perspectives are incorporated in feminist academic approaches to migration in Italy. The historical articulations between feminism and migration, though, are far from being linear or unproblematic. Since the 1970s, feminism and migration in Italy have been the driving forces of social and political changes, which have profoundly reshaped the Italian society. As a political and epistemological project, feminism has pursued a struggle for rights and emancipation of women, but above all a politics of liberation based on political practices among women. Likewise, international migratory flows to Italy affect Italian economy, politics and cultural life by creating a new social landscape marked by ethnic boundaries as well as new forms of collective belonging based on a reinvention of an "Italian national identity." However, "immigration and feminism are rarely, if ever, coupled in popular discussion, social movements, or academic research" (Hondagneu-Sotelo 2000, 112).

Despite increasing female migration to Italy in the 1970s, migrant women and the relevance of the experiences of non-western women in general remained invisible in feminist theorizations (Maher 1989, 9–10) until the 1990s, when Italian feminists began incorporating the notion of ethnicity into gender analysis and political practices. At first, the desire to include a cross-cultural perspective within feminist reflections emerged in the search for transnational alliances with activists throughout the world (Borghi 2006, 26–27). Italian feminists, indeed, started problematizing the concepts of development, global economics and universal human rights—regarded as laden with ethnocentric assumptions.[5] The Fourth World Conference on Women (Beijing, 1995) and the National Forum "Natives and Migrants: Citizens of the World"[6] (Turin, 1996) represented a turning point in redefining feminist agendas which led many Italian feminist groups to envision a new politics of relationship on a global stage.

In the United States, "women of color" and black feminists involved in the women's groups in the 1970s challenged white feminists' essentialist notions of "sisterhood" or "common oppression" by voicing the power relations among women within the movement (Davis 1981; hooks 1981, 1984; Moraga and Anzaldua 1983; Smith 1983). Such conflicts led to persistent divisions and tensions, but also to compelling theorizations about difference and power among women. As Italian feminist Lea Melandri (2002) noted, the articulations of the philosophy of sexual difference[7] became hegemonic in Italy during the 1980s; this trend obscured other practices

---

[5] This turn is marked by the emergence of a feminist literature on the topic (e.g. Libera Università delle Donne di Milano 1994; Dalla Costa and Dalla Costa 1996).

[6] The original title is *Native e Migranti: Cittadine del Mondo.*

[7] Lea Melandri refers in particular to the work of Luce Irigaray and the Italian articulations of the philosophy of sexual difference developed by the Diotima Philosophical Community at the University of Verona and the Women's Bookstore Collective in Milan.

and discourses such as those developed within the *gruppi di autocoscienza* (self-consciousness-raising groups). Participants in self-consciousness-raising groups started dealing with the contradictions embedded in the universal category of "woman," and hence facing the tensions generated by multiple differences among women (Melandri 2002, 17). This shift, as well as the uneasy relations between feminism and transsexual and lesbian movements (Borghi 2006), may help to situate Italian feminist reflections on "differences *among* women," and its multiple trajectories in terms of theoretical tools and political agendas. Feminism in Italy is, indeed, conceived as a complex set of competing theoretical positions, political practices and experiences developed through various paths over almost 40 years (Spagnoletti 1974; Mapelli and Seveso 2003; Bertilotti et al. 2006).

Feminist activists sought different ways to dialogue with migrant women in the last few decades. However, a systematic reflection on the challenges that migrant women pose to feminism still stands at the margin of Italian debates (Pojmann 2006, 50). I do not assert that the articulation of gendered subjectivity as a site of differences (De Lauretis 1999) neither affected Italian feminist debates nor shifted feminist agendas. From a theoretical perspective, Italian feminists engage in debates on queer theory and postcolonial critiques of the white western feminism since the 1990s. These encounters enable Italian scholars a nuanced understanding of the lived experience of "crossing borders" and of the complex ways in which migrant women and men negotiate subject positions and power relations in their everyday lives. Rather, by exploring the multiple sites of engagements between feminism and migration, I pay attention to the relational practices that different groups of Italian activists try to establish with migrant women and vice versa.

13.3 Migrant Women's Associations: Gendered Alliances, Enduring Conflicts

Over the last four decades, Italy has become one of the main destination countries of migrants and refugees in Southern Europe. In 2010, there were 4,570,317 migrants originating from about 190 countries (Caritas-Migrantes 2011). Until the 1990s, a widespread perception of migratory flows as a transitory phenomenon[8] legitimized *de facto* the enactment of partial policies[9] towards migrants and refugees (Macioti and Pugliese 2003), that have recently shifted[10] in the direction of

---

[8] During the late 1980s and early 1990s, both academic scholars and politicians started recognizing immigration as a structural phenomenon within the Italian society.

[9] For instance, migrants' political rights are subordinated to the obtainment of Italian citizenship, which is a very long and complicated bureaucratic process. Non-EU (European Union) citizens have to demonstrate they had stayed in Italy legally for 10 years.

[10] Italian legislation has always been oriented by the search for equilibrium between inclusionary rhetoric and the European Union's pressure toward border control; the need for ensuring at the same time a labor force and the electoral strategies that mobilized anti-immigrant sentiments.

discrimination and of restriction of rights (Dal Lago 2004). Neoliberal assumptions affect Italian immigration policy and the widespread popular comprehension of the experience of human mobility (Palidda 2008). The increasing presence of migrants poses several challenges to national politics and local government, not only in terms of policies of border control, security and electoral interests but also in terms of inclusive citizenship rights and the promotion of an intercultural society (Giusti 2001). The Italian government pursued the politics of recognizing cultural differ-ence (Grillo and Pratt 2002), for example, founding "cultural mediation." The cul-tural mediator is a professional figure established by Testo Unico (Law n. 40/1998) to facilitate the interactions of migrants—with whom she/he shares the cultural or national background—with Italian institutions. By providing culturally-sensitive linguistic translation, access to social services, healthcare, schools, and local admin-istrations or police services are mediated.

A hegemonic representation of migrant women as "dependent subjects" (Salih 2002, 141), though, informs policies by which the local government deals with interpretations of cultural difference with regard to several aspects of their lives. Few studies address the issues of migrants' political participation or explore their emergent self-organizations (Basso and Perocco 2003; Mantovan 2007) and hardly any studies focus on the trajectories of migrant women's activism and their emer-gence as political subjects. Theorists and activists maintain that Italian-run associa-tions and Catholic voluntary organizations play a prominent role in the local management and the social inclusion of migrant population. They underline the significant trust and financial support from local governments to the detriment of migrants' associations (Caponio 2005, 2006). Some scholars recently explore the relations between feminism and migrant women's self-organizations in Italy. Jacqueline Andall's study (2000) may be considered as one of the first attempts to include gender, class and ethnicity into the analysis of migrant women employed in the domestic sector in relation to Italian families' attitudes and national gendered politics. Andall sheds light on the contradictory outcomes of Italian women's access into the labor market: the ambivalent rewards of western women's liberation obtained through a "new service caste" of non-western domestic servants. This illu-minates the enduring interdependences and hierarchies between reproductive and productive work in terms of *class* and *ethnicity* (Andall 2000, 247; Ongaro 2001; Andall 2003, 50). Wendy Pojmann (2006) reconstructs the historical trajectories of feminism in Italy and its relationships with the emergent migrant women's self-organized groups since the 1970s. By providing a cartography of the migrant wom-en's organizations, as well as discussing the alliances established between Italian and migrant women, Pojmann (2006, 162) highlights the feminists' tendency to approach migrant women as "pupils to be educated in the ways of western feminist emancipation."

In her ethnographic account, Heather Merrill (2006) describes the genealogy and the social life of the *Alma Mater* association, formed in Turin in 1992 by a group of Italian and migrant women from several countries, within the context of an increas-ingly racist Italy. She shows the difficulties that characterize the relationships among migrant women, as well as the precarious alliances established with Turin feminists who supported the project of *Alma Mater* from the onset. For Merrill, feminists' approach to migrants was benevolent and paternalistic, while they continued to maintain the most influential positions in *Alma Mater*. Thus, they often failed to recognize migrant women as equal interlocutors. As Merrill (2006, 162) states, "Italian feminists often overlook the activist experiences migrant women had in their countries of origin and disallow their understanding of gender oppression and feminist practices."

These studies contribute to opening up the debate on the ways in which feminism and migration in Italy intersect along multiple sites of engagement, engendering both conflicts and forms of alliance. The most enduring alliances among Italian and migrant women seem to rest in the intercultural dialogue as the main practice of their relationship. Yet several key issues require further scrutiny. Firstly, the consequences of Italian "liberated" women's delegation of reproductive work to migrant women in terms of possibilities of establishing cross-cultural alliances remain a problematic issue. Secondly, there are current internal debates among different feminist groups in Italy. Beyond the dominant feminist desire to emancipate migrant women, some Italian feminist groups have engaged in critical reflection on the ambiguous complicity that ties feminism, gendered economics and migration. By doing so, they have endeavored to envision new political practices based on reciprocity and mutual recognition. Moreover, the implications of the alliances between feminism and the politics of cultural difference remain unexplored. Although intercultural projects aim to contrast racism by contesting ethnocentrism, several scholars underline the ambiguities inherent in such politics (Salih 2002, 139–157; Pinelli 2008). Often based on a concept of culture as a bounded entity, they implicitly demand that migrants mobilize ethnic identity in order to be recognized as citizens and gain access to public spheres (Però 2007).

13.4 Milanese Activisms: "Thinking Globally, Acting Locally"

Milan is an industrialized city in Northern Italy where the movements of migrants and refugees from different countries intersect with internal migratory flows in the last four decades. Milan has a population of 1,322,750 in 2010 of whom 217,284 are foreign citizens.[11] Aside from ethnic restaurants, clothes and food shops, there are roughly 113 migrants' associations, plus religious and informal groups in Milan and its province.[12] Since the early 1990s, some Milanese women's organizations began paying attention to the presence of migrant women and emphasize the necessity of creating a dialogue with them. The Fourth World Conference on Women and the

---

[11] These data, collected by the Municipality of Milan (31.12.2010), do not represent the actual number of migrant population since it does not take into consideration the number of undocumented or illegal aliens, in addition to naturalized citizens.

[12] Data produced by Provincia di Milano (http://www.provincia.milano.it/cultura/progetti/integrando).

National Forum in Turin provided the opportunity for tightening a (trans)national network of activists around a sense of common interests and agenda. The awareness of the interconnections existing between "North" and "South" engendered new reflections on the importance of "thinking globally and acting locally."[13] Moreover, the feminists' desire to build up relationships with migrant women they meet at schools, hospitals or women health centers and the emergence of migrant women's associations in Italy created sites of alliances as well as challenges and conflicts.

While it is not possible to explore the complex dynamics of those encounters or the multiple positions assumed by feminist groups in Milan, I briefly sketch the case of the *Libera Università delle Donne* (Free University of Women or LUD), one of the main sites of Milanese feminism.[14] LUD plays a critical role in the search for new paths of relationship and alliances among women from different countries; it promotes group-discussion, seminars and public events to reflect upon the connections existing among gender economies, women's intimate lives and migration. The association pays close attention to the rise of racism in Italy and to the appropriation of female bodies as the site of anti-immigrant political discourses. In 1996, a group of women of LUD set up the *Crinali* cooperative in order to promote intercultural dialogue and to engender practices and projects sensitive to both gender and cultural differences.[15] Understanding the crucial role that work plays in migrant women's lives, they try to enhance job opportunities for migrant women even in professional sectors or involving them as cultural mediators.

Notwithstanding the desire to include migrant women within the feminist movement, the actual capability of cementing political relationships with them remains a critical issue. According to Lucia, an activist of LUD,[16] the absence of a public place of encounter for women's associations sharpens the fragmented nature of feminist movement in Milan. Apart from migrant women with previous experiences of activism, the encounters between Italian feminists and migrant women often occur on the bases of perceived migrants' needs. The attempts to turn the hierarchical relationship based on feminist response to migrant women's needs into a practice of political relationship faces many obstacles. Migrant and Italian native women at LUD agree about the crucial role of carework in their lives as it ambivalently creates dependency and independency, forms of emancipation and power relations among

---

[13] In particular, I refer to a collective paper published by the Libera Università delle Donne after the Fourth World Conference entitled "Pensare globalmente, agire localmente" (Thinking globally, acting locally). See Percovich and Damiani (1995).

[14] LUD was established in 1987 by a group of feminist activists within *corsi delle 150 ore* (150-h courses), women centers, and women health centers.

[15] *Crinali* was formed in 1996 with the aim of promoting intercultural dialogue in Italian society, by supporting migrant women and their children in healthcare, education and legal assistance, and offering help in the search of professional work. It is autonomous but connected with *Libera Università delle Donne* (Free University of Women), engaged in a work of cultural mediation, research and training in the fields of healthcare, education, and maternity.

[16] I meet Lucia (a pseudonym) at her home in Milan on April, 14, 2010. She kindly gave me the papers written by several women's organizations during the National Forum in Turin and afterwards.

women. For Lucia, the difficulties in voicing issues connected with power relations among women result in a general tendency of articulating conflicts in terms of "us" versus "them" and, at times, this prevents women from seeing each other as individual persons. Lucia further asserts that being politically active nowadays has become a luxury even for many Italian women. By and large, the encounter of Milanese feminists with migrant women's self-organizations in rethinking the politics and practices of the feminist movement remains a challenging issue.

In what follows, I explore the experiences of two groups of migrant women organized in formal associations; namely, the *Filipinas' Movement for Progress* and *Donne in Movimento* (Women on the Move). By interrogating the ways in which they have described themselves, their daily lives and their interactions with Italian society, I provide further insights into the uneasy positions these groups of women occupy as both vulnerable and agentive subjects. The collective strategies through which those women struggle to overcome their condition of social vulnerability disclose the ambivalent rewards that permeate their experiences of migration. Meanwhile I wish to call attention to the plural subjectivities they affirm, contesting the reductionist category of "migrant woman" in which Italian debates and social interventions tend to situate them. Indeed, they articulate the difference among migrant women in terms of social class, professional skills and education.

13.4.1   Crafting Professionals: Reversing Marginal Positions[17]

Filipinas' Movement for Progress (FMP) is an association organized in Milan in 2004 by a group of university-educated Filipinas in order to improve the difficult living and working conditions they experience as domestic servants. Since the 1970s Catholic institutions and religious organizations in the Philippines acted as informal mediators between Filipinas and Italian families, creating and consolidating migratory chains of women recruited as domestic workers (Andall 2000). In the province of Milan, Filipinos are one of the most numerous groups, comprising 48,600 in 2006 (ISMU 2011). Thus, FMP is situated within and in relation to an ongoing and multifaceted social landscape that includes youth rock bands, informal groups, churches and several formal associations. With these words Joanna synthesizes[18] the combination of aspirations that led a group of well-educated migrant women to gather together in a formal association:

> The Filipinas' Movement for Progress started two years ago with the intention of … we've formed a group of Filipino women who finished university, because when we arrived here

---

[17] A preliminary elaboration of the ethnographic data on migrant women's self-organization in Milan was presented in Menin's (2008) "Leadership femminili, desideri e strategie d'inclusione. I percorsi associativi di due gruppi di donne migranti a Milano" (Women's Leadership, desires and strategies of inclusion: The self-organizing paths of two groups of migrant women in Milan).

[18] I use the "ethnographic present" even though four years have passed since I carried out my research. In 2009, I tried to contact both the associations but I was not able to work out and verify whether they are still operating or not.

in Italy we saw the situation of Filipino women, doing jobs as house servants. A lot of Filipinas said: 'I am so tired of doing domestic work, only domestic work, and our brains don't work . . . only for cleaning, washing, taking care of elderly.' We thought: "We should do more!" Women think: 'Let's do more, because we studied at university, we should think more! We need to use our brains more!'[19]

Joanna is a 40-year-old Filipina who came from Manila, and has lived in Milan since her arrival in 2001. She worked as a domestic servant for a wealthy family for many years, taking care of their house, and also of their children, to whom she was required to speak in English. Joanna's account above unfolds the discrepancies between her previous expectations and present situation. Joanna thought of migration as a strategy for resolving her plight when she lost her job in the Philippines. As a chartered accountant, she aspired to find a similar job in Italy. Milan, imagined as starting point for envisaging a new lease of life, turned out to be a place of loneliness and suffering.

The majority of Filipinas in Italy are recruited as domestic servants or *badanti* (caregivers for the elderly). This sector is so ethnicized and gender segregated (Vicarelli 1994; Andall 2000; Salazar-Parreñas 2000; Ongaro 2001) that the term *Filippina* has become the slang equivalent of "domestic servant" in Italian. The life-stories of some Filipinas I met are characterized by situations of precariousness and invisibility.[20] Having arrived in Italy with a tourist visa or undocumented, they were unable to legalize their status for years due to the difficulties in obtaining regular contracts as hourly paid or live-in domestic workers.[21] These conditions prevent them from being entitled to a set of rights in Italy—i.e., maternity protection, insurance payments, contributions and sickness benefits. As undocumented migrants, their status of *non-citizens* enforces dependency on the family they work for, thus institutionalizing the structural inequality between employer and employee. Other documented women feel exploited by the Italian families they work for and complain about the low wages or *in nero* salary[22] they receive. Joanna maintains that this condition of marginality frustrates educated women, especially professionals.[23]

---

[19] The quotations referring to Joanna here and elsewhere in the text are extrapolated from a long interview conducted on May, 15, 2007. As Joanna did not speak Italian well and felt more comfortable in speaking English, the interview was conducted mainly in English.

[20] Such precariousness and invisibility is not completely new or simply linked to the contemporary forms of the post-capitalist organization of the labor market. On the contrary, it stems from the asymmetrical conditions of employment that have historically characterized the main informal sector in the Italian re-productive economy (Andall 2000, 88–109).

[21] Restrictions in definition of the annual entry quota system lead to continuous enactment of *sanatoria* by which Italian government regularizes retrospectively the undocumented migrants drawn by the informal labor market in Italy.

[22] "In nero" is an Italian expression that refers to a cash-in-hand wage; it may be weekly or monthly cash payments, but with no regular contract.

[23] As Rhacel Salazar Parreñas (2001, 2006) argues, the majority of Filipinas employed in domestic service in Italy belongs to the middle-class, and had been working as teachers, professionals and business entrepreneurs in their country prior to migration. Thus, for middle-class women the decision to migrate is related to the desire to maintain, rather than to shift, the socio-economic status they were used to.

Nevertheless, she does not describe or perceive herself as a "weak subject." Joanna's memory of her identity as a professional, educated and capable woman leads her not to recognize herself in the subject positions she has been occupying hitherto as an unskilled and low-wage worker (Pinelli 2008). Rather, she calls for the active role women should play to shift their position of invisibility, as her words testify: "We women, we should be here for us […] we women should do it, we should help our life here in Italy."

The FMP involves 65 Filipino members who were acquaintances in the Philippines or in Italy. The majority migrated alone or left behind their family and children. Those who applied for family reunification (*ricongiungimento familiare*) are facing the difficulties of rebuilding their daily lives after long periods of separation. On the first Sunday of each month, when they have a day off, the women meet in a rented space in different Milanese parishes, since FMP does not have its own headquarters nor can it afford a monthly rent. Over the years, women have been involved in self-training[24] and now one group is studying the Italian laws in order to understand how to modify the articles of their association so as to take out a banking loan and run their own business. They yearn to define an *ethnic niche* like setting up a travel agency, as Joanna explained to me: "Now we are concentrating on training. We want to engage in business. We women should do our business here, because the other Blacks, the Africans, the Chinese are doing business, so why shouldn't Filipinos run their own business?"

The FMP pursues a gender politics that defines the criteria of inclusion: it is an association *for* and *of* women. Thus, it does not involve men as they are not considered reliable partners in any projects. Joanna said, "We think that women can do better than men. In the Philippines, women are a little bit active and they think better. Men talk, talk, drink, they go around, oh no!" She added that even in the Philippines, women are regarded as more capable and reliable; women migrate nowadays and are expected to be economically responsible for the extended family left behind. By sending remittances, they enhance their family's quality of life, meet the costs of children's education and support their own cost of living. Nevertheless, such a portrait of Filipinas as strong and independent subjects conceals tensions that women experience either in long-distance relations or in negotiating the conflicting images of "motherhood" and "womanhood" that permeate their mobility and the "ideology of domesticity" in their country (Salazar Parreñas 2008, 31–39). In other words, women's sacrifice to the nation pushes them beyond its borders, thus constructing them as breadwinners and "modern heroines" of global mobility. On the other hand, they suffer the material and emotional consequences that a border crossing entails in terms of the transgression of gender ideologies and behaviors constructed as "inappropriate" (Salazar-Parreñas 2006, 95–115, 2008). While they are engaged in invisible jobs like carework in Italian households, they neglect their own reproductive

---

[24] In some cases, the women receive help from the Philippine consulate, which provides free use of facilities and space, but not financial support.

roles and subordinate their rights of motherhood. Especially for live-in workers, being always under their employers' control may undermine the women's independence and intimacy, thus sharpening the feelings of loneliness connected with the transnational dislocation of family ties.

Joanna disclosed that some women have love affairs and relationships with Italian men, "forgetting the family left behind." Consequently, FMP has planned to provide women and their husbands with a program of values formation[25] in order to help them to tackle with the problems that couples may go through. The loss of Philippine and Christian values is interpreted as a consequence of the social breakup tied to migration and to the engagement with a Western life-style, which she perceives ambivalently. Women's social activities encompass collective reading of the Bible, as well as celebrations of national and religious festivities. These are regarded as a social time for themselves. Joanna said: "It is our only consolation. We forget our troubles, our work in the houses. I think it is good to spend our time together, sometime you forget your worries, your children."

Within the trajectories of migration, national and cultural gender ideologies are not simply reproduced in the context of arrival, but they are reinterpreted and reflected upon within the encounter with the Italian society and its own discourses on femininity. Not only do migrant women renegotiate their self-perceptions and social identities in relation to new subjectivities and subject positions they take up (e.g., migrants, caregivers, bread-winners, long-distant mothers), but they deal with hegemonic definitions of modernity and emancipation. Although FMP may stir up desires of emancipation for all Filipinas, Joanna insisted in drawing a distinction between those who are university-educated and those who are "uneducated," by which she means non-university graduates. Access to membership in the organization is restricted to the former. Joanna declares, "FMP is only for professionals. We have to study! We must carry on. We have to build a stronger group." FMP believes that the presence of other women would slow down the process of self-training, since Joanna asserts that "we want to train the other women, but not the all other women can be trainers." After setting up a company, they envisage involving other women, providing them with vocational training as *badanti* and waitresses. The decision to limit the participation to professionals elicits incomprehension and criticisms amongst migrants who regard the group as elitist. Although described as a temporary and necessary choice by FMP, the exclusion of other Filipinas may express the desire to create or consolidate a socio-economic leadership, by reaffirming the material and symbolic boundaries that set them apart from the broader Milanese Filipino community. Joanna now works as a bookkeeper in a small Italian enterprise, while the majority continues to work as domestics.

By emphasizing the deflected attention on the issue of *classism among women* in white feminist scholarship, bell hooks (2000, vii, 101–110) defines class an "uncool subject". Paying attention to class divide within Filipino women's groups in Milan

---

[25] Divorce is forbidden in the Philippines. As stated in the article of the association, the respect of moral norms and values is a condition for membership.

provides further insights into FMP's search for collective agency. The Italians' widespread perception of Filipinas as a unitary category conceals the fact that the Philippines is a class-tiered society, whose internal differences are both shifted and reproduced in Italy. Although they share the job of domestic servants, FMP articulate their subjectivity and the differences existing among migrant Filipinas in terms of social class, professional skills and education.

13.4.2   Re-appropriating Culture: The "Cultural Self" and Its Ambiguities

The *Donne in Movimento* (DM) association is a non-profit organization formed in 2002 by a group of Italian and migrant women living in Milan. Marisa, a 38-year-old Brazilian of Italian descent, has played a significant role in promoting and supporting the association from the outset. In 1994 Marisa arrived in Italy, searched for a job and then she met her Italian husband with whom she has two children now. Since her arrival, she had collaborated as an educator in different Italian nongovernment organizations (NGOs) and cooperatives. Dissatisfied with her precarious working conditions, especially when she became pregnant, Marisa and one Italian friend decided to set up an association with a group of university-educated migrant women from countries such as Russia, Brazil, Algeria and China. Despite their high level of education, they found it very difficult to obtain professional jobs. Marisa and other women started meeting informally, and, later on, around 87 families living in a peripheral district of Milan became involved. They meet in one another's homes, exchange experiences and help each other on daily errands. As Marisa explained:

> I decided to form an association for women who could have managed in the place where they live, I mean, women who had got their university degree, who might have made use of their own resources within their territory, that is, to activate something within the place where they live, like cleaning the squares, ok? We could have helped each other in taking care of the children, learnt Italian cuisine and so on…Everything happened at home.[26]

When it got difficult to manage the informal meetings, the women decided to formalize their group with the creation of an association that promotes respect for cultural differences in a multicultural society. Through a municipal competition for assignment of public spaces to associations and NGOs at a cheap monthly rate, they obtained a place in the district where Marisa lives—a small first-floor flat with two rooms.[27]

---

[26] The quotations referred to in the text are extrapolated from a long interview carried out with Marisa at the headquarters of *Donne in Movimento* in Milan on May, 14, 2007. Quotations from the other members of the association are part of a focus group held on the same day.

[27] Currently registered at the Provincia of Milano, the association at times succeeded in getting financial support from the Italian national and local governments for their projects like Italian language courses for foreign women.

Marisa provided training in intercultural education, sharing with the other women the knowledge that she had developed in Brazil and Italy as a professional educator. The women then started to propose educational projects that aim to deconstruct prejudices and racist stereotypes about migrants and people from different countries in Milanese primary schools. The association organizes courses in guitar, Chinese and Italian languages for foreign women, and events which involve the residents of the district. These activities aim to promote dialogue among people and the knowledge of different cultures through the direct involvement of migrant women.

According to Marisa, it is precisely the informal character as well as women's high level of education that distinguish the group: "*Donne in Movimento* has become anomalous because we are all graduate migrant women, who have Italian citizenship, who work, who have studied here and there, and now we are starting to make our voice heard." Marisa and the other women I met stressed their efforts to develop relationships that would be based on a sensitive and sympathetic approach towards other women, thus, creating a relation of trust. As mentioned above, Marisa's decision to work with educated migrant women was inspired by the desire to valorize their professional qualifications, to enhance their inner potentials, and to encourage their self-empowerment. From Marisa's standpoint, educated migrant women may risk losing control over their lives because of the conditions of marginality they experience in Italy. She commented:

> It was not a decision against men [...] I was looking at a picture and I thought 'I want to find the other women who go on, who generate, because I am a woman,' I want to bring the family, the men [...] how is it possible to create a kind of politics . . . to do all these things within a kind of politics that is not for the women, which forbids? This occurred here, with this mentality, but for the other women who come from other countries . . . I come from Brazil, there are movements, there is a kind of . . . .do you know what I mean?

Marisa expressed her discomfort about Italian gendered politics, which disregards the experiences of migrant women and women in general. By endorsing a representation of migrant women as resourceful subjects, Marisa gives voice to a counter-hegemonic discourse that subverts emancipator narratives that focus on migrant women only as subjects in need of help. She describes women as holders of specific gendered knowledge, hence evoking the *natural* female qualities of creativity and giving birth. DM was established with the purpose of involving educated migrant women, precisely "to hold together people who are at risk [...] because they do not succeed in integrating into Italian society despite their high level of education." However, in recent years, their activity has focused on intercultural education in the schools.[28] The encounter with other members presents more point of views, desires and expectations. They explained that their job as cultural mediators within the association offers them the possibility of giving a new meaning to their lives. In their view, working with the association not only enables them to build up relationships and share projects with other women, but provides the opportunity to deepen

---

[28] Some educated migrant men collaborate as intercultural educators, and their participation contribute to redrawing the imagined borders of the group based on gender.

their knowledge of their own culture. Describing their experience as intercultural educators in schools, many women stress the importance of the presence of a person who "represents her own culture." For instance, Alina, a woman in her 30s and of Russian origin, notes: "[at school] there's a need for such *authenticity* that only a person who comes from a different country can provide!" While thinking over her personal experience as an intercultural mediator, she adds:

> I hadn't known my own culture until I joined the association. Working with other women, I went into the details of my own culture [...] through those projects I learnt to know myself better. Besides, it's a pleasure, a great discovery that I can share with children in schools. I mean, as a foreigner, I receive something here, but I can give as well, so there's room for exchange and that's such a gorgeous thing! But also, through these intercultural laboratories, I discover myself.

Alina described her involvement in the intercultural projects as a significant opportunity for fulfillment and self-becoming, as her work with children enables her *rediscovering* of her cultural belonging. Nevertheless, the search for "her own culture" has led Alina toward a process of "objectification" that contains various ambiguities as it leads to crystallize some traits of "the Russian culture and identity." Furthermore, by claiming the specificity of a new professional job as an intercultural mediator, Alina and other migrant women actively appropriate the multiculturalist idiom that inhabits the politics of cultural difference and the public discourses on migration in Italy. On the one hand, this idiom enables women to articulate their experiences, giving voice to their inner sentiments of estrangement and belonging. Women's claim for "cultural authenticity" based on national belonging may even express a quest for public recognition and visibility. But it risks endorsing an image of culture as a fixed and bounded essence, thus reducing migrants to belonging to a shared community or national group instead of recognizing them as *persons*. Put another way, their strategy fits and challenges at the same time the paradigms of a multicultural society. Feminist reflections on the notion of subjectivity during the last two decades highlights the complexity and variety of the subject positions people occupy in shifting sets of power relations. On the contrary, multicultural paradigm jeopardizes a dynamic understanding of cultural processes and of subjective formations, by upholding essentialist interpretations of identities and forms of belonging (Salih 2003, 138–152).

13.5 Toward a Politics of Relationship: Feminist Cross-Cultural Encounters

Far from being a linear trajectory toward empowerment and modernity, migration is a multifaceted and contradictory phenomenon in women's lives. The ambivalent sentiments that permeate the daily lives of the majority of Filipinas I met, as well as the desires that inhabit their collective agencies, are continuously articulated and reworked in the geographical and imagined movements between the Philippines and Italy. However, the fact that their lives are intrinsically transnational does not necessarily entail a process of empowerment in their everyday lives. Nor does it enable these "global workers" to cross the national boundaries as easily as some enthusiastic narratives would suggest. On the contrary, the precarious conditions in which most of them live as underpaid, undocumented or *in nero* workers situate them in a position where empowerment and disempowerment ambivalently intersect. In other words, they experience not only a "conflicting class mobility"[29] (Salazar Parreñas 2001, 150–196), but I underline as well the feelings connected with their precarious working conditions, and the ways those affect their subjectivities and self-perceptions.

In many ways, migrant women's agency interrogates several assumptions that inform narratives and practices of Italian feminism, by revealing the persistent tensions between universalism and particularism. By depicting the educated migrant women as disempowered *due to* the marginal positions they came to occupy in Italy, activists in FMP and DM show the limit of emancipatory rhetoric that surrounds the representation of "Third world women." The two groups feel that, despite their high-educational qualifications, their difficulties in moving out of the domestic sector are intrinsically connected with their gender and ethnicity. The intricate ways in which power relations linked to ethnicity, class and gender interlock in women's everyday lives create "simultaneity of oppressions" (Smith 1983, xxxiv, 272–282).

Women of FMP and DM experience different levels of vulnerability: economic, social, political and emotional. The experiences of the women engaged in self-organized groups reveal the structural obstacles that most of them encounter in their personal trajectories, as well as the identity strategies they pursue to shift their marginal positions. Indeed, interlocking oppressions contextually define specific subject positions available as well as possibilities of personal and collective agency (Moore 1994, 50). The women's associations represent the forum where they share the sentiments of daily lives, define collective strategies and create ties of friendship and solidarity. Their decision to set up an association *of* and *for* women expresses the desire to transform their subaltern positions, involving university-educated migrant women as members. Their forms of gendered activism disclose the different subject positions that differentiate migrant women from their stereotypical representation in Italy. As they define themselves as professionals and educated, these women claim other subjectivities beyond those in which they find themselves confined and negotiate for broader forms of recognition.

Both the groups' narratives are infused with the notions of gender, ethnicity and culture, yet they contextually mobilize these categories in different ways and for different purposes. Although Filipino women's access to the labor market is deeply ethnicized, FMP refuses the identity of house servants and struggle to define a Filipino business ethnic niche to run a company. DM works with educated women from several countries to promote their self-empowerment by training them as

---

[29] Rhacel Salazar Parreñas (2000, 574) points out in this regard: "They earn more than they ever would have if they had stayed as professional women in the Philippines. Yet, at the same time, they experience a sharp decline in occupational status and face a discrepancy between their current occupation and actual training."

cultural mediators. By narrating their own *rediscovery* of their culture, participants construct national belonging as a trait of "cultural authenticity" which they perceive as a valued skill in intercultural mediation. Appropriating and reversing multicultural discourses enable them to engender counter-hegemonic narratives as well as to recover their sense of self. However, FMP and DM pursue strategies of social inclusion that only shift, instead of altogether removing, forms of ethnicization, since they enter into the public space as "ethnic others" instead of citizens or members of a working class.

Reflecting upon the history of almost 40 years of neo-feminism in Italy, Barbara Mapelli (2003) regards black feminist and post-colonial feminist critiques as the ambiguous yet necessary legacy of Italian feminism. She calls upon feminists to keep open the reflection on the competing meanings of being a female subject, by theorizing, negotiating and voicing such differences within the encounters with men's groups, young generations of feminists and migrant women (Mapelli 2003, 357). I wish to continue this conversation by pinpointing legacies and envisioning paths of these challenges to feminists. Feminism established the personal as the political domain, theorizing personal experiences as sites of knowledge and social critique. In this regard, the life stories of the migrant women I worked with shed light on the contradictory gendered politics that regulate the Italian nation-state. It implicitly promotes the return of carework within the domestic sphere and delegates it to migrant women instead of supporting workers by implementing social services, such as public childcare services or nursery schools at work. Moreover, being workers does not necessarily enable women to renegotiate with their male partners the burden of domestic tasks, which largely remain a female responsibility. The chains of "transnational transfer of caretaking" (Salazar Parreñas 2001, 61), produced by the international division of reproductive work, unfold the costs of women's access to the global labor market throughout the world.

The concern with lived experience should not be limited to the analysis of transnational gendered hierarchies and inequalities; rather, it is worthwhile paying attention to the complex subjectivities and agencies emerging within and at the margins of carework (Decimo 2006, 90). Migrant activists are indeed calling for the recognition of their experiences and professional skills to the Italian state. Both FMP and DM include participants based on their educational attainment and aim to promote their socio-economic improvement by creating alternative jobs for migrants. However, the former involves only Filipino women while the latter incorporates groups of women from different countries.

Encounters with activists from different countries and migrant women's groups enable Italian feminists to compare further ways of practicing feminism and empowerment. Migrant women, indeed, do not necessarily recognize themselves in the feminist agenda or in the model of the "emancipated" women in Italy. Their narratives show the multiple ways of experiencing gender oppressions, but also express different modes of conceptualizing "agency," "selfhood," "community," and "resistance" in daily life (Mohanty 2003, 45). The recognition of "others" as authoritative subjects of history and knowledge possibly results in negotiating and sharing reinterpretations of the legacy of feminism. This aspect introduces another point. The prevalent emphasis on cultural identities, or the promotion of intercultural dialogue, which largely marks the practices of encounter between Italian feminists and migrant women, may mask, instead of disclose, the power relations that mold their daily interactions (Maher 2006, 115). A close look at the pervasive mechanics of power relations, and the ways these work on women's bodies and their intimate lives, may open room for envisioning new paths of political struggle. For instance, the term *precarietà* (precariousness) has been at the core of the young generation of Italian feminists' reflections to capture the experience of living and working under flexible regimes of labor. Young feminists pose "gender, racist and classist exploitation to the centre of a feminist reading of precariousness" (Andall and Puwar 2007, 10) and focus on the subjectivities and imaginative practices stemming from this field of tensions and possibilities. Precariousness may represent a terrain of encounter for third-wave feminists, migrant activists and an emergent generation of women born in their parents' country of immigration. In challenging the dilemmas between universalism and particularism, feminism should continue the counter-hegemonic critique it has historically pursued in the analysis of *any* power relations, whatever form they take.

References

Andall, J. (2000). *Gender, migration and domestic service: The politics of black women in Italy.* Aldershot: Ashgate.

Andall, J. (Ed.). (2003). *Gender and ethnicity in contemporary Europe.* Oxford: Berg Publisher.

Andall, J., & Puwar, N. (Eds.). (2007). Italian feminisms [Special Issue]. *Feminist Review, 87,* 1–165.

Anthias, F., & Yuval-Davis, N. (1983). Contextualizing feminism: Gender, ethnic and class divisions. *Feminist Review, 15,* 62–75.

Barth, F. (2000 [1994]). Enduring and emerging issue in the analysis of ethnicity. In H. Vermeulen & C. Govers (Eds.), *The anthropology of ethnicity: Beyond ethnic groups and boundaries* (pp. 11–32). Amsterdam: Het Spinhuis.

Basso, P., & Perocco, F. (2003). *Gli immigrati in Europa: Diseguaglianze, razzismo, lotte.* Milano: Franco Angeli.

Bertilotti, T., Galasso, C., Gissi, A., & Lagorio, F. (Eds.). (2006). *Altri femminismi: Corpi, culture, lavoro.* Roma: Manifestolibri.

Borghi, L. (2006). Tramanti non per caso: Divergenze e affinità fra lesbo-queer e terzo femminismo. In T. Bertilotti, C. Galasso, A. Gissi, & F. Lagorio (Eds.), *Altri femminismi: Corpi, culture, lavoro* (pp. 19–36). Roma: Manifestolibri.

Brah, A. (1996). *Cartographies of diaspora: Contesting identities.* London: Routledge.

Caponio, T. (2005). Policy networks and immigrants' associations in Italy: The cases of Milan, Bologna and Naples. *Journal of Ethnic and Migration Studies, 31*(5), 931–950.

Caponio, T. (2006). *Città italiane e immigrazione: Discorso pubblico e politiche a Milano, Bologna e Napoli.* Bologna: Il Mulino.

Caritas-Migrantes. (2009). *Dossier statistico immigrazione.* Roma: Caritas Migrante.

Castles, S., & Miller, M. J. (1993). *The age of migration: International population movements in the modern world.* London: Macmillan.

Dal Lago, A. (2004[1999]). *Non-persone: L'esclusione dei migranti in una società globale.* Milano: Feltrinelli.

Dalla Costa, M., & Dalla Costa, G. (Eds.). (1996). *Donne, sviluppo e lavoro di riproduzione: Questioni delle lotte e dei movimenti.* Milano: FrancoAngeli.

Davis, A. (1981). *Women, race and class*. New York: Random House.
De Lauretis, T. (1999). *Soggetti eccentrici*. Milano: Feltrinelli.
Decimo, F. (2006). Le migranti, le reti, la mobilità: Sguardi dislocati di ricerca sociale. In T. Bertilotti, C. Galasso, A. Gissi, & F. Lagorio (Eds.), *Altri femminismi: Corpi, culture, lavoro* (pp. 85–100). Roma: Manifestolibri.
Fabietti, U. (2004). *Elementi di antropologia culturale*. Città di Castello: Mondadori.
Giusti, M. (2001). *L'educazione interculturale nella scuola di base*. Milano: La Nuova Italia.
Grillo, R., & Pratt, J. (Eds.). (2002). *The politics of recognizing difference: Multiculturalism Italian-style*. Burlington: Ashgate.
Hondagneu-Sotelo, P. (2000). Feminism and migration. *The Annals of the American Academy of Political and Social Science, 57*(1), 107–120.
hooks, b. (1981). *Ain't I a woman: Black women and feminism*. Boston: South and Press.
hooks, b. (1984). *Feminist theory: From margin to center*. Boston: South and Press.
hooks, b. (2000). *Where we stand: Class matters*. New York: Routledge.
ISMU [Iniziative e Studi sulla Multietnicità]. (2011). *Decimo Rapporto sull'immigrazione straniera nella Provincia di MIlano*. Milano: Ismu.
Libera Università delle Donne di Milano. (1994). *Donne del nord/donne del sud: Verso una politica della relazione fra diversità, solidarietà, conflitto*. Milano: Franco Angeli.
Macioti, M. I., & Pugliese, E. (2003). *L'esperienza migratoria: Immigrati e rifugiati in Italia*. Roma/Bari: Laterza.
Maher, V. (1989). *Il potere della complicità: Conflitti e legami delle donne nordafricane*. Torino: Rosemberg & Sellier.
Maher, V. (2006). Conoscenze di seconda mano. In M. Deriu (Ed.), *Sessi e culture: Intessere le differenze: Oltre gli stereotipi per una politica dell'incontro* (pp. 109–130). Parma: Edicta.
Mantovan, C. (2007). *Immigrazione e cittadinanza: Auto-organizzazione e partecipazione dei migranti in Italia*. Milano: Franco Angeli.
Mapelli, B. (2003). L'eredità del femminismo. In B. Mapelli & G. Seveso (Eds.), *Una storia imprevista* (pp. 355–414). Milano: Guerini.
Mapelli, B., & Seveso, G. (2003). *Una storia imprevista*. Milano: Guerini.
Melandri, L. (2002). *Come nasce il sogno d'amore*. Torino: Bollati Bolinghieri.
Menin, L. (2008). Leadership femminili, desideri e strategie d'inclusione: I percorsi associativi di due gruppi di donne migranti a Milano. *Achab: Rivista di Antropologia, 13*, 51–56.
Merrill, H. (2006). *An alliance of women: Immigration and the politics of race*. Minneapolis: University of Minnesota Press.
Mills, M. B. (1999). *Thai women and global labor force: Consuming desire, contested selves*. New Brunswick/New Jersey/London: Rutgers University Press.
Mohanty, C. T. (1984). Under western eyes: Feminist scholarship and colonial discourses. *Boundary, 12*(3), 333–358.
Mohanty, C. T. (2003). *Feminism without borders: Decolonizing theory, practicing solidarity*. Durham: Duke University Press.
Moore, H. (1994). *A passion for difference: Essays in anthropology and gender*. Bloomington: Indiana University Press.
Moraga, C., & Anzaldua, G. (1983). *This bridge called my back: Writings by radical women of color*. New York: Kitchen Table: Women of Color Press.
Nussbaum, M. C. (2000). *Women and human development: The capabilities approach*. Cambridge/New York: Cambridge University Press.
Okin, S. M., Cohen, J., Howard, M., & Nussbaum, M. C. (Eds.). (1999). *Is multiculturalism bad for women?* Princeton: Princeton University Press.
Ongaro, S. (2001). *Le donne e la globalizzazione: Domande di genere all'economia globale della ri-produzione*. Catanzaro: Rubbettino.
Osella, F., & Osella, C. (2000). Migration, money and masculinity in Kerala. *The Journal of the Royal Anthropological Institute, 6*(1), 115–133.
Osella, F., & Osella, C. (2006). Once upon a time in the West? Narrating modernity in Kerala, South India. *The Journal of the Royal Anthropological Institute, 12*, 569–588.

Palidda, S. (2008). *Mobilità umane: Introduzione alla sociologia delle migrazioni*. Milano: Cortina.

Percovich, L., & Damiani, C. (Eds.). (1995). *Pensare globalmente, agire localmente (dopo Pechino): Atti del convegno*. Milano: Libera Università delle Donne.

Però, D. (2007). *Inclusionary rhetoric/exclusionary practices: An ethnographic study of the discourses and practices of the Italian left in the context of migration*. Munich: Berghahn Books.

Pessar, P., & Mahler, S. (2001). Gendered geographies of power: Analyzing gender across transnational spaces. *Identities: Global Studies in culture and Power, 7*, 441–459.

Pinelli, B. (2008). Etnografia della vulnerabilità: Storie femminili dell'immigrazione forzata. In M. Van Aken (Ed.), *Rifugio Milano* (pp. 131–161). Milano: Bottega Carta.

Pojmann, W. A. (2006). *Immigrant women and feminism in Italy*. Aldershot: Ashgate Publishing.

Provincia di Milano. (n.d.). http://www.provincia.milano.it/cultura/progetti/integrando. Accessed January 10, 2010.

Robertson, R. (1994). Globalization or glocalization? *Journal of International Communication, 1*(1), 33–52.

Salazar Parreñas, R. (2000). Migrant Filipina domestic workers and the international division of reproductive labor. *Gender and Society, 14*(4), 560–581.

Salazar Parreñas, R. (2001). *Servants of globalization: Women, migration ad domestic work*. Stanford: Stanford University Press.

Salazar Parreñas, R. (2006). Caring for the Filipino family: How gender differentiates the economic causes of labour migration. *Women and Migration in Asia, 14*, 95–115.

Salazar Parreñas, R. (2008). *The force of domesticity: Filipina migrants and globalization*. New York/London: New York University Press.

Salih, R. (2002). Recognizing difference, reinforcing exclusion: A 'family planning center for women and their children' in Emilia-Romagna. In R. Grillo & J. Pratt (Eds.), *The politics of recognizing difference: Multiculturalism Italian-style* (pp. 139–157). Burlington: Ashgate.

Salih, R. (2003). *Gender in transnationalism: Home, longing and belonging among Moroccan migrant woman*. London/New York: Routledge.

Smith, B. (Ed.). (1983). *Home girls: A black feminism anthology*. New York: Kitchen Table: Women of Color Press.

Spagnoletti, R. (1974). *I movimenti femministi in Italia*. Roma: La Nuova Italia.

Vicarelli, M. G. (Ed.). (1994). *Le mani invisibili: La vita e il lavoro delle donne immigrate*. Roma: Ediesse.

Willis, K., & Yeoh, B. (Eds.). (2000). *Gender and migration*. Cheltenham/Northampton: Edward Elgar Publishing.

Yeoh, B. (2005). Transnational mobilities and challenge. In L. Nelson & J. Seager (Eds.), *A companion to feminist geography* (pp. 60–73). Malden: Blackwell Publishing.

Part IV
Religion for Change

Chapter 14
'Sister Agnes was to go to Ghana in Africa!' Catholic Nuns and Migration

Katharina Stornig

14.1 Introduction

Despite the recognition of their long-standing participation in (national and international) migration as well as in the creation of transnational female networks across borders (Hüwelmeier 2004, 2005), feminist scholarly literature paid little attention to Catholic nuns over the last decades. In part, this can be explained by Catholicism's ambiguous relationship to feminism (e.g. its role in the (re)production of patriarchy) in general and the conventional treatment of nuns as largely passive and ahistorical research objects in particular (Braude 2004; Hollywood 2004). As anthropologist Saba Mahmood (2001, 2004, 2005) points out, feminist scholars face analytical problems when dealing with accounts of women's agency within religious historiographies that are rooted in the secular and liberal biases of feminist tradition.

Recent works, however, challenge the marginal role assigned to religious women in the history of feminism (Thorne 1999). Nuns feature in this scholarship in several directions. Some scholars have shown that women religious were actually involved with the second wave feminist movement (Weaver 1986; Ebaugh 1993; Braude 2004). Others, in turn, departed from the nuns' peculiar way of life in relative independence from men and turned them into some kind of proto-feminists. Feminist scholars have discussed women's convents as important institutional and social spaces for feminine self-assertion, social mobility and collective action in the long run (Weaver 1986; Ebaugh 1993, 401; Lutkehaus 1999; Meiwes 2000; Brosnan 2004). Although embedded in the male-centered hierarchy of the Catholic Church, the ecclesiastical ideal of female self-administration constituted the ground on which women religious were able to negotiate their roles. Sociologist Helen Rose Ebaugh (1993, 400) has used Deniz Kandiyoti's (1988) concept of "patriarchal

K. Stornig, Ph.D. (✉)
Institute of European History, Alte Universitätsstraße 19, 55116, Mainz, Germany
e-mail: katharina.stornig@eui.eu

G.T. Bonifacio (ed.), *Feminism and Migration: Cross-Cultural Engagements*,
International Perspectives on Migration 1, DOI 10.1007/978-94-007-2831-8_14,
© Springer Science+Business Media B.V. 2012

bargains" to describe the ways in which American nuns actively and/or passively resisted oppression and gained access to resources, informal power and status throughout the twentieth century. Altogether, these studies, in one way or another, have used the "personal is political" paradigm for they relate the history of nuns to the emergence of a new kind of feminine self that set women beyond the relational terms of the family (Bamidele Erlandsson 1997; Shebi 1997; Sullivan 2005). Accordingly, the historical and present figure of the nun served (and still serves) as a model of femininity that emphasizes women as autonomous subjects and constitutes an alternative to marriage, motherhood and domesticity. In her substantial volume on the history of nuns over two millennia, Jo Ann McNamara (1996, 6) describes the history of nuns as conditional to the emergence of modern feminisms because they "created the image and reality of the autonomous woman."

Based on research conducted in the archives of the Servants of the Holy Spirit, a congregation of missionary nuns, this chapter proposes a feminist approach to the involvement of nuns with migration in historical and contemporary contexts.[1] I explore the ways in which migration and cross-cultural collaboration have shaped the congregation's history and empowered women through the exercise of personal agency. Agency and empowerment in this context are thought broadly incorporating religious and secular aspects. While feminist scholarship largely acknowledges the experience of migration as a liberating move for women religious in secular terms (Bowie 1993; Huber and Lutkehaus 1999; Bötzinger 2004), it paid less attention to religious aspects. Sabah Mahmood (2001, 208) convincingly argues for an equal consideration of religion by departing from the work of black feminists who have expanded the notion of "self-realization/self-fulfillment," making considerations of class and race constitutive of its understanding. Departing from a critical reflection on the gendered conception of the missionary, this chapter looks at the interaction of Catholic nuns with indigenous girls and women in Northern New Guinea and explores the ways in which the experience of movement and mobility have empowered women from different ethnic background, who migrated for religious reasons, throughout the twentieth century.

14.2   Women and Missions

Since the late nineteenth century, Catholic women actively strove to get access to the missionary profession. This was reflected in the Servants of the Holy Spirit's founding history. Significantly, it was already in the same year, 1875, in which Father Arnold Janssen founded the first Catholic mission-sending society for priests in Germany (Society of the Divine Word), that the first women missionaries appealed to him. Janssen, however, who was not at all about to establish an associated women's congregation at

[1] This chapter is based on archival work conducted in the Servants of the Holy Spirit's historical archives in Rome, Stockerau (Austria) and Steyl (Netherlands). I would like to express my gratitude to all responsible archivists for their friendly assistance, support and hospitality during my extended visits. All unpublished materials cited are filed in the congregation's general archive in Rome. Translations from German are my own. I also thank the editor for her insightful comments on earlier drafts of this chapter.

that time, reacted negatively at first. It was only after young Helena Stollenwerk (1852–1900), a farmer's daughter from a small village in North Rhine-Westphalia, addressed herself to him and brought forward her "burning desire to become a missionary in China" (Soete 1953, 15) that Janssen started to change his mind. Consequently, he invited Helena over to the society's headquarters in the Dutch town of Steyl, where he offered her an appointment as a kitchen maid. In hope of approaching the fulfillment of her missionary vocation, Helena stood up to the initial resistance of her parents, left her home and inheritance and moved to the society's headquarters. There, she performed the hardest work for 7 years. Ultimately, Janssen founded the Servants of the Holy Spirit in 1889 and the kitchen maid became a novice (Volpert 1951, 11–17; Soete 1953, 25–26).

Although the life-long desire to become a missionary in China dominated her narrative of vocation, Helena Stollenwerk never left Europe. Instead, she became the congregation's first novice directress. Helena's successors nonetheless referred to her missionary vocation and honored her contribution to the congregation's founding process. In her history of the congregation, Sister Assumpta Volpert wrote about Mother Maria Helena Stollenwerk, who was soon recognized as one of the congregation's co-foundresses, that, although her gender prevented her from acting out her life's desire to become a missionary in China, she, in her words:

> was to become the spiritual mother of thousands and thousands of virgins, who, following the calling of the Lord, wandered out until the boarders of the universe in order to gain souls for the kingdom of Christ on all continents. (Volpert 1951, 8–9)

The establishment of the Servants of the Holy Spirit in 1889 appealed to many women. Candidates from all over Germany, the Netherlands, and Austria applied for admission. By 1914, there were 1,000 members dispersed in over five continents. While 216 postulants and novices as well as 269 professed nuns resided in Europe (Germany, Netherlands and Austria), 316 Servants of the Holy Spirits settled in the Americas (USA, Argentina and Brazil). By then, 148 European nuns had also moved to Africa (Togo and Mozambique), Asia (China, Japan, Philippines and Indonesia) or Oceania (New Guinea). Besides, the congregation had already started to train nuns from German migrant families in the US, Argentina and Brazil, where 51 young women stayed in its postulates and novitiates (Soete 1953, 199). Considering the great response of Catholic women to the mission venture and their enthusiastic disposition to leave Europe for good irrespective of health and other risks, suggests examining the history of the missionary profession from a feminist perspective.

14.3 Gender and Mission: The Case of Papua New Guinea

The first group of four nuns left the congregation's motherhouse for what was then German New Guinea in 1899.[2] Upon arrival, they not only established the first women's convent in the region but also started to create a female Catholic

---

[2] The congregation's New Guinean mission field at first concentrated on the part of the mainland that formed part of the German colony "Deutsch Neu-Guinea." In 1920, the colony became a League of Nations mandated territory of Australia. Papua New Guinea gained full independence in 1975.

infrastructure. Although the founder, Janssen, assigned nuns in missions to a merely assisting function,[3] the nuns stationed in New Guinea transcended this narrow concept of feminine mission work (Huber 1999; Lutkehaus 1999). In fact, the Catholic ideal of separated spheres of work for nuns, monks and priests constituted the ground on which women missionaries erected and managed their religious institutions. They established girls' schools and apothecaries. Although the frontier conditions demanded the location of women's convents in proximity to the priests' houses and the nuns always ran the risk of enlarged male supervision, the ecclesiastical ideal of self-administration of women's congregations allowed them to negotiate their position with the male ecclesiastical hierarchy.[4] By 1945, there were 130 European nuns who migrated to New Guinea, where they founded 17 convents (Soete 1953, 216–217). Residing in the small and scattered convents, mission life not only allowed but demanded self-initiatives and creativity. Nuns in missions encountered a considerable scope for autonomy in organizing their day-to-day lives. Some also managed to pursue professional achievements.

The educated members of the Servants of the Holy Spirit created important positions within the mission organization. Teacher-trained nuns set up and headed girls' schools. They entered the field of pedagogy in an institutional setting and assumed official responsibility on the sector of colonial education. From the outset, priests not only acknowledged the teaching nuns' contribution to evangelization but praised their aptitude in the elementary schools. In 1906, Prefect Apostolic Eberhard Limbrock wrote to founder Janssen that the nuns are "of extraordinarily great importance" to the mission venture in New Guinea for they "have a much better spirit than, for example, our young priests."[5] He related this assessment precisely to the nuns' engagement in education. According to him, nuns were able to "dedicate themselves more to education, for which they have more patience and perseverance, prepare themselves with more zeal, and so achieve more and better results than most priests do."[6] While Limbrock primarily evoked virtues that the Catholic discourse connoted with femininity, teaching nuns also emphasized their professional accomplishments (i.e. language skills).[7] Similarly, trained nuns also took outstanding positions in the developing missionary medical scheme

---

[3] According to the first constitution of the congregation issued by its founder, Janssen, the primary purpose of the nuns was to support the priests through prayers and works (Soete 1953, 19).

[4] This can be observed well in 1910, when a document was issued that codified the relationship between nuns and priests. Accordingly, the nuns were responsible to the ecclesiastical head of the prefecture as well as they had to consult the priests in charge concerning all questions of missionary practice. Their internal affairs (e.g. the training and place of action of the single nuns), however, should be decided by their own leading committee (See *Über das Verhältnis der ehrwürdigen Schwestern zur Mission und unserer Kongregation* S.V.D. In Arch.Gen.SSpS SVD– SSpS. Gründerzeit 0006.1 SVD-SSpS 1909–1911, 29).

[5] See Eberhard Limbrock to Arnold Janssen, 19.5.1906. (Alt 2001, 342–343).

[6] See Eberhard Limbrock to Arnold Janssen, 19.5.1906. (Alt 2001, 343).

[7] For example, Sister Hermengilde Simbürger (1891–1934), a teacher, managed several indigenous languages and even translated parts of the bible (See Arch.Gen.SSpS PNG 6201 Korrespondenz 1911–1975. Sister Hermengilde Simbürger 27.12.1924 and 5.9.1926).

establishing and managing dispensaries and hospitals. The mission nurses' professional identity can be observed in their writings that witness the cultivation of self-esteem through qualified achievements.[8] Significantly, it was the professions introduced by the nuns that were the first spheres of employment open to indigenous women on the postwar labor market. These nuns grounded their individual life choices on a vocation they derived from a transcendental will or divine calling. Consequently, their dedication to a life-long service within the mission venture (and its male dominated structure) could be understood as acting upon the desire to realize this individually experienced divine calling.

As Valentine Cunningham (1993, 89) points out, the term *missionary* in the Christian context originally was "a male noun" for "it denoted a male actor, male action, male sphere of service." In Catholicism, the male conception of the missionary related primarily to clerical authority and a gendered definition of ministry and discipleship. Women were banned from preaching the gospel and delivering the sacraments. Over centuries, the feminine apostolate concentrated on the inner domains of prayer, religious exercises and spiritual support. Most clearly since the period of Catholic reformation, the Church had assigned the external world to priests and placed nuns within the "private" domain of the cloister (McNamara 1996; Evangelisti 2007). Thus, the entry of nuns into the mission force not only meant the transcendence of the cloister, but allowed women for the first time to participate in those activities that were closely associated with the clergy. Through migration, these nuns actually became *missionaries*, thus people religious, who, referencing the biblical Great Commission (the instruction of the resurrected Christ to his apostles to spread his teachings to all the nations), travelled the world for religious reasons. Nuns departing for missions usually referred to the realization of their missionary vocation as the "aim of the lives" for it allowed them to actively contribute to what they perceived to be the holiest venture of their times. Hence, migration empowered these women in an essentially religious sense because it made them *missionaries*. As such, they functioned as the visible, mobile and publicly recognized ambassadors of the Catholic Church and engaged in an activity they perceived to be the favored path on the way to their own sanctification.

The exceptional organization of the Catholic mission in Northern New Guinea constituted a framework in which many nuns managed to engage in those spiritual works that were traditionally associated with priests. Due to the limited number of priests in the region and their broad engagement in material works, nuns collaborated in some of their central duties (Huber 1987, 1999). They gave religious instruction to students of both sexes and prepared catechumens for baptism or the reception of other sacraments. The proselytizing activities of single nuns were sometimes

---

[8]During her years of training to become a nurse in the congregation's hospital in Haan (Netherlands), Sister Arildis Engelbrecht (1903–1943) stated in a letter to her relatives that sick-nursing had become the "entire world" to her. After her arrival to New Guinea in 1931, she explicitly referred to medical work as her "profession" and expressed considerable pride about her medical achievements (See Arch.Gen.SSpS 6204 SSpS Briefe. Briefe von Schwester Arildis Engelbrecht an ihre Familie; i.e. 16.11.1930).

even appreciated by priests, who lauded them for "doing a men's job" when they regularly travelled around on horseback in order to give religious instruction.[9] Moreover, when visiting sick persons, women missionaries administered the rite of emergency baptism to the terminally ill. In Catholicism, the sacrament of baptism makes the candidate a child of God and, thus, a partaker of all the privileges flowing from the redemptive act (Fanning 1907). By administering emergency baptism, the nuns essentially 'saved souls' for the kingdom of Christ. Hence, if mission activity in the New Guinean frontier constituted an empowering experience of liberating quality for nuns because they managed to create new public roles in society as teachers and nurses, this was even more the case when it came to the religious realm. Although clergymen denied them official pastoral status, they constructed their identities as women *missionaries* who followed a religious vocation that led them overseas as the ambassadors of the Catholic Church. By then, the Catholic Church had recognized that it needed its women in order to reach the female half of the non-Christian world whose conversion was given growing importance. Western nuns emphasized their disposition to dedicate their lives to the religious salvation of the female populations in the non-Christian world. This very concept of the other's salvation through conversion, however, necessarily denigrated her original condition for it not only depended on a firm sense but hierarchic interpretation of difference (McNamara 1996, 595–598).

14.3.1 Converting Women

Emphasizing their own importance to the mission venture, "white" nuns constructed the image of the other—"black" and "heathen"—woman in need of liberation. Similar to secular colonial women who propagated their own advancement by emphasizing their difference to non-western women (Dietrich 2006), nuns constructed their identities vis-à-vis those women they had set off to convert. They took for granted their privileged positions as "whites" in a colonial society constructed on inequality. A peculiar western interpretation of the state of indigenous women in what Europeans called "primitive" societies featured as the marker of their level of civilization. In other words, the nuns in New Guinea fell back on a secular discourse of both "cultural" and "racial" difference in order to describe their unequal relationship to indigenous females. They saw themselves at the forefront of what they called the liberation of the New Guinean woman. Up to 1960, however, missionary notions of female "liberation" meant conversion and, more precisely, the transformation into Catholic wives and mothers. Western nuns criticized what they called the "low status" of a woman in the indigenous culture as the "maidservant rather than the equal companion of the man," which found expression in social practices that were incompatible with Catholic life norms, such as

---

[9] See Arch.Gen.SSpS PNG 6201 Korrespondenz 1911–1975. Father Andreas Puff 7.4.1922.

polygamy, divorce, abortion or infanticide (Neuß 1914, 180). Missionaries saw the conversion of women as the key to change the religious and moral system of non-Christian societies. This was linked with the early twentieth century Christian ideal of gender roles in society and gendered spheres of work within the family. Accordingly, women, as wives and mothers, were to form the "heart of the house" for they constituted the most important influence on their family's aptitude for piety (Thorne 1999, 43). Practically, this implied that the nuns' attempt to "liberate" women through mission Christianity also contributed to their denigration and the creation of new dependences in the long run.[10]

The Catholic ideal of women's roles in Church and society also formed the basis of the mission's early educational approach, which explicitly targeted different goals for the sexes. While male students were trained to take on official responsibilities as teachers or catechists, females were prepared to become wives and mothers (Lyons Johnson 1993). Apart from religious instruction, domestic work constituted the most important subject on the missionary girls' schools syllabi.[11] Hence, somewhat paradoxically, Catholic nuns functioned as the role models for indigenous females to become Christian mothers and wives. Whether wanted or not, staying at the convents, unencumbered by husbands and children, the nuns introduced an alternative model of womanhood to the family-centered societies in the New Guinean cultural setting (Lutkehaus 1999, 228). At their convents, they created a female dominated space in which indigenous women experienced alternative social roles than the one of the village mother. The nuns' peculiar way of life in combination with the high esteem that some of them managed to acquire in the eyes of the villagers, impacted on the local sociocultural constructions of gender identity. For example, anthropologist Camilla Wedgewood, who stayed in the region in 1933 researching the cultural impact of colonialism on the lives of women and children, related the decision of a teenage girl to remain unmarried in the presence of local nuns. In contrast to conventional women's roles in society that centered on marriage and motherhood, the girl in question rejected motherhood and declared childbearing as a tiresome business. Wedgwood (1937, 411ff), however, interpreted the girls' standpoint in relation to her particularly great admiration for one of the local nuns.

Starting in the 1930s, the nuns in New Guinea also reported on some schoolgirls who had expressed interest in celibate life. By then, however, such responses to female missionary presence were neither appreciated nor encouraged by the nuns, who, joining a secular discourse of racial difference that oversexualized indigenous women, perceived their virtue in danger outside marriage. Declaring western-Christian mores as universally true and absolutely superior, the nuns perceived indigenous sexual practices as morally threatening. The long-term exclusion of indigenous women from the congregation of the Servants of the Holy Spirit suggests

[10] Huber and Lutkehaus (1999, 7) call this "one of the many ironies of colonialism," namely that the "the same enterprise that aimed to dignify and liberate their subjects could also contribute to their denigration and dependence."

[11] Anthropologists suggest that missionaries built the base for the enduring disadvantage of indigenous women in education (Lyons Johnson 1993, 185).

exploring women's roles in the (missionary) Church by making considerations of race and ethnicity important.

By then, race and ethnicity played a crucial role in religious community building in New Guinea. Within the women's convents a racial divide not only marked the individual's status in the community but was, moreover, institutionalized. As Patricia Hill Collins (1991, 225) points out, the substitution of an interlocking research model of oppression for an additive one allows us to fully grasp the significance of intersecting systems of domination. Such an approach enables the exploration of shifting (or even dual) roles of individuals who were potentially both at once oppressor and oppressed. In the mid twentieth century missionary context in colonial New Guinea, race and gender constituted the main systems of domination. While the Servants of the Holy Spirit ultimately were relatively powerless in relation to male religious and secular authority, they nonetheless headed their convents and affiliated institutions. Within the local female religious infrastructure, they constituted a ruling class that commanded over resources and represented themselves as the indigenous girls' educators or employers. Western nuns reproduced the colonial order of "white" domination and "black" subordination. Representing indigenous women as in need of supervision, they denied them any form of self-definition or representation. Western nuns set the terms of what was considered to be a proper behavior of Catholic females. Hence, to be a good Catholic meant to behave and to pray like German Catholic women did. Cultural difference was thought of hierarchically. Ultimately, the female Catholic community's division by race was institutionalized in 1950 when a separate institution was established for indigenous nuns. The Servants of the Holy Spirit still refused admission to New Guinean women at this time.

Elements of race featured centrally in this context for it were precisely "black" women that were banned from entering the congregation. Significantly, despite Catholic universalism, neither African nor New Guinean or "black" American candidates were admitted in 1960.[12] Simultaneously, however, the congregation got increasingly diverse with regard to the national origin of its members. In 1948, it encompassed members from 27 nationalities and maintained novitiates in several European nations, the Americas (Argentina, Brazil, Chile and United States) and Asia (China, Japan, Java and the Philippines).[13] The increasing diversity within the congregation was also reflected in the national formation of its New Guinean branch. While most nuns came from Germany, Austria and the Netherlands before the Second World War, the postwar community comprised of women from the United States, the Philippines, Eastern Europe and Argentina.[14] Although spiritual and cultural unity continued to be emphasized as an important feature of religious sisterhood, cross-cultural collaboration (e.g. teaching of the English language) gradually emerged as a feature in day-to-day community life. Constructions of "race," however, continued to feature as an important

---

[12] See Arch.Gen.SSpS 100 General chapter 5 1960, 5–1002. Protokoll, 72.

[13] See Arch.Gen.SSpS 100 General chapter 4 1948, 4–1002. *Allgemeiner Bericht über die äußere Entwicklung der Genossenschaft* 1934–1948, 1–4.

[14] See the list of nuns in Coles and Mihalic (1999, 49–56).

factor in community building. Even if they refused admission of indigenous women to their own institution, western nuns were engaged in the foundation of the Rosary Sisters. The Congregation of the Rosary was chronologically the first local congregation for indigenous nuns.[15] Since individual Servants of the Holy Spirit functioned as the secular and religious educators of the Rosary Sisters as well as took on leadership positions, both institutions related to each other vertically. New Guinean women, nonetheless, responded positively to the new foundation. Despite the contested place of the consecrated celibate woman in the family-centered societies, growing numbers of indigenous women asked for admission.

The new congregation provided indigenous women with opportunities that appealed to them. The Rosary Sisters engaged successfully in mission work in which their language skills and ethnic origin turned out to be advantageous. Western nuns, however, continued to occupy all leadership positions. The canonical status of both institutions also diverged. While the Servants of the Holy Spirit's New Guinean branch was part of a well-organized, female-administered, transnational religious network established with ample resources and training opportunities in Europe and elsewhere, the Rosary Sisters were directly subordinated to the authority of the bishop and limited to the institutional framework provided by the diocese. Most importantly, the diocesan ties geographically limited the activities of these indigenous nuns, who were banned from succeeding their western sisters and going abroad in an official religious function.

14.3.2   Difference in the Creation of Sisterhood

In the second half of the twentieth century, the nuns in New Guinea started to gradually redefine their approach to mission strategies with regard to women. For the first time, leading nuns challenged the policies set by the priests. Contrary to male ecclesiastical authorities who favored the training of men, these nuns emphasized the necessity to create an institutional framework that enabled indigenous women to get education and gain access to the labor market. In an official report dated in 1960, the local head of the nuns complained to the congregation's European leading committee that the male missionaries in the area not only prioritized the education of boys but even demanded the nuns' collaboration for it. This, again, took away the nuns' time to teach girls.[16] Many priests, therefore, failed to support the girls' schooling. The nuns, however, challenged this standpoint of male-centered education and withdrew their teaching materials from a boys' school precisely with the objective to establish another one for girls. The report not only calls to mind the

---

[15] Still in the 1950s, a second indigenous congregation, the Sisters of St. Therese, was established in Madang close to the Servants of the Holy Spirit's New Guinean headquarters in Alexishafen.

[16] See Arch.Gen.SSpS 100 General chapter 1960 5 1960, 5–1002. *Berichte Provinzen/Regionen, Berichterstattung an das fünfte Generalkapitel der Dienerinnen des Heiligen Geistes*. Holy Ghost convent Alexishafen Madang Region Neu Guinea, 3.

fact that nuns in general "were intimately familiar with patriarchal authority in its most overt form" (Braude 2004, 563), but also shows that the Servants of the Holy Spirit in New Guinea were conscious about the institutionalized disadvantages they faced as women in the missionary Church in 1960.

During the 1960s, the nuns in New Guinea started to question the male missionary policies and related their own subordinate position with the oppression faced by other women. This change in the nuns' attitudes to gender roles and gendered policies in the missionary Church could be explained by the large number of new (and young) nuns from diverse national backgrounds who arrived in New Guinea since 1945. As well, the beginning process of political decolonization worldwide led the Catholic Church to announce the end of "Church colonialism" and increasingly propagated indigenous participation (Mantovani 1984, 3). The Second Vatican Council (1962–1965) not only represented a milestone with regard to the Catholic discourse on cultural plurality and inter-religious dialogue but also the nuns' roles in Church and society. After the Council, the papacy encouraged nuns to get out of their convents and be engaged in up-to-date social issues (Braude 2004; Hüwelmeier 2008). Like other women's congregations at that time, the Servants of the Holy Spirit initiated a period of profound renewal. They started to re-interpret the spirituality of the founding generation and their mission charism in the light of contemporary understanding. They generally declared their solidarity to women and marginalized people. In addition, nuns started to rework the constitution of their own congregation according to their shifting visions of nuns' roles in a globalized world.

Scholars have pointed out (McNamara 1996; Braude 2004; Hüwelmeier 2008) that nuns by then, unlike secular groups of women, did not have to build or reorganize women's religious networks anew. On the contrary, due to their peculiar history, they were well-structured groups of educated women that provided social support to its members and commanded over trained leaders (Ebaugh 1993). Most importantly, however, the Servants of the Holy Spirit constituted a transnational religious institution, the leaders of which came together on a regular basis in order to update its members about contemporary issues. Consequently, nuns in both (the newly independent nation of) Papua New Guinea and Europe demanded the start of a formation program for indigenous women to become members of the congregation in 1978. The Servants of the Holy Spirit organized what they called "live-ins" to screen the candidates. "Live-ins" were weekends during which interested indigenous women could stay with the nuns in order to learn about convent life and to get acquainted with each other (Coles and Mihalic 1999, 38). In 1983, the Servants of the Holy Spirit's language of sisterhood in New Guinea became a reality: the first two indigenous candidates were admitted to the novitiate.

14.3.3 New Missionary Careers

One of the novices was Agnes from the village of Tambanum, which is situated along the Sepik River in the mainland's interior. Tambanum came into regular contact with the Catholic mission only after the Servants of the Holy Spirit had established a convent in the 2-hour canoe ride distant town of Timbunke in 1953. Three nuns based in Timbunke established a school and a dispensary, and regularly visited another village, Tambanum. Mission activity there was significantly linked with the name of Sister Mertia, an Austrian Servant of the Holy Spirit and former missionary to China, who had moved to New Guinea for political reasons due to the rise of communism. Sister Mertia set up a village school in Tambanum, where she taught over two decades. Every Monday morning, she left the women's convent in Timbunke for Tambanum. There she stayed on her own in a small house next to the village school until Thursday afternoon, when she returned to the convent and fellow sisters. Due to her isolated position on weekdays, Sister Mertia even received a special permission from ecclesiastical authorities to keep the Blessed Sacrament in her Tambanum dwelling and to administer herself communion.[17] Obviously, her independent lifestyle as a single woman, village teacher, and religious emissary featured as an important role model to young local women Catholics. Agnes attested that it was the nun's example which influenced her decision to dedicate her life to God (Coles and Mihalic 1999, 32).

The examination of Sister Agnes' subsequent career as a missionary highlights a high degree of national and international mobility. This was partly linked with the new guidelines decreed by congregational elites concerning the religious formation of the novices and young nuns. Accordingly, every novice spends a period of 6 months in one of the congregation's regional outpost places in order to gain community experience. Both pioneer indigenous Papua New Guinean novices at first were appointed for two mountain stations in the country's interior, where they stayed in the Servant's of the Holy Spirit's sub-branches. In 1986 they took their first vows and received their work and study appointments. Since both nuns were trained as teachers, they subsequently taught at different local settings until 1992, when they entered what the Servants of the Holy Spirit call the "tertianship."[18] The "tertianship" characterizes a period of formation that the nuns go through in preparation to take their perpetual vows. Since the last two decades, the tertianship ideally takes place in an alien cultural missionary context. Therefore, both Papua New Guinean nuns moved to the community's branch in Manila, Philippines where they stayed for almost a year in preparation to make their final commitment to God and the congregation.

Finally, the novices' perpetual profession was an important event held at the congregation's historical headquarters in Papua New Guinea. It concerned all local missionaries and was celebrated by the entire Catholic community.[19] The significance of the event was even greater because Sister Agnes was simultaneously appointed to the congregation's mission in Ghana. She was the first national missionary who was appointed overseas, an event that the nuns in New Guinea interpreted as "going full circle" of their missionary commitment. A nun wrote, describing the bystanders reaction after the head of the nuns in New Guinea announced that one of the newly professed was about to stay,

---

[17] See Arch.Gen.SSpS PNG Chronicles. Timbunke, November 1969.

[18] See Arch.Gen.SSpS PNG Chronicles. Alexishafen, 29.3.1992.

[19] The chronicler recorded the event and mentioned it in the local Catholic newspaper.

Sister Agnes was to go to Ghana in Africa! On hearing this, at first the audience was stunned
into dead silence, and then it reacted with thunderous applause. Fr. Joe Sakite, SVD, a
native Ghanaian who was concelebrating at the Mass, broke out onto a spontaneous dance
right in the sanctuary. (Coles and Mihalic 1999, 41)

On the occasion of her missionary appointment to Ghana, an additional ceremony
was held in her home village of Tambanum, in the cause of which her relatives and
clanspeople saw her off festively. The local bishop, priests and nuns from
13 nationalities participated in the celebrations with the villagers.[20]

The enthusiastic response of the non-western Catholics to Sister Agnes' mission
appointment suggests the high symbolic importance of the event for it assigned non-
western people in general and women in particular official roles in the globalized
Church. By migrating to Ghana in an official religious function, Sister Agnes has
become herself the visible emissary of both the congregation and the Catholic
Church. She crossed symbolic and racial boundaries, because, as discussed earlier,
the missionary profession was originally reserved for "white" men. To migrate for
religious reasons and to serve people from different cultural background constitute
the absolute missionary commitment for Catholics in the long run. In their capacity
as women missionaries, nuns have claimed their roles as women disciples in historical and present religious contexts. Nowadays, some members of the congregation
adopt an outspokenly feminist language in order to claim women's roles as spiritual
equals to men by arguing for an inclusive conception of ministry and discipleship.
Proposing a feminist reading of the New Testament, they argue that the authority of
the apostles consists in the primacy of testimony, not in that of power or domination,
and highlight the biblical roles of women as prophets or witnesses. Most importantly, the nuns relate this demand for the re-examination and establishment of
women's leadership and discipleship roles in the early Church to overcome the age-
long invisibility, alienation and silence of women, and the renewal of the present
Catholic conception of mission. As Sister Bernadette Dere Nulenpaala (2009, 71),
a Ghanaian Servant of the Holy Spirit and feminist theologian puts it: "We cannot
think of mission in the third millennium without awakening ourselves to the alien-
ated experience of half of the human family."

According to a document issued on the occasion of the congregation's twelfth
general chapter in 2002, the Servants of the Holy Spirit define themselves as a
"religious missionary community of women disciples in an international congregation."[21] Subsequent to the chapter, which was held in Rome under the presence of
delegates from all branches worldwide, the capitulars returned to their fields of
work and echoed its outcome in their respective communities. Apart from the topics
of spiritual formation and HIV/AIDS, "women" constituted a main theme in the
chapter. This was related with the nuns' ongoing attempt to redefine their roles as
women missionaries in the light of today's globalized world. In Papua New Guinea
in 2002, all nuns were invited to collectively think about themselves being "prophetic

---

[20] See Sepik nun is first PNG missionary to Ghana. In *Wantok* 1315/94, 11 August 1994.
[21] See Missionary Sisters Servants of the Holy Spirit (2002a).

women reflecting the feminine face of God."[22] They expressed their solidarity with oppressed women in New Guinea and offered prayers to those who suffer, as well as collected concrete proposals to improve the social position of rural women by providing them with better access to education.[23] In an open session, some participants also expressed their appreciation that "women" were addressed as a special subject during the chapter and raised the issue of women's rights in the Church.[24]

Nuns emphasize the importance of women's presence in a globalized world in their capacity as peacemakers and friendly persons who listen, give support and encouragement. The Servants of the Holy Spirit evoke virtues that Christian tradition associates with femininity (e.g. motherhood, intuition, tender-hearted, gentleness, etc.) and situate these into a global political and human context. In human nature, they argue, both sexes can share divine qualities and women "are called to share the feminine face of God."[25] The participants in the twelfth general chapter have reformulated the congregation's mission statement in similar terms. For example, Point 5 of the document is titled "mission spirituality of presence" and states:

> A spirituality of presence as active but not overbearing service; of kenosis as self-emptying, in a position of powerlessness, non-defense, yet different from submission; of reconciliation in the sense of being agents of healing, of building bridges, as especially women do in areas of conflicts; of a Christian human vision in answer to a world crying out for a new vision of all that is truly human; of a cosmic vision which is a committed spirituality, attentive to the cosmic voice of God within all that exists.[26]

These nuns understand the re-conception of mission and appropriation of ministerial roles for all as renewing forces to restructure the globalized Church, which needs "a response and a radical commitment of persons inspired and infused by the Spirit to foster human dignity, equality, and freedom for all, both women and men" (Dere Nulenpaala 2009, 71). This involves the inclusion of women, and an active concern with diversity and cross-cultural collaboration.

14.4 Nuns, Feminism and Migration

Two themes are derived from the Servants of the Holy Spirit's historical and present experience with and practice of migration. Firstly, an active engagement with cultural diversity and internationality characterized the congregation's collective

---

[22] See Missionary Sisters Servants of the Holy Spirit (2002b).

[23] See Session 11 Group discussion. Arch.Gen.SSpS PNG 6106 Province chronicles. Prophetic women in mission 2002. For the social disadvantage of rural women in Papua New Guinea due to the lack of access to education, see Lyons Johnson 1993.

[24] See Session 9. Open Session. Arch.Gen.SSpS PNG 6106 Province chronicles. Prophetic women in mission 2002.

[25] See Session 9. Open Session. Arch.Gen.SSpS PNG 6106 Province chronicles. Prophetic women in mission 2002.

[26] See Missionary Sisters Servants of the Holy Spirit (2002b).

identity and recent religious politics. This is most clearly expressed in a number of formation programs and renewal courses based on cross-cultural collaboration and experience, which were introduced in the early 1980s. For the cause of their novitiate the nuns stay 6 months in outpost places to gain community experience. The so-called tertianship, the preparation period for the perpetual vows, is organized in an international framework because it usually takes place in other mission provinces than one's home region. New Guinean nuns, for example, travel to the Philippines, Indonesia or Europe in order to absolve their tertianship. Many nuns appreciate these international formation courses as spiritually and personally enriching experience precisely because it involves the fostering of personal relationships with fellow sisters from diverse cultural and national backgrounds.[27] In addition, a program called "Cross-Cultural Mission Experience" was developed by congregational leaders. This program grants young nuns up to a 5-year stay abroad in order to complete their professional and spiritual formation. This type of cultural exchange program has worked and continues across regions: nuns from Papua New Guinea go to Africa, Asia or Europe while European and American nuns spend a couple of years in other continents. In addition, the congregation's single branches are established with funds to enable nuns to further their formal education in Rome or elsewhere.[28] A range of international or regional cooperation programs and joint events foster the collaboration of women missionaries worldwide. For instance, the Servants of the Holy Spirit in Papua New Guinea actively promote a transnational dialogue in the framework of the congregation's Asia-Pacific Assembly, which involves among others its provinces in Australia, Indonesia and India.

Considering these efforts to promote cultural diversity and dialogue in day-to-day religious life, one is reminded of the work of the German anthropologist Gertrud Hüwelmeier (2008, 106), who accurately speaks about contemporary nuns as cosmopolitans pointing out their efforts to mediate between the "local, regional and national loyalties" of fellow sisters. Parallel to the steady process of "internationalization" of the congregation, which nowadays maintains branches in 46 countries worldwide and defines its universal character as essential,[29] the democratization of internal structures is also observed. Initiated in the aftermath of Vatican II, non-western nuns negotiated their roles and power within the institution. In this case study of the Servants of the Holy Spirit in a Papua New Guinean province, recent shifts in internal power relations are visible. While German nuns still supplied all leadership positions by mid 1980s, the last years witness shifts in this context. The actual provincial leader, for example, is a Filipina nun who has stayed in the region since 1981. Her assistant, in turn, is from the local area with an equally impressive

---

[27] Remarks like this can be found in the regular annual reports that record the return of the nuns to their home province.

[28] For example, Sr. Bernadette, the author of the theological study quoted earlier, is a Ghanaian nun who left Ghana for Rome in 2003. In Rome, she stayed with the Servants of the Holy Spirit's local community and studied biblical theology at the Pontifical University of St. Thomas Aquinas in Urbe Anglicum.

[29] See Missionary Sisters Servants of the Holy Spirit (2002a).

mobile career. Born in Papua New Guinea in 1962, Sister Helen took her first vows in 1988. Like her local predecessors, she completed her 1-year tertianship in the Philippines and consequently moved to Ghana, where she gained 4 years of mission experience. Before returning to Papua New Guinea in 2003, she travelled to Rome, where she visited the congregation's local community and participated in the canonization of its founder, Arnold Janssen. Since her return to Papua New Guinea, Sister Helen has been occupying the major office of the novice directress and thus been in charge of the formation of future nuns. In addition, nuns from Poland, Indonesia and India are among the actual community leaders in the single convents in the province. Altogether, the New Guinean branch of the congregation is actually composed of nuns from 14 different nationalities coming from Oceania, Asia, the Americas and Europe. All of them are trained and employed as teachers, university lecturers, librarians, pastoral workers, nurses, and counselors.[30]

The nuns' involvement with migration, frequent travel and transnationalism shaped their congregation's history and collective identity in very basic terms. Up to a certain extent, this applies also to their host societies. Since the late nineteenth century, nuns on the move have spread the image of the autonomous, celibate woman throughout the globe (McNamara 1996, 611). With the establishment of convents, they created institutional spaces in which women could realize alternative life-styles, get access to education, professional training and the possibility to travel. Significantly, while religious vocations in the West decline steadily, growing numbers of "third world women" enter religious institutions. Nowadays, the Servants of the Holy Spirit promote a model of the "prophetic woman," one who resides in an international female community and dedicates her service to the oppressed and marginalized people in society.

The experience of migration and mobility for religious reasons has empowered Catholic women since the late nineteenth century. They entered the missionary profession, built transnational female networks and assumed leadership positions within an increasingly globalized framework. However, the history of the Servants of the Holy Spirit shows that, once we adopt an international perspective, no linear path towards emancipation can be observed because mobility and migration were the privilege of westerners for the larger part of the twentieth century. It was only after a period of profound renewal initiated in the 1960s that the nuns started to redefine their collective lives and developed a more inclusive vision of mission and religious community building. Nowadays, religious women's congregations act as social support groups of women that provide platforms for collective action, the fostering of global and transnational dialogue, and the achievement of individual and common goals in diverse social, political and theological arenas.

---

[30] According to the list of sisters dating from December 31, 2009, nuns of the following nationalities resided in Papua New Guinea: Nationals (27), German (13), Polish (6), Indonesian (5), Italian (4), Austrian (3), Indian (3), USA (3), Timor (2), Bolivian (1), Filipino (1), Dutch (1), Slovakian (1) and Argentinean (1). See Arch.Gen.SSpS.Papua New Guinea: List of sisters in various communities December 31st 2009, courtesy of the archivist in Rome.

References

Alt, J. (Ed.). (2001). *Arnold Janssen—Letters to New Guinea and Australia*. Nettetal: Steyler Verlag.
Arch.Gen.SSpS 100 General chapter 4 1948, 4–1002. *Allgemeiner Bericht über die äußere Entwicklung der Genossenschaft 1934–1948*.
Arch.Gen.SSpS 100 General chapter 5 1960, 5–1002. *Berichte Provinzen/Regionen, Berichterstattung an das fünfte Generalkapitel der Dienerinnen des Heiligen Geistes*. Holy Ghost convent Alexishafen Madang region Neu Guinea.
Arch.Gen.SSpS 100 General chapter 5 1960, 5–1002. Protokoll.
Arch.Gen.SSpS PNG 6106 Province chronicles. Prophetic women in mission 2002.
Arch.Gen.SSpS 6204 SSpS Briefe. *Briefe von Schwester Arildis Engelbrecht an ihre Familie*.
Arch.Gen.SSpS Papua New Guinea: List of sisters in various communities December 31st 2009.
Arch.Gen.SSpS PNG 6201 Korrespondenz 1911–1975.
Arch.Gen.SSpS PNG Chronicles. Alexishafen.
Arch.Gen.SSpS PNG Chronicles. Timbunke.
Arch.Gen.SSpS SVD–SSpS. Gründerzeit 0006.1 SVD-SSpS 1909–1911.
Bamidele Erlandsson, U. (1997). In search of women's dignity and greater freedom. Fieldwork on women and identity among the Catholic Fatima Sisters in Jos, Nigeria. In E. Evers Rosander (Ed.), *Transforming female identities: Women's organizational forms in West Africa* (pp. 136–147). Stockholm: Gotab.
Bötzinger, V. (2004). *"Den Chinesen ein Chinese werden" Die deutsche protestantische Frauenmission in China*. Stuttgart: Franz Steiner Verlag.
Bowie, F. (1993). Introduction: Reclaiming women's presence. In F. Bowie, D. Kirkwood, & S. Ardener (Eds.), *Women and missions: Past and present. Anthropological and historical perceptions* (pp. 1–22). Providence/Oxford: Berg Publishers.
Braude, A. (2004). A religious feminist—Who can find her? Historiographical challenges from the National Organization for Women. *The Journal of Religion, 84*(4), 555–572.
Brosnan, K. A. (2004). Public presence, public silence: Nuns, bishops, and the gendered space of early Chicago. *The Catholic Historical Review, 90*(3), 473–496.
Coles, D., & Mihalic, F. (1999). *Sent by the spirit. Missionary sisters, Servants of the Holy Spirit. 1899–1999*. Wewak: Wirui Press.
Cunningham, V. (1993). 'God and nature intended you for a missionary's wife': Mary Hill, Jane Eyre and other missionary women in the 1840s. In F. Bowie, D. Kirkwood, & S. Ardener (Eds.), *Women and missions: Past and present. Anthropological and historical perceptions* (pp. 85–105). Providence/Oxford: Berg Publishers.
Dere Nulenpaala, B. (2009). *The Samaritan woman and Mary Magdalene: Two models of female discipleship—A comparative study*. Thesis, Pontifical University of St. Thomas Aquinas in Urbe Anglicum Rome.
Dietrich, A. (2006). Konstruktionen weißer Weiblichkeit. Emanzipationsdiskurse im Kontext des Kolonialismus. In M. Bechhaus-Gerst & S. Gieseke (Eds.), *Koloniale und postkoloniale Konstruktionen von Afrika und Menschen afrikanischer Herkunft in der deutschen Alltagskultur* (pp. 33–44). Frankfurt: Peter Lang Verlag.
Ebaugh, R. H. (1993). Patriarchal bargains and latent avenues of social mobility: Nuns in the Roman Catholic Church. *Gender and Society, 7*(3), 400–414.
Evangelisti, S. (2007). *Nuns. A history of convent life 1450–1700*. New York: Oxford University Press.
Fanning, W. (1907). Baptism. *The Catholic encyclopedia*. http://www.newadvent.org/cathen/02258b.htm. Accessed March 30, 2010.
Hill Collins, P. (1991). *Black feminist thought. Knowledge, consciousness, and the politics of empowerment*. London: Routledge.
Hollywood, A. (2004). Gender, agency, and the divine in religious historiography. *The Journal of Religion, 84*(4), 524–528.

Huber, M. T. (1987). Constituting the church: Catholic missionaries on the Sepik frontier. *American Ethnologist, 14*(1), 107–125.

Huber, M. T. (1999). The dangers of immorality: Dignity and disorder in gender relations in a northern New Guinea Diocese. In M. T. Huber & N. Lutkehaus (Eds.), *Gendered missions: Women and men in missionary discourse and practice* (pp. 179–206). Ann Arbor: University of Michigan Press.

Huber, M. T., & Lutkehaus, N. (1999). Introduction: Gendered missions at home and abroad. In M. T. Huber & N. Lutkehaus (Eds.), *Gendered missions: Women and men in missionary discourse and practice* (pp. 1–38). Ann Arbor: University of Michigan Press.

Hüwelmeier, G. (2004). Global players—Global prayers. Gender und Migration in transnationalen religiösen Räumen. *Zeitschrift für Volkskunde, 100*(2), 161–175.

Hüwelmeier, G. (2005). "Nach Amerika!" Schwestern ohne Grenzen. *L'Homme. Europäische Zeitschrift für feministische Geschichtswissenschaft, 16*(2), 97–115.

Hüwelmeier, G. (2008). Negotiating diversity. Catholic nuns as cosmopolitans. *Schweizerische Zeitung für Religions- und Kulturgeschichte, 102*, 105–117.

Kandiyoti, D. (1988). Bargaining with patriarchy. *Gender and Society, 2*(3), 274–290.

Lutkehaus, N. (1999). Missionary maternalism: Gendered images of the Holy Spirit Sisters in colonial New Guinea. In M. T. Huber & N. Lutkehaus (Eds.), *Gendered missions: Women and men in missionary discourse and practice* (pp. 207–235). Ann Arbor: University of Michigan Press.

Lyons Johnson, P. (1993). Education and the 'new' inequality in Papua New Guinea. *Anthropology & Education Quarterly, 24*(3), 183–204.

Mahmood, S. (2001). Feminist theory, embodiment, and the docile agent: Some reflections on the Egyptian Islamic revival. *Cultural Anthropology, 16*(2), 202–236.

Mahmood, S. (2004). Women's agency within feminist historiography. *The Journal of Religion, 84*(4), 573–579.

Mahmood, S. (2005). *Politics of piety. The Islamic revival and the feminist subject.* Princeton: Princeton University Press.

Mantovani, E. (1984). Traditional religions and Christianity. In E. Mantovani (Ed.), *An introduction to Melanesian religions. A handbook for Church workers* (pp. 1–23). Goroka: Melanesian Institute.

McNamara, J. A. K. (1996). *Sisters in arms. Catholic nuns through two millennia.* Cambridge/London: Princeton University Press.

Meiwes, R. (2000). *"Arbeiterinnen des Herrn" Katholische Frauenkongregationen im 19, Jahrhundert.* Frankfurt/New York: Campus Verlag.

Missionary Sisters Servants of the Holy Spirit. (2002a). *Our identity.* http://www.worldssps.org/our_identity.html. Accessed March 30, 2010.

Missionary Sisters Servants of the Holy Spirit. (2002b). *Official communications No. 199 on the SSpS 12th General Chapter.* This is our vision of mission. http://www.worldssps.org/our_mission.html. Accessed March 30, 2010.

Neuß, P. (1914). *Die Steyler Missionsschwestern Dienerinnen des Heiligen Geistes. Ein schlichter Kranz zu ihrem silbernen Jubelfest.* Steyl: Selbstverlag der Missionsschwestern.

Sepik nun is first PNG missionary to Ghana. In Wantok, 1315/94, 11 August 1994.

Shebi, E. (1997). A Nigerian sisterhood in the transformation of female identity. In E. Evers Rosander (Ed.), *Transforming female identities. Women's organizational forms in West Africa* (pp. 123–135). Stockholm: Gotab.

Soete, S. (1953). *Geschichte der Missionsgenossenschaft Dienerinnen des Heiligen Geistes.* Dissertation, University of Vienna, Vienna.

Sullivan, R. (2005). *Visual habits: Nuns, feminism, and American postwar popular culture.* Toronto: University of Toronto Press.

Thorne, S. (1999). Missionary imperial feminism. In M. T. Huber & N. Lutkehaus (Eds.), *Gendered missions: Women and men in missionary discourse and practice* (pp. 39–66). Ann Arbor: University of Michigan Press.

Volpert, A. (1951). *Ein Rebenhang in Wahren Weinberg. Geschichte der Missionsgenossenschaft Dienerinnen des Heiligen Geistes 1889–1951*. Steyl: Missionsdruckerei Steyl.

Weaver, M. J. (1986). *New Catholic women: A contemporary challenge to traditional religious authority*. San Francisco: Harper & Row.

Wedgwood, C. (1937). Women in Manam I. *Oceania. A Journal Devoted to the Study of the Native Peoples of Australia/New Guinea and the Islands of the Pacific Ocean, 7*(4), 401–439.

Chapter 15
Exploring the Activism of Immigrant Muslim Women in Chicago: Continued Frontiers of Engagement

Jackleen M. Salem

15.1 Introduction

It is often perceived that women had little role in or contribution to immigration in general (Marquez and Padilla 2004; Kibria 2008). This is partially due to the fact that men historically initiated and led the immigration of the family to the new land. However, women also participated immensely in many aspects of immigration both at home and in host societies. In early periods, men generally migrated and settled first, and brought the family later; but there were cases of women who arrived independently (Gualtieri 2009). This, too, has changed due to women's role in today's global society.

Muslims began migrating to Europe and America as the Ottoman Empire fell into decline in the late nineteenth century (Orfalea 1988). Well before their arrival on American shores, Western views of Muslims were established and they were considered barbaric, lascivious, violent, and incapable of self-governance (Said 1978). In addition, the perception of Muslim women was problematic in travel literature during the height of colonialism in the nineteenth century which gave accounts of harems and sexual slavery. Considering the Western perception of women in Islam—a product of the Orientalist movement—it is not implausible to think how little Muslim women might have contributed to the immigration of Muslim families throughout history (Said 1978). One of the misconceptions of the Orientalist theory is that Muslim women are restricted to their homes and have none or little contribution to the public sphere except serving the needs of their

J.M. Salem, Ph.D.(✉)
Department of History, University of Wisconsin-Milwaukee,
Milwaukee, WI, USA
e-mail: jsalem@uwm.edu

G.T. Bonifacio (ed.), *Feminism and Migration: Cross-Cultural Engagements*,
International Perspectives on Migration 1, DOI 10.1007/978-94-007-2831-8_15,
© Springer Science+Business Media B.V. 2012

husbands.[1] However, Muslim women participate in many aspects and spheres of life which are not necessarily documented and studied (Gualtieri 2009). Historically, Muslim women have been active since the inception of Islam in the early 600s and there has been an ongoing movement for women's rights and place in Muslim societies (Abd-Allah 2004). There are documented accounts of women who were knights, soldiers, scholars, queens, and much more (Roded 1994; Brooks 1995; Abd-Allah 2004). They participated in daily life and even challenged the societal norms. Amira al-Azhari Sonbol, professor at Georgetown University, "through her research in court documents and archives, has demonstrated that historically Islamic law was flexible and in many cases served to work in favor of women's full participation in the economy" (cited in Haddad et al. 2002, 151). In addition, women actively attended court (Sonbol 2001). This idea that the liberation of women in Muslim countries came with the feminist movement occurring in America, or with colonialism, or twentieth century military involvement in the Middle East, is particularly unfair to Muslim women of the region. After September 11, 2001, the State Department began to specifically address the education and liberation of women in the Middle East by providing funding for programs to educate them and bring groups of Muslim women to the United States (U.S.) to learn about democracy and equality (Geaves et al. 2004). This, however, was not received well by most Muslim women who felt this to be condescending since they viewed themselves as liberated on their own terms. According to Ron Geaves and colleagues:

> One delegation of high powered Arab women included the mayor of a North African city, the vice mayor of a Palestinian town, and a banker from the Gulf. Some in the group expressed indignation at the presumption that they needed empowerment. Their message was that the American government should change its policies to promote economic development in the area, rather than create a gender divide. (Geaves et al. 2004, 105)

The idea of a Middle Eastern woman as subservient, covered, and continually sequestered is more of an Orientalist stereotypical projection of the Muslim woman than the reality of her engagement in society. Some feminists suggest that "A critical analysis of and opposition to the uniformity of technological, industrial culture—capitalist and socialist—is crucial to feminism, ecology, and the struggles of indigenous peoples" (King 1992, 117). In order to break down the ideology behind how women are viewed in America and the Middle East, it is necessary to challenge the ideas behind these cultures.

Muslim women are not necessarily mute recipients of the change needed in their societies but active participants in the process. In particular, the head covering or *hijab* of Muslim women has been depicted in Western media as a sign of Islam's

[1] Orientalism holds that in the early eighteenth and nineteenth centuries, Westerners in academia, government, and literature, as heirs of an ethnocentric education, viewed the Orient (The Middle East and Asia) as a place where backward and ignorant people sequestered their women in harems. Edward Said (1978) argued that the Orientalists' xenophobic and misguided romanticized perspective informed the academic study of the Middle East and Asia well in to the twentieth century.

oppression to women. Groups of Muslim women on college campuses in the U.S. have tried to challenge such notions by wearing t-shirts that say, "We cover our hair, not our brains" (Haddad et al. 2002, 10). The vast majority of Muslim women in America and the Middle East do not wear *hijab* and, according to Islam, it cannot be coerced. For Muslim women in America who choose to wear *hijab*, they believe it is liberating for them to do so because it focuses attention on their actions and inner beauty as opposed to outer, bodily features. They believe *hijab* frees them from the global obsession in the media of female objectification (Haddad et al. 2002). Hijab does not limit Muslim women from obtaining education, involvement in politics, and other forms of participation in society.

Using feminist theories, this chapter explores Muslim women and their participation in the private and public spheres, including education, work, religion, society, and politics. It provides a historical analysis on the diverse roles of Muslim women immigrants in the U.S. from the early periods of the nineteenth century to the present. The significance of their contributions to the American Muslim community is discussed through a particular emphasis on contemporary activism of Muslim women in Chicago. Using oral history methodology, this chapter presents the historical evolution of immigrant Muslim women's activism in Chicago through three specific periods: (1) from the early 1900s; (2) from the 1950s to 1980s; (3) and from 1990s to present. In this oral history project, there were over ten participants who were interviewed but only four are cited here: three are Palestinians and one Iranian. The educational background and professions of these immigrant Muslim women varies from teachers, social workers, factory workers, and cashiers to environmentalists. They have been active members of their communities and continuously work for the improvement and empowerment of American Muslim women and their children in the areas of human rights, education, work, religion, socioeconomy, environment, women's rights, and politics. Profiles of their activism are viewed based on different feminist orientations. The conclusion presents a discussion on the future directions and challenges for Muslim women in American society in general and the Muslim community in particular.

15.2 Feminism, Theory and Activism

Feminism is a phenomenon often associated with women's rights, equality, and women's activism. Bell Hooks defines feminism as "a struggle against sexist oppression" (2000, 26), and adds:

> it is necessarily a struggle to eradicate the ideology of domination that permeates Western culture on various levels, as well as a commitment to reorganizing society so that the self-development of people can take precedence over imperialism, economic expansion and material desires. (Hooks 2000, 26)

The literature on Western feminism identifies three main historical eras or "waves" of the movement. The first wave of the feminist movement in the United States began in the early eighteenth century when American women fought for the right to vote, which was granted in 1920. The second wave of feminism was, supposedly, between the 1950s and 1980s and it focused on the inequality between men and women in various aspects of society.[2] These inequalities result from the entry of American women in the labor force. They gained economic freedom yet remained constrained by social policies and practices in a male-dominated business society. The third wave of feminism began in the early 1990s and is often considered a continuation and a response to the failures of the previous waves (Krolokke and Sorensen 2005).

As a result of the feminist movement, different theories of feminism have been introduced including, but not limited to, liberal feminism, socialist feminism, and multicultural and global feminism. First wave feminism led mainly to liberal feminist theory which argues for the equality of all human beings. Liberal feminism aims to eradicate inequalities between men and women, and works for the equal access of women in all domains of public life (Kirp et al. 1986; Epstein 2002). According to Chris Beasley (1999, 52), "[p]ublic citizenship and the attainment of equality with men in the public arena is central to liberal feminism." Second wave feminism resulted in the development of socialist feminist theory which views economic dependency as a form of oppression under capitalist patriarchy, and calls for women to enter the labor force as a way to gain independence from men (Fuentes and Ehrenreich 1983; Eisenstein 1987). A socialist feminist approach integrates the issue of gender with socio-economic class to bring a different dimension in achieving gender equality. The general idea is that women occupy inferior positions, both at home and at work, and through their economic liberation such gender and class barriers are potentially eliminated. The social feminist approach asserts that "women's subordination pre-dated the development of class-based societies and hence that women's oppression could not be caused by class division" (Beasley 1999, 62). The third and the current wave of feminist movement brought, among others, multicultural and global feminism. Instead of solely focusing on gender, these threads of thought focuses on all kinds of differences and extend its scope to class, ethnicity, and age, to mention a few. Rosemarie Tong (2009, 300) writes, "Multicultural, global, and postcolonial feminists push feminist thought in the direction of both recognizing women's diversity and acknowledging the challenges it presents." Some view feminism as "a protest against women's oppression" and others see it as an issue of equality, class, or race (Evans 1995, 1). Muslim feminism is another emergent area of study under the rubric of multicultural feminism. It aims to address the issues and problems associated with the rights of Muslim women and work for social justice against various oppressive cultural norms and governmental practices. Muslim feminist movement often utilizes Islamic law as the basis for justifying the equality of Muslim women.

[2] Women during the second wave of feminism fought for reproductive rights in *Roe vs. Wade* in 1973 but also affirmative action, making marital rape illegal, and educational equality (Brownmiller 2007; Murray 2007). There is a disagreement between feminist scholars as to the exact dates of the second wave of feminism. Some argue that we are still in the second wave of feminism, while others hold it ended and we have moved into the third wave of feminism.

There are many scholars who have worked on Muslim feminism, such as Yvonne Y. Haddad and others (2002), Fatima Mernissi (1987), Leila Ahmed (1993), Amira El-Azhary Sonbol (2001), Lila Abu-Lughod (1998), Amina Wadud (1999), and Lois Lamya al Faruqi (1991). Muslim feminist thought varies from those who argue for full equality based on the Western model to those who suggest that Islam, in the Qur'an, provides equality for men and women but cultural influences have to be weeded out. Sonbol (2001, 122) argues in her article,, "Rethinking Women and Islam," that Muslim women are given equality with men in the Qur'an but that it has been the legal analysis of scholars from patriarchal dominated societies and the misuse of certain *hadiths* (sayings of the Prophet Muhammad) throughout Islamic history that altered the message of the Qur'an and the place of Muslim women in society. Al Faruqi (1991, 28–29) believes that Western feminism is incompatible with Muslim societies because it views religion as the enemy of women's rights and cannot be exported to other parts of the world with divergent cultures. In addition, Al Faruqi holds that,

> any feminism which is to succeed in an Islamic environment must be one which does not work chauvinistically for women's interest alone. Islamic traditions would dictate that women's progress be achieved in tandem with the wider struggle to benefit all members of the society. The good of the group or totality is always more crucial than the good of any sector of the society. In fact, the society is seen as an organic whole in which the welfare of each member or organ is necessary for the health and well being of every other part. (Al Faruqi 1991, 30)

For the Muslim women included in this chapter, their work and activism is based not on the Western model but on a wider struggle that include the benefits and needs of the whole community. Consistent with Sonbol's (2001) argument, these women do not believe Islam deprives them of their rights to equality but that, instead, patriarchal societies have diminished the role of Muslim women. The women in this chapter, however, do not view themselves as "feminists" but as Muslims standing for what they see as their inherent rights.

15.3   Muslim Women and the Great Migration, Early 1900s–1950s

The first wave of Muslim immigration to the U.S. was between 1870 and 1924. The largest groups of Muslims to arrive in the late 1800s were mainly men between the ages of 14 and 40 from the region of Greater Syria (today Syria, Lebanon, Jordan, Iraq, and Palestine). Of the 350,000–500,000 Arab immigrants who came to the U.S., about 80–90% were Christians while the other 10–20% were Muslims (Read 2003). Similar to the journeys of other immigrants during this period, these Muslims came to America because of economic hardships in their own lands and heard stories of great opportunities in the United States. The Middle East—as it is called today—was still part of the Ottoman Empire during the late 1800s and early 1900s. The region suffered political, economic, and religious instability. There was a high birthrate and little arable land to support the growing population (Naff 1985). Over 100,000 people died of starvation in the Middle East, especially during World War I (Orfalea 1988). Taxes increased and so did the laws of conscription in 1909. Sectarian violence increased between 1820 and 1860 among Christian Maronites and Druze (Orfalea 1988).[3] These conditions propelled many Christian and Muslim Arabs to escape and emigrate in search of stability and better opportunities to lift their families out of poverty and insecurity.

Among Muslims in America, Arab men were the first migrants (except for the forced migration of African Muslim men who came during the trans-Atlantic slave trade during the 1600s–1800s). Most of them were unmarried and lived for many years in America supporting their parents and siblings back in the Middle East. A few years after they arrived and realized they were not about to leave soon, Muslim men started to return home to marry. They either left their wives for sometime or brought them back to America. Muslim immigrants, especially men, were often focused on pursuits of wealth and economic stability in order to take care of their families in America as well as their extended families overseas. Many Muslim men started their careers in peddling but also worked in the automobile industry in the Detroit area and silk factories in the East Coast. The average income for a Muslim peddler was about US$1,000 a year (Naff 1985). As Muslims began to make money in peddling, automobile factories, and other industries, they began to send for other family members—a brother, uncle, cousin, or brother-in-law. Cases of chain migration to the United States came from certain areas of Greater Syria and were instrumental in creating a support structure for Arabs, whether Muslims or Christians, such as the villagers from Beitunya in Chicago (Al-Tahir 1950).[4]

Muslim women migrants in America were not simply housewives; they contributed to the educational, economic, and social growth of their families and communities. These women often immigrated to the U.S. after their husbands, brothers, and fathers (Gualtieri 2009). Although there are some cases of Muslim women coming independently, most came concurrently with or 2–10 years after their husbands' or fathers' arrivals. After 1899, there was a steady increase in the percentage of women immigrating to the U.S. Between 1899 and 1910, over 32% of Arab immigrants were women; and between 1919 and 1930, about 47% were Arab women (Gualtieri 2009). Some Arab women did arrive autonomously from men to work and help support the migration of their mother, sister, or brother to the U.S.; while other women were widowed and journeyed with their children, or sent them ahead to the States (Gualtieri 2009).

---

[3] Maronites are a Christian group who reside mainly in Lebanon and represent the majority of the Lebanese population. Maronites still follow the Catholic Church in Rome. Druze refers to a group of people who embrace a religion that was once considered a sect of Sunni Islam but has separated itself and developed its own belief system. Druzes are found in Israel, Lebanon, and Syria.

[4] Beitunya is a small village west of Ramallah in the West Bank. According to Abdul Jalil Al-Tahir (1950), many Arabs immigrated to America from this village and a considerable number came to the Chicagoland area.

Some Muslim women in the U.S. also peddled or worked in the store—either independently or with their husbands. Women were often more convincing salespersons than their husbands since most of their customers were women (Naff 1985). Women helped select the items to be sold, like bed linens and women's undergarments, which made the bulk of income for the peddler. They even sold souvenirs from the Holy Land. In some cases, some women traveled independently and tried to peddle, work in factories, bake and sell their own bread, and sew and sell aprons and other materials. Women played a vital role in sustaining the household economy. In the U.S., Muslim men came to depend on their wives even more than they did in their homelands. Women's work, especially wives, carried new responsibilities and meanings in America—she earned money, traveled, and learned English at the same time her husband did (Haddad et al. 2002). Alixa Naff (1985, 176) states, "Women were, by far, the most valuable economic asset to the trade (peddling)." Around 75% of women peddled during this early period of U.S. immigration (Naff 1985). Their economic participation challenged the traditional role of the husband as the sole breadwinner and leader of the family. Working Muslim women presented a serious dilemma for some Muslim men because of the cultural beliefs associated with protecting a woman's honor. Muslim Arab men were alarmed over how women dressed; how far they travelled to peddle; whether or not they spent the night outside the house; and how they conducted themselves outside the home (Gualtieri 2009). Most Arab men, Muslim or Christian, prefer their wives or daughters to work at home as a homemaker or assume responsibilities in the family business (though often behind the scenes). However, as more Muslim women settled in the United States, they wanted to assist the family by working outside the home. Single Muslim immigrant women wanted to have their own income to support themselves, their siblings, and adjust to American society, in addition to supporting their parents.

15.4 Chicago Muslim Women, 1950s–1980s

Being in America presented great economic advantages to Muslim women, as well as difficulties. As a minority in the U.S., Muslim women faced the challenge of maintaining their traditions, native languages, and religious practices. Muslim men dealt more with the economic hardships of providing for their immediate families in America and extended families in the Middle East. This placed Muslim women in a multi-faceted position. First, they attended the children and the home. Second, they worked with their husbands in their businesses or in their own businesses. Third, Muslim women ensured their children learned and retained their cultural traditions, languages, and religious practices. Fourth, they helped form a Muslim community through organizing community events—Eid prayers, funerals, cooking for weddings, and fundraising for buildings—by selling food and going door to door. Moreover, these women often did all of this with five to nine children in tow. These women viewed it as a necessity to fill the gap and address the needs of the community. In this regard, two Muslim women are notable for their activities in the Chicago area from 1950 to 1980: Shamsa Zayed and Sorya Shalabi.

Shamsa Zayed of Chicago, Illinois is a Muslim mother of nine. She was born in 1929 in Beitunya, Palestine and came to America in 1949 on her British Mandate papers together with her baby girl of 40 days and two male family friends from Beitunya (S. Zayed, Personal interview, March 16, 2010). She married her husband Khalil Zayed in 1947 right before the establishment of the state of Israel and the war for control of Palestine. She journeyed from Beitunya in the West Bank to Beirut, Lebanon with her baby girl to secure papers to travel to America. She took an Air France flight from Damascus, Syria to Paris, France and stayed there for 3 days before finally travelling to New York City. Her husband bought her tickets unknowingly only to New York City. When she arrived there, she had no money (nor did the men with her), and did not know how to contact her husband living in Chicago. She asked around until she found some Muslims from Ramallah, from the Ba'ith family. They owned a wholesale business in New York City. They invited them to a Middle Eastern restaurant and asked her where she was from. When she told her story and the name of her father—Ahmed Hammada—they smiled in excitement because they had worked with her father many times and believed him to be a very honest man. They gave her the money for her ticket, her daughter's, and her friends without requesting any payment in return. Her own father was an important man in Beitunya who owned stores in Chicago and lots of land in Jerusalem. He had journeyed to America seven times in the 1920s on business and it garnered suspicion. He was imprisoned in New York City for a short time allegedly as a spy. He had never brought his wife and children and simply traveled back and forth between New York City and Beitunya, and in the process became a successful businessman.

When Shamsa settled in Chicago, she discovered that there were very few Muslim families living in the area. There were between 150 and 200 Muslim families in the Chicagoland area (Al-Tahir 1952). It was very difficult to go from living communally in Beitunya, Palestine to independently in Chicago. Her husband worked all day from 10 am until 10 pm as a door to door peddler. The dominant view of the role of women was that "women's natural function of childbearing prescribes their domestic and subordinate place in the order of things" (Pateman 1987, 109). However, in Shamsa's case and many others like her, women had more than just domestic duties. Due to her husband's long workday peddling, Shamsa was left to do many things on her own—shopping, taking care of school needs for the children, resolving health concerns, organizing holiday events, and overseeing everyday needs of life. Although some of these activities were part of her duties before she came to America, she did not have to organize holiday events or manage the children's school activities. Being in a foreign country added a new dimension of difficulty since she could not also speak English. However, Shamsa began to operate outside the confines of the home when she realized two things early on: her children were not learning their native language, culture, and religion, and the Muslim community on the Southside of Chicago needed their own space for their activities. Shamsa used to meet with other Muslim women and discussed issues facing the immigrant Muslim community: "We used to sit and talk on the stairs with other Muslim women about how our children were losing their identity and our dream of building a mosque."(S. Zayed, Personal interview, March 16, 2010.) To address these growing concerns, she joined the

Arabian Ladies Society (later changed to the Arabian American Ladies Society) in 1953 with a few other women and started on a path of community organizing.

The Arabian Ladies Society was established in 1947 by an American Jewish woman married to a Palestinian immigrant, Mr. Mahmoud Falahat, in order to assist the educational and societal needs of the Arab community in Chicago and abroad (Al-Tahir 1950). Traditionally, "[a]dult women remained almost entirely within the private sphere, defined politically, economically, and socially by their familial roles" (DuBois 1987, 129). But Shamsa ventured beyond her socially prescribed roles and decided to actively attend to the needs of the Muslim community. Her efforts to make lives better for her children and other Muslim women in a new society would make Shamsa a liberal Muslim feminist, but not from a conscious effort of standing up for women's rights. Al Faruqi (1991, 29) argues that if feminism is to work in Muslim societies or communities, "it must be an indigenous form of feminism, rather than one conceived and nurtured in an alien environment with different problems and different solutions and goals." Shamsa is, as al Faruqi (1991, 29) describes, providing an "indigenous" feminism unique to Muslims and the community they were establishing in Chicago. Shamsa was motivated to find a space for inclusion in the community based on their particular religious, cultural, and societal needs. This does not mean her actions were accepted by all members of the community because she received criticism from many of the male members for her fundraising activities.

Sarah Shalabi, nicknamed Sorya, was also active during this period. She left Beitunya in the West Bank on November 1, 1955 and arrived in America on November 4, 1955. She came with her two young daughters—Hanan was 4 years old and Hayat was 3 years old—to follow her husband already living in Chicago for 5 years (S. Shalabi, Personal interview, April 10, 2009). Her father came to Chicago in the early 1920s and commuted back and forth from Beitunya. Her uncles, brothers and sister-in-laws were also in Chicago when she arrived.

Sorya received her high school diploma in 1945 from the Schmidt's Girls College in Jerusalem. She intended to continue her bachelor's degree but her trip to America prevented her from doing so. After she arrived in Chicago, she registered for college and attended two semesters in 1956. But with her husband working from 10 am to 10 pm, she found it difficult to manage schoolwork with her two daughters and decided to quit. Sorya recalls, "I opened up a little store, a neighborhood grocery on 57th and Carpenter to help my husband."(Ibid.) She worked at the store accompanied by her daughters (S. Shalabi, Personal interview, April 10, 2009). Although she could not keep up with her studies, Sorya still joined the Arabian American Ladies Society in 1956. Arab Muslim ladies sought to make their children learn and retain proficiency in Arabic language, Arab culture, and Muslim faith. In 1959, each woman paid 50 cents in monthly dues and the group elected Sorya as president because she was highly educated. Sorya also knows how to drive, which was a great advantage since many Arab women could not drive at that time.

Shamsa and Sorya wanted a mosque or center as a venue to hold weddings, celebrate Eid holidays, teach their children, and hold events for the Muslim community. It was of utmost importance during this period that Muslims have a place of their own to ensure that their cultural and religious heritage is practiced, especially among children. These women *felt the pressure of preserving their culture, fall upon them.* Hence, the Arabian American Ladies Society decided it was crucial to establish a school for their children to learn and improve their knowledge of the Arabic language and Arab culture. They also felt a religious imperative that their children learn and practice Islam. To achieve this, they collected US$5,000 in 2 years and rented out a building for a weekly Sunday school (S. Shalabi, Personal interview, April 10, 2009). While the men were busy working, Muslim women on the south side of Chicago took matters in their own hands and raised funds. As Denise Riley (1987, 195) states, the lack of "[s]ymmetry between women as parents and men as parents are neither timeless, universally true nor incapable of being eroded." The idea that Muslim men were responsible for specific duties like work or business, and women concerned themselves solely with domestic work and children gradually changed as a result of their participation in various aspects of life.

Aside from caring for their children and the home, Muslim women had a variety of different roles back in their villages which included farming, going to the market, and conducting business transactions on behalf of the household. Shamsa and Sorya defined their roles as they saw fit, without considering the social acceptability of their actions but responded to a need in Chicago. It was part of what they believed to be their duty as mothers—to impart their cultural and religious heritage to their children. Consequently, Shamsa, Sorya, and other members of the Arab American Ladies Society started to bake and collect money for their planned mosque. They solicited funds, conducted a door to door campaign among the Arab Muslims in the community. In addition, most of these women had over five children on average; Sorya had six and Shamsa had nine. One of Shamsa's eldest daughters, Miriam, drove her mom and other women around to different homes and businesses every Sunday, leaving their children in the house. Shamsa said,

> We would take Miriam's daughters on our laps so she could drive us around. They would stay in the car while we went from house to house getting ten to five dollars. My poor daughter Miriam. She would take us in the car to give us practice (S. Zayed, Personal interview, March 16, 2010).

Sorya also drove some women throughout the Chicagoland area—North, South, and West—to local Arab groceries or other businesses asking for financial support. Their husbands did not object to these activities and supported them in general, but they did not necessarily always seek their permission. However, they often received negative reactions from other Muslim men in society. Some Muslim men were more traditional and disliked women outside of the home or involved in activities they deemed inappropriate. On one occasion, Shamsa described going to an Arab coffeehouse in Chicago, the Middle East Club:

> We used to go to the coffee house, me and a couple of other women. The coffee house on Damen. We would see them playing cards and we would tell them, "Please help us, we want to build a mosque" and the men would say, "Do you have any shame that would keep you indoors? Go away. You made us forgot our game!" And we were fasting, too (S. Zayed, Personal interview, March 16, 2010).

The men chastised these Muslim mothers for daring to enter the club and distract them from their game. According to Zillah Eisenstein (1987, 83), "[w]oman is instead reared for obedience and self-sacrifice to others rather than taught how to assert her own needs." When women do assert their needs, their actions are considered shameful. However, men's behavior at the coffeehouse was more inappropriate on a cultural and religious level because they were playing cards during the holy month of Ramadan instead of attending to their family or work. Coffee houses in the Middle East are considered the cultural domain of men, and women entering it would be viewed as highly improper, despite their noble cause or their location in America. Sorya and Shamsa, together with other Muslim women, showed a clear sign in the transformation of women's traditional roles. Although women in the Middle East are also active in re-defining their roles, certain places were considered the exclusive domain of men, including the coffeehouse. In the Middle East, society is communal and extended family—cousins, uncles, aunts, and in-laws—functioned jointly. Neighbors took care of neighbors or fellow villagers; a support structure had been in place for centuries. Immigrant Muslim women in America seek to re-create these support structures by first taking more responsibilities and new roles, such as, fundraising, organizing, and educating their children in public spaces.

Through the efforts of Shamsa, Sorya, their husbands, and others, the Mosque Foundation of Chicago was established in 1954. Its organization represented both men and women's efforts to establish a mosque and community center in the South side of Chicago. But the women were the ones who raised the money. Shamsa and Sorya, with the Arabian American Ladies Society, raised over US$50,000 to purchase the land initially strewn with garbage in Bridgeview, Illinois, a suburb in the southwest area of Chicago. It would take them another 27 years before the mosque would be built and opened its doors in 1981. During that time, Sorya and the Arab American Ladies Society continued to raise funds. Once the mosque was built, Sorya continued her activism in the Muslim and Arab communities. She even met with the former Illinois Governor Jim Edgar to find a way for Arab students in the public schools of Chicago and its suburbs to learn Arabic (S. Shalabi, Personal interview, April 10, 2009). She had met many times with Mayor Richard M. Daley to advocate for the rights of Arab Americans in Chicago. Sorya also raised funds to buy an ambulance for her village in Beitunya (S. Shalabi, Personal interview, April 10, 2009). While men in the Muslim community assisted in fundraising, Sorya, Shamsa and the American Arabian Ladies Association were the backbone of the project. For these women, there was never a thought out organized effort to be activists for the Muslim community. They saw the need and sought to address it without ever believing it was either a man or a woman's job. As women, they are leaders of their communities who were concerned with identity, culture, and social status of Muslim women.

15.5   Muslim Women in Chicago, 1990–Present

Muslim women of the post-1965 generation in the U.S. have more access to education, economic opportunities, and political involvement than previous generations of immigrant Muslim women. The passage of President Lyndon B. Johnson's *Civil Rights Act* of 1964 banned racial segregation in public facilities, such as schools, businesses, government, and other institutions. The *Civil Rights* Act facilitated economic, political, and social changes toward equality for all human beings. It was the impetus for changing immigration legislation, the quota system, and gender discrimination. In 1965, the *Immigration and Nationality Act* allowed the entry of non-whites, including 20,000 people from each country in Asia, the Middle East, and Africa. It granted preferential treatment to skilled laborers and family members of United States' citizens—their parents, spouses, siblings, and children under 21 who were not considered part of the quota for each country (Ameri and Ramey 2000). Although immigrants from the Indian subcontinent began arriving in the U.S. at the turn of the century, the civil rights legislation brought additional Muslims from Pakistan, Bangladesh, Sri Lanka, China, Afghanistan, Malaysia, Indonesia, Turkey, and other countries (Smith 2009). Between 1970 and 1994, over ten million immigrants entered the U.S. Of this number, 400,000 were Arabs from Egypt, Jordan (80% Palestinian refugees), Syria, Iraq, and Yemen (Ameri and Ramey 2000). Smaller numbers came from Algeria, Morocco, Bahrain, Libya, Sudan, Tunisia, Oman, and Saudi Arabia. Since 1965, Muslims have comprised 75% of the Arabs who have migrated to the U.S. compared to the Arabs during the Great Migration when 80% to 90% were Christians (Read 2003). According to statistics by the U.S. Department of State (2010), Muslims can be divided into the following ethnic categories: 33% South-Central Asian, 30% African American, 25% Arab, 3% African, 2% European, and 7% other.

Muslim American women since 1965 are not only homemakers but also educators, doctors, actors, lawyers, pharmacists, journalists, politicians, and community fund-raisers and organizers (Haddad et al. 2002). Of the Muslim women who migrated to America during the twentieth century, the post-1965 generation represents the most diverse, ethnically and professionally. Itedal Shalabi and Shireen Pishdadi migrated in this period. Itedal Shalabi was born in 1961 in Amman, Jordan but had migrated from the occupied West Bank. She eventually came to America at the age of nine with her family due to the civil unrest in Jordan in 1970 between the Hashemite monarchy's King Hussein and certain Palestinian groups (I. Shalabi, Personal interview, March 20, 2010). Although her father, Taha Shalabi, served the family of the King as a teacher, their status as Palestinians left them in a vulnerable situation. When her parents received an opportunity for an American green card through her mother's brother, they took it. In the U.S., Itedal got married and had three children before she finished her bachelor's degree from the University of Illinois at Chicago. Then she completed a master's degree in social work from Jane Adam's College of Social Work at the University of Illinois. At present, she is the Executive Director and co-founder of Arab American Family Services (AAFS) in Bridgeview, Illinois. This nonprofit organization was founded in 2001 and works to provide "support in the areas of public benefits, immigration, domestic violence, mental health, and elderly services and sponsors outreach programs to build healthier families and communities."[5] In addition, it provides programs like cultural training and youth activities.[6]

---

[5] American Arab Family Services (2010). About Us (http://www.arabamericanfamilyservices. org/aboutus.asp)

[6] Ibid.

Itedal decided to return to school after the birth of her youngest son. In 2001, she began the Arab American Family Services (AAFS) and, in the same year, also lost her husband in a traffic accident. Since then, she has been raising her children on her own. Itedal describes social work as a calling, something that chose her.

> It really was a calling. The women in the neighborhood and in my building used to come to me because I was one of the only ones who spoke English. So, they would bring their letters from school and ask me, "could you read this?"(I. Shalabi, Personal interview, March 20, 2010)

But it was a much deeper event in her life that led her to study social work seriously. In the early 1980s, after Itedal had married, there was a problem with one of the Muslim women in the apartment building she was living in, predominantly occupied by Muslims. Rent money was stolen from various people throughout the building (Ibid.). One mother finally realized that her son was stealing the money. When she confronted him, he denied it. In punishment, she slightly burned him thinking it would teach him a lesson for stealing. When the mother took him to the doctor for treatment, the nurse called the Department of Child and Family Services (I. Shalabi, Personal interview, March 20, 2010). As a result, her two younger children were taken away and the 12-year old boy was sent to a juvenile residential facility. This Muslim mother had to attend court and parenting classes, often all in English. Itedal reflects,

> Here is an immigrant woman that doesn't drive, doesn't have a husband that can take off because he leaves work at 7 am and doesn't come home until 11 pm. He can't take off or he loses his job. They're already financially burdened; don't know how to communicate effectively with the social worker. So she started coming to me and asking me, "would you go with me and can you take me?"(Ibid.)

Itedal started to attend the court dates and classes with her neighbor to help her translate, and everyone thought she was her social worker (Ibid.). She was in her early twenties then, just married with her first child when she started helping this woman; the impetus for her career in social work.

Itedal realized that the American system and its way of life were new to Muslim immigrants. They needed help, especially for those who could not speak English, who had many children, and with husbands who worked all day. She claims, "We (Arabs) didn't understand the system. And I think that is a huge part of why me and Nareman (co-founder) started the Arab American Family Serves." Today, Itedal extends services from merely helping immigrants fill out forms with Medicaid, food stamps, other public benefits, and translating documents to helping victims of domestic violence, sexual abuse, and the elderly. AAFS also provides services to Hispanic and Latino immigrants. Their domestic abuse department has grown in recent years and, as of 2011, has over 2,500 clients. One of their present challenges is related to Muslim and Arab men using Islam to justify their emotional and physical abuse of their wives. Maha Azzam (1996, 219) notes: "A woman will often find it difficult to bring charges against her husband to court and if she does, she will frequently arouse social condemnation and not receive justice in the courts." Many women are afraid to leave their husbands because they view Islam and culture as one. It is difficult for them to differentiate between these two and make a stand for their rights. They also have to deal with familial and societal pressures including parents, siblings, cousins, and uncles who think it is culturally and religiously inappropriate to divorce their husbands, in spite of abuse. Furthermore, most immigrant Muslim women in the U.S. do not seem to know their rights, whether rights allotted to them according to Islam or American law. Itedal says about her work,

> What we found is that a lot of women didn't know their Islamic rights … Immigrant women and Muslim women, you have to understand, also grew up in a patriarchal society; where there is a very fine line between understanding Islam and living Islam. Theory and practicality sometimes don't go hand in hand. It is a shame we are living in a time where Islam theoretically gives women so many rights and I love it when you have Arab or Muslim men who talk about how Islam gave women the right to education 1,400 years ago, the right to a job, the right to inheritance, the right initiate a marriage, the right to initiate a divorce but does it happen? You can talk about it theoretically, yes, we do have all those rights but most women don't even know they have those rights… It is not important just that our women know they have rights but that they exercise those rights, too (I. Shalabi, Personal interview, March 20, 2010).

Education has been an integral part of Itedal's work. Muslim women who recently immigrated often allow cultural conventions to take precedence over the rights accorded to them in Islam and American law. What many of these Muslim women do not realize is that economics is often directly related to these cultural conventions. In liberal feminist interpretation, "both sex and class power have a material aspect, that is, they both are conceived as having an economic form," which is not just about culture and religion (Beasley 1999). Itedal is also involved in fighting domestic violence not only with the Arab community but all communities in Chicago. She has been on the committee for Domestic Violence Advisory Council, on the executive committee of the Chicago Battered Women's Network, and the Illinois Coalition against Domestic Violence (I. Shalabi, Personal interview, March 20, 2010). Based on her actions, Itedal could be considered as a social feminist because she challenges the government, societal, and cultural institutions and beliefs for the welfare of women, children, the elderly, and other marginalized groups. Jean Bethke Elshtain (1995, 270) notes, "In affirming the dignity of the human subject, beginning with the needs of children, social feminism challenges irresponsible corporate power and a politics of group self-interest." However, Itedal does not see herself as a feminist, simply a Muslim woman standing for what is right (I. Shalabi, Personal interview, March 20, 2010). Applying al Faruqi (1991) in this context, Itedal has established her own brand of feminism in the Muslim community and identifies herself as a Muslim and American. She has served as a board member of the Mosque Foundation and Universal School in Bridgeview, Illinois. Her professional career involved a variety of activities, making her one of the many contemporary Muslim women activists in Chicago. Itedal's activism comes from a deep sense of social justice and responsibility ingrained by Islamic principles taught by both her parents, such as helping those in need without expecting anything in return, and challenging social and moral injustices (I. Shalabi, Personal interview, March 20, 2010).

Shireen Pishdadi is another example of a Muslim woman working beyond the stereotypical frame attributed to Muslim women in the West. Shireen has been fighting for increased awareness about the environment, food, the treatment of animals, and corporate agricultural practices for many years. All of these coalesced into a single cause, economic justice. According to Karen J. Warren, the environment and feminism have much in common as they are both a form of domination, and notes:

> On this view, it is oppressive and patriarchal conceptual frameworks (and the behaviors which they give rise to) which sanction, maintain, and perpetuate the twin dominations of women and nature. Revealing and overcoming oppressive and patriarchal conceptual frameworks as they are manifest in theories and practices regarding women and nature are important tasks of feminism, environmentalism, and environmental ethics. (Warren1996, xii)

Some scholars argue that feminism can be used to better comprehend humankind's domination over the environment. However, Shireen's motivation for her environmental work comes from her belief that the capitalist structures upon which our global economy is based, puts the wealth and power in the hands of a few giant corporations which exhibit abusive labor, environmental practices and others (S. Pishdadi, Personal interview, March 25, 2010). Shireen is a biochemist by training but her profession became advocating for the just treatment of the environment by opposing monocropping—an agricultural practice in which the same crop is planted year after year without practicing crop rotation or resting the soil, the inhumane treatment of animals in the American meat industry, and the biopiracy of seeds (S. Pishdadi, Personal interview, March 25, 2010). According to Shireen, monocropping is an aggressive form of farming by corporations which depletes the topsoil and fresh water. She believes that "sustainable land cultivation is a profoundly effective means to reverse climate change and rebalance the environment, bringing back the abundance of our naturally wholesome planet."(Ibid.) Shireen notes that the environment has been irrevocably damaged by corporate practices. In this vein, feminist ideology holds that how women and the environment have been mistreated are very similar. Considering ecology and feminism together, women and nature are seen as subjects to the destructive socio-economic and technological systems of a modern male-dominated society (Mellor 1997).

Shireen was born in Jeddah, Saudi Arabia to an Iranian father and Palestinian mother. She came to America in 1982 at the age of 11. She lived in England, Jordan, and Saudi Arabia before settling in the United States. She finished her bachelor's degree at Chicago State University and began to work at Faith in Place in Chicago (S. Pishdadi, Personal interview, March 25, 2010). Faith in Place seeks to give "religious people the tools to become good stewards of the earth. We partner with religious congregations to promote clean energy and sustainable farming."[7] At Faith in Place, Shireen was the director and founder of Taqwa Eco-Food Cooperative and the Muslim Outreach Coordinator, which helped connect Muslims in the Chicagoland with local farmers to give them humanely treated and well-fed meats but also connect religious congregations with environmental living (S. Pishdadi, Personal interview, March 25, 2010). She gave talks and lectures at local mosques, churches, synagogues, and other congregations about the importance of sustainable

---

[7] Faith in Place (2010). "Mission Statement." http://www.faithinplace.org/about/mission-statement

farming and locally grown food. Shireen and the director of Faith in Place, Reverend Clare Butterfield, helped convince over 200 congregations from various faith groups in the Chicago area to become "guardians of the earth."[8] She convinced some religious organizations to invest in solar panels and geothermal heating and cooling systems.[9] Shireen and Reverend Butterfield encouraged a synagogue to become the first fully functioning green synagogue in the nation.[10]

Through her work, Shireen instantly became passionate about the disturbing effects of the practices of food corporations and the monocropping by local farmers—pesticides in food, grain fed cows with higher fat and cholesterol levels, chickens shocked into laying eggs, hormones and antibiotics in the food (S. Pishdadi, Personal interview, March 25, 2010). Shireen believes that the environment and how animals are treated in the meat industry are important "because it is all linked in with social justice and living Islamically."(Ibid.) The Islamic way of life means respecting the earth and all its living creatures, to abuse any would abruptly affect the equilibrium of the environment. Mary Mellor (1997, 196) says, "Responsibility and reciprocity would mean that in a limited world no one has any right to more than they need, and all provisioning would be direct and responsible as possible (labor to consumption to disposal)." Shireen views our everyday lives as directly linked with the treatment of animals and the earth, since humans consume these inhumanely treated animals and live on the earth. People's consumption of ill-treated meat directly affects their health—with heart attacks and high cholesterol, to name a few—and the environment—deforestation to graze animals, the hole in the ozone, and more. She has even spoken out against the *Halal Food Act* passed in 2001 in Illinois because it fails to ensure that the slaughtered animals were humanely treated and fed, and had a vague description of what constituted slaughtered meat according to Islamic regulations. While many Muslims disagreed with Shireen, she maintained her ground. Shireen prefers not to be called an 'activist' because what she does is what everyone should do—show concern for the environment. Shireen's activism comes from her convictions regarding social justice and environmentalism. She was featured in a documentary, on the radio, in various articles online and in print, and was *Chicago Magazine's* Green Award Honoree for 2007. Today, she still advocates for the environment and holds the view that educating children to be kind and just to the environment, animals, people, and to stand for social injustices is an important form of activism. She is busy raising her daughter and producing her own locally grown food in her backyard.

---

[8] Geoffrey Johnson, "Green Awards 2007 Honorees," Chicago Magazine. [Online Article retrieved 4/16/10.] (http://www.chicagomag.com/Chicago-Magazine/April-2007/Green-Awards-Honorees/index.php?cp=5&si=4&cparticle=4&siarticle=3#artanc)

[9] Ibid.

[10] Ibid.

15.6 Conclusion

The examples of immigrant Muslim women in Chicago demonstrate a form of activism based on the needs of their community as well as the importance of social justice in society at large. While it is recognized that there are women in Muslim countries who remain oppressed and uneducated by Western standards, gender inequality appears to be a universal pattern in many parts of the world—regardless of religious beliefs. Stereotypical representations of Muslim women in the West negate the multifaceted nature of different Muslim societies and the complex reality of Muslim women's lives upon migration.

The stories of Shamsa Zayed, Sorya Shalabi, Itedal Shalabi, and Shireen Pishdadi prove otherwise and defy the negative views of Muslim women as subservient, domesticated, and male dependent in host communities like Chicago. Although their actions to improve their lives in the U.S. could well be considered as "feminists," they chose not to embrace the term. Hooks (2000, 72) said, "The focus on feminism as a way to develop shared identity and community has little appeal to women who experience community, who seek ways to end exploitation and oppression in the context of their lives." Shamsa, Sorya, Itedal, and Shireen utilize their shared identity as Muslims and affirm the principles of equality in Islam unbounded by patriarchal culture. These women seek to make changes in their everyday lives that may seem small but affect their communities, the environment and the larger society. The feminist lenses used in this chapter helps to frame their actions and understand the actions of immigrant Muslim women from the point of view of a western scholar in the twenty-first century. For these women, Muslim activism is largely based on less fighting for the rights of gender but more on championing the values of social justice and reform. Muslim activism is largely based on the Muslim faith, which for them is consistent with the values of social justice in the U.S.

References

Abd-Allah, U. F. (2004). *Famous women in Islam*. Chicago: Nawawi Foundation, CD.
Abu-Lughod, L. (1998). *Remaking women*. Princeton: Princeton University Press.
Ahmed, L. (1993). *Women and gender in Islam: Historical roots of a modern debate*. New Haven: Yale University Press.
Al Faruqi, L. L. (1991). *Women, Muslim society, and Islam*. Indianapolis: American Trust Publications.
Al-Tahir, A. J. (1950). *The Arab community in the Chicago area: The Muslim Palestinian community*. Master's thesis, University of Chicago, Chicago.
Al-Tahir, A. J. (1952). *The Arab community in the Chicago area, a comparative study of the Christian-Syrians and the Muslim-Palestinians*. Dissertation, University of Chicago, Chicago.
Ameri, A., & Ramey, D. (Eds.). (2000). *Arab American encyclopedia*. Detroit: The Gale Group.
American Arab Family Services. (2010). About us. *American Arab family services*. http://www.arabamericanfamilyservices.org/aboutus.asp. Accessed March 17, 2010.
Azzam, M. (1996). Gender and the politics of religion in the Middle East. In M. Yamani (Ed.), *Feminism and Islam: Legal and literary perspectives* (pp. 217–230). Berkshire: Ithaca Press.

Beasley, C. (1999). *What is feminism? An introduction to feminist theory*. Thousand Oaks: Sage.

Brooks, G. (1995). *Nine parts of desire: The hidden world of Islamic women*. New York: Anchor Books.

Brownmiller, S. (2007). Against our will: Men, women and rape. In E. Freedman (Ed.), *The essential feminist reader* (pp. 311–317). New York: Modern Library.

DuBois, E. (1987). The radicalism of the women suffrage movement. In A. Philips (Ed.), *Feminism and equality* (pp. 127–138). New York: New York University Press.

Eisenstein, Z. (1987). Elizabeth Cady Stanton: Radical-feminist analysis and liberal-feminist strategy. In A. Philips (Ed.), *Feminism and equality* (pp. 77–102). New York: New York University Press.

Elshtain, J. B. (1995). Feminism, family, and community. In P. A. Weiss & M. Friedman (Eds.), *Feminism and community* (pp. 259–272). Philadelphia: Temple University Press.

Epstein, B. L. (2002). The successes and failures of feminism. *Journal of Women's History, 14*(2), 118–125.

Evans, J. (1995). *Feminist theory today: An introduction to second-wave feminism*. Thousand Oaks: Sage.

Faith in Place. (2010). *Mission statement. Faith in Place*. http://www.faithinplace.org/about/mission-statement. Accessed April 15, 2010.

Fuentes, A., & Ehrenreich, B. (1983). *Women in the global factory*. Cambridge: South End Press.

Geaves, R., Gabriel, T., Haddad, Y., & Idleman Smith, J. (2004). *Islam & the west post 9/11*. Burlington: Ashgate Publishing.

Gualtieri, S. M. A. (2009). *Between Arab and white*. Berkley: University of California Press.

Haddad, Y., Smith, J. I., & Moore, K. M. (2002). *Muslim women in America*. New York: Oxford University Press.

Hooks, B. (2000). *Feminist theory: From margin to center*. Cambridge, MA: South End Press.

Johnson, G. (2007). Green awards 2007 honorees. *Chicago magazine*. http://www.chicagomag.com/Chicago-Magazine/April-2007/Green-Awards-Honorees/index.php?cp=5&si=4&cparticle=4&siarticle=3#artanc. Accessed April 16, 2010.

Kibria, N. (2008). Muslim encounters in the global economy: Identity developments of labor migrants from Bangladesh to the Middle East. *Ethnicities, 8*(4), 539–556.

King, Y. (1992). Healing the wounds: Feminism, ecology, and nature/culture dualism. In A. M. Jaggar & S. R. Bordo (Eds.), *Gender/Body/Knowledge: Feminist reconstructions of being and knowing* (pp. 115–141). New Brunswick: Rutgers University Press.

Kirp, D. L., Yudoff, M. G., & Strong Franks, M. (1986). *Gender justice*. Chicago: University of Chicago Press.

Krolokke, C., & Sorensen, A. S. (2005). *Gender communication theories and analyses: From silence to performance*. Thousand Oaks: Sage.

Marquez, R. R., & Padilla, Y. C. (2004). Immigration in the life histories of women living in the United States-Mexico border region. *Journal of Immigrant and Refugee Services, 2*(1), 1536–2957.

Mellor, M. (1997). *Feminism & ecology*. New York: New York University Press.

Mernissi, F. (1987). *Beyond the veil*. Indianapolis: Indiana University Press.

Murray, P. (2007). Testimony, house committee on education and labor (United States 1970). In E. Freedman (Ed.), *The essential feminist reader* (pp. 283–287). New York: Modern Library.

Naff, A. (1985). *Becoming American: The early Arab immigration experience*. Carbondale: Southern Illinois University Press.

Orfalea, G. (1988). *Before the flames*. Austin: University of Texas Press.

Pateman, C. (1987). Feminist critiques of the public/private dichotomy. In A. Philips (Ed.), *Feminism and equality* (pp. 103–126). New York: New York University Press.

Read, J. G. (2003). *Culture, class, and work among Arab-American women*. El Paso: LFB Scholarly Publishing LLC.

Riley, D. (1987). The serious burdens of love? Some questions on child-care, feminism and socialism. In A. Philips (Ed.), *Feminism and equality* (pp. 176–197). New York: New York University Press.

Roded, R. (1994). *Women in Islamic biographical collections: From Ibn Sa'd to who's who.* Boulder: Rienner Publishing.

Said, E. (1978). *Orientalism.* New York: Vintage Books.

Smith, J. I. (2009). *Islam in America.* New York: Columbia University Press.

Sonbol, A. E. (2001). Rethinking women and Islam. In Y. Y. Haddad & J. L. Esposito (Eds.), *Daughters of Abraham: Feminist thought in Judaism, Christianity, and Islam* (pp. 108–146). Gainesville: University of Florida.

Tong, R. (2009). *Feminist thought: A more comprehensive introduction* (3rd ed.). Boulder: Westview Press.

U.S. Department of State. (2010). *Patterns of Muslim immigration.* U.S. Department of State. http://infousa.state.gov/education/overview/muslimlife/immigrat.htm. Accessed March 15, 2010.

Wadud, A. (1999). *Qur'an and woman: Re-reading the sacred text from a woman's perspective.* New York: Oxford University Press.

Warren, K. J. (1996). Ecological feminist philosophies: An overview of the issues. In K. J. Warren (Ed.), *Ecological feminist philosophies* (pp. ix–xiv). Indianapolis: Indiana University Press.

Index

CPSIA information can be obtained at www.ICGtesting.com
Printed in the USA
LVOW080019191112

307902LV00006B/13/P